NGOs have been challenging international relations theory for some time, and this essential volume clearly articulates the many ways it has. More importantly, it also charts a path for future theorizing.

Michael Barnett, University Professor of International Affairs and Political Science, George Washington University

This new volume on NGOs provides a root and branch critique of how all the major IR theories overlook the politics of NGOs. Redeploying core themes of power and practice, it provides an in-depth understanding of the global order, locating the 'bridging' role that NGOs play for many issues and across many societies. The chapters offer new insights into the strategies and impacts of NGOs in international affairs, and the conclusion synthesizes the various ways in which NGOs force radical reorientations of IR theory. This book should be read by any student or scholar of international relations.

Anthony F. Lang, Jr., Chair in International Political Theory and Director of the Centre for Global Constitutionalism, University of St Andrews

The NGO Challenge for International Relations Theory

It has become commonplace to observe the growing pervasiveness and impact of Non-Governmental Organizations (NGOs). And yet the three central approaches in International Relations (IR) theory, Liberalism, Realism, and Constructivism, overlook or ignore the importance of NGOs, both theoretically and politically.

Offering a timely reappraisal of NGOs, and a parallel reappraisal of theory in IR, this book uses practice theory, global governance, and new institutionalism to theorize NGO accountability and analyze the history of NGOs. This study uses evidence from empirical data from Europe, Africa, Latin America, the Middle East and Asia and from studies that range across the issues of peacebuilding, ethnic reconciliation, and labor rights to show IR theory has often prejudged and misread the agency of NGOs.

Drawing together a group of leading international relations theorists, this book explores the frontiers of new research on the role of such forces in world politics and is required reading for students, NGO activists, and policy-makers.

William E. DeMars is Professor and Chair, Department of Government, Wofford College, USA.

Dennis Dijkzeul is the Research Coordinator of the Institute of International Law of Peace and Armed Conflict and Professor of Conflict and Organization Research at Ruhr University Bochum, Germany.

Global Institutions

Edited by Thomas G. Weiss
The CUNY Graduate Center, New York, USA
and Rorden Wilkinson
University of Sussex, Brighton, UK

About the series

The "Global Institutions Series" provides cutting-edge books about many aspects of what we know as "global governance." It emerges from our shared frustrations with the state of available knowledge—electronic and print-wise, for research and teaching—in the area. The series is designed as a resource for those interested in exploring issues of international organization and global governance. And since the first volumes appeared in 2005, we have taken significant strides toward filling conceptual gaps.

The series consists of three related "streams" distinguished by their blue, red, and green covers. The blue volumes, comprising the majority of the books in the series, provide user-friendly and short (usually no more than 50,000 words) but authoritative guides to major global and regional organizations, as well as key issues in the global governance of security, the environment, human rights, poverty, and humanitarian action among others. The books with red covers are designed to present original research and serve as extended and more specialized treatments of issues pertinent for advancing understanding about global governance. And the volumes with green covers—the most recent departure in the series—are comprehensive and accessible accounts of the major theoretical approaches to global governance and international organization.

The books in each of the streams are written by experts in the field, ranging from the most senior and respected authors to first-rate scholars at the beginning of their careers. In combination, the three components of the series—blue, red, and green—serve as key resources for faculty, students, and practitioners alike. The works in the blue and green streams have value as core and complementary readings in courses on, among other things, international organization, global governance, international law, international relations, and international political economy; the red volumes allow further reflection and investigation in these and related areas.

The books in the series also provide a segue to the foundation volume that offers the most comprehensive textbook treatment available dealing with all the major issues, approaches, institutions, and actors in contemporary global governance—our edited work *International Organization and Global Governance* (2014)—a volume to which many of the authors in the series have contributed essays.

Understanding global governance—past, present, and future—is far from a finished journey. The books in this series nonetheless represent significant steps toward a better way of conceiving contemporary problems and issues as well as, hopefully, doing something to improve world order. We value the feedback from our readers and their role in helping shape the on-going development of the series.

A complete list of titles appears at the end of this book. The most recent titles in the series are:

21st Century Democracy Promotion in the Americas (2014)
by Jorge Heine and Brigitte Weiffen

BRICS and Coexistence (2014)
edited by Cedric de Coning, Thomas Mandrup, and Liselotte Odgaard

IBSA (2014)
by Oliver Stuenkel

Making Global Institutions Work (2014)
edited by Kate Brennan

Post-2015 UN Development (2014)
edited by Stephen Browne and Thomas G. Weiss

Who Participates in Global Governance? (2014)
by Molly Ruhlman

The Security Council as Global Legislator (2014)
edited by Vesselin Popovski and Trudy Fraser

The NGO Challenge for International Relations Theory

Edited by
William E. DeMars and
Dennis Dijkzeul

LONDON AND NEW YORK

First published 2015
by Routledge
2 Park Square, Milton Park, Abingdon, Oxon OX14 4RN
and by Routledge
711 Third Avenue, New York, NY 10017

Routledge is an imprint of the Taylor & Francis Group, an informa business

© 2015 William E. DeMars and Dennis Dijkzeul for selection and editorial matter; individual contributors for their contributions.

The right of William E. DeMars and Dennis Dijkzeul to be identified as editors of this work has been asserted by them in accordance with the Copyright, Designs and Patent Act 1988.

All rights reserved. No part of this book may be reprinted or reproduced or utilized in any form or by any electronic, mechanical, or other means, now known or hereafter invented, including photocopying and recording, or in any information storage or retrieval system, without permission in writing from the publishers.

Trademark notice: Product or corporate names may be trademarks or registered trademarks, and are used only for identification and explanation without intent to infringe.

British Library Cataloguing in Publication Data
A catalogue record for this book is available from the British Library

Library of Congress Cataloging in Publication Data
The NGO challenge for international relations theory / edited by William DeMars and Dennis Dijkzeul.
  pages cm. – (Routledge global institutions series ; 92)
Includes bibliographical references and index.
  1. Non-governmental organizations. 2. International relations–Philosophy. I. DeMars, William E. (William Emile), 1953- editor of compilation. II. Dijkzeul, Dennis, editor of compilation.
  JZ4841.N347 2015
  327.101–dc23
                    2014031081

ISBN: 978-1-138-84529-9 (hbk)
ISBN: 978-1-138-84530-5 (pbk)
ISBN: 978-1-315-72815-5 (ebk)

Typeset in Times New Roman
by Taylor & Francis Books

Printed and bound by CPI Group (UK) Ltd,
Croydon, CR0 4YY

Contents

List of illustrations	xi
List of contributors	xiii
Acknowledgments	xvi
Abbreviations	xviii

PART I
Introduction   1

   Introduction: NGOing   3
   WILLIAM E. DEMARS AND DENNIS DIJKZEUL

PART II
Theory   39

1 How to study NGOs in practice:
   a relational primer   41
   MORTEN SKUMSRUD ANDERSEN

2 Global governance and NGOs: reconceptualizing
   international relations for the twenty-first century   65
   KAREN A. MINGST AND JAMES P. MULDOON JR.

3 Network institutionalism: a new synthesis for
   NGO studies   82
   ANNA OHANYAN

PART III
Crosscutting evidence: history, region, accountability 105

4 The co-evolution of non-governmental and
  intergovernmental organizations in historical perspective 107
  BOB REINALDA

5 Being an NGO in the OECD 130
  ELIZABETH A. BLOODGOOD

6 The accountability and legitimacy of international NGOs 159
  CRISTINA M. BALBOA

PART IV
Case evidence: NGOs and networks 187

7 Theoretical and practical implications of
  public– private partnerships for labor rights advocacy 189
  SHAREEN HERTEL

8 NGOs in peacebuilding: high expectations, mixed results 211
  PATRICE C. MCMAHON

9 Follow the partners: agency and explanation in
  the color revolutions 237
  WILLIAM E. DEMARS

10 Heart of paradox: war, rape and NGOs in the DR Congo 262
   DENNIS DIJKZEUL

PART V
Conclusions and implications 287

11 Conclusion: NGO research and International
   Relations theory 289
   WILLIAM E. DEMARS AND DENNIS DIJKZEUL

   Index 317
   Routledge Global Institutions Series 325

List of illustrations

Figures

I.1	State/society bridging effects for one NGO in two countries	27
6.1	Principal–agent relationships of global governance	165
11.1	Cycle of NGO social construction	310

Tables

I.1	How conventional IR theories reduce and obscure NGO politics	13
I.2	How NGO anchoring practices conceal their particularity and politics	26
3.1	Comparative overview of policy network theories	88
5.1	NGO identities across the OECD	137
5.2	NGO procedures for establishment	141
5.3	Government oversight of NGOs across the OECD	143
5.4	Case studies	146
6.1	Three questions of accountability	168
9.1	Theoretical questions on replication and change in NGOs and networks	241

Contributors

Morten Skumsrud Andersen is a research fellow at the Norwegian Institute of International Affairs (NUPI). His research interests include the study of empires in IR, conceptual history, and philosophies of science. He is author of "Legitimacy in Statebuilding," *International Political Sociology* 6, no. 2 (2012): 205–219; and co-author with Iver B. Neumann of "Practice as Models: A Methodology with an Illustration Concerning Wampum Diplomacy," *Millennium: Journal of International Studies* 40, no. 3 (2012): 456–480. He is also book review editor for *Internasjonal Politikk*.

Cristina M. Balboa is Assistant Professor in the School of Public Affairs, Baruch College CUNY. She is currently conducting a baseline assessment of the size and scope of New York City's international NGO sector through Baruch's Center for Nonprofit Strategy and Management. She is author of "How Successful Transnational Nongovernmental Organizations Set Themselves Up for Failure on the Ground," *World Development* (2014); and co-author with Graeme Auld, Steven Bernstein and Benjamin Cashore of "The Emergence of Non-State Market Driven (NSMD) Governance: A Cross Sectoral Assessment," in Magali Delmas and Oran Young, eds, *Governance for the Environment: New Perspectives* (Cambridge, 2009).

Elizabeth A. Bloodgood is Associate Professor at Concordia University, Montreal. She is author of "The Interest Group Analogy: International Non-Governmental Organizations in International Politics," *Review of International Studies* 37, no. 1 (2011): 93–120; and co-author with Hans Peter Schmitz of "The INGO Research Agenda: A Community Approach to Challenges in Method and Theory," in Bob Reinalda, ed., *Routledge Handbook of International Organization* (Routledge, 2013). She is collaborating to create several new datasets

xiv *List of contributors*

on national NGO regulation and the evolution of international NGO populations.

William E. DeMars is Professor and Chair of the Department of Government at Wofford College. He previously taught at Earlham College, the American University in Cairo, Egypt, and the University of Notre Dame. He has observed NGOs working in Europe, Africa, the Middle East, Latin America, and East Asia. He is author of "War and Mercy in Africa," *World Policy Journal* 17, no. 2 (2000); *NGOs and Transnational Networks: Wild Cards in World Politics* (Pluto Press, 2005); and "Transnational Humanitarian Heroes in the Early Twentieth Century: The Congo Reform Movement," in Luc Reydams, ed., *The Global Activism Reader* (Continuum, 2011).

Dennis Dijkzeul is Professor of Conflict and Organization Research and Research Coordinator of the IFHV at Ruhr University Bochum, Germany. He is author of "Transnational Humanitarian NGOs? A Progress Report," in Ludger Pries, ed., *Rethinking Transnationalism: The Meso-Link of Organisations* (Routledge, 2008); co-author with Claude Iguma Wakenge of "Proselytizing as Spoiling from Within? Comparing Proselytizing by UN Peacekeepers in the Sudan and the DR Congo," *Journal of International Organizations Studies* 5, no. 1 (2014); co-editor with Yves Beigbeder of *Rethinking International Organizations: Pathology and Promise*, 2nd edition (Berghahn, 2015); and co-editor with Jürgen Lieser of *Handbuch Humanitäre Hilfe* (Springer Verlag, 2013).

Shareen Hertel is Associate Professor of Political Science and Human Rights at the University of Connecticut. She has served as a consultant for foundations, NGOs and United Nations agencies in the United States, Latin America and South Asia. She is author of *Unexpected Power: Conflict and Change Among Transnational Activists* (Cornell, 2006); co-editor with Lanse P. Minkler of *Economic Rights: Conceptual, Measurement and Policy Issues* (Cambridge, 2007); and coeditor with Kathryn Libal of *Human Rights in the United States: Beyond Exceptionalism* (Cambridge, 2011). Hertel is editor of *The Journal of Human Rights*.

Patrice C. McMahon is Associate Professor and Director of Global Engagement, College of Arts and Sciences, at the University of Nebraska–Lincoln. She is author of *Taming Ethnic Hatred: Ethnic Cooperation and Transnational Networks in Eastern Europe* (Syracuse, 2007); co-editor with Courtney Hillebrecht and Tyler White of *At Home and Abroad: How States Respond to Human Security* (Routledge, 2013); and co-editor with Jon Western of *The International Community and Statebuilding: Getting Its Act Together* (Routledge, 2012). In addition, her research articles have appeared in *Foreign Affairs, Political Science Quarterly,* and *Human Rights Review.*

Karen A. Mingst is the Lockwood Chair Professor at the Patterson School of Diplomacy and International Commerce at the University of Kentucky. Her widely used textbook, *Essentials of International Relations* (W. W. Norton, 2013) has been translated into Chinese, Portuguese, Polish, Spanish, Korean, and Albanian. She is also author of *Politics and the African Development Bank* (University Press of Kentucky, 1990); and coauthor with Margaret P. Karns of *The United Nations in the 21st Century* (Westview, 2011), and *International Organizations: The Politics and Processes of Global Governance* (Lynne Rienner, 2009).

James P. Muldoon, Jr is Vice-Chair of The Mosaic Institute in Toronto. He is author of *The Architecture of Global Governance: An Introduction to the Study of International Organizations* (Westview, 2003); and co-editor with JoAnn Fagot Aviel, Richard Reitano and Earl Sullivan of *Multilateral Diplomacy and the United Nations Today* (Westview, 2005), and *The New Dynamics of Multilateralism: Diplomacy, International Organizations, and Global Governance* (Westview, 2010).

Anna Ohanyan is Associate Professor and Chair of the Department of Political Science and International Studies at Stonehill College. She is the author of *Networked Regionalism as Conflict Management* (Stanford University Press, forthcoming), and *NGOs, IGOs, and the Network Mechanisms of Post-Conflict Global Governance in Microfinance* (Palgrave Macmillan, 2008). In addition, she has published widely on international organizations, conflict resolution and peacebuilding in such settings as Kosovo, Bosnia and Herzegovina, and Afghanistan. She was a Fulbright Core Scholar for Armenia in 2012–13.

Bob Reinalda is a Senior Researcher at Radboud University, Nijmegen, The Netherlands, and a member of the Institute for Management Research of the Nijmegen School for Management. He is editor of the *Routledge Handbook of International Organization* (2013); *The Ashgate Research Companion to Non-State Actors* (2011); and the *Routledge History of International Organizations: From 1815 to the Present Day* (2009). He is also ongoing editor of the online IO BIO Project, *The Biographical Dictionary of Secretaries-General of International Organizations.*

Acknowledgments

This edited volume began at an International Studies Association (ISA) conference in Chicago. Several of us shared our experience that International Relations (IR) theory was consistently of little use to help us understand NGOs and their impact. At this early stage we realized that two areas in particular were seriously undertheorized. The first area was the phenomenon of NGOs "partnering" with an extremely wide range of other actors—varying from senators on Capitol Hill to bureaucrats in Brussels, from warlords to rape victims, from global UN organizations to local democracy activists. This phenomenon is not captured by policy studies of NGOs that examine conditions for success or failure in achieving their mandates, because whether or not they make a huge impact concerning their mandates, NGOs *always* generate skeins of local and transnational relationships that change social and political structures in unpredictable ways. Only much later did we recognize that here was a failure of liberalism to theorize international institutions, and of constructivism to theorize international change.

The second area overlooked by IR theory was the way that these "networks" of NGOs and their various partners almost always incorporate a great deal of contestation and competition along with the cooperation that they embody. This was a more obvious failure of realist theory and its competitors to recognize complex political realities. Paradoxically, through their partnering with manifold actors, NGOs bridge both cooperation and competition, just as they bridge many other conceptual divides in their everyday practice.

We recognized from the beginning that the study of NGOs in world politics needed better theory to illuminate both their activities and their impact. However, we realized more gradually, in the dialogue with each other, that our findings could contribute to renewing IR theory itself; that the NGO challenge could be *for* IR theory. And so we wish to underscore that the arguments in this book—and particularly for us as editors—have developed in a process of interaction and reconceptualization with our coauthors over several years. Their insights and patience have made this a more coherent and profound book.

We would like to thank ISA for a Workshop Grant that enabled our first meeting and exchange with coauthors preliminary to the ISA Annual Convention. This volume would not have been possible without the association's support.

Finally, all of us involved with this book are grateful to the NGO officials—at headquarters, and especially in the field—who have taken the time to explain their work and their aspirations. Our response is to take seriously the full social and political context of their principles and their partners.

When we had already submitted this volume to Thomas G. Weiss and Rorden Wilkinson, the editors of this series, we came across their 2014 article in *Global Governance*, in which they argue that the field of international relations "teeters on the edge of an abyss of irrelevance ... IR as an academic pursuit has become disparate and fragmented. Those of us in the discipline have ceased to pursue greater clarity in the way that we understand the world around us."[1] Weiss and Wilkinson propose the study of global governance as a possible way out of this growing irrelevance. In this volume, we pursue a complementary strategy toward the same goal by examining and theorizing NGOs and the networks in and through which they partner.

Although many hands contributed to this book, the usual disclaimer holds that the errors and omissions are ours alone.

> Dennis Dijkzeul, Ruhr University Bochum, Germany
> William E. DeMars, Wofford College, USA

Note

1 Thomas G. Weiss and Rorden Wilkinson, "Global Governance to the Rescue: Saving International Relations?" *Global Governance* 20, no. 1 (2014): 19.

Abbreviations

BiH	Bosnia and Herzegovina
CANVAS	Centre for Applied Nonviolent Action and Strategies
CC	Carter Center
CCC	Clean Clothes Campaign
CDDRL	Center on Democracy, Development, and the Rule of Law
CEP	Council on Economic Priorities
CFO	Comité Fronterizo de Obreras
CIA	Central Intelligence Agency
CIS	Commonwealth of Independent States
CIVICUS	World Alliance for Citizen Participation
CNSP	Comparative Nonprofit Sector Project
CRC	UN Convention on the Rights of the Child
CRS	Catholic Relief Services
DRC	Democratic Republic of the Congo
ECOSOC	Economic and Social Council
EU	European Union
FAO	Food and Agriculture Organization
FIFA	International Federation of Football Associations
FLA	Fair Labor Association
GAP	Global Accountability Project
GBV	gender-based violence
GONGO	government organized NGO
HIV	human immunodeficiency virus
IAEA	International Atomic Energy Agency
ICC	International Chamber of Commerce
ICC	International Criminal Court
ICCPR	International Covenant on Civil and Political Rights
ICCR	Interfaith Center for Corporate Responsibility

ICESCR	International Covenant on Economic, Social and Cultural Rights
ICNC	International Center on Nonviolent Conflict
ICNL	International Center for Not-for-Profit Law
ICRC	International Committee of the Red Cross
ICVA	International Council of Voluntary Agencies
IFAD	International Fund for Agricultural Development
IGO	intergovernmental organization
ILO	International Labour Organization
ILRF	International Labor Rights Fund
IMF	International Monetary Fund
IO	international organization
IR	International Relations
IRC	International Rescue Committee
IRS	Internal Revenue Service
ISO	International Standards Organization
JACO	Japan Association of Charitable Organizations
JCIE	Japan Committee for International Exchange
KLA	Kosovo Liberation Army
KPMG	Klynveld Peat Marwick Goerdeler
LDP	Liberal Democratic Party (Japan)
LOA	law on associations
MNC	multinational corporation
MSF	Médecins Sans Frontières
MAD	Multiple Accountability Disorder
MONUC	United Nations Mission in the Democratic Republic of the Congo
MONUSCO	United Nations Stabilization Mission in the Democratic Republic of the Congo
NAACP	National Association for the Advancement of Colored People
NAALC	North American Agreement on Labor Cooperation
NATO	North Atlantic Treaty Organization
NGO	non-governmental organization
NLCR	New Life Children's Refuge
NPM	new public management
OECD	Organisation for Economic Co-operation and Development
OHR	Office of the High Representative (Bosnia)
ONE	ONE Campaign to End Extreme Poverty
OSI	Open Society Institute
PA	principal–agent (theory)

PIU	public international union
PPPs	public private partnerships
TWN	Third World Network
UK	United Kingdom
UN	United Nations
UNDP	United Nations Development Programme
UNEP	United Nations Environment Programme
UNHCR	United Nations High Commissioner for Refugees
UNICEF	United Nations Children's Fund
UNMIL	United Nations Mission in Liberia
US	United States
USAID	United States Agency for International Development
USAS	United Students Against Sweatshops
WFP	World Food Programme
WfWI	Women for Women International
WHO	World Health Organization
WRC	Worker Rights Consortium
WTO	World Trade Organization
YMCA	Young Men's Christian Association

Part I
Introduction

Introduction
NGOing

William E. DeMars and Dennis Dijkzeul

- The NGO challenge ... for International Relations theory
- The three traditions revisited
- Anchoring practices of NGOing
- Conclusion: about this book

The global surge of non-governmental organizations (NGOs) since the 1990s is still accelerating, as they proliferate in numbers, new issue-areas, and regions of the world. Some NGOs have captured the public imagination with a compelling leader and dramatic narrative—Princess Diana campaigning against land mines, Bono ending extreme poverty, or George Clooney and Angelina Jolie protecting human rights and refugees.[1] However, NGOs may have expanded their scope, responsibility, and celebrity beyond the limits of their operational capacity. While some NGOs now function almost as local and state governments,[2] other governments are pushing back to limit NGO authority.[3]

Indeed, NGOs are facing a paradoxical crisis of trust. On the one hand, their external credibility has never been stronger. According to the 2014 Edelman Trust Barometer, NGOs are revered globally as the most trusted institution, while faith in governments and corporations has plummeted.[4] On the other hand, more observers are questioning the presumptive legitimacy accorded to NGOs, which claim to hold states and other actors accountable in global governance while their own accountability remains elusive. Even some of those who know NGOs best are voicing deep disenchantment with their usefulness and promise.[5]

In this volume we offer a timely reappraisal of NGOs, and a parallel reappraisal of International Relations (IR) theory. Too much of the scholarship in IR either ignores the role of NGOs in world politics, or reiterates NGO self-understanding in theoretical form. As a consequence, even as NGOs spread to fill the interstices of world politics, their significance and impact are still enigmatic. This book is an attempt to prepare the theoretical ground to better understand NGOs.

International Relations theory is our point of departure to address NGOs, because IR comprehends, in principle if not yet in practice, the entire spectrum of social, economic, and political relations entailed by NGOs and their transnational networks as global phenomena. IR theory has attempted to address NGOs, but the relationship remains deeply problematic. We have seen this in our own professional lives and affiliations. One disturbing sign is to meet IR scholars—some with years of operational experience with NGOs—who return from field research to discover that the main lines of IR theory cannot explain much of what they have seen NGOs do. This appears to be a growing problem, particularly among young scholars entering the field. In spite of efforts to bridge the gap, there remains an embarrassing dearth of studies that are both empirically rich and also theoretically engaged with the central debates of IR theory. This presents a challenge to the IR field as a whole, which claims to describe and explain world politics.

This book thus serves a dual purpose: to better understand NGOs; and to inform and renew IR theory through the challenge of understanding NGOs. Hence, the NGO challenge *for* International Relations theory.

Compared to any other category of actor in world politics, NGOs demonstrate an unparalleled capacity to connect with both political and societal actors ("partners" in NGO parlance) in several countries. This transnational partnering imperative is always pursued in the name of a universal normative mandate. For a simple example, consider the signature proposal of the ONE Campaign: "Join the fight against extreme poverty."[6] The slogan comprises both an invitation to partner with the NGO (Join the fight ...), and a universal normative purpose (... against extreme poverty). These two practices—a private actor claiming to serve a universal public purpose, and then partnering with societal and political actors in several countries—are vital for making NGOs happen. We propose that they are the two *anchoring practices* that constitute the process or activity of "NGOing."[7]

Starting with practice means looking intensely at what particular NGOs do. In the NGO world, the discourse of "partners" and "partnership" is as pervasive as it is problematic.[8] Savvy activists and observers are well aware of the irony of asserting the mutuality of "partnership" in relationships that are marked by asymmetric power, conflict, and mutual political and economic instrumentalization. Having found no clearly superior alternative, we continue to use the terminology of partnership, with its inherent ironies accentuated by our analysis of network politics.

NGOs characteristically work in a networked context with a transnational menagerie of other partners/actors/parties/stakeholders ranging from informal neighborhood groups to warlords and governing elites to businesses and United Nations agencies to ethnic and religious communities. Some "partners" may be hidden in some way, or may not share all the values and norms by which network members identify each other. By raising the controversial questions of hidden partners and heterogeneous networks, we challenge leading theoretical approaches in international relations that tend to overstate the homogeneity of collective norms or the uniform rationality among actors in a network. Through partnering and forming networks, NGOs find themselves almost effortlessly bridging seven critical divisions in world politics:

1 between state and society, and the shifting boundary between public and private;
2 within society, between family and market;
3 between normative and material;
4 between religious and secular;
5 between agency and structure;
6 between conflict and cooperation; and
7 between national and international.

These divides, while resisting theoretical comprehension, are easily bridged by real NGOs in the everyday performance of their anchoring practices, that is, by NGOing. Through bridging, NGOs generate a loose and variegated network form of international institutionalization.

As their *anchoring practices* lead NGOs to *bridge divides* in world politics, a third dynamic emerges. By bridging, NGOs generate myriad transnational encounters where power is at play. Belying their idealist and anodyne image, transnational NGOs create the occasion for, and often veil from scrutiny, a growing arena of *complex power relationships* in world politics. In this way, NGOs and their networks institutionalize both conflict and cooperation. These three conceptual touchstones—*practice, bridging*, and *power*—are the foci of the book.

Why examine theoretically marginalized NGOs for leverage to broaden IR theory? The central debates of the field are conventionally understood as a conversation between the three traditions of Liberalism, Realism and Constructivism. Practitioners of each tradition or school of thought focus intensely on a particular set of empirical phenomena. Realists look for the role of power in world politics, liberals focus on the influence and spread of international institutions, and constructivists concentrate on discerning and explaining profound change in the actors or practice of world politics. Each tradition carries a professional responsibility to illuminate and understand its central empirical bailiwick. However, our empirical work on NGOs suggests that all three theoretical traditions are often distorted, and their blind spots reinforced, by the conventional structure and practice of theoretical debate in IR. By marginalizing NGOs, each overlooks a significant sector of precisely those international phenomena with which it is most centrally concerned. We propose that each school, by bringing NGOs in theoretically and empirically, can better carry out its academic, pedagogical, and policy responsibilities. A new theory is not needed; instead, we propose to refine and enrich the practice of all three traditions. Specifically:

- our approach enriches the realist tradition by revealing overlooked power relationships in the transnational networks built by bridging NGOs;
- we bring to the liberal tradition a much broader conception of international institutions by illuminating these transnational institutional networks; and
- the significance of NGO practice in world politics can bolster the constructivist tradition's ability to discern and explain international political change.

This introduction undertakes two tasks. First, we critically examine the state of IR theory relevant to NGOs, showing how all three theoretical traditions are often distorted, and their blind spots reinforced, by their inattention to NGOs. Second, we unpack the central practices of NGOs themselves, drawing on multiple disciplines, to explain how they generate bridging effects and set up complex power dynamics. Each of the contributors to this volume will show how an empirical case, a comparative study, or a mid-level theory addresses the triptych of *practice, bridging*, and *power*.

The NGO challenge ... for International Relations theory

How and why does so much IR theory obscure—render opaque and invisible—the complex politics of NGOs? What apertures exist in IR theory for glimpsing the politics of NGOs, and how can those be thrown open for a wider and clearer view? To address these questions, we first review conventional IR theoretical traditions that severely reduce the politics of NGOs, and we map and explain their blind spots. We then reexamine the same traditions, identifying select studies that manage to integrate more of the politics of NGOs.

Myopic realism

Many realist scholars ignore NGOs altogether. According to Stephen Walt, realism, "depicts international affairs as a struggle for power among self-interested states and is generally pessimistic about the prospects for eliminating conflict and war."[9] Although there are many "realisms," twin premises prevail: pervasive conflict in world politics, and states as the most important actors. These starting points leave all types of international organizations at the margins of the realist world. Most marginalized are NGOs, which appear to be the actors that possess the least resources and rely most on international cooperation. Some realists argue that NGOs address issues with which states are not concerned, or that NGOs are political epiphenomena acting on behalf of state interests. For such hardline realists, neither NGOs nor other international organizations or institutions produce any significant impact on world politics. Unsurprisingly, hardline realism generates little research on NGOs. The watchword of realism may be to debunk the "false promises" of international institutions, or the "false dawn" of global civil society.[10] Realism's language of national interests reiterates the discourse of states, or heads of state, facing serious security or economic threats.

Among realist scholars, Kenneth Waltz, in particular, has been a defining figure. His 1959 book *Man, the State, and War*[11] argued that "third image" explanations of war based on the anarchic structure of the international system were superior to both "first image" accounts that attributed war to human nature, and also to "second image" approaches that explained war by the internal structure of states. Through its assault on first and second image explanations, this book may have done more than any other work to foreclose the study of political theory by later generations of IR scholars. Waltz reinforced the conceptual primacy of third image explanations in his 1979 *Theory of International Politics*, with its focus on the enduring bipolar structure of the international system.[12] Although the theory's prescience is questionable after the demise of bipolarity in 1989, the parsimony of structural realism continues to seduce.

In many ways, Waltz's "neorealism" helped to institutionalize IR as an autonomous academic discipline. Yet the "American discipline" of IR actually has a long history of borrowing from the related social sciences of economics, sociology, history, and law. Waltz himself cited several studies in game theory and economics in his 1959 book.[13] In the 1983 volume, *International Regimes*, Ernst Haas proposed an "organic model" of world politics characterized by a capacity for adaptive learning that he derived from sociobiology and structural sociology.[14] In the same book, Donald Puchala and Raymond Hopkins offered a distinctively sociological take by proposing the reality of "diffuse" or "informal" regimes.[15] In the 1986 volume, *Neorealism and Its Critics*, some critics embraced a "neoliberal" view that shares many assumptions with neorealism. But others, including John Ruggie, Richard Ashley and Robert Cox, drew extensively from the European structural sociologists Durkheim and Giddens, and from critical theorists Bourdieu and Gramsci. Ashley, for example, emphasized that neorealist structuralism ignores historical factors that he summed up as "process, practice, power, and politics."[16] Our emphasis on practice and power is an attempt to revive this kind of attention to the detail of what political actors actually do.

Ashley also launched a blistering critique of the *rationalist ontology* and *positivist epistemology* of Waltz's neorealism. The critique resonates today, although taken up by constructivism. Rationalist theory relies on the assumption that "instrumental rationality provides the crucial link between the environment and actor behaviour."[17] Positivism assumes that the only reliable way of knowing is by direct observation, frequently understood as quantitative measurement (epistemology), with the implication that everything real can be measured (ontology). Rationalism and positivism together reinforce a methodological individualism that assumes actors (states for neorealists and neoliberals) are autonomous and unaffected by interactions with other actors with respect to their conceptions of interests, their *rationality* for calculating how to achieve their interests, and their capabilities for pursuing them.[18] Both neorealists and neoliberals apply methodological individualism to states, to the point of treating states as "black boxes" whose internal dynamics can be assumed and therefore ignored. We are more sympathetic with a view (derived from sociology or anthropology rather than economics) that all actors in world politics are "socially constructed." That is, they are constituted by their interactions with other actors.

We find that an assumption of homogeneity among actors in an NGO network is the single theoretical preconception that most blinds scholars to the politics in the network. The surprise is that this assumption of homogeneity is shared by *both* rationalists (like Waltz) and also by many who take a more sociological approach.[19] Both fail to look beyond the issue-areas publicly articulated by NGOs and their partners. Sociological approaches assume that all the actors in the NGO network share the same *normative* commitments and discourse. But rationalists assume that all actors share a common rationality. NGO discourse of issue-areas and mandates is construed as common norms by one view, and common rationality by the other. In the end, therefore, both methodological individualism and methodological collectivism can lead (by divergent paths) to the assumption of homogeneity among actors.

In sum, IR theoretical debate since the 1950s has been richer than sometimes comes forward in the canonical narrative. However, it is paradoxical that this record of rich interchange with economics, sociology and history has left a strikingly sterile legacy for contemporary IR, requiring current scholars to rediscover or reinvent what has been marginalized. Our book's themes resonate with these earlier critiques, which we seek to revive and build upon.

Given the attention that scholars of international organizations give to myopic realism as a foil, it may be ironic that the real but overlooked nemesis all along has been liberalism.

Liberal institutionalism

A major source of the marginalization of NGOs in IR theory may well be the curious inhospitality of *liberal theory* toward the study of NGOs. After all, the natural home for NGOs and the scholars who study them would seem to be liberalism, with its emphasis on interstate cooperation, the possibility of reasoned progress toward binding international norms, the influence of global public opinion, and the participation of a diverse cast of actors beyond states in world politics. In fact, however, liberal theory has actively discouraged NGO scholarship for several decades.

For example, two surveys of IR theory published in the 1980s contain nary a reference to NGOs.[20] The literature on "international regimes," which dominated liberal theory through the 1980s, focused on the causal power of international norms, but remained resolutely state-centered. NGOs were almost completely ignored in the seminal regime literature, even in studies concerning the emergent human rights regime, where NGOs were already playing leading roles.[21]

Why has liberalism ignored NGOs? Liberal institutionalism, one of several liberal variations, at its core holds that the spread of international institutions progressively builds global peace and cooperation. International institutions are understood to include the "Kantian triangle" of economic interdependence through free trade, electoral democracy, and intergovernmental agreements and organizations.[22] Each of these three institutional forms is spread primarily by the actions of states, and particularly major power states, even if one of the consequences of their spread is to empower nonstate actors like NGOs and multinational corporations. This statist premise—that states are causes while international institutions are consequences—explains the paradox that, while liberalism acknowledges a multiplicity of kinds of actors in world politics, it only rarely directs serious attention beyond states.

The ingrained state-centrism of liberalism is illustrated by its flirtation with "nonstate actors" in the 1970s. While this *first transnationalism* broke new ground, its leading lights did not point to the distinctive significance of NGOs among other nonstate actors.[23] The first transnationalism failed to launch a sustained research agenda on NGOs in world politics because it failed to escape the gravitational pull of both realist and liberal state-centrism. As quickly as it had appeared, transnationalism disappeared from the central debates of the discipline in the 1980s. Today, global elites refer to NGOs as useful adjuncts and cheerleaders for the liberal "Davos consensus" of expanding global interdependence, but this recognition has not led to sustained scholarship on what real NGOs do.

Constructivism

If both realism and liberalism fail to take NGOs seriously, who does? In their surveys of IR theory, both Stephen Walt and Jack Snyder place transnationalism and NGO scholarship squarely in the *constructivist* camp, derived from the marriage of idealism and Marxism. Snyder brands contemporary constructivism as a revival of idealist theory from before World War II.[24] Both constructivism and idealism emphasize the causal role of norms, ideas and values in shaping world politics. Walt highlights the other genealogy—that constructivism inherited the mantle of radical theory from a defunct Marxism. In their common radicalism, both Marxism and constructivism seek "a blueprint for fundamentally transforming the existing international order."[25] The irony is that this form of constructivism turns Marx on his head by trading his materialism for idealism.[26] Today there is strong consensus in IR that constructivism is essentially idealist, emphasizing the influence of ideas, values, and discourses in shaping political identities, beliefs and interests.[27]

While the *first transnationalism* of the 1970s did not lead to major change, a *new transnationalism* burgeoned when constructivism met NGOs in the 1990s.[28] Civil society actors, including NGOs, had been implicated as leaders in bringing about the "Third Wave" of democratization. Almost anything seemed possible with the rise of "global civil society" after the Cold War. Tens of thousands of NGOs teamed up with the UN to change the world at a series of global conferences. New forms of transnational cooperation and "global governance" emerged across many fields. The NGO boom of the 1990s was matched by an exploding literature on their growing influence in world politics.

Much of the scholarship from the new transnationalism falls into two camps, which we identify as *pluralist* and *globalist*, both versions of idealist constructivism.

In the *pluralist* school of idealist constructivism, NGOs are understood as the articulate and organized element of transnational civil society, acting largely independently of government. Pluralists portray NGOs as servants of the poor in grassroots development, or prophetic voices of the voiceless lobbying governments and the UN, or transnational pilgrims in an emancipatory passage from oppressive rule to self-regulating community. Pluralism reiterates, in abstract theoretical terms, the representative claims articulated by NGOs themselves. However, the pluralist causal narrative truncates the full range of NGO politics, highlighting only the *single axis of political conflict between society and state.*[29] For pluralists, power flows bottom-up from society to the state. Although pluralists regularly exaggerate the normative homogeneity of NGO networks, persistent critics from the radical left reveal the broader political heterogeneity of networks, and the complexity of NGO power relations.

If power erupts from the bottom up in pluralist imagery, it flows from the top down in accounts from the *globalist* school of idealist constructivism. Global norms are "implemented" or "enforced" by NGOs collecting information on norm compliance by states, multinational corporations and other actors.[30] In another version, NGOs and other international organizations "socialize" states into accepting and complying with global norms.[31] In the process, elements of world government, or at least global governance, emerge above states. Globalist policy analysis is written as if the United Nations were becoming a unitary bureaucracy pursuing rational policy objectives for the sake of global human interests. Under these assumptions, NGOs are the UN's extension agents, bringing authority and order to the hinterland. Globalism portrays NGOs as obediently implementing and enforcing the global norms that descend from UN organs and multilateral agreements, as from the "heavens" of ancient faiths and philosophies.

Globalism views NGOs through the lens of UN institutional interests, and reiterates the discourse of UN multilateralism. In this "New York view," characteristic of career UN civil servants, NGOs may be useful to fill the enforcement gap in multilateral agreements and to lend legitimacy to the UN itself. Globalism is concerned primarily with the *politics of building normative consensus* within multilateral fora, and secondarily with the *politics of enforcing normative compliance* on the recalcitrant subjects of global authority. The watchword of globalist approaches might be global governance.

Idealist constructivism, in both its pluralist and globalist variations, recognizes that NGOs and networks exist and exercise agency in world politics, but truncates NGO politics to fit theoretical preconceptions. It stresses *vertical* political axes, with power brought to bear on states either from below by civil society, or from above by global norms and institutions. Pluralism and globalism greatly overstate the normative homogeneity of NGO networks, and then tell researchers to stop looking for network partners when they run out of actors that publicly declare the normative consensus.

We need constructivist NGO studies to reveal and explain the full gamut of global political change and stability, not merely to reiterate the self-descriptions of NGO activists or UN civil servants and to legitimate their projects. As illustrated in the subsequent chapters, NGO networks may accomplish much less than they promise in some respects, and much more in others, even transforming states materially and ideologically. A constructivism that ignores these broader effects betrays its own theoretical promise.

In sum, each of the leading approaches prejudges the politics of NGOs in a restrictive way that obscures their full complexity:

- *realists* prejudge all NGO power as insignificant compared to the power of states;
- *liberal institutionalists* prejudge all NGOs as merely accompanying the spread of international institutions but not significantly constituting or shaping them;
- *pluralist constructivists* prejudge NGO power as flowing in a single direction from societies upward to states; and
- *globalist constructivists* prejudge NGO power as flowing largely from international norms downward to states.

Table 1.1 How conventional IR theories reduce and obscure NGO politics

Theory	Theory reduces NGO politics to	Theory reiterates discourse of	Theory watchword	For theory, impact of NGO boom	Theory highlights NGO reality	Theory obscures
Realist	State-to-state power relations	Head of state facing security threat	"False dawn"	Negligible	Pervasive conflict and inadvertent consequences	NGO transnational networks institutionalize power relations
Liberal institutionalist	Legitimating spread of markets, democracy and civil society	International diplomats and business-persons	"Interdependence"	Pliable legitimacy and accountability for global elites	NGOs accompany spread of cooperation and institutions	NGO transnational networks embody international institutions
Pluralist/ constructivist	Bottom-up, representing societies to states	NGO activists	"Transnational civil society"	Democratize world politics	NGOs exercise agency and link to societal partners	NGO transnational networks transform states and other actors
Globalist/ constructivist	Top-down, enforcing global norms on states	UN career civil servants	"Global governance"	Strengthen UN	NGOs reinforce global norms and institutions	normatively and materially

14 *Introduction*

All four conventional approaches wrongly assume the homogeneity of NGO networks, whether in terms of norms, rationality or power. Consequently, researchers who follow conventional approaches *fail to look for the politics that is embodied in variances of norms, rationality or power*. Table I.1 summarizes our critique of how conventional IR theories reduce and obscure the politics of NGOs.

A new theoretical point of departure is needed. Realists concerned about power must be able to perceive and explain how transnational NGO networks sometimes generate new actors, reshape existing ones, and create and modify relationships among actors, whether on their own initiative or as tools of other powerful actors. Liberal theoretical conceptions of both international institutions and international cooperation must be expanded to encompass the complexity and dynamism of NGO bridging institutions. And both pluralist and globalist constructivists must rework their conceptions of power and norms to comprehend the enormous fields of transnational politics embedded in the encounters between NGOs and their partners.

The three traditions revisited

On our second tour of NGO scholarship and IR theory, we turn to a selection of more nuanced works in all three theoretical schools. They share a healthy hybridization across traditions, mixing and fusing elements of the realist focus on power, the liberal attention to institutions, and the constructivist concern for change. Some of them take NGOs seriously, while others ignore NGOs in interesting ways.

Beyond realism as foil

A growing body of scholarship takes NGOs seriously while retaining distinctively realist sensibilities.[32] These studies portray NGOs and networks as institutionalizing asymmetric power relationships, combining both material and ideational power, and generating unintended consequences.

Daniel Drezner asks "Who regulates the global economy?"[33] At one level, the answers are squarely in the realist tradition. States are the most important actors in world politics; however, the United States and the European Union are the major powers of regulation, dictating global norms when they agree, or blocking norms when they disagree. "Global civil society" lobbies these powers, but they follow their own interests. Drezner finds that powerful actors often seek to instrumentalize or selectively empower international organizations (IOs including both non-governmental and intergovernmental organizations). IOs can be used as agents to accomplish their explicit organizational goals; or to create "sham standards" that foster the illusion of effective action; or for some extraneous purpose apart from either success or failure in their explicit goals. For Drezner the major players—the United States, the EU, and "Global Civil Society"—are unitary actors whose interest preferences are given and exogenous to interaction with each other. Such methodological individualism lumps together all the NGOs and networks concerned with a particular issue. Drezner shows that black box treatment of global civil society can be useful to a point. However, his rationalist premises lead him to overlook scenarios of IO influence in which the actors are transformed by their encounter, which we address in the next section on constructivism.

In contrast to Drezner, Clifford Bob sees global civil society not as a unitary actor with a single set of preferences on each global issue, but as a politicized arena filled with contention and asymmetric power relations. Bob affirms the agency of local social movements, showing how they compete aggressively for NGO representation to a global audience. Northern NGOs also exercise agency in their choice and "marketing" of southern partners.[34] This process bears some resemblance to the "framing" activity that transnational social movement theory attributes to NGO activists.[35] However, Bob's approach undermines the representative claims of NGOs which the framing literature legitimates. According to the latter, northern and southern activists negotiate to agree on a frame that will both represent the poor and also resonate with global civil society. In sharp contrast, Bob "denies the meritocracy of suffering, with the worst-off groups necessarily getting the most help."[36] Representation is highly selective and arbitrary in practice, he argues, leaving most groups in obscurity. Today, activists on the left frequently face a counter-network of right wing opponents who also use framing effectively. If framing alone cannot explain policy outcomes, Bob infers, then the relative effectiveness of the two opposing sides must depend on other power factors such as the relative strength of resources and state ties in rival networks.[37] Bob's empirical research shows the necessity of mapping NGO networks by looking well beyond only those actors that voice the shared values and common discourse of a network defined by *normative homogeneity*. While he finds that the high level of conflict among NGOs in global civil society limits the effectiveness of many campaigns, Bob fails to open up the individual NGO to reveal internal contention between the latent agendas of NGO partners. His NGOs remain hard-shelled, autonomous actors.

Comparing these two realists, Bob attributes to NGOs much more independent agency and influence than does Drezner, but much less representation. Neither one finds significant inadvertent consequences of NGO action. The expectation of inadvertent or even tragic consequences of well-intended action is found in the classical realists E. H. Carr, Reinhold Niebuhr, and Hans Morgenthau.

Such a tragic sensibility reminiscent of classical realism can be found among several contemporary scholars of NGOs (who do not identify themselves as realists). Alex de Waal has long opposed humanitarian military intervention and indictments by the International Criminal Court for creating counterproductive, inadvertent consequences.[38] Alan Kuperman goes much further in attributing negative consequences to humanitarianism, arguing that rebel groups deliberately provoke their opponents into genocidal reactions, hoping to draw in the international community on their side of civil wars.[39] DeMars argues that the international humanitarian network, across refugee, relief, and human rights organizations, has served as the "default state maintenance system" for collapsed states in Africa, forming an inadvertent, mutually reinforcing relationship with warlord conflict practices.[40]

These studies make a compelling case that realism must take NGOs seriously if it is to give a competent account of power relations in world politics. To do so, however, realism must absorb elements of liberalism and constructivism.

Which constructivism?

Constructivism—with its complex genealogy, bewildering internal debates, and seemingly endless variants—actually consists of a few core ideas. Constructivist scholars are interested in change—explaining change that has occurred, and promoting progressive change. Constructivists are dissatisfied with traditional theories in terms of ontology, epistemology, and methodology.

Ontology is about what exists, what realities and processes are out there in society that we need to understand. For IR, world events since 1989 have demonstrated dramatically that a "superpower" can quickly and radically redefine its interests, or even dissolve itself. In addition, small countries can suddenly be born, be rebuilt by the international community, or collapse into forms of warlord anarchy. Neither neoliberalism nor neorealism could explain these changes. Scholars and students sought new ontological premises for understanding which actors are important in world politics and what drives change.

Epistemology is about how we can know the social realities that concern us. Constructivists participate in a broader "interpretive turn" which questions rationalist and positivist research programs in social science. After 1989 and 1991, when Russia gave up without a fight first its European empire and then its Soviet empire, constructivists have found it impossible to accept that state rationality is unvarying over time, unaffected by interaction with other actors, and easily read by observers. Constructivists also reject positivism, which holds that only what is observable and measurable can be known, or needs to be known. Instead, reality is socially constructed, and is therefore contingent and subject to change. After 1989, such an approach promised to account for the rapid pace of global change better than rationalism or positivism.

However, our review of selected realist/rationalist approaches to studying NGOs and networks (particularly Drezner and Bob) shows that in the right hands they can be very fruitful. Problems arise from the exclusivity often associated with rationalism and positivism, which leads to denial of any other way to know, or anything else worth knowing, and results in homogenizing actor rationalities and norms. Consequently, we are loath to abandon either rationalist or interpretivist modes of understanding world politics.

Methodology is about how professional scholars actually observe and analyze the social realities that interest them, and explain their conclusions to one another. Our sense is that IR epistemological debates since the 1980s have yielded little new understanding. The priorities for scholars ought to be more methodological and ontological: get into the field, avoid theoretical preconceptions that homogenize the actors and obfuscate the politics, and distrust models that dictate that you stop looking for the politics. As explained below, the most useful rule of thumb for studying NGOs may be methodological in the simplest sense: *follow the partners.*

Most constructivism in IR leans earnestly toward idealist ontology, and is concerned largely with the influence of ideas, values, norms and discourse in shaping state conceptions of national interests.[41] We challenge this commitment to idealism. Constructivism has opened up the "minds" of states and other actors to explore how they form interests, but has largely ignored state "bodies" in the sense of material realities like land, borders, food, demographic realities, energy sources, and also the human bodies of citizens, immigrants, internally displaced persons, and refugees. Rationalism and positivism assumed too much about actors, their motives and means, and did not look hard enough at all the available sources of evidence. In light of this negative legacy, it seems important that constructivism be broader than the interpretive turn or the linguistic turn, to include (as a constructivist might say) "material practices" as well as linguistic practices.[42]

Margaret Keck and Kathryn Sikkink's 1998 book, *Activists beyond Borders*, portrays politically effective NGOs in a sophisticated constructivist account that can be generalized by scholars as theory, and by activists as an organizational model.[43] "Transnational advocacy networks" are led by NGOs but may include other kinds of actors, all bound together by "shared values, a common discourse, and dense exchanges of information and services."[44] Transnational advocacy networks mount campaigns toward a common goal and against a common target, in which members "develop explicit, visible ties and mutually recognized roles."[45] For these authors, members of the network must be normatively homogeneous; the network excludes NGOs that do not engage in public advocacy, and denies the existence of hidden or normatively anomalous partners.

While we agree that networks are led by NGOs and may contain other kinds of actors, the most distinctive element of our approach is to stipulate that a network incorporates *all those actors that share any common partners*. Thus our approach encompasses all kinds of NGOs, not only advocacy groups, and allows for network members that may be hidden from other members, or may deviate from the network's common norms, values, or discourse.

We draw on constructivism to discern NGO politics and renew international theory. However, we seek a common sense constructivism that is light enough to leave the office and take "on the road," encourages field research, takes seriously both the ideas and the material practices of actors, pays attention to both formal and informal institutions, and recognizes that the social construction of actors may be mutual and at the same time involve conflict and asymmetric power.

Several scholars have already explored aspects of our itinerary. Ralph Pettman's "commonsense constructivism" recommends that scholars move dialectically between three positions: theorizing with critical distance, conducting fieldwork, and engaging in committed political action.[46] In the 1993 book, *Ideas and Foreign Policy*, John A. Hall counsels a middle ground, suggesting that, "Ideas and [material] circumstances are held to interrelate and interpenetrate in ways both deep and subtle."[47] Samuel Barkin admonishes researchers of international organizations "to remember to look, and to remember to look beyond the obvious, at all the potential sources and forms of power."[48]

Michael Barnett and Martha Finnemore in their 2004 book, *Rules for the World: International Organizations in Global Politics*, propose to refocus the subfield of IO on real international organizations, and redefine constructivism along the way. Although academics, Barnett was working at the UN during 1994 while Finnemore was researching the World Bank in Washington, DC. Comparing experiences, they concluded that their IR graduate training "had not prepared us for what international organizations were *really* like."[49]

Barnett and Finnemore's research strategy utilizes organizational and bureaucratic theory imported from sociology to assert the autonomy of intergovernmental organizations (IGOs) to exercise agency and make and enforce rules independent of state interests and pressures. They also seek to reveal the bureaucratic pathologies of which international organizations are capable when they betray their missions. The book is important because it takes power seriously, it exposes the longstanding indifference of IR theory to real international organizations, and it sets a productive research agenda by posing the questions of organizational autonomy and pathology.

Yet there are serious problems. Barnett and Finnemore pay little attention to NGOs, which possess much less authority than international organizations to "constitute social reality."[50] In effect, they reproduce a marginalization of NGOs much like the marginalization of IGOs that they overturn. They examine each IGO in isolation, an approach with limited value for studying NGOs that inhabit networks with many other kinds of actors. Their concept of pathology, leading to therapy and reform, fails to capture the extremes of inadvertent and tragic consequences that exercising power can and does generate in the international environment. Finally, there is a more fundamental ontological issue in using bureaucratic theory to diagnose the pathologies of IGOs. As socially engaged scholars, their aspiration is to a world of UN agencies that are hard-shelled, rational bureaucracies, reformed of their pathologies, and exercising power with states, and sometimes against them. Even if this is what some IGOs are, or can be, it does not represent the full reality of NGO ontology.[51]

NGOs are not wholly rational bureaucracies, and their most important activity is not making or enforcing rules. The institutional reality of NGOs is expressed much more through their imperative to affiliate with far-flung societal and political partners. NGOs therefore assume institutional forms that are more fluid and protean than rational bureaucracies, even when they present a bureaucratic face to the world. NGOs, as constituted by all their partners at any particular moment, are ontologically interwoven with their partners. NGOs and their partners are part of one another. This by no means leads to a denial of NGO agency or power. But NGO agency often emerges out of an appearance of weakness and an ontology of relationship.[52]

20 *Introduction*

Two scholars have penetrated the multilayered ambiguity of NGO ontology and epistemology with exceptional depth. Brian H. Smith wrote in 1990 about dozens of NGOs with headquarters in Europe and North America and operations in Latin America.[53] Smith followed an idiosyncratic comparative approach, shaped by his many years of experience working as a missionary in Chile, surrounded by NGOs. Dorothea Hilhorst, trained as an anthropologist, spent three years in participant observation of a single NGO in the Philippines.[54] Both authors watched NGOs very carefully for a very long time, and they arrive at strikingly similar conclusions about what NGOs are and how to study them.

Smith opens up NGOs to reveal internal organizational conflict between partners in the societies and governments of their home countries, and also among their Latin American host country societies and governments:

> There are multiple agendas being pursued by several groups at once, and several of the actors are not unitary but made up of clusters of subgroups with different objectives that must be balanced, sometimes in creative tension.
> ... Moreover, some of the multiple goals of the actors are manifest and public, while others are latent and sometimes hidden to public view—even to other partner groups in the system.[55]

Smith portrays NGOs as permeable, internally divided, and pervaded by both open and hidden conflict among their partners. Partners pursue both open and latent agendas. Holding the network together requires that some partners not know too much about what other partners are really doing. Dorothea Hilhorst, too, sees NGOs as multiple realities:

> NGOs present different faces to different stakeholders, for instance in relating with donor representatives, clients or colleagues. Which is the real face, or in case they are all real, what does that mean for our understanding of NGOs?
> To unravel these questions, we have to take on board a more dynamic approach to organizations. This starts with treating organizations not as things, but as open-ended processes ... Rather than taking organizations at face value, we have to ask and observe how the claims and performances of NGOs acquire meaning in practice. NGOs are not things but processes and instead of asking what an NGO is, the more appropriate question then becomes how "NGO-ing" is done.
> ... However, when looking at NGO practice, the boundaries that surround organizations and activities become vague or may

evaporate altogether. The NGO may shrivel to proportion of a mere post box, or ... become an only slightly distinguishable part of a larger whole.[56]

Hilhorst argues that NGOs are multiple realities, but that many of those realities can be known. Therefore, the fundamental research challenge is not *epistemological*, as some strands of constructivism argue. NGO reality is not inherently elusive or opaque. Instead the core research challenges are *ontological*—avoiding misleading models of NGOs as hard-shelled bureaucracies or of networks as normatively homogeneous, and especially *methodological*—getting into the field with enough time and determination and other resources to observe all the faces of NGO practice. Both Smith and Hilhorst spent several years observing NGOs in the field. They followed the partners. For them, the organizational boundaries of NGOs are not hard-shelled, and NGOs are not exclusively or primarily rule-making bureaucracies.

Like Smith and Hilhorst, we open up NGOs and their networks to reveal their permeable ontology. NGOs are already ontologically linked to the states and other actors with which they interact, and which they mutually constitute. However, this does not necessarily mean that a sophisticated research design could not utilize a mix of approaches, selectively tightening and relaxing black-box assumptions for individual organizations, networks, and global civil society as a whole.

The accelerating interpenetration of national and global realities in transnational politics demands a serious and sustained dialogue across subfield boundaries, and across the social sciences.[57] In some respects, the mindset and explanatory toolkit of comparative politics may be useful for illuminating the politics of NGOs, in combination with IR approaches.[58] Discovering the real impact of NGOs demands penetrating field research on the politics and societies of host countries, which may be available only to nationals or anthropologists who are immersed in the language and culture, or to investigative reporters or former NGO practitioners.[59]

Precisely because NGOs are themselves "multiple realities," and also because NGOs bridge and link to so many different kinds of other actors across nations and across levels of the international system, therefore no single social theory can illuminate everything that NGOs do and everything they influence. At the end of the day, constructivism is about *actors under construction*, so it must address the whole actor (both material and normative dimensions) and all the relationships that shape it.

Whence liberalism?

With respect to NGO research, the locus for cutting-edge theorizing may have passed from liberalism to constructivism. However, we find a growing number of studies that partake of the traditional liberal interest in international norms and institutions, but that push the envelope in their empirical research.

Many recent studies continue to trace and catalogue the growing ambit of global NGO influence, often under a larger category of actors and processes, such as nonstate actors, global civil society, transnational activism, or global governance.[60] Another group includes works that present the growing number and influence of NGOs within a particular issue-area or policy field, such as human rights, international development, humanitarianism, environmentalism, women's rights, or peacebuilding.[61]

These books have empirical value, and the best ones push past the conventional limits of IR research on NGOs. For example, Abdelrahman shows that a high proportion of NGOs in Egypt, across rural and urban and several issue areas, have a board member or significant patron linked to the government's Ministry of Social Affairs.[62] Donini lifts the veil on pervasive attempts by governments, warlords, and even public opinion to manipulate and instrumentalize humanitarian agencies in conflict situations.[63] Hall examines the power of NGOs operating at local, national and international levels to reduce armed violence.[64] And Magone, Neuman and Weissman reveal for the first time the humanitarian negotiations that one NGO (MSF) has undertaken over the past decade with actors that attempted to instrumentalize them.[65]

These more empirically adventurous works show the need for our book. Each of them pursues empirical research on NGO political and/or societal partners farther than others had before attempted.[66] We seek to theorize these new directions in liberal research.

Anchoring practices of NGOing

A research agenda taking practice, rather than actors, as its point of departure may better comprehend the complex politics of NGOs.[67] By engaging in two *anchoring practices*, NGOs generate complex *bridging effects* in world politics, which set the stage for distinctive *power dynamics*. Thus, the three conceptual touchstones of *practice, bridging*, and *power* that inform our critique of NGO studies also guide our itinerary to renew International Relations theory.

Each chapter of this book shows how an empirical case or mid-level theory addresses these anchoring practices, bridging effects, and power dynamics. Hence: NGOing.

International NGOs happen when:

a private actors claim to pursue public purposes; and
b they link with societal and political partners in at least two countries.

These two anchoring practices happen simultaneously, and every moment of the life of an NGO. An NGO that is not engaging in these practices is defunct or fraudulent. At the same time, every NGO has to sustain these practices, repeating them and thereby reproducing itself, always in relation to its partners. These are relational practices. Highlighting these two practices may appear to be so obvious as to be banal. But starting here, rather than with NGO normative claims and aspirations, has profound implications for revealing the institutional reality and power of NGOs and their networks.

Private actors claim to pursue public purposes

This anchoring practice is readily recognizable as Tocqueville's "associationalism" in America; "Mr. Smith Goes to Washington"; or Gandhi marches to the sea. By this anchoring practice, NGOs are distinguishable from corporations (private actors pursuing private profit), and also states, as well as political parties and revolutionary movements trying to take over states (public actors addressing public purposes). This practice of NGOing presumes the autonomy of civil society from the state, or entails the risk to act as if such an autonomous civil society exists, or can be brought into being.

All NGOs today replicate the two generic normative claims of representation and enforcement that are implicit in the first anchoring practice of a private actor claiming to pursue a public purpose. NGOs need not go out of their way to do this, because these claims are inherent in NGOing. To be in the NGO game entails making a *representative claim*, to speak for the people or species at the grassroots, and a *secular sanction claim*, to invoke or enforce global norms from above. All NGOs reenact these dramatic gestures, imitating other NGOs.

Each explicit normative claim is linked to an implicit causal claim about how the world works. Behind each NGO's normative claim of representation is a causal claim of *empowerment causality*—that the NGO actually and consistently mobilizes the power of those it claims to represent. Behind the normative claim of secular sanction is a claim of *enforcement causality*—that the intentions of the NGO to enforce particular norms actually create those effects, everywhere, consistently.[68] The normative claims implicitly—and therefore structurally—veil the causal claims in their far-flung NGO networks across different countries. It is transparently implausible to claim that a single organization—even Amnesty International—can consistently empower the weak and enforce global norms anywhere regardless of local political or societal conditions. But NGOs regularly make such claims, and supporting or belonging to an NGO entails suspending disbelief is such claims.

As private actors claiming to pursue public purposes, NGOs enacting the first anchoring practice also generate direct bridging effects. Precisely by crossing between *private* actors and *public* purposes, all NGOs bridge society and state. The claim of empowerment causality is reiterated and legitimated pre-empirically by pluralist constructivism, and the claim of enforcement causality is reiterated and legitimated pre-empirically by globalist constructivism. Our practice approach problematizes what pluralists and globalists assume.

This first anchoring practice also entails direct power dynamics. In the interfaces between society and state, power relations can take many forms. NGO self-descriptions, and the dominant pluralist and globalist schools of NGO theory built upon them, would emphasize and restrict the flow of power to two vertical paths: from below in representative empowerment causality; and from above in norm enforcement causality. However, many other paths and forms of power are possible. For example, a state may co-opt the legitimacy of a societal actor for another purpose, or use an NGO as a surrogate to extend its reach, or (paradoxically) to renounce political responsibility for some outcome.

This particularity of any NGO's relational links is crucial. The first two causal claims (empowerment and enforcement causality) generate an illusion of general, uniform progress that *conceals the heterogeneous particularity* of each local situation, and often obscures the genius of singular NGO responses to a particular historical moment.[69]

NGOs link with societal and political partners in several countries

This second anchoring practice occurs simultaneously and continuously with the first. The universalist moral reason of NGOs demands that they take whatever they do "on the road," seeking to expand across the world, which requires linking with far-flung societal and political partners. This universalist faith is vividly expressed in the most mimicked NGO names:

[Dandelions] International; [Dandelions] Watch, [Dandelions] Without Borders, Save The [Dandelions], and more recently, Global [Dandelions].

This second anchoring practice of linking with societal and political partners entails two additional characteristic NGO normative claims that are essential to establish the authority of the NGO to partner globally. The claim of *global moral compass* is an act of "self-authorization," appointing oneself as a global moral authority in a given issue area ("I am Jimmy Carter and I know what you need").[70] The claim of *modular technique* is a set of practices that an NGO can bring to bear to alleviate unmet needs or unprotected rights anywhere in the world ("I am Jimmy Carter and my people already know what to do: conflict mediation, election monitoring, mosquito netting for malaria"). The package must be replicable and portable, that is, modular.[71]

Each normative claim is linked to an implicit, or partially veiled, causal claim. Behind the normative claim of *global moral compass* is the claim of *circumscribed causality*—that the NGO's operations or presence will have no side effects on the target country's politics or society. Behind the normative claim of *modular technique* is the claim of *magic bullet causality*—that the technique will in fact create its intended effect regardless of the political or societal context.

These causal claims are not optional for NGO activity. The very existence and functioning of every NGO depends utterly on each of its crucial partners suspending disbelief in the claims that its operations are pristinely insulated in both directions from their social and political environments; that NGO operations will not influence the context, and that the context will not affect the operations. Because these causal claims are inherently implausible, NGOs wisely keep the focus on their normative claims.[72] This whole process involves relational practices between mutually constituting actors—NGOs and their political and societal partners.

So, NGOs link themselves to societal and political partners *by the authority of* their normative claims, that is, their principled mandates. But the full spectrum of real politics can be discerned only by taking one's eyes *off* the mesmerizing vision of the NGO's heroic principles and aspirations, and paying more attention to actual partner relationships. This is really quite difficult to do, which is why so few NGO boosters or detractors manage to achieve it. To "follow the partners" is the single most important methodological imperative for conducting penetrating research on the politics of NGOs. The reason is that politics plays out in the power dynamics of the bridging relationships that NGOs create as they partner.

Table I.2 How NGO anchoring practices conceal their particularity and politics

NGO anchoring practices	(a) Private actor claims to pursue public purposes			(b) Links with societal and political partners in several countries	
Explicit normative claim	Representative claim	Secular sanction		Global moral compass	Modular technique
Implicit causal claim	Empowerment causality	Enforcement causality		Circumscribed causality	Magic bullet causality
What claims conceal	Conceal the particularity of NGO relationships			Conceal the full spectrum of NGO politics	
Specific overlooked bridging effects:	(1) between state and society; (2) between family and market; (3) between normative and material; (4) between religious and secular; (5) between conflict and cooperation; (6) between agency and structure; and (7) between national and international.				

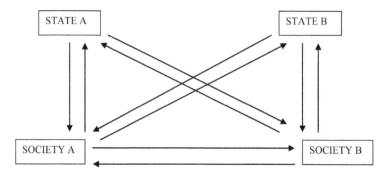

Figure I.1 State/society bridging effects for one NGO in two countries

The effects of the NGO on its local environment are available to be captured, resisted or shaped by local actors. The second pair of NGO claims (circumscribed causality and magic bullet causality) actively obscures the very political plasticity of NGOs that makes them most interesting to potential partners. And scholars who reiterate those NGO claims theoretically—the pluralist and globalist schools of idealist constructivism—inadvertently reinforce this political inattentiveness. Through the structural requirement that NGOs must assert universal normative claims, both NGOs and scholars inadvertently help to *conceal the full spectrum of real politics* in which NGOs are immersed.

Table I.2 summarizes how the two anchoring practices conceal NGO power and particularity. The second anchoring practice also entails multiple, direct bridging effects. A single NGO operating in two countries must have at least one societal partner and one political partner in each country. (The political partnership may entail only the permission of the government, rebel group or warlord to be present and operate.) Each relationship entails causal effects in both directions. In this simplest of models, one NGO embodies ten distinct bridging effects between two states and their societies (as illustrated in Figure I.1). The NGO stands between the state and society of each state (four vertical effects), links the two societies (two horizontal effects), and also embodies relationships between each state and the other society (four transverse effects).

This abstract schematic does not specify which of innumerable societal actors and national or local governmental institutions are linked to a particular NGO. All of these are empirical questions whose answers may vary from case to case, and from time to time in the same case. In broad terms, an NGO may bridge religious and secular actors within one society, or between several societies. Families or corporate business actors within one or several societies may also be bridged to each other and to states.

Because the modular technique of an NGO often has a physical/material dimension, many NGOs bridge the normative and material gap in several countries. NGOs shape the material infrastructure of human societies and states in profound ways, which are immediately evident in the work of environmental NGOs (air, water, land, energy, species) and humanitarian NGOs (hunger, refugees, mass murder, torture). For example, in humanitarian and refugee affairs, NGOs can decisively structure the material relationship between national population and territory that is constitutive for states.[73] All of these ways in which NGO networks can constitute states are missed by both myopic realists who ignore international organizations, and by idealist constructivists who ignore the material "bodies" of states in favor of their ideas and ideals.

While most scholars of NGOs conceptualize networks as normatively homogeneous, we conceptualize NGO networks as including any common partners, including hidden or normatively discordant partners. Conventional views overlook the reality that normative and material relationships between NGO partners in the network become available to be mobilized for the movement of information, material resources, people, norms and responsibility. Taking into account several NGOs in several countries, the web of links, and potential power implications, expands exponentially.

The making of (potential) networks is not something that NGOs do only some of the time when they decide to launch a campaign or cooperate in an aid operation. Instead, they make potential networks every day, just by NGOing. Which relationships are politically significant in a particular case or network varies over time and is always a matter of empirical investigation. Researchers are ill-served by IR or other theories that presumptively truncate the range of relationships where power might be found at play.

The second anchoring practice thus generates profound power dynamics. It is clear that we need a broad understanding of power as multidimensional, relational, and sometimes hidden and paradoxical.[74] We need to be able to discern power at play through the lenses of realism (sticks), liberalism (carrots) and constructivism (seeds). In our view, the study of NGOs, with an emphasis on practice, offers a particularly favorable opportunity for integrating rationalist and constructivist approaches to understanding world politics.[75]

As NGOs make networks every day, their relationships are politically significant even before they are mobilized in a campaign or operation.

Crucially, political actors in each country vigilantly watch these NGO relationships with other actors, with a view to *either capturing them for their own purposes or neutralizing them for use by their rivals*. Every category of bridging effect identified above creates an interface that is politically significant. Every encounter generated by NGOs may have a power dynamic of some kind. The interfaces and encounters include the four distinct bridging relationships between states and societies; links between families, market actors and states; religious and secular actors; normative and material realities. Across any of those relationships bridged by NGOs, there is the potential for a power encounter entailing, and institutionalizing, both cooperation and conflict. All of these bridged actors and realities constitute a network. The number and kinds of power encounters are not "infinite," strictly speaking, but they are "unlimited" in the sense that any attempt to create a taxonomy of NGO tactics will have a short half-life measured by the time it takes other NGOs and other actors to counter the old tactics with innovative ones.

Successful NGO professionals learn complex scripts to keep their partners in the game by not totally discouraging partners' hopes for attaining latent agendas. Ethical and competent NGO professionals channel their partners' often conflicting latent agendas into fueling the cooperative, salient agenda of the NGO official mission.

In sum, every NGO is itself a power-laced encounter, a nexus of several other cooperating *and* competing actors, with complex interests and agendas, often from halfway around the world. The global is local, and the political uses to which this encounter may be put are radically up for grabs. This is why NGO research is so interesting, and also so challenging. The "realist" who thinks that NGOs are epiphenomena of the power politics between states, is just not paying attention to what states really do. The United States conducts foreign policy in a sea of domestic and international NGOs, in a constant process of negotiation and mutual manipulation. Middle power states are busy networking with NGOs to create treaties and IGOs without the United States (landmines, child soldiers, greenhouse gases). The weakest, collapsed states of sub-Saharan Africa are sometimes held together—population and territory—by networks of humanitarian NGOs and IGOs. International NGOs routinely link states, or groups within a state, that are in conflict or even at war with each other.

The most profound and elusive bridging effect—and therefore, also power dynamic—is that between agency and structure. Because NGOs link societal and political actors, the agency and structural dynamics enfold them as well. We return to this question of NGO social construction in the conclusion of this book.

Conclusion: about this book

The scholars writing in this book share an affinity for NGOs. They want to understand and reveal their fascinating politics and unexpected influence. They share the view that NGOs are more important than either their detractors or their boosters claim.

Part A analyzes the strengths and weaknesses of several alternative theoretical approaches to the study of NGOs and their networks.

Morten Andersen proposes in Chapter 1 the benefits of following a practice approach to construe and explain international NGOs. The relational ontology of the emerging "practice turn" in IR allows an observer to better understand NGOing as fluid and intermingling relational processes. NGO effects are seen as emanating from interactions themselves, rather than from the attributes of static entities. A case study illustrates how NGOs engage in informal relational practices that can blur the boundaries between actors.

Governance processes beyond the state have been emerging strongly in world politics, and IR theory, since the 1990s. Karen Mingst and James Muldoon argue in Chapter 2 that global governance offers a synthetic conceptual framework to incorporate these changes. Global governance recognizes non-state actors in a multi-actor framework; incorporates transnational and international spheres and processes; brings power back in, conceptualized as transnational outcomes of governance processes; and demands normative assessment of global governance institutions. All four dimensions implicate NGOs— as significant actors in transnational institutions that exercise power and participate in processes of accountability.

In Chapter 3, Anna Ohanyan integrates insights from the three major strands of new institutionalist theory—rational choice, sociological, and historical institutionalisms—for understanding NGOs. She argues that NGOs exercise agency by bridging, and at the same time their bridging creates structural effects on NGOs themselves and other actors in the network. Gradually, NGOs institutionalize their bridged relationships with donors, host governments, and societal partners.

In Part B, we approach NGOs by evaluating cross-cutting evidence through history, across regions, and in terms of accountability.

Bob Reinalda takes a long historical view in Chapter 4, surveying the expansion of both NGOs and IGOs since the American and French revolutions. This approach shows major power governments creating new IGOs in the aftermath of major wars, and the societies of the same powers generating waves of international NGOs. As IGOs and NGOs have "co-evolved," they have constituted networks, and have instrumentalized each other to realize their various goals.

Elisabeth Bloodgood, using theories of new institutionalism and the new economics of organization, examines in Chapter 5 the effects of national regulations on the identities and legal personalities of NGOs in the OECD, with a particular focus on the United States, Japan, and Poland. National NGO regulations are a useful object of study because they provide concrete illustrations of NGO bridging practices between states and societies, and of the power dynamics that accompany NGO interactions with states.

In Chapter 6, Cristina Balboa examines the growing problem of NGO accountability. Who holds the NGOs accountable? She analyses a wide range of theoretical approaches to NGO accountability, arguing that many of them would impose such heavy demands that NGOs could not comply and still keep all their essential partners in the game. Paradoxically, but inevitably, there are severe limits to the degree of accountability that can be imposed on NGOs.

Part C presents case evidence on NGOs and their networks, revealing fascinating paradoxes of NGO effectiveness and partnering.

In Chapter 7, Shareen Hertel surveys and analyzes the growing phenomenon of public–private partnerships (PPPs) in global rule-making on labor rights. Drawing on both scholarship and field-level examples, Hertel explores the origin and evolution of PPPs, and demonstrates their relevance for IR. She develops a three-fold typology for mapping the domains in which PPPs operate, each of which combines cooperation and conflict. PPPs constitute a large arena of "constrained governance" in world politics.

Patrice McMahon examines in Chapter 8 the role of NGOs in Bosnia after the 1995 Dayton Peace Accords. She finds that NGOs consistently failed to bridge interethnic divides at the societal level in Bosnia, even as donors continued to fund their programs that claimed to do so. In this context, she critically evaluates the claims of principal–agent theory to explain both accountability and unaccountability in donor–NGO relations.

William DeMars in Chapter 9 analyzes the role of NGOs and networks in the "color revolutions" since 2000. In each successful revolution, democracy activists faced a formidable domestic social structure of security bureaucracies supporting a dictatorial regime. The activists then exercised social agency to draw in transnational partners and create a new social structure that transformed the meaning and consequences of the regime's authoritarian practices. DeMars uncovers several layers of "hidden partners" in the democracy network.

Dennis Dijkzeul in Chapter 10 compares three NGOs that addressed the needs of survivors of gender-based violence (GBV) in the eastern

Democratic Republic of the Congo during the 2000s. Based on field research over several years, he analyzes the emergence of GBV and describes the successes and inadvertent consequences of NGO operations in an environment of ongoing violence. NGOs both embody and resist instrumentalization by political and societal partners, inadvertently extending a limited form of global governance into the region.

In the Conclusion, we analyze the arguments of the contributors to this volume, examine the ontological, epistemological, and methodological implications, and explore directions for further research. Incorporating their insights, we return to the argument that conventional IR theory hides the politics of NGOs, and that an alternative practice approach to understanding international NGOs can better explain the politics missed by IR theory. We address the problem of conceptualizing NGOs and networks as international institutions, while balancing both structure and agency.

This book demonstrates that NGOs offer a privileged fulcrum for scholarship to leverage IR theory, not only to illuminate its theoretical blind spots, but also to renew its relevance to real politics.

Notes

1 Andrew F. Cooper, *Celebrity Diplomacy* (Boulder, Colo.: Paradigm, 2008); Kenneth R. Rutherford, Stefan Brem and Richard A. Matthew, eds, *Reframing the Agenda: The Impact of NGO and Middle Power Cooperation in International Security Policy* (Westport, Conn.: Praeger, 2003).
2 Cristina M. Balboa, "When Non-governmental Organizations Govern: Accountability in Private Conservation Networks," Ph.D. Dissertation in Environmental Governance, Yale University, 2009.
3 For example, in Putin's Russia and Morales' Bolivia.
4 Edelman Trust Barometer 2014 (www.slideshare.net/EdelmanInsights/2014-edelman-trust-barometer).
5 Stephen Hopgood, *The Endtimes of Human Rights* (Ithaca, NY: Cornell University Press, 2013); Antonio Donini, ed., *The Golden Fleece: Manipulation and Independence in Humanitarian Action* (Sterling, Va.: Kumarian Press, 2012); Aziz Choudry and Dip Kapoor, eds, *NGOization: Complicity, Contradictions and Prospects* (London: Zed Books, 2013); Claire Magone, Michael Neuman and Fabrice Weissman, eds, *Humanitarian Negotiations Revealed: The MSF Experience* (New York: Columbia University Press, 2012); Lyla Mehta and Steve Rayner, eds, *The Limits to Scarcity: Contesting the Politics of Allocation* (London: Routledge, 2013); and Thomas G. Weiss and Rorden Wilkinson, "Global Governance to the Rescue: Saving International Relations?" *Global Governance* 20, no. 1 (2014): 19–36.
6 www.one.org.
7 Dorothea Hilhorst, *The Real World of NGOs: Discourses, Diversity and Development* (London: Zed Books, 2003); and Bertil Dunér, "The Art of NGO-ing," Research Report 32, Stockholm: Swedish Institute of International Affairs (1999).

Introduction 33

8 Brian H, Smith, *More Than Altruism: The Politics of Private Foreign Aid* (Princeton, N.J.: Princeton University Press, 1990); Alan Fowler, "Beyond Partnership: Getting Real about NGO Relationships in the Aid System," *IDS Bulletin* 31, no. 3 (2000): 1–13; Tom Harrison, "The Role of Contestation in NGO Partnerships," *Journal of International Development* 19, no. 3 (2007): 389–400; and Issa G. Shivji, *Silences in NGO Discourse: The Role and Future of NGOs in Africa* (Oxford: Fahamu Books, 2007).
9 Stephen M. Walt, "International Relations: One World, Many Theories," *Foreign Policy* no. 110 (1998): 31.
10 John J. Mearsheimer, "The False Promise of International Institutions," *International Security* 19, no. 3 (Winter 1994/95): 5–49; and David Rieff, "The False Dawn of Civil Society," *The Nation*, 22 February 1999.
11 Kenneth N. Waltz, *Man, the State, and War: A Theoretical Analysis* (New York: Columbia University Press, 1959).
12 Kenneth N. Waltz, *Theory of International Politics* (New York: McGraw-Hill, 1979).
13 Waltz, *Man, the State, and War*, 201–210.
14 Ernst B. Haas, "Words Can Hurt You: Or, Who Said What to Whom about Regimes," in *International Regimes*, ed. Stephen D. Krasner (Ithaca, NY: Cornell University Press, 1983), 33.
15 Donald J. Puchala and Raymond F. Hopkins, "International Regimes: Lessons from Inductive Analysis," in Krasner, *International Regimes*, 63–65.
16 Richard K. Ashley, "The Poverty of Neorealism," in *Neorealism and Its Critics*, ed. Robert O. Keohane (New York: Columbia University Press, 1986), 290.
17 Peter J. Katzenstein, Robert O. Keohane and Stephen D. Krasner, "International Organization and the Study of World Politics," *International Organization* 52, no. 4 (1998): 679.
18 Alexander Wendt, "Collective Identity Formation and the International State," *American Political Science Review* 88, no. 2 (1994): 384–396.
19 John Ruggie observed that Waltz himself had deliberately embedded his 1979 structural theory within a "Durkheimian problematic" of the relation of structure to unit in a social system: John Gerard Ruggie, "Continuity and Transformation in the World Polity: Toward a Neorealist Synthesis," in *Neorealism and Its Critics*, ed. Robert O. Keohane (New York: Columbia University Press, 1986), 133.
20 James E. Dougherty and Robert L. Pfaltzgraff, Jr., *Contending Theories of International Relations: A Comprehensive Survey*, 2nd edition (New York: Harper & Row, 1981); and Paul R. Viotti and Mark V. Kauppi, *International Relations Theory* (New York: Macmillan, 1987).
21 Stephen D. Krasner, ed., *International Regimes* (Ithaca, NY: Cornell University Press, 1983); Jack Donnelly, "International Human Rights: A Regime Analysis," *International Organization* 40, no. 3 (1986): 599–642; and Conway Henderson, "Human Rights Regimes: A Bibliographic Essay," *Human Rights Quarterly* 10, no. 4 (1988): 525–43.
22 Bruce Russett and John R. O'Neal, *Triangulating Peace: Democracy, Interdependence, and International Organizations* (New York: W.W. Norton, 2001).
23 Robert O. Keohane and Joseph S. Nye, Jr, eds, *Transnational Relations and World Politics* (Cambridge, Mass.: Harvard University Press, 1972); and Richard W. Mansbach, Yale H. Ferguson and Donald E. Lampert, *The*

Web of World Politics: Non-State Actors in the Global System (Englewood Cliffs, N.J.: Prentice Hall, 1976).
24. Snyder, "International Relations: One World, Rival Theories," 59.
25. Walt, "International Relations," 32.
26. Ironically, idealist constructivism has come full circle, as Marx had famously "turned Hegel on his head" by rejecting Hegelian idealism for dialectical materialism as the engine of history.
27. Martha Finnemore and Kathryn Sikkink, "Taking Stock: The Constructivist Research Program in International Relations and Comparative Politics," *Annual Review of Political Science* 4 (June 2001): 391–416.
28. William E. DeMars, *NGOs and Transnational Networks: Wild Cards in World Politics* (London: Pluto Press, 2005), 35–40.
29. Thomas Risse-Kappen, ed., *Bringing Transnational Relations Back In: Non-State Actors, Domestic Structures and International Institutions* (Cambridge University Press, 1995); Laura MacDonald, *Supporting Civil Society: The Political Role of Non-Governmental Organizations in Central America* (New York: St. Martin's Press, 1995); Paul Wapner, *Environmental Activism and World Civic Politics* (Albany, NY: State University of New York Press, 1996); Jackie Smith, Charles Chatfield and Ron Pagnucco, eds, *Transnational Social Movements and Global Politics: Solidarity Beyond the State* (Syracuse, NY: Syracuse University Press, 1997); Julie Fisher, *Nongovernments: NGOs and the Political Development of the Third World* (West Hartford, Conn.: Kumarian Press, 1998); and Ann M. Florini, ed., *The Third Force: The Rise of Transnational Civil Society* (Washington, DC: Carnegie Endowment for International Peace, 2000).
30. Peter Willetts, ed., *'The Conscience of the World': The Influence of Non-governmental Organizations in the UN System* (Washington, DC: Brookings, 1996); Thomas G. Weiss and Leon Gordenker, eds, *NGOs, The UN, and Global Governance* (Boulder, Colo.: Lynne Rienner, 1996); Kerstin Martens, "NGO Participation at International Conferences: Assessing Theoretical Accounts," *Transnational Associations*, issue 3 (2000): 115–126; Ann-Marie Clark, *Diplomacy of Conscience: Amnesty International and Changing Human Rights Norms* (Princeton, N.J.: Princeton University Press, 2001).
31. Martha Finnemore, *National Interests in International Society* (Ithaca, NY: Cornell University Press, 1996).
32. A few realists have taken the political significance of international institutions seriously: Samuel P. Huntington, "Transnational Organizations in World Politics," *World Politics* 25, no. 3 (1973): 333–68; and Stephen D. Krasner, "Power Politics, Institutions, and Transnational Relations," in *Bringing Transnational Relations Back In*, ed. Thomas Risse-Kappen (Cambridge University Press, 1995), 257–279.
33. Daniel W. Drezner, *All Politics is Global: Explaining International Regulatory Regimes* (Princeton, N.J.: Princeton University Press, 2007).
34. Clifford Bob, *The Marketing of Rebellion: Insurgents, Media, and International Activism* (Cambridge: Cambridge University Press, 2005).
35. Margaret E. Keck and Kathryn Sikkink, *Activists beyond Borders: Advocacy Networks in International Politics* (Ithaca, NY: Cornell University Press, 1998); and David A. Snow and Robert D. Benford, "Ideology, Frame Resonance, and Participant Mobilization," in *From Structure to Action: Comparing Social*

Movement Research across Cultures, ed. Bert Klandersman, Hanspeter Kriesi and Sidney Tarrow (Greenwich, Conn.: JAI Press, 1988), 197–217.
36 Bob, *The Marketing of Rebellion*, 6.
37 Clifford Bob, *The Global Right Wing and the Clash of World Politics* (Cambridge: Cambridge University Press, 2012); Keck and Sikkink, *Activists beyond Borders*; and DeMars, *NGOs and Transnational Networks*.
38 Alex de Waal and Rakiya Omaar, "Can Military Intervention Be 'Humanitarian'?" *Middle East Report*, no. 187/188, (1994): 2–8; and Alex de Waal, "No Such Thing as Humanitarian Intervention," *Harvard International Review*, 21 March 2007 (http://hir.harvard.edu/archives/1482).
39 Alan Kuperman and Timothy Crawford, eds, *Gambling on Humanitarian Intervention: Moral Hazard, Rebellion, and Civil War* (New York: Routledge, 2006).
40 William DeMars, "War and Mercy in Africa," *World Policy Journal* 17, no. 2 (Summer 2000): 1–10.
41 Michael Barnett, "Social Constructivism," in *The Globalization of World Politics: An Introduction to International Relations*, 4th edition, eds John Baylis, Steve Smith and Patricia Owens (Oxford: Oxford University Press, 2008); and Emanuel Adler, "Constructivism in International Relations," in *Handbook of International Relations*, eds Walter Carlsnaes, Thomas Risse and Beth A. Simmons (London: Sage, 2002).
42 For a project to theorize both material and symbolic/normative power, see Michael Barnett and Raymond Duvall, eds, *Power in Global Governance* (Cambridge University Press, 2005), especially Michael Barnett and Raymond Duvall, "Power in Global Governance," 1–32; and Ronnie D. Lipschutz, "Global Civil Society and Global Governmentality," 229–48.
43 Keck and Sikkink, *Activists beyond Borders*; Thomas Risse, Stephen C. Ropp and Kathryn Sikkink, eds, *The Power of Human Rights: International Norms and Domestic Change* (Cambridge: Cambridge University Press, 1999); and Thomas Risse, Stephen C. Ropp and Kathryn Sikkink, eds, *The Persistent Power of Human Rights: From Commitment to Compliance* (Cambridge: Cambridge University Press, 2013).
44 Keck and Sikkink, *Activists beyond Borders*, 2.
45 Ibid., 7.
46 Ralph Pettman, *Commonsense Constructivism: Or the Making of World Affairs* (Armonk, NY: M. E. Sharpe, 2000).
47 John A. Hall, "Ideas and the Social Sciences," in *Ideas and Foreign Policy: Beliefs, Institutions, and Political Change*, eds Judith Goldstein and Robert O. Keohane (Ithaca, NY: Cornell University Press, 1993), 32 and 45.
48 J. Samuel Barkin, *International Organization: Theories and Institutions* (New York: Palgrave Macmillan, 2006), 25; and J. Samuel Barkin, *Realist Constructivism: Rethinking International Relations Theory* (Cambridge: Cambridge University Press, 2010).
49 Michael Barnett and Martha Finnemore, *Rules for the World: International Organizations in Global Politics* (Ithaca, NY: Cornell University Press, 2004), vii.
50 Ibid., 31.
51 In other works, Michael Barnett has taken positions, particularly on humanitarian issues and NGOs, in tension with the positions in Barnett and Finnemore: Michael Barnett, "Evolution Without Progress?

Humanitarianism in a World of Hurt," *International Organization* 63, no. 4 (October 2009): 621–663; Michael Barnett, "Humanitarianism Transformed," *Perspectives on Politics* 3, no. 4 (December 2005): 723–40; and Michael Barnett, *Empire of Humanity: A History of Humanitarianism* (Ithaca, NY: Cornell University Press, 2011).

52 Such relations of mutually constituted actors point to larger patterns of "structural power." See Barnett and Duvall, *Power in Global Governance*, 18–20.

53 Brian H, Smith, *More Than Altruism: The Politics of Private Foreign Aid* (Princeton, N.J.: Princeton University Press, 1990).

54 Hilhorst, *The Real World of NGOs*; and Dorothea Hilhorst, "The Art of NGO-ing: Everyday Practices as Key to Understanding Development NGOs," in *Reconceptualising NGOs and Their Roles in Development*, eds Paul Opoku-Mensah, David Lewis and Terje Tvedt (Aalborg, Denmark: Aalborg University Press, 2007), 297–325.

55 Smith, *More Than Altruism*, 279–81.

56 Hilhorst, "The Art of NGO-ing," 297–300.

57 David A. Lake, "Rightful Rules: Authority, Order, and the Foundations of Global Governance," *International Studies Quarterly* 54, no. 3 (2010): 587–613.

58 For exemplary NGO case studies by a comparativist, see Shareen Hertel, *Unexpected Power: Conflict and Change among Transnational Activists* (Ithaca, NY: Cornell University Press, 2006). On integrating comparative and international approaches, see Peter Gourevitch, "The Second Image Reversed: The International Sources of Domestic Politics," *International Organization* 32 (1978): 881–912; Robert D. Putnam, "Diplomacy and Domestic Politics: The Logic of Two-Level Games," *International Organization* 42 (Summer 1988): 427–460; Gabriel A. Almond, "The International-National Connection," *British Journal of Political Science* 19, no. 2 (1989): 237–259; and Harald Müller and Thomas Risse-Kappen, "From the Outside In and from the Inside Out: International Relations, Domestic Politics, and Foreign Policy," in *The Limits of State Autonomy: Societal Groups and Foreign Policy Formulation*, eds David Skidmore and Valerie M. Hudson (Boulder, Colo.: Westview Press, 1993), 25–48.

59 For example, see Maha M. Abdelrahman, *Civil Society Exposed: The Politics of NGOs in Egypt* (London: Tauris, 2004); Masooda Bano, *Breakdown: How Aid Is Eroding Institutions for Collective Action in Pakistan* (Stanford, Calif.: Stanford University Press, 2012); Mark Schuller, *Killing with Kindness: Haiti, International Aid, and NGOs* (New Brunswick, N.J.: Rutgers University Press, 2012); Samantha Power, *A Problem from Hell: America and the Age of Genocide* (New York: Basic Books, 2002); and David Kennedy, *The Dark Sides of Virtue: Reassessing International Humanitarianism* (Princeton, N.J.: Princeton University Press, 2005).

60 Peter Willetts, *Non-Governmental Organizations in World Politics: The Construction of Global Governance* (London: Routledge, 2011); Helen V. Milner and Andrew Moravcsik, eds, *Power, Interdependence, and Nonstate Actors in World Politics* (Princeton, N.J.: Princeton University Press, 2009); Mary Kaldor *et al.*, eds, *Global Civil Society Yearbook* (London: London School of Economics, annually 2001–2012); and Sidney Tarrow, *The New Transnational Activism* (Cambridge: Cambridge University Press, 2005).

61 Claude E. Welch, Jr, ed., *NGOs and Human Rights: Promise and Performance* (Philadelphia, PA: University of Pennsylvania Press, 2000); Thomas Lyon, ed., *Good Cop/Bad Cop: Environmental NGOs and Their Strategies toward Business* (London: Routledge, 2010); Tina Wallace, Fenella Porter and Mark Ralph-Bowman, eds, *Aid, NGOs and the Realities of Women's Lives: A Perfect Storm* (Rugby: Practical Action, 2013); and Henry F. Carey, *Privatizing the Democratic Peace: Policy Dilemmas of NGO Peacebuilding* (New York: Palgrave Macmillan, 2012).
62 Abdelrahman, *Civil Society Exposed*.
63 Donini, *The Golden Fleece*.
64 Rodney Bruce Hall, *Reducing Armed Violence with NGO Governance* (London: Routledge, 2013).
65 Magone, Neuman and Weissman, *Humanitarian Negotiations Revealed*.
66 Mary Kaldor, *Global Civil Society: An Answer to War* (Cambridge: Polity Press, 2003); Deborah D. Avant, Martha Finnemore and Susan K. Sell, eds, *Who Governs the Globe?* (Cambridge: Cambridge University Press, 2010); Randall W. Stone, *Controlling Institutions: International Organizations and the Global Economy* (Cambridge: Cambridge University Press, 2011); Sarah S. Stroup, *Borders Among Activists: International NGOs in the United States, Britain, and France* (Ithaca, NY: Cornell University Press, 2012); Emilie M. Hafner-Burton, *Making Human Rights a Reality* (Princeton, N.J.: Princeton University Press, 2013); and Benjamin Stachursky, *The Promise and Perils of Transnationalization: NGO Activism and the Socialization of Women's Human Rights in Egypt and Iran* (London: Routledge, 2013).
67 Ann Swidler, "What Anchors Cultural Practices," in *The Practice Turn in Contemporary Theory*, eds Theodore R. Schatzki, Karen Knorr Cetina and Eike von Savigny (London: Routledge, 2001), 74–92; and Ole Jacob Sending and Iver B. Neumann, "Banking on Power: How Some Practices in an International Organization Anchor Others," in *International Practices*, eds Emanuel Adler and Vincent Pouliot (Cambridge: Cambridge University Press, 2011), 231–254.
68 In the theoretical debate about the primacy of *principled ideas* about right and wrong, justice and injustice, in NGO activity, versus *causal ideas* about how the world works, we take a hybrid position that principled ideas are primary, but also serve to veil causal claims. On principled ideas, see Keck and Sikkink, *Activists beyond Borders*. On causal ideas, see Peter M. Haas and Ernst B. Haas, "Learning to Learn: Improving International Governance," *Global Governance* 1, no. 3 (1995): 255–285.
69 Our point of departure is *not* the common premise that all NGOs seek organizational survival above all. In our experience, the imperative to maintain partner relations ontologically precedes NGO organizational interests and is essential for achieving them. Financial donors are not necessarily the most critical partners. The misleading premise of organizational survival plays into the rationalist homogenization of actors. In reality, the interests and norms governing the social and political partners of a single NGO may conflict with each other, and can change, perhaps transforming or even killing the NGO. See Alexander Cooley and James Ron, "The NGO Scramble: Organizational Insecurity and the Political Economy

of Transnational Action," *International Security* 27, no. 1 (2002): 5–39; and Thomas G. Weiss, *Humanitarian Business* (Cambridge: Polity Press, 2013).
70 John Boli and George M. Thomas, eds, *Constructing World Culture: International Nongovernmental Organizations Since 1875* (Stanford, Calif.: Stanford University Press, 1999), 37.
71 Sidney Tarrow, *Power in Movement: Social Movements and Contentious Politics*, 2nd edition (Cambridge: Cambridge University Press, 1998), 29–42.
72 DeMars, *NGOs and Transnational Networks*, 6–33.
73 Michael Barnett and Thomas G. Weiss, eds, *Humanitarianism in Question: Politics, Power, Ethics* (Ithaca, NY: Cornell University Press, 2008); Fiona Terry, *Condemned to Repeat? The Paradox of Humanitarian Action* (Ithaca, NY: Cornell University Press, 2002); and DeMars, "War and Mercy in Africa," 1–10.
74 Barnett and Duvall, *Power in Global Governance*; Felix Berenskoetter and M. J. Williams, eds, *Power in World Politics* (London: Routledge, 2007); Steven Lukes, *Power: A Radical View*, 2nd edition (New York: Palgrave Macmillan, 2005); and Harold H. Saunders, *Politics Is about Relationships: A Blueprint for the Citizens' Century* (New York: Palgrave Macmillan, 2005).
75 Daniel L. Nielson, Michael J. Tierney and Catherine E. Weaver, "Bridging the Rationalist–Constructivist Divide: Re-engineering the Culture of the World Bank," *Journal of International Relations and Development* 9, no. 2 (2006): 107–139; and Alex Thompson, Michael J. Tierney and Catherine Weaver, eds, *The Politics of International Organizations: Bridging the Rationalist–Constructivist Divide* (forthcoming).

Part II
Theory

1 How to study NGOs in practice
A relational primer

Morten Skumsrud Andersen[1]

- **Ontologies of NGOs: substantialism and relationalism**
- **NGOs and IR theory**
- **Why we need a relational approach to NGOs**
- **NGOs in practice**
- **Conclusion**

One evening, at a beachfront condo in Monrovia, Liberia, off a dusty road, I attended what was presented to me as an "NGO wig party." These NGO parties were supposedly (in)famous and had become something of a tradition. It seemed like everyone there was already acquainted with each other. However, the NGO party was not for NGO workers exclusively—quite the opposite. It was a curious mix of employees from different NGOs, from the different sections of the UN country mission (UNMIL), from the many different UN agencies operating in the country, researchers doing fieldwork (like myself), immigrant workers, and diplomats—all gathering under UN portable shelters conveniently converted into party tents for the occasion. This speaks to the inherent interrelatedness of internationals having in common that they work with broadly similar issues in a small and demanding environment (for me perhaps exacerbated by the fact that everyone was wearing wigs). But the fact that it was referred to as an "NGO party" despite not being one, was more puzzling. This indicates how NGOs are often associated with exactly such informal relations and intermingling, something happening "below" the level of formal organizations and bureaucracies under a common umbrella (or party tent, as in this case). These *relational* aspects of NGOs are the point of departure for this chapter. How is it possible to study relations between disparate entities as a core feature of what NGOs do, and still to connect the empirics to a systematic, theoretical approach to NGOs?[2]

A frequent critique of dominant International Relations (IR) theories is exactly this; that they are not making the transition from theoretical assumptions to empirics explicit enough. So-called rationalist theories set out to identify actors' underlying incentives and preferences, which is often just as difficult as constructivism's attempt to determine the impact of ideas, norms, and values on identities and interests.[3] I argue that all three dominant theories of IR—neorealism, neoliberalism, and constructivism[4]—have problems with effectively combining theoretical accounts with empirical investigations of NGO practices. As the title of this book indicates, NGOs can be seen as an empirical challenge to IR theory, and NGO workers return from the field to find that current theories are discordant with "ground truths" and practical experiences. Why is this?

In this chapter, I investigate how two different ontological starting points found within the social sciences—what have been called *substantialism* and *relationalism*—can lead to different ways of doing research on NGOs. I will argue that given the characteristics of what we can call the NGO field of investigation, an ontology of relations can be more effective in explaining the various ways in which NGOs are operating, and in connecting empirics and theory within this particular area of studies.

The concern in this chapter is the potential benefits of analytically starting with relations when studying NGOs, rather than with predetermined entities which, I will show, is the modus operandi of much IR scholarship. In short, it can be analytically useful and effective to think about relations before entities. Even if it is in principle unproblematic to talk about entities called "NGOs," I argue that it is time for this notion to be unpacked to make the most out of the "NGO challenge for IR theory."

Hence, I first introduce two distinct ontological positions regarding NGOs. They can be seen as relatively fixed *entities* possessing certain properties or, alternatively, as sites for specific investigations of *relations*. The objects of investigation depend on the ontological starting point one chooses. Second, I show how a substantialist ontology predominates in traditional IR theories, and critique the limitations of a substantialist point of departure in studying NGOs. With illustrative detours to Liberia, I then argue that given the difficulties in delineating NGOs, and with their multiple connections with other actors in society, starting from a relational ontology might produce more useful knowledge about NGOs. I suggest that emerging "practice approaches" to the study of the social might serve as a useful guideline. In conclusion, starting out with a different analytical priority can open up the "black box" of NGOs and promote a more comprehensive understanding of both NGOs and their networked local and global environment. The purpose of this chapter is to map some alternatives on a theoretical-ontological level and suggest how to treat NGOs analytically.

Ontologies of NGOs: substantialism and relationalism

Many fundamental questions posed in this book do not concern the study of NGOs only. They are basic questions about the investigation of social life in general. The debates over ontology, the agency–structure problem, the normative versus the material, and the role of power, are issues in almost any discipline studying human communities. However, the issues under discussion in this chapter, I argue, have a particular relevance for the study of NGOs.

A basic ontological issue divides approaches to IR and to NGOs: the difference between substantialism and relationalism. On the one hand, a substantialist ontology starts out *a priori* with objects or concepts as possessing some defining features, a "collection of properties, held together at their core by some bare and propertyless substantial existence, a dispositional 'being-that' around which the object's different qualities are arranged."[5] The initial point of departure for this approach is the different "things" existing out there, and only later does one investigate how these "things" act, interact, or relate.[6] This is an ontology with a long, philosophical history—from Descartes and Spinoza, to Putnam and Kripke.[7]

The claim that a certain entity exists, hinges on first identifying a set of stable properties that define that entity. How these entities *are*, or in what ways they interact with each other, produce effects. However, the effects are not seen as emanating from the interaction itself. The effects or results of interaction can be traced back in the last instance to the attributes of the entities. One example of this way of thinking is methodological individualism, where the human mind is treated as a self-contained entity. From the properties of this entity, then, springs social action.

Today, a second ontological position, which we can call relationalism or a relational ontology, is increasingly being accepted in IR as a productive alternative to substantialist ontologies, as indicated by the ongoing "relational turn" or "practice turn" in the field.[8] A relational ontology posits that "nothing is without being in relation, and that everything is—in the way that it is—in terms and in virtue of relationality."[9] Things are not first entities, and then start interacting.[10] Such a relational ontology turns from looking at entities as a collection of static attributes in isolation, to taking the dynamic and observable relational processes in which the entity is a part (and a product), as the primary object of investigation. The entities are embedded in and produced by relations that constantly reproduce the entity. This relational line of thought has some of its philosophical antecedents in the thinking of Hume, Nietzsche, Simmel, and Heidegger.[11]

When talking about NGOs, or indeed anything else, one will inevitably set some boundaries for that of which one is talking. Still, I will not make any claims about what an NGO *really* is or corresponds to, nor claim any deep philosophical reason for saying that relations come before or after entities. In short, the main aim of this chapter is not to engage in a philosophical discussion over whether NGOs are in some sense "real" or not, whether our concepts may or may not correspond to a potentially objective world beyond the gaze of the researcher, or whether relations in a really real way come before entities, but is concerned with the content of our theories, which are by definition models that set intellectual and analytical priorities and leave other aspects out.[12]

The point that affects our concrete research is that the basic ontological categories researchers include in their theories constrain the empirical studies and empirical claims they can consistently make. Relationalism finds it more useful to treat relations as the primary ontological focus, especially when studying phenomena that might include unit-level changes,[13] for example revolutions, social movements, the evolving role of the state or even the international system, or how NGOs or not-for-profit organizations are becoming more standardized and bureaucratized with the surge in managerialism.[14] Relations in turn are producing and reproducing the objects. Relationalist research does not *start* with the objects. One begins by looking at relations as the foci for study, so that it is possible to investigate also how the objects came about and how they might be changing. As I will show, this is something that substantialism has problems in doing because the "essential" or "constitutive" properties of the units cannot be opened up for study, as this would undermine the whole theoretical enterprise by questioning the starting assumption—the objects under study as defined in the theory.

Seen from within a relational ontology, the entities are involved in constant transactions, often in what is conceptualized as networks.[15] The meaning and identity of the entities come as a direct result of the changing functional roles they play within those transactions or networks.[16] From such a starting point, it is nonsensical to speak of entities as existing *before* the transactions or relations take place, as they cannot be taken out of the relational context within which they operate. Entities gain their characteristics not from what is inherently inside them, but what is between them—that is, through their relations.

Consequently, a further characteristic of a relational ontology is that relations are most often seen as unfolding processes, and not as static ties.[17] This does not mean that everything is changing all the time, or that relations never stabilize and become enduring. Whether this is the case, however, is an empirical question. The default setting of a relational ontology is that the social is never coherent, but constantly in a process of change. The central question for relationalists, then, is what makes relations take on a stable and enduring form? Instead of assuming order, and aiming to explain change, they take change for granted and explore the dynamics and power processes involved in the (history of) institutionalization or sedimentation of certain relations.

As I will show, most IR approaches studying NGOs still prefer substantialism, as when applying rational choice theories, constructing models of "norm diffusion" between entities, or analyzing variables and comparing units for the purpose of generalizations. All of these approaches imply that entities, analytically speaking, come before the relations between them.

NGOs and IR theory

On a general level, the purpose of theory is to highlight what is taken to be of special importance to the field under consideration, and deliberately to leave other elements out. For that reason, there are no *a priori* right or wrong theoretical approaches in the study of NGOs, but it is important to be aware of the implications of one's ontology—what objects are component parts of our theories—when conducting scientific research. This will have implications for our subsequent empirical investigations, and how those can be connected to our theories.

In the following, I will briefly look at how the dominant theories of IR have treated NGOs. The take-home message of this exercise is that constructivism is the one dominant IR theory that can be said to have treated NGOs more or less consistently but that—just as neorealism and neoliberalism—constructivism often leans on a substantialist ontology when studying NGOs. This has the effect that constructivism also has troubles explaining NGOs in an efficient way, and explaining what happens when "the books hit the ground."

These three dominant theories of IR are state-centric theories. This means that the state is the natural and obvious reference point, no matter how one weighs the influence of NGOs relative to it. The debate often concerns the issue of how much power states have as relative to other actors and processes, and the nature of the ensuing order this creates.

The debate over these issues has most often involved a critique of the neorealist concepts of the states-system and the power of states. Neorealism sees states as self-interested rational actors operating in international anarchy, which implies a self-help environment and perpetual inter-state power struggles.[18] In this narrative, NGOs have extremely limited independent power as they are political epiphenomena of these interstate power struggles. Typically, a realist argument would be that the autonomous agency of NGOs is only realized if granted by states, which have the final say based on their national interests. The potential impact of NGOs or intergovernmental organizations (IGOs) is then only as instruments for states. Behind the seemingly humanitarian or altruistic operations of NGOs, there is always the dominating context of great power interests. Whenever there is a conflict of interest between NGOs and states, the latter will win. If a role is granted to NGOs within neorealism, it could be as entities trying to influence the big powers—influencing the *really* important players that actually can affect outcomes.[19] However, this does not explain how or whether states might choose to promote the goals of NGOs,[20] and as such is still within the limits of a neorealist logic.

Like neorealism, neoliberalism in IR focuses on states as the most important actors of world politics. Still, in the liberal spirit of reasoned compromise, the theory holds that IGOs might function as arenas for states to meet and coordinate their interests to reach mutually beneficial solutions. However, NGOs have seldom been an object of study for liberal scholars, unless they are involved somehow in the above dynamics. The scholarship on interdependence and transnational relations in the 1970s focused mostly on the rise of multinational corporations. One of the first works within liberalism focusing explicitly on NGOs[21] treated them as equivalent to "interest groups."[22] Later neoliberal work has focused mainly on the possibility for state cooperation under anarchy. In any case, liberalism mainly excludes NGOs from the central processes of interdependence or transnationalism.

The emergence of constructivism within IR in the 1980s led to a greater focus on non-state actors and their role in constituting world politics. Constructivism focused mainly on issues of identity and ideas, and challenged many of the established truths of IR scholarship. Constructivism is now the only mainstream IR theory in which NGOs figure prominently. For constructivism, NGOs do have power as independent actors. Constructivism puts emphasis on the dynamics behind the spread of norms and ideas in the international system, and NGOs play a central role in this. NGOs embody values and are acting independently of governments. They function as norm entrepreneurs[23] and norms transmitters within what many see as an emerging global civil society. Constructivism calls attention to the frequent interactions between NGOs and states. As such, the goal is not to replace the state-centrism of earlier theorizing, but to focus on "governance without government."[24] Much of constructivist NGO scholarship investigates their impact on the macro level of governance and interstate relations, while little is being done on the specific dynamics of NGO relations with other kinds of actors.[25]

These dominant theories make a central analytical point of clearly drawing boundaries between the outside and the inside of NGOs (and states). Crucially, all of these traditional IR theories in general treat the context, that is the outside, as causally more important than the inside of NGOs. In all analyses of NGOs as actors in the context of a system of states, the inside/outside distinction is the defining issue.[26] Whether talking about the international system, states versus NGOs, or interactions between these, the "essential" properties of the actors are defined *a priori*. Often, NGOs are seen instrumentally as tools that can be wielded to further a variety of goals or as vehicles for challenging the present order, as "speaking truth to power."[27] What is doing the acting in all these accounts, are not really the actors themselves, but the variables or their "second-order" properties. The *modus operandi* of these theories is substantialism. The question then becomes, is this a problem, and, if so, why?

Why we need a relational approach to NGOs

Constructivism, many would argue, is the only dominant theory that takes NGOs seriously, but I suggest that constructivism's substantialist ontology hampers many of the efforts to explain the roles and effects of NGOs in world politics, and to connect theory to empirics.

Alexander Wendt's work is the reference point for much constructivism. His version is often described as "structural" or "thin" constructivism, as he explicitly takes on Kenneth Waltz on his home turf ("*Social* Theory of International Politics") and tries to find a (positivist) middle way between "rationalism" and more "radical" forms of constructivism and post-structuralism.[28] It is, however, difficult to study NGOs within his framework, because the theory is professed as state-centric.[29] More fundamentally, even if Wendt is attentive to identity, ideas, and change in world politics, the entities remain stable at some level.[30] Wendt is substantialist, and in his framework it is difficult to explain the origin of changes in what is taken to be the properties of units, in this case norms and ideas as properties of states.

48 *Theory*

In effect, definitions are not based on observed, empirical practice, but rather demarcating boundaries between the inside and outside of the entities being defined. What happens if one tries to apply his framework to the study of multifaceted NGOs? Even if the attributes "inside" of NGOs might change, the constitutive properties of NGOs as entities would remain. What *is* changing are the contents, or the variables, of NGOs, be it their identity, interests or norms. The preferences of an entity might shift as they seek out new goals, but the entities do not change in the least, and explaining the origins of such identity, interests or norms becomes equally problematic. The variables—different ideas or material phenomena or norms—form, clash, converge and interact within the unreceptive arena of entities.[31]

Recent work suggests a growing awareness of the problems of such an approach, by stressing how entities are both constructed by, and themselves construct, the world in which they operate. However, some work remains limited by not being fully relational, and by upholding an *a priori* inside/outside distinction. For example, Barnett and Finnemore[32] give greater analytical weight to the inside of international organizations. They try to address the shortage of IR theories by explaining the inner workings of IGOs. IGOs, they argue, do have autonomy to influence state behaviour. This is contrary to neorealist claims. IR theories in general, they argue, are not able to prepare IGO officials for what IGOs really are.[33] This is reaffirmed in the Introduction to this book, which observes that NGO researchers returning from the field find that current theories are discordant with the "ground truths" and their experiences. Barnett and Finnemore postulate that IGOs are autonomous actors and that IGOs as such "are able to use their authority, knowledge, and rules to regulate and constitute the world that subsequently requires regulation," and they go on to identify three mechanisms by which IGOs are able to do this: they can classify the world, fix meanings, and diffuse norms.[34] The power of IGOs lies in their ability to use these mechanisms independently of states and other actors. Through three case studies of the IMF, the UNHCR, and the UN secretariat, they show the specific ways in which IGOs are using their power. Through autonomous practices like IMF conditionality, and decisions to intervene or not intervene in specific contexts, IGOs can form the environment in which states act in fundamental ways, and set the conditions for the debate and even for state interests.

The emphasis is on the use of independent authority as a defining characteristic of the nature of IGOs, but not on how this authority is reproduced or changing over time and place. The focus is on what IGOs are that can make them relevant as explanatory variables or actors in our theories. Other factors that might be involved through the relations IOs uphold with other entities and actors, are treated as "context."

In short, how norms are formed, used, or adapted, how norms are changing, constituting, and influencing both IGOs and other interacting partners, are not central to the analysis. Norms, in short, are not problematized, but are assumed to manifest as another variable, so they can be used and spread. IGOs, Barnett and Finnemore argue, "often act as conveyor belts for the transmission of norms and models of good political behaviour."[35] However, as has been amply studied, in sociology for example, norms are contradictory and changing, and not unitary variables that automatically produce effects, such as a convergence of interest.[36]

Barnett and Finnemore show how power is actually used by IGOs, a highly valuable contribution to debates about non-state actors. They explain that the bureaucratic power of IGOs involves both "constitutive power," as in creating new categories and relationships while persuading actors to alter their preferences, and also "power as domination," as in using rules, regulations, information, and decrees to compel others to act.[37] However, this sophisticated conceptualization is used to explain a one-way flow of power from IGOs to other entities, such as states.[38] The relational properties of power are not given much empirical attention, and power becomes something actors may or may not have. Relationalism, in contrast, would argue that power always involves acting towards another entity, and is therefore defined by both the set-up of relations and the distribution of capabilities within them. Classifying the world, fixing meanings, and articulating and diffusing norms cannot be done by IGOs alone. In short, how IGOs gain their power and authority in practice is not particularly clear.

Their argument that "we can better understand what IOs do if we better understand what IOs are"[39] indicates that a substantialist ontology is the starting point for the analysis. The emphasis is mainly on the inner force and dispositions of IOs as what is driving them to spread and pursue norms given in advance. This is indeed a valid analysis, but I argue that adopting a relationalist ontology might explain even more.

NGO relations in Liberia

This became even clearer when I visited an international NGO in Liberia, doing fieldwork for a study of local ownership in peacebuilding.[40]

In 1978, Jimmy Carter made a visit to Liberia to negotiate behind enemy lines, and continued his visits to the country in the following years, with the result that the Carter Center (CC) in Liberia has been established since 1992. At the invitation of President Ellen Johnson Sirleaf, the CC is now working with the justice system in Liberia, which is not traditionally a focus area for the CC. They established a pilot project with community legal advisors—locally trained Liberians working to resolve disputes in local villages and referring people to the authorities—in partnership with the Catholic Justice and Peace Commission in Liberia. The CC's activities steadily expanded. Using community legal advisors was difficult in cases of grave breaches of the law or cases more apt for the formal justice sector, so the CC teamed up with the American Bar Association to strengthen the program. The CC later expanded their activities to include cooperation with theatre groups dramatizing rule-of-law dilemmas in local villages, and with community radios in collaboration with the county attorneys and others. They expanded geographically, with mobile legal advisors on motorbikes around the country. The most recent development was to team up with traditional chiefs, the CC serving as intermediaries between the local chiefs and Monrovia, and educating them in Liberian statutory law. It was "wildly successful," and the chiefs wanted the CC to implement the same model in every county. As "no one reaches out to them, they are happy for this," the CC explained. The NGO workers are on constant alert with their cell phones, responding to calls from village chiefs around the country on matters of how to deal with rule-of-law problems and paradoxes that might emerge. Then, the HQ of the National Traditional Council, headed by the supreme chief, was rebuilt with the support of the CC. The CC staff is also working on capacity building in the Ministry of Justice, training the police and prosecutors, and training public defenders through the "judicial institute" at the University of Liberia. As such, the CC workers use a "bottom up" approach, collaborating with a host of local personalities and organizations.

As the CC in Liberia has developed relations with local actors and other NGOs, its traditional borders have become increasingly blurred, and the organization and its purpose have been constantly changing. Apart from the purely infrastructural aspects—offices and cars—it was difficult to empirically establish where the boundaries between the NGOs and other actors lay. In some cases, this was difficult even for infrastructure. When visiting the headquarters of the National Traditional Council (established with the help of the CC) an NGO worker hinted that it might be time to go back to the CC. The supreme chief responded "this *is* the Carter Center," laughing heartily.

The CC in Liberia has become central within a network of actors loosely related to the field of rule-of-law projects in Liberia. As the CC employees explained, relations have over time become more numerous and have expanded and changed in the process. From a modest beginning as a facilitator for community legal advisors, the CC now has routine relations with the American Bar Association, the local university, all UN agencies, the local government, various ministries, the National Traditional Council in Liberia, local village chiefs, and the local drama groups and radio stations. At the time, the newly appointed head of the CC was coming from the role as an international advisor to the Liberian Ministry of Justice, and in turn expanded the density of relations and links.

I participated in a field trip, organized by the CC, to observe various rule-of-law projects in operation in a rural village. Here, a network of relations was activated in implementing the local project that day: local chiefs, the supreme chief, the local governor, village elders, a drama group, the district commissioner, the CC local office in Gbarnga in Bong county, two other Liberian NGOs, community legal advisors with their personal relationships with villagers, and ourselves, being greeted as a visiting "rule-of-law team," all made part of what can uneasily be termed one project.

Given the above, a fruitful starting point would be to look at the NGO as a *site* in which various relations and networks intersect, rather than starting out with a scholarly definition of NGOs as the object for investigation. Starting with the relations, a rather different research agenda on NGOs opens up, one in which the NGO as such is less interesting than what is happening *through* it.

As NGOs are constantly changing, participating in overlapping networks, and different relations,[41] it is difficult to find common characteristics of NGOs. If we are to use a substantialist ontology, claiming that we can operate with self-sustaining entities, it requires us to treat them as having a core set of stable attributes. We would have to define their existence in advance to use them as variables. After having set the definition, we would have to go looking for cases that correspond with our definitions.

Such a substantialist starting point is even less pertinent for NGOs than for IOs, as the Introduction argues that most NGOs are not rational bureaucracies, and are not there to enforce rules. As seen, if the operation of NGOs is more about affiliating with different partners, we can expect their institutional forms to be distinctly heterogeneous. It then becomes important to explore the boundaries of NGOs, and how they are made and *changing*.

What practices are making these borders possible, what are the enabling conditions for them? It becomes necessary to investigate, for example, how networks in which NGOs operate are constitutive of their boundary conditions, and the much related boundary conditions for other actors in the network, such as states, civil society, or any other project.[42]

A "relations first" approach can be more effective in explaining NGOs and other phenomena involving changes in the unit of investigation. A relational ontology permits us to problematize the NGOs themselves, and account for them in a theoretically informed way because their very borders, which in substantialism are part of their constitutive and given nature, are open for scrutiny.[43]

In a field actually calling itself "International Relations," a focus on relations should not be an improper suggestion. There is no deep ontological *necessity* to do so, but neither is there a necessity to start with entities. It would be worth the risk, at least, to adopt a relational sensibility when setting out to investigate a phenomenon like NGOs, which might seem difficult to handle in the traditional ways of IR.

The substantial point is that using power, spreading or making norms, promulgating new ideas, creating status and trust, changing structures and incentivizing actors, cannot be done by NGOs as actors alone. This significant point must be included in the analysis, and adopting a substantialist ontology hampers this effort. Instead of trying to define the substance of NGOs, or to leave unchallenged the supposed causal powers of either the inside or the outside context, one should focus analytical attention on the practices of NGOs constituting the very borders between the inside and outside, so often taken for granted in traditional IR theories.

NGOs in practice

If, as I have argued, it is problematic to treat entities as existing before transactions or relations take place, as they gain their characteristics through their relations, then how do we explain outcomes? How do we study NGOs in a way different from traditional IR theories? If we are to focus on relations, we must somehow pin down and understand people's communal activities and experiences.[44] The challenge facing us "is to consider non-governmental organizations as one specific possible form of collective action and human community and to set the stage for a comparative analysis of the different configurations these forms of collective action have taken and are taking in a complexly woven field of translocal flows."[45]

If we are not to operate with a substantialist ontology, the alternative is to look at the NGO practices themselves, and through them, both NGOs and their environment—what others would call the "context."[46] Fortunately, there is a developing literature that might guide us in this endeavour.

A "practice approach" or "practice theory" in the social sciences is "a loose, but nevertheless definable movement of thought that is unified around the idea that the field of practices is the place to investigate such phenomena as agency, knowledge, language, ethics, power and science."[47] It often embraces a concept of the social as "a field of embodied, materially interwoven practices centrally organized around shared practical understandings."[48] Thus, a practice approach differs from both individualistic and structural theory because the former locates its "smallest theoretical unit" not in minds, discourses, interactions, structures or systems, but in practices that, however, can function as instantiations of all of the above.[49]

Practice theory is a counter-measure to "armchair analyses" of discourses, and abstract and structural theoretical constructs.[50] Practice theory pays attention to what practitioners do through interactions. In NGO networks, "shared interests are constructed in and through political discourses, persuasions, negotiations and bargains,"[51] that is, through practices. For example, NGO workers can make a joint effort to identify and collect practical tricks and "lessons learnt" into a "best practices" knowledge base. On the other hand, the same NGO workers might also meet regularly in informal settings, like over lunch (or at wig parties). Here, they are not necessarily aware that their discussions might be a major source of developing knowledge on how to deal with issues that regularly arise in their work. In both cases, they are developing common narratives and a common repertoire of practices, even if not consciously doing so in the latter case.[52] Paying attention to these repeated interactional patterns, on what is going on "on the ground," how people solve everyday problems, is the core of practice approaches and the point of departure for investigation.

Because of this empirical sensibility, it is important not to isolate units. For example, instead of the traditional focus on agents and structures as two different kinds of entities, practice approaches direct attention to the relations between entities. Acting is not only that of a self-contained individual, but is taking place within the context of the expectations, traditions or routines of others.

Using the notion of practices as a guideline can help address one central difficulty or problem that comes with using a relational ontology. I started the outline of relationalism in the first part of the article by saying that setting boundaries for objects is inevitable in research—and in everyday life in general. When trying to apply relationalism in practice, we quickly come up against the problem of marking out our objects of research.

What is an NGO, then?

One might think that relationalism sounds great, but how do you know what you are looking for if you cannot start with a definition of the object? Where do you find the relations? Where do you start? How do you define the borders? How do you recognize an NGO when you see one? There are basically two strategies for doing this. One might start with a definition as a tool, as shorthand to facilitate the research. On the other hand, it is also possible to make the production of definitions themselves objects for analysis. The question, in short, is who specifies what an NGO is?

First, what one might call a "normative" approach sees the main sources of defining NGOs as being a categorization exercise done by the scholars. What NGOs think they are doing themselves is not so important. One can look at second-hand accounts, historical analyses, or other data to try and construct one's own, covering, scholarly definition of an NGO.[53]

Second, some would see the objects as defined by how participants in NGO processes operate and see themselves. This can be termed an "empirical" or "sociological" identification of an NGO, more concerned with social practices in specific contexts.[54] The reflections of the object's participants are central. Different societal norms, appropriateness, morality, modes of operation, etc. can be more or less important in defining NGOs, but that is an empirical question. Consequentially, the self-conceptions of NGO participants in specific locales put constraints on the conceptualization of analysts, and make the borders of what an NGO is or isn't rather blurry and difficult to determine. The way to assess NGOs is therefore inductively through looking at processes "on the ground," how participants actually reflect on what they do as NGO workers, rather than deductively from the view of the scholar. I find this approach to delimitation most convincing when treating NGOs in relational ways.

NGOs do not only participate as self-contained actors in practices, but their very actions are a part of what constitutes them as NGOs. No deductive logic is applied, but an investigation of the "grammar" of NGO practices—how people actually *use* the concept of NGO to make sense of the world.

As Shrum maintains, echoing Bourdieu's notion of competitive social fields, NGOs "spring from a variety of other entities, and are not

How to study NGOs in practice 55

a 'sector' until they begin to compete and strive for recognition, which allows other organizations to perceive them as similar."[55] NGOs are a collection of relations within a network that "agrees" that certain practical activities count as "NGOs." In that respect, instead of talking about NGOs, we should here actually talk about "NGO*ing*."[56] In similar ways, William Fisher gives attention to "the political implications of discourses about NGOs, the complex micro-politics of these associations, and the importance of situating them as evolving processes within complexes of competing and overlapping practices and discourses."[57]

What are the constitutive practices of an NGO? (Some) facts depend on rules, so constitutive rules are conditions of possibility for a fact. As normally understood, then, a constitutive rule says that something counts as X in a context Y. For the present purpose, an important feature of constitution is that practices play an important role in continuously confirming that an NGO is what it is. If you want to become an NGO, there are certain practices that other NGOs and actors expect of you in order for the social recognition of NGO status to occur. The practices must therefore be publicly performed, even if not consciously as practices explicitly reaffirming NGO status. There will be arguments over exactly what these practices are—and that is exactly the subject matter of research.

In their Introduction, DeMars and Dijkzeul suggest that NGOing is associated with two central practices: "International NGOs happen when (a) private actors claim to pursue public purposes, and (b) they link with societal and political partners in at least two countries." That is a valid point of departure, also in relational research, but it does not necessarily explain and follow how participants in "NGO-ing" creatively conceptualize and specify NGOs or their activities in their projects. In short, defining an NGO can be a useful tool for scholars, but also for the participants. The methodological question here is therefore: whose tool is it?[58] In the latter case, one could ask how NGOs function as narrative resources or repertoire for participants to act in and interact with their social environment,[59] successfully or not. In Russia, for example, a pro-Kremlin think tank helped a state-controlled hydropower giant create an "NGO" pretending to represent the Evenkia people to prevail over local resistance to a new dam project. This was quickly decertified as a "false NGO."[60] Some have categorized Al-Qaeda as an NGO, based on strict definitions.[61] Importantly, then, "NGOing" should be recognized as valid from day to day also by other actors ("societal and political partners") with which one is relating as an NGO.

Then there is also the other side to the coin. An NGO can be negatively defined as non-governmental, and other constitutive practices could be NGOs themselves emphasizing how very different they are from other entities operating within similar fields or areas. Particularly as new relations surge and the field of operation of an NGO expands, this need for differentiation to reproduce the particular role of the organization becomes more acute.

Returning to Liberia, NGO workers repeatedly stressed how "we are different" from the UNDP, USAID, or other agencies they interacted and collaborated with—and also different in their relations. While other organizations were afraid of getting too involved with local village chiefs and the problems of traditional systems of justice versus human rights, the CC had the exact opposite policy. Their policy was to engage in relationships with as many local actors as possible, including the "bad" people who had not "internalized the rule-of-law standards." The ethos of the CC seemed to be opposed to any strict interpretation of principles that might obstruct interaction and pragmatic relationships with local chiefs. As one said, "we would never condone" human rights violations, but instead of condemning such violations, would point out the practical implications of choices, and make the logic behind what the CC proposed explicit, using practical examples. Furthermore, some CC staff members expressed their doubts about the UN bureaucracy. As one employee asserted, "coordination works better in the South because it is more isolated. There we cannot worry about mandates." Further, "in (the capital) Monrovia, there are so many UN agencies with specialized functions and certain responsibilities." They made, in short, a case for relations, and against bureaucratic specialization. It was also explicitly mentioned that USAID, after having been skeptical of the CC's approach, now considered it an important actor and came to accept and adopt its approaches. "We have seen a change in many partners," one employee explained, "for example USAID and the US embassy, from a critique of our involvement with chiefs on grounds of human rights, to more acceptance." Others were said to be "gravitating towards our approach, and becoming part of the process." The CC explicitly defined itself as different from other actors in the field in their practices of NGOing. Nevertheless, the CC saw itself as exercising an increasing influence on these other actors, as the CC's status as a well-connected actor grew. It drew on both exclusion and inclusion at the same time.

As such, it is less important to find an exact definition of what an NGO is than to find out what they do and how they talk about it, and how it affects the NGO, other actors, and dynamics within the relational network of which they are part. We need to start with working definitions as shorthand for what we want to study. In academic practice as in our everyday lives, we need categories to make sense of what is going on. Some social practices define what NGOs are in practice, and these must continue over time to uphold and reproduce the entity. However, and importantly, these might be changing. Most definitions in circulation "distinguish NGOs from non-NGOs and fake-NGOs, with the result that they do not analyze how such distinctions are constructed and used in practice."[62] It will therefore be important to establish—with attention to detailed empirical case studies—how these patterns are reproduced or change, in order to understand the dynamics of NGOs.

The entry point for study of these reproductions or changes is the empirical micro-level "doings" or practices of NGOs in the field, and not sweeping generalizations, so often seen in the study of NGOs.[63] This can help us be more effective in explaining and understanding "local and translocal connections that enable and constrain flows of ideas, knowledge, funding and people" in NGO networks, as well as connections between the personal and the political, citizenry, associations, and the state.[64] Putting empirical processes first is one of the central markers of a practice approach. Doing the opposite would be postulating a range of theoretical claims about the workings of some entities and institutions, and then going about a traditional, empirical study with little relevance for our preconceived theoretical frameworks.

Norms and power in practice

Asking concrete questions about concrete cases of NGO practice, focusing on relations and ties concerning the formation of boundaries and the constitution of NGOs, implies the study of power, as such questions presuppose that the actors involved could have chosen to act otherwise.[65] As the Introduction to this book emphasizes, norms and power are central to the operation of NGOs. Adopting a relational ontology opens up interesting analytical spaces in which to investigate power mechanisms in networks.

For example, it is easy to assume that power lies with the funding agency in a particular donor–NGO relation. If investigated as a set of practices, another picture might emerge. States and donors might be equally dependent on the NGO. Looking at power as relational might open up for empirical investigation how different NGO–donor relationships are reproduced and change in different ways.[66]

This approach explains things as concrete practices in relations, and not by variables. If economic power is seen as a variable, it could be expressed as the proposition that "because NGO X is economically dependent on donor funding, Y follows." No one is acting, there are

58 *Theory*

no practices, and all the explanatory force is placed upon the variable "presence or absence of donor funding." The agent in this case is the abstract entity of "the variable," and not the NGO.[67] If seen as relations, however, funding arrangements are an arena of power struggles and competition.[68]

These funding agencies are often states, and the traditional concern of IR theories is the relative power of NGOs to that of states. Much literature on global governance argues that as non-state actors gain increasing leverage, the influence and reach of states is waning. However, we must not overestimate the demise of the state. Some studies have focused on how the state is not losing power, but how the ways in which power is *used* are changing and remaking traditional relationships in new ways. For example, outsourcing tasks from states to NGOs concerning welfare or development, does not necessarily mean "handing over power" in any sense.

Neumann and Sending[69] examine precisely these transformations, using a relational approach to investigate NGOs as an expression of the evolving nature of global governance. They argue that NGOs have gone from being elite institutions, instrumental for state purposes, to focusing on grassroots activities directed toward individuals. This places them in a new logic of power vis-à-vis states. As opposed to Keck and Sikkink's[70] claims that states are losing power to non-state actors, they argue against the "standard cases" of how NGOs use their power to coerce and shame governments. What is going on today, they argue, is not a "power shift" from states to non-state actors but rather an expression of a new way for the state to govern. It is missing the point, they argue, to focus only on "the knowledge and expertise produced and brought to bear by NGOs as a case of how non-state actors challenge state supremacy and control." Instead, they look at how NGO knowledge and expertise relates to other actors and institutions. NGOs are not discrete units influencing state action, and neither are NGOs co-opted and brought into the official government sphere. Rather, the fact that they are viewed as independent actors is exactly what facilitates their participation in the practices of governments.[71] Processes of governing, they argue, are increasingly operating *through* rather than *on* NGOs.

This means that NGOs are at the same time both objects and subjects of governance. Through their practices and diverse associations and relations—emphasized as the objects of investigation in this chapter—NGOs may create spaces of agency for different parts of the state, and in this way perform a governance function. They are opponents and collaborators at the same time. In this way, power itself is studied relationally. Power surges through practices in relations, and must not be conceptualized primarily as intentional acts of dominance by rational actors. The analytical question shifts from "Who is exercising power?" to "How is power exercised?"

For the Carter Center in Liberia, relations deepened and new relationships were formed, particularly with local chiefs and other NGOs. In this process, the CC "started working as intermediary between the local level and Monrovia," and actually assumed a national governance function, in collaboration with, but at the same time opposed to, the Liberian Ministry of Internal Affairs and the UN. Another international NGO operating in Liberia was even able to implement local rule-of-law projects and projects related to land reform, going to the heart of national sovereignty, without receiving the approval of the Liberian government. Not only do NGOs and states influence each other in opposition, but also state governance mechanisms often work through and with NGOs. NGOs can provide governance functions that are not explicitly mandated by the state, but that surge in relations with numerous actors and different parts of the state.

Power in this view is not only applied to NGOs or by NGOs, but also passes through NGOs. This logic creates new types of NGO; or, rather, it may redefine what an NGO does and thereby the parameters of what it means to be one. This, Neumann and Sending argue, must be investigated by focusing on "micro-level relations and interactions between the state and non-state actors,"[72] and, one might add, between NGOs and other actors in their relational networks.

Conclusion

The ongoing "relational turn," or "practice turn" in IR bodes well for the study of NGOs, and should be taken on board as a direct response to the NGO challenge for IR theory. In this chapter, I have argued that the dominant IR theories have limited potential for connecting theory to empirical evidence and effectively explaining the workings of NGOs because of their substantialist ontology. This hampers the study and explanation of norms, power and change, that are crucial issues for the study of NGOs.

In a relational approach, an NGO is not treated as a thing, nor a category of observation or analysis, but a site in which to investigate practices. And such practices, in turn, give shape to relations, and not to properties.[73] Social practices make certain relations possible. This has some important implications for the NGO challenge for IR theory.

First, the processes of making NGOs into substances and "things" are themselves worthy of empirical investigation, because such processes in general have effects, and more importantly, they seem to be particularly important for NGOs, because they are explicitly defining themselves both inclusively as important "nodes," and exclusively in opposition to other actors.

Second, how the NGO becomes an actor with an identity is not due to the NGO alone, but emerges from the myriad relationships it entertains with other actors. Changes in the relations between actors and groups can explain how NGOs become what they are, and do what they do.

Third, the task, then, would be to identify such relational mechanisms that create, transform, and activate the political identity of NGOs. How do NGOs form coalitions by searching for strategic opportunities within the NGO network? Does an NGO broker between groups and actors (such as the government and local actors)? How are the borders between the inside and outside of NGOs as actors emerging and changing in the process?

In all of this, one is not specifying *a priori* how certain properties of NGOs could come to have effects on relations, or tracing relations and effects back to an essence. Rather, we can capture the formation of and alterations in stable relations, and how such change or stability creates both constraints on and possibilities for political action.

The point of analysis is therefore not "what NGOs are good for, nor whether a specific association is or isn't an NGO ... but an understanding of what happens in specific places and at specific times."[74] Such an approach can also help scholars understand and make public the connections NGOs have to various other levels and fields, drawing our attention to flows of money, knowledge, ideas and people involved in these shifting relations and associations.[75] These are visible practices of NGOs—particular and temporally constrained multiple relations with effects. NGOs are not only socially constructed entities, but are constantly in the making.

Notes

1 The author is grateful for feedback on this chapter from the editors, Iver B. Neumann, Neil F. Ketchley, Lars Raaum, Håkon Lunde Saxi, and Ole Jacob Sending, with whom I conducted the fieldwork for this chapter. The Norwegian Ministry of Foreign Affairs provided financial support.
2 "Empirics" here broadly refers to the empirical facts that are produced—assessable knowledge about the world under investigation. As such it distinguishes itself from normative evaluations or standards, or the theoretical and analytical concepts one might use to make sense of the empirics.
3 Richard K. Herrmann, "Linking Theory to Evidence in International Relations," in *Handbook of International Relations*, eds Walter Carlsnaes, Thomas Risse, and Beth Simmons (London: Sage, 2002), 119.

4 Richard Jordan, Daniel Maliniak, Amy Oakes, Susan Peterson, and Michael Tierney, *One Discipline or Many? TRIP Survey of International Relations Faculty in Ten Countries* (Williamsburg, Va.: The Institute for the Theory and Practice of International Relations, The College of William and Mary, 2009).
5 Patrick T. Jackson, "How to Think About Civilizations," in *Civilizations in World Politics: Plural and Pluralist Perspectives*, ed. Peter Katzenstein (London: Routledge, 2009), 181.
6 Mustafa Emirbayer, "Manifesto for a Relational Sociology," *The American Journal of Sociology* 103, no. 2 (1997): 281–317.
7 Nick Huggett and Carl Hoefer, "Absolute and Relational Theories of Space and Motion," in *The Stanford Encyclopedia of Philosophy*, ed. Edward N. Zalta (2009) (http://plato.stanford.edu/entries/spacetime-theories/).
8 See inter alia Yosef Lapid, "Introduction: Identities, Borders, Orders: Nudging International Relations Theory in a New Direction," in *Identities, Borders, Orders. Rethinking International Relations Theory*, eds Mathias Albert, David Jacobson and Yosef Lapid (Minneapolis: University of Minnesota Press, 2001), 1–20; Emmanuel Adler and Vincent Pouliot, "International Practices: Introduction and Framework," in *International Practices*, eds Emmanuel Adler and Vincent Pouliot (Cambridge: Cambridge University Press, 2011); T. Baumgartner, W. Buckley and T. Burns, "Relational Control: The Human Structuring of Cooperation and Conflict," *Journal of Conflict Resolution* 19, no. 3 (1975): 414–40; Emirbayer, "Manifesto," 281–317; Patrick T. Jackson and Daniel Nexon, "Relations before States: Substance, Process and the Study of World Politics," *European Journal of International Relations* 5, no. 3 (1999): 291–332; Iver B. Neumann, "Returning Practice to the Linguistic Turn: The Case of Diplomacy," *Millennium* 31, no. 3 (2002): 627–51; Daniel Nexon, "Relationalism and New Systems Theory," in *New Systems Theories of World Politics*, eds Mathias Albert, Lars-Erik Cederman, and Alexander Wendt (London: Palgrave Macmillan, 2010); Margaret R. Somers, "The Narrative Constitution of Identity: A Relational and Network Approach," *Theory and Society* 23, no. 5 (1994): 605–649; and Charles Tilly, "International Communities, Secure or Otherwise," in *Security Communities*, eds Emanuel Adler and Michael Barnett (Cambridge: Cambridge University Press, 1998), 397–412.
9 Michael Dillon, "Poststructuralism, Complexity and Poetics," *Theory, Culture and Society* 5, no. 17 (2000): 4.
10 Brent D. Slife, "Taking Practice Seriously: Toward a Relational Ontology," *Journal of Theoretical and Philosophical Psychology* 24, no. 2 (2004): 159.
11 Ibid., 160.
12 Morten Skumsrud Andersen and Iver B. Neumann, "Practices as Models: A Methodology with an Illustration Concerning Wampum Diplomacy," *Millennium* 40, no. 3 (2012): 457–481.
13 Jackson and Nexon, "Relations before States," 292.
14 George Lawson, *Negotiated Revolutions: The Czech Republic, South Africa and Chile* (Aldershot: Ashgate, 2005); Jens Bartelson, *A Genealogy of Sovereignty* (Cambridge: Cambridge University Press, 1995); and Walter W. Powell and Richard Steinberg, eds, *The Non-Profit Sector. A Research Handbook* (New Haven, Conn.: Yale University Press, 2006).

62 *Theory*

15 DeMars and Dijkzeul; Ohanyan in this volume.
16 Emirbayer, "Manifesto," 287.
17 Ibid., 289.
18 Kenneth N. Waltz, *Theory of International Politics* (Reading, Mass.: Addison-Wesley, 1979).
19 Stephen Krasner, "Sovereignty, Regimes, and Human Rights," in *Regime Theory and International Relations*, ed. Volker Rittberger (Oxford: Clarendon Press, 1993), 139–67.
20 Thomas Risse, "Transnational Actors and World Politics," in *Handbook of International Relations*, eds Walter Carlsnaes, Thomas Risse and Beth Simmons (London: Sage, 2002), 264.
21 Peter Willetts, ed., *Pressure Groups in the Global System: The Transnational Relations of Issue-Orientated Non-Governmental Organizations* (London: Palgrave Macmillan, 1982).
22 Risse, "Transnational Actors," 258.
23 Martha Finnemore and Kathryn Sikkink, "International Norms Dynamics and Political Change," *International Organization* 52, no. 4 (1998): 887–917.
24 Risse, "Transnational Actors," 259; and James N. Rosenau and Ernst-Otto Czempiel, eds, *Governance without Government: Order and Change in World Politics* (Cambridge: Cambridge University Press, 1992).
25 Risse, "Transnational Actors," 259.
26 Ole Jacob Sending and Iver B. Neumann, "Banking on Power: How Some Practices in an International Organization Anchor Others," in *International Practices*, eds Emmanuel Adler and Vincent Pouliot (Cambridge: Cambridge University Press, 2011), 231–254.
27 William F. Fisher, "Doing Good? The Politics and Antipolitics of NGO Practices," *Annual Review of Anthropology* 26 (1997): 444–45.
28 Alexander Wendt, *Social Theory of International Politics* (Cambridge: Cambridge University Press, 1999), 39–40.
29 Ibid., 7–22.
30 Ibid., 112, 189.
31 Jackson and Nexon, "Relations before States," 293–94.
32 Michael Barnett and Martha Finnemore, *Rules for the World* (Ithaca, NY: Cornell University Press, 2004)
33 Ibid., vii.
34 Ibid., 31.
35 Ibid., 33.
36 Ann Swidler, *Talk of Love: How Culture Matters* (Chicago, Ill.: University of Chicago Press, 2001); and "What Anchors Cultural Practices," in *The Practice Turn in Contemporary Theory*, eds Theodore R. Schatzki, Karin Knorr Cetina, and Eike von Savigny (London: Routledge, 2001), 74–92.
37 Barnett and Finnemore, *Rules for the World*, 165; see also Michael Barnett and Raymond Duvall, *Power in Global Governance* (Cambridge: Cambridge University Press, 2005).
38 Barnett and Finnemore, *Rules for the World*, 29–34.
39 Ibid., 9.
40 Morten Skumsrud Andersen and Ole Jacob Sending, "Liberia," in *Learning to Build a Sustainable Peace: Ownership and Everyday Peacebuilding*, ed. Ole Jacob Sending (Bergen, Norway: Chr. Michelsen Institute, 2010), 23–29; Morten Skumsrud Andersen and Ole Jacob Sending,

"Governmentalisation of Sovereignty," paper presented at the International Studies Association Annual Convention, New Orleans, La., 17–20 February 2010. The empirical data from Liberia are based on interviews with NGO workers, including staff from the Carter Center, and the National Traditional Council, conducted by the author and Ole Jacob Sending during a field visit between 29 September and 4 October 2009.

41 See Mingst and Muldoon in this volume.
42 Jackson and Nexon, "Relations before States," 304; and Mustafa Emirbayer and Jeff Goodwin, "Network Analysis, Culture, and the Problem of Agency," *The American Journal of Sociology* 99, no. 6 (1994): 1411–1454.
43 Jackson and Nexon, "Relations before States," 292.
44 Robert Prus, *Symbolic Interaction and Ethnographic Research: Intersubjectivity and the Study of Human Lived Experience* (Albany, NY: State University of New York Press, 1996).
45 Fisher, "Doing Good?" 459.
46 Jackson, "How to Think About Civilizations"; and Hans Joas, *The Creativity of Action* (Chicago, Ill.: University of Chicago Press, 1996), 161–62.
47 Theodore R. Schatzki, "Introduction," in *The Practice Turn in Contemporary Theory*, eds Theodore R. Schatzki, Karin Knorr Cetina, and Eike von Savigny (New York: Routledge, 2001), 13–14.
48 Ibid., 3.
49 Andreas Reckwitz, "Toward a Theory of Social Practices: A Development in Culturalist Theorizing," *European Journal of Social Theory* 5, no. 2 (2002): 243–63; and Schatzki, "Introduction," 3.
50 Neumann, "Returning Practice," 627–51.
51 Nikolas Rose and Peter Miller, "Political Power beyond the State: Problematics of Government," *British Journal of Sociology* 43, no. 2 (1992): 184.
52 Etienne Wenger, *Communities of Practice: A Brief Introduction* (Wenger-Trayner, 2009) (http://wenger-trayner.com/theory/).
53 See Jackson, "How to Think About Civilizations."
54 Morten Skumsrud Andersen, "Legitimacy in Statebuilding: A Review of the IR Literature," *International Political Sociology* 6, no. 2 (2012): 205–219.
55 Wesley Shrum, "Science and Story in Development: The Emergence of Non-Governmental Organizations in Agricultural Research," *Social Studies of Science* 30, no. 1 (2000): 106.
56 Dorothea Hilhorst, "The Art of NGO-ing: Everyday Practices as Key to Understanding Development NGOs," in *Reconceptualising NGOs and Their Role in Development: NGOs, Civil Society, and the International Aid System*, eds Paul Opoku-Mensah, David Lewis, and Terje Tvedt (Aalborg, Denmark: Aalborg University Press, 2007), 297–325.
57 Fisher, "Doing Good?" 439.
58 Jackson, "How to Think About Civilizations," 185–187.
59 Swidler, *Talk of Love*.
60 Joshua Keating, "Kremlin 'Think-Tank' Creates Fake NGO, then Brags About It," *Foreign Policy* Blog, 8 April 2009 (http://blog.foreignpolicy.com/posts/2009/04/08/kremlin_think_tank_creates_fake_ngo_then_brags_a bout_it); and Maria Antonova, "RusHydro Linked to Dubious Activism," *The Moscow Times*, 8 April 2009, (www.themoscowtimes.com/sitemap/free/2009/4/article/rushydro-linked-to-dubious-activism/376006.html).
61 Moisés Naím, "Al Qaeda, the NGO," *Foreign Policy* 129 (2002): 99–100.

62 Hilhorst, "The Art of NGO-ing," 305.
63 Tina Wallace, Lisa Bornstein and Jennifer Chapman, *The Aid Chain: Coercion and Commitment in Development NGOs* (Rugby: Practical Action Publishing, 2007).
64 Fisher, "Doing Good?" 441.
65 Stefano Guzzini, "The Concept of Power: A Constructivist Analysis," *Millennium* 33, no. 3 (2005): 495–522, 497, 508–09.
66 Alnoor Ebrahim, *NGOs and Organizational Change: Discourse, Reporting, and Learning* (Cambridge: Cambridge University Press, 2005).
67 Jackson and Nexon, "Relations before States," 291–332.
68 Hilhorst, "The Art of NGO-ing," 312–313.
69 Ole Jacob Sending and Iver B. Neumann, "Governance to Governmentality: Analyzing NGOs, States, and Power," *International Studies Quarterly* 50, no. 3 (2006): 651–672.
70 Margaret E. Keck and Kathryn Sikkink, *Activists beyond Borders: Advocacy Networks in International Politics* (Ithaca, NY: Cornell University Press, 1998).
71 Sending and Neumann, "Governance to Governmentality," 668.
72 Ibid., 664.
73 John Shotter, *Conversational Realities* (London: Sage, 1993), 122.
74 Fisher, "Doing Good?" 449.
75 Arjun Appadurai, "Global Ethnoscapes: Notes and Queries for a Transnational Anthropology," in *Recapturing Anthropology: Working in the Present*, ed. Richard G. Fox (Santa Fe, N.M.: SAR Press, 1991), 191–210; and Scott Lash and John Urry, *Economies of Signs and Space* (London: Sage, 1994).

2 Global governance and NGOs
Reconceptualizing international relations for the twenty-first century

Karen A. Mingst and James P. Muldoon, Jr.

- **Reinterpretations of traditional IR theories**
- **Global governance perspective**
- **Conclusion**

International Relations (IR) theorizing is a journey, where the classical theories of realism, liberalism, radicalism, and constructivism are continuously expanded and modified in response both to new ideas by theorists and changes in the real world. Neo-realism, liberal institutionalism, dependency theory, and social constructivism, for example, have emerged from this process. These expansions, modifications, and reinterpretations are an iterative process which is continually contested. Nowhere is this contestation more evident than in IR theorizing about the role and place of non-state actors. Both classical realism and liberalism emphasize the primacy of the state, the former in terms of an international state system and the latter in terms of a state system which left room for domestic political processes. Yet each theory has gradually opened space for non-state actors, albeit slowly and in different ways.

This chapter, like the Introduction to this volume, takes IR theory as the point of departure, showing how traditional theories have evolved. We go on to show how one synthetic framework, global governance, offers a useful analytic that enables us to better describe and explain the changing contours of international relations. A global governance approach enriches liberal theorizing of international institutions, draws on the realist emphasis on power, and utilizes constructivist concepts and approaches.

In this chapter, global governance is developed as a reconceptualization of IR theory for the twenty-first century. Global governance offers four unique and interrelated perspectives:

66 *Theory*

- a multi-actor framework where non-state actors can fit;
- the incorporation of transnational processes which engage the various actors;
- a reincorporation of power in terms of global governance outcomes; and
- concepts for normative assessment of global governance.

Reinterpretations of traditional IR theories

Traditional IR theories (e.g., realism and liberalism) share one important characteristic—the overriding significance of the modern nation-state in world politics and world order. This focus on states and their interactions reflected the predominant theoretical perspective of the IR discipline from its earliest days, which took as axiomatic that the nation-state form of political organization was the highest possible and that the interests, objectives, and capabilities of nation-states are what shape world politics. According to Thompson:

> The twentieth century is a history of one established intellectual discipline following another in successive attempts to make thinking in international relations more coherent and relevant. International law and organization studies supplanted diplomatic history as the dominant approach in the 1930s and 1940s, and international politics and theory came into its own in the postwar period. Much as governments hailed the study of politics, with its focus on the political process within the nation-state, as an advance over constitutional law, postwar students of international politics announced that power, its determinants, and the normative and political constraints on power were essential for understanding the international political process.[1]

It was in 1971, with the publication of the special issue of *International Organization* entitled *Transnational Relations and World Politics* that major IR theorists identified a multi-actor framework including sub-units of states, international governmental organizations (IGOs), and non-state actors.[2] Non-state actors (both non-governmental organizations and multinational corporations) were acknowledged as being part of the "global political terrain" and as having a role in and influence on international politics.[3] That conceptual breakthrough resulted in case studies of these new actors, but theorizing about different political processes incorporating these actors and their impact on IR theory lagged far behind.

In 1977 Keohane and Nye identified key relevant transnational processes in *Power and Interdependence*.[4] Those processes included linkage strategies when outcomes vary by issue area; agenda-setting strategies where international and domestic interests were intertwined, and multiple channels connecting transnational and transgovernmental actors, including new roles of IGOs. While these earlier works followed from liberal theorizing, complex interdependence included a healthy dose of power and power relations. The roots of systematically including nongovernmental organizations (NGOs) and other non-state actors, especially multinational corporations (MNCs), were planted, but the plant grew ever so slowly, largely confined to studies of relations among wealthy democratic states.

During the 1980s two factors explain the slow uptake of theorizing non-state actors. First, in the highly regarded book, *After Hegemony: Cooperation and Discord in the World Political Economy*, Robert Keohane laid out for the first time the theory of liberal institutionalism.[5] While positing that international institutions or regimes provide critical functions (reducing the costs of transactions, facilitating bargaining across issue areas, providing information to reduce cheating), the theory remained state-centered. Cooperation is seen as a rational response by *states* (note by states), even if a hegemonic state is absent.[6] These ideas paved the way for a decade of research on international regimes, a debate on whether they exist or not, and on the impact they have on the *international state system*. While the introduction of international regimes opens the door for acknowledging important roles for international institutions, the focus is on how *states* benefit from these institutions, and NGOs were generally not included.

Second, part of the reason why NGOs remained absent from that analysis is that even as recently as the 1980s, there was a dearth of information about NGOs as a global phenomenon. (Even though by this time, NGOs were already important in limited sectors and regions, such as humanitarian NGOs in Africa, human rights NGOs in Latin America, and environmental NGOs among North Atlantic states.) Gathering systematic empirical data on states was already a task undertaken by international governmental organizations and think tanks; nothing comparable existed for the non-state sector, much less for NGOs. This lack of empirical data on NGOs was a key factor in the lack of attention to NGOs in IR theorizing. Indeed, the omission of NGOs from IR theories during the 1980s was perhaps a logical extension of state-centric theorizing and a pragmatic response to the lack of empirical data.

68 *Theory*

Since the 1990s, however, neither IR theorists nor practitioners can afford to neglect non-state actors, especially NGOs. Widespread recognition of globalization, understood as the thickening of relations among different units in the international system, has led to a variety of interdependence issues where states themselves control neither the information nor the resources, and a qualitative shift in the international system. NGOs have responded to this interdependent world, expanding in number, scope of activities, and developing enhanced expertise. Due to their ability to collect and disseminate information, mobilize key constituencies, and target resources on a broad range of issue areas—from human rights and economic development to the environment and disarmament—NGOs have developed the capabilities to address the challenges and opportunities of globalization, providing them an avenue for influence. With the Cold War's end and the spread of democracy, these actors had more political space to develop and operate. The UN-sponsored global conferences with their parallel NGO forums spurred networking among participating groups and provided aid for Southern-based NGOs. And the communications revolution—first the fax, the cell phone, the internet, and then the web and Twitter—accelerated this growth of real-world NGOs, changed how they communicated, and opened up their activities to researchers who found NGO influences where none had been found before.[7]

How have IR theorists responded? Only a few, such as John Mearsheimer, have dismissed international institutions (IGOs, and by extension NGOs) by saying they only reflect underlying power and the interests of states, and therefore exert no independent influence of their own.[8] Rather, most liberal institutionalists and constructivists have begun the arduous task of middle-range theorizing and developing nuanced case studies. The struggle now is to (re)conceptualize international relations with non-state actors, relevant transnational processes, assessment of outcomes, and evaluative normative criteria. Global governance offers such a wide-ranging perspective.

Global governance perspective

A global governance perspective offers a theoretically encompassing analytical framework, with the potential to be a paradigm shift. The key is found in the notion of governance: it involves complex networks of actors and institutions that include both multiple levels of government and actors outside of government; it recognizes the blurring of responsibilities and boundaries between the public and private; it recognizes different forms of power relationships and the possibility of autonomous self-governing networks of actors.[9] Perhaps the Commission on Global Governance defined governance most succinctly, as:

> the sum of the many ways individuals and institutions, public and private, manage their common affairs. It is a continuing process through which conflicting or diverse interests may be accommodated and cooperative action may be taken. It includes formal ... as well as informal arrangements that people and institutions have agreed to or perceive to be in their interest.[10]

As Rosenau articulated, "It embraces governmental institutions but it also subsumes informal, nongovernmental mechanisms whereby those persons and organizations within its purview move ahead, satisfy their needs, and fulfill their wants."[11] In short, governance is a multi-level collection of activities, rules and mechanisms, formal and informal, public and private. It may be both a top-down or bottom-up activity.

The global governance approach thus represents an important new ontology that breaks with the orthodoxies of IR theory, which recognized only "a narrow band of entities"—nation-states and international organizations—in world politics. It provides an analytical framework for exploring the status of collective political identities and of civil society and the relative importance of state and non-state actors in emerging structures and forms of global governance.[12] According to Dingwerth and Pattberg:

> global governance can be a useful concept to guide our analysis of political processes beyond the state ... Rather than presuming a priori a hierarchy between international and transnational spheres of political activity, a global governance perspective is based on the premise that both spheres have equal ontological status. In short, a global governance perspective acknowledges that world politics is neither international governance plus transnational actors nor transnational governance plus international actors.[13]

DeMars and Dijkzeul in the introduction to this volume suggest that NGOs perform bridging behavior; global governance accommodates this behavior and the multifaceted linkages that it creates, highlighting the bridges among the global, transnational, state, and sub-state, as well as the bridges between the public and the private, and within society, between family and market. Global governance posits *a priori* no hierarchy among the levels; it is pluralistic in that there is no one locus of authority; it is structurally complex with many sources of rule-making and power.[14] Global governance introduces four different areas through which IR theories may be better integrated with each other and with the changing realities of global politics.

Multi-actor framework

First, global governance is a multi-actor framework, but much more expanded from the theorizing in the 1970s. It has a more sophisticated typology of actors. It includes states, since states continue to be key actors in global governance, carrying out many of its activities. States alone have sovereignty, even though the state is more porous than realists admit. States alone create IGOs; it is states that officially create international law and norms and generally determine their effectiveness through their compliance or lack thereof. With differentials in power, their importance is not uniform, however. Global governance includes IGOs, both as reflections of great powers as Mearsheimer suggests, or as elite pacts,[15] or as even autonomous bureaucracies.[16] Also included is an array of non-state actors such as NGOs, MNCs, and social movements. Increasingly, this wider array of other actors establishes habits and norms that may become commonly accepted as soft law or customary law.

Even a realist such as Drezner acknowledges that governance processes are influenced by non-state actors.[17] Actors including NGOs, MNCs, and IGOs affect governance processes, trying to change state preferences, blocking preferred routes of governance, forcing great powers to substitute among different global governance structures. If prominent states are in agreement, they may delegate authority to IGOs and non-state actors to give legitimacy or lock in their preferences through club-like institutions. If preeminent states disagree among themselves, there is more opportunity for IGOs and non-state actors to advance their own interests. Or in some cases, where there is no global agreement or when sham agreements or standards are passed, then non-state actors may provide imperfect enforcement or try to generate their own codes and standards. But the greater the number of non-state actors within global civil society, the greater the coordination problems within each of these processes and the more they have to compete either to protect their own turf or for scarce resources. Yet Drezner's theory is confined to discussion of the specific issues of global regulatory regimes.

In sum, there is a broader categorization of actors in global governance, including not just states and IGOs, but also subnational and local jurisdictions, transgovernmental networks, and epistemic communities. Furthermore, there is a more nuanced typology of non-state actors which includes not only NGOs, but also transnational networks of experts, foundations, multistakeholder arrangements, multinational corporations, and social movements.[18] And among these actors, there is the absence of a defined hierarchy. On some issues, states may dominate; on others, IGOs; and on still others, NGOs or MNCs.[19]

Transnational processes

Second, global governance offers a more extended discussion of transnational processes that form bridges among the various actors and different levels. How non-state actors influence governance processes is of key relevance. Sociologists have long contended that for many organizations—all types of organizations—the most important part of the environment is their cooperative and conflictual relations with other organizations. Organizational interdependence emerges from the shared need for resources (money, specialized skills, and markets), overlapping missions, or the desire to add new specialties at reduced cost. In response, organizations may innovate to exclude rivals or increase coordination and cooperation.

Thus, the study of interorganizational relations examines how and why organizations, often working within the same environment or on the same type of problems, may both clash and cooperate. These theorists are also interested in coordination problems between and among organizations, arising in part from interdependency of resources. Many of the chapters in this volume trace precisely that, the bridging behavior of the various actors across different levels. These scholars have turned to both networks and constructivist learning as illustrations of prominent transnational processes.

Networks

Part of understanding how organizations interact is recognizing that they may interact not just with each other, but within broader social networks. The sociological literature on networks examines the various links between organizations and individuals (both private and public), domestic and international. Often there is a linking-pin organization or a node in the network, wherein coalitions on particular issues are mobilized or where bargaining occurs. Such organizations have seldom been delegated much authority, but are able to legitimize their actions with respect to the specific issue area.

For Keck and Sikkink, a specific type of network—transnational advocacy networks—share "the centrality of values or principled ideas, the belief that individuals can make a difference, the creative use of information, and the employment by nongovernmental actors of sophisticated political strategies in targeting their campaigns." They are "bound together by shared values, a common discourse, and dense exchanges of information and services."[20] These networks also consciously try to set the terms of international and domestic debate, influence international and state-level policy outcomes, and alter the behavior of states, international organizations, and other interested parties.

Generally, network forms of governance encompass both international and domestic actors and processes, linking individuals and groups. The study of network governance has benefited enormously from the information available on the web and new methodologies developed in network analysis, using relational data to show graphically the interconnections among the nodes.

Ohanyan masterfully defines networks as, "inter-organizational coalitions formed among individual international governmental and non-governmental organizations, private consulting firms, commercial banks and others, bound together by financial resource flow and formalized relationships. They are 'incentive compatible' institutional arrangements because constituent members create, change, and adhere to the institution of the network in order to advance their respective organizational goals."[21] For Ohanyan, in contrast to Keck and Sikkink's transnational advocacy networks, members of the networks may not always share common values, discourse or objectives. Coalitions may form for instrumental reasons or to coopt material or nonmaterial resources. In these cases, the "network" may be little more than an inter-organizational coalition. Both DeMars and Dijkzeul in this volume envision networks as even more deeply conflicted. For them, networks can include entities—such as warlords, smugglers, or national intelligence agencies—that are not known to some or all of the NGOs, and that instrumentalize the network for either corrupt purposes or to gain advantage in a war or a diplomatic conflict.

Ohanyan also poses key questions that are critical to an expanded global governance framework: How is authority organized and power exercised in the institutionalized networks? How is power altered within the network? How do the networks affect policy outcomes? Are the outcomes compatible with normative criteria of governance, like promotion of democracy? A network-based approach is essential to understanding the centrality of NGOs, their relationship to other actors, and how networks function. As Ohanyan states in this volume, "Greater appreciation of NGO embeddedness in institutional networks is paramount for furthering NGO studies in meaningful ways, which will also serve to expand the analytical scope of the studies in international organizations and global governance."[22] Networks provide a valuable analytic description and explanation of transnational processes where there are multi-layered processes of governance.

Transnational learning

A second transnational process prominent in the constructivist literature is rooted in the sociological literature on organizational change. Organizations may adapt by adding new activities to their agendas, sometimes muddling through with little attention to the changing underlying bases of the organization and its values. Or as sociologists have pointed out, organizations can, in fact, learn. With learning, members or staff question earlier beliefs and develop new processes. Thus, learning involves redefinition of organizational purposes, reconceptualization of problems, articulation of new ends, and organizational change based upon new, underlying consensual knowledge. As Kapur points out:

> Change may also occur simply due to organizational learning ... Competition, failures, and changing norms, and epistemologies are all likely to spur learning. The consequences of an international institution's own actions may lead to wider systemic learning which, in turn can shape future change in that institution ... Institutional learning is likely to be Bayesian, that is, institutions update their beliefs in response to new information. However, the ability to process information is not equal across IOs. A large literature on organizational learning stresses the importance of an organization's capabilities in affecting learning. Capabilities, in turn, depend on a variety of factors ranging from recruitment criteria (the stock of human capital), organizational structure and systems of authority, and staff and managerial turnover.[23]

Building on this foundation, social constructivists are concerned with how new norms and ideas are learned by the various actors and how those ideas are diffused across time and space. In particular, the non-state actors are examined to find the origins of the new norms, how these new norms are diffused, whether or not the new norms are internalized or socialized in other relevant actors, and with what effects. Human rights, environmental protection, and democratization are issues often singled out for special attention. In each case, non-state actors and networks of NGOs have played key roles in the learning process. Yet, both networks and constructivist learning processes have been criticized for their lack of attention to underlying power dynamics.

Transnational outcomes, bringing power back in

While global governance has been criticized for its neglect of power, that is changing. A third perspective of global governance is that power can be brought back in. Drezner does that when he differentiates between governance processes and governance outcomes.[24] Drezner's position is that outcomes in global regulatory regimes reflect great power interests, consistent with realist expectations. But that may not be true across all issues. So how can global governance bring power back into the discussion, an ingredient so often missing in the non-state actor and NGO literatures and not the major emphasis in the network literature?

To answer that question, we return to the concept of governance. Governance is the process of managing affairs, where conflicting and diverse interests are at stake. More specifically, governance is, according to Hurrell, mediation of difference, promotion of common interests, and management of power.[25] State power remains an essential component in that states enjoy not only significant material resources, but also shape the legal order as well as institutional forms and choices. States decide to participate in networks or not; states can promote learning or choose to not change in relation to lessons learned. But the power of states over other actors is not all the same, and the power of different states varies enormously. To more systematically delve into power, another perspective may be useful.

Principal–agent models

One way to assess relative power of states, IGOs, and NGOs is to utilize rationalist principal–agent models. Economists' work on the theory of the firm, from which principal–agent is derived, posits that principals (in politics, decision-makers) delegate authority to an agent (e.g. a bureaucracy), empowering the agent to act on behalf of the principal(s). Principals delegate such authority for a number of reasons: to benefit from the agent's specialized knowledge, enhance certitude, resolve disputes, or enhance their own credibility. Yet principals need to be careful of agent autonomy, that is, of the agents taking independent actions that the principals do not want. Much of this literature discusses ways the principals control the agents (establishing rules and incentives, monitoring and reporting, inserting checks and balances) and ways in which agents can become independent, autonomous actors.

Scholars of both IGOs and NGOs have turned to principal–agent theory to examine how states as collective principals delegate authority and control to IGOs and the ways that the agents (both IGOs and

NGOs) can exert autonomy.[26] The theory has been used to show how agents interpret mandates, reinterpret rules, expand permeability to third parties, and create barriers to principals' monitoring. While much of this literature to date has focused on a few IGOs, it provides tools to assess the nuances of power more generally.

While NGOs have been examined in principal–agent theory to only a limited extent, the results are promising. Some writers have found that NGOs have agency—the ability to choose among different courses of action, learn from experience, and effect change, which may be independent of states. Some cases in this volume reflect that position. Yet, as Cooley and Ron warn, that may be dysfunctional.[27] Other scholars are not so sure of NGO independence, as other cases show. While NGOs may be crucial intermediaries between states and international organizations, they may not be independent actors that change preferences; in short, they are not sufficiently powerful.[28] Thus, principal–agent theorists are concerned with examining the degree of independence and autonomy of the agent. Generally they find principals limiting their agents and agents acting rationally and strategically to try and expand their authority. Although there are other ways to focus on power relationships, principal–agent theory makes power a paramount concern.

The global governance approach permits us to explore NGOs as potentially both agents and principals. From a legal perspective, NGOs are agents, given authority to operate within a particular jurisdiction and subject to laws of taxation, property, and reporting. That regulatory framework circumscribes NGO approaches and behaviors, as Bloodgood (this volume) examines. Yet, NGOs are also agents of their funders, which may include states and IGOs as well as independent contributors, such as wealthy individuals or private foundations and trustees. Thus, many NGOs have multiple principals, who enjoy the controls they exert over the agents—the laws, the administrative procedures, the ability to budget funds and reduce those funds and target money for specific purposes, and monitor the behavior of the NGO.

But NGOs do have some power in this relationship. They often have specialized expertise needed by the principal or principals, especially because they often operate closer to the grassroots. They may have more local information than the principals, and their ability to exploit this information gives them power. Hence, NGOs may enjoy more credibility than the principals because of their unique positioning and their "perceived" independent status. Because of their smaller size with more targeted goals and interests, NGOs may be more efficient operators than the principals. And the fact that NGOs have multiple principals gives them more leeway—more power—to either select or adapt to one principal over another, to frame arguments for particular audiences, or to get the principals fighting amongst each other to obtain a privileged agent. Having the advantage of information asymmetry, NGOs are able to act autonomously and to exploit the differences among the principals, utilizing the rules of the principal which best matches the interests of the NGO. In short, NGOs may have the power to influence outcomes. And a global governance perspective demands consideration of outcomes.

NGOs are also the principals providing aid and services to local individuals or groups, the aid recipient being the agent. NGOs as principals may have the power to determine who may be the recipients, the procedures through which aid is dispensed, and the conditions given for the assistance. Sometimes there will be multiple NGOs involved in the project—and then the agents, just as described above, have the ability to pick and choose among the most suitable or among those having personal ties, much as Clifford Bob found.[29]

Have NGOs acted independently by developing rules and guidelines that do not follow exactly from the principals or is the organizational culture fully congruent with the principals? Has the NGO exercised independence by trying to change the normative environment? Has the NGO acquired the ability to create space for independent maneuvering? Has the NGO been able to overcome an organizational culture which may impede adaptation and learning, including "a cultural bias towards action rather than reflection; a focus on immediate project concern rather than the wider environment; a lack of emphasis on listening and participation; and the rapid turnover of staff, particularly those in decision-making positions"?[30] Only close empirical research including interviews and participant observation, as conducted by authors in this volume, will uncover the NGOing. A global governance perspective demands such deep consideration of processes and outcomes.

Individual practices

Another way to examine the processes and practices of specific NGOs, states, and IGOs, in networks and beyond, is to focus on the practices of individuals. As Hilhorst describes this constructivist approach,

> We must try to make sense of people's motivations, ideas and activities by taking into account their past and present surroundings, social networks and histories. And we must observe the way they deal with NGO-ing, because this conveys practical knowledge, implicit interpretations and power processes taking place in their organizations.[31]

Global governance and NGOs 77

To examine global governance outcomes, then, rationalist principal–agent models and social constructivist approaches with emphasis on individual practices might be fruitfully combined. The contributors to a forthcoming volume edited by Tierney, Thompson and Weaver attempt to do just that.[32] Weaver takes the first steps toward such a synthesis in the case of the World Bank.[33] She examines both the bank's external environment, using the principal–agent model, and the internal environment, the bank's bureaucratic and intellectual culture, including individuals, using a social constructivist approach. By examining how bank personnel think and what the institution wants, we can see why the bank might deviate from both the ideas and policies of the principals. Particularly useful is Weaver's discussion of how international organizations get slippage leading to autonomy, by having expertise and control over information, and from preference heterogeneity among multiple or collective principals. In this volume, NGOs are put under the same scrutiny. And global governance accommodates both rationalist and constructivist theorizing.

The normative framework

Finally, global governance demands normative assessments. While principal–agent theory is popular in some circles because of its discussions about accountability, as Cristina Balboa in this volume asserts, accountability, legitimacy, and effectiveness are core normative concerns of global governance.[34] A global governance approach probes these key issues from various perspectives.

For whom is global governance working? Are global governance actors and processes accountable? To whom? Ironically, NGOs themselves have raised the accountability issue for states and IGOs; yet many also question the accountability of NGOs and other transnational actors. For example, Sperling finds that while transnational social movements and judicial institutions have had positive effects on governmental accountability, the effects are limited.[35] And in other globalizing issues, including economic development and democracy promotion, the effects of transnational activity on accountability are negative. In many cases, therefore, neither states nor transnational actors are held accountable. More research is called for in this realm of global governance.

Is global governance legitimate? To be so, various structures and processes of governance must accommodate widespread participation and some degree of consent. The challenge of legitimizing global governance structures is not just one of formal procedures or legal safeguards. It depends on the diversity and breadth of support. With participation, people have a sense of ownership and stake in outcomes of policy-making.[36] A necessary part of legitimacy then is how and to what degree NGOs and other civil society actors have broadened participation, as illustrated in this volume. Yet to be considered legitimate, global governance cannot be considered an American, Western, or liberal economic project that is only compatible with the power and preferences of the United States, MNCs, Northern NGOs, or Western-trained experts. Moreover, it is the imperative to deliver "global" public goods that shapes people's view of the legitimacy of global governance institutions. As Buchanan and Keohane argue:

> It is important not only that global governance institutions be legitimate, but that they are perceived to be legitimate. The perception of legitimacy matters, because, in a democratic era, multilateral institutions will only thrive if they are viewed as legitimate by democratic publics. If one is unclear about the appropriate standards of legitimacy or if unrealistically demanding standards are assumed, then public support for global governance institutions may be undermined and their effectiveness in providing valuable goods may be impaired.[37]

Legitimation of global governance organizations seems to rest increasingly upon these organizations being accountable and inclusive through "consultative" processes or "stakeholder" engagement. This approach reflects the widespread belief that the management of international organizations and of private-sector entities is analogous. "While the consultative process approach may involve political risks—it is likely to create, on the part of the stakeholders, an expectation of accountability—it also establishes a direct and more formalized relationship between the organization and its stakeholders, thus bringing the organization closer to the 'people' and enhancing the perceived legitimacy of its decision-making."[38] However, the legitimacy of hybrid governance organizations, such as transnational public–private partnerships, is not necessarily "automatic" because they are inclusive and/or transparent; rather, it is "derived through effective problem solving" in that a hybrid governance organization attains legitimacy if and when its decisions prove to be effective.[39]

Finally, is global governance effective? Do governance institutions actually address and manage the interdependence issues of the twenty-first century, including human insecurity and inequality? Although assessment of effectiveness of global governance institutions is in its infancy, the literature on evaluation and effectiveness in both the public and private sectors offers a variety of methods and approaches for developing criteria to measure governance activities and impact of global governance institutions and organizations. There are many different research traditions on evaluation and effectiveness that emphasize different approaches, namely rationalistic and hermeneutic: "Rationalistic approaches rely heavily on deduction of causal relations and ex post-evaluation research has developed a broad array of relatively simple to highly sophisticated methods, models, techniques and tools for tracking down such causal relations. In the hermeneutic approach relations are not deductively arrived at, but induced by observation and interpretation."[40] The challenge is to make full use of both types of evaluation methodologies in assessing the effectiveness of global governance institutions.

Conclusion

This volume provides a fruitful step in providing answers to the woefully neglected subject of NGOs and international relations. Global governance provides a useful overarching analytic for this study: a multi-actor framework, an incorporation of the transnational processes of networks and social learning, an analysis of power relationships through principal–agent theory, and incorporation of key normative concerns of accountability, legitimacy, and effectiveness. As a reconceptualization of IR theory for the twenty-first century, the global governance approach opens up research on international relations to the full range of state and non-state actors, though it is also necessary to take seriously the reality of both cooperative and conflictive relations in global governance.[41]

Notes

1. Kenneth Thompson, *Traditions and Values in Politics and Diplomacy: Theory and Practice* (Baton Rouge: Louisiana State University Press, 1992).
2. Robert O. Keohane and Joseph S. Nye, Jr, eds, *Transnational Relations and World Politics* (Cambridge, Mass.: Harvard University Press, 1972).
3. Charles W. Kegley, Jr and Eugene R. Wittkopf (1981) *World Politics: Trend and Transformation* (New York: St. Martin's Press, 1981), Chapter 6, "Nonstate Actors in the Interstate System"; and Peter Willetts, ed., *Pressure Groups in the Global System: The Transnational Relations of Issue-Orientated Non-Governmental Organisations* (London: Pinter, 1982).
4. Robert O. Keohane and Joseph S. Nye, *Power and Interdependence: World Politics in Transition* (Boston, Mass.: Little, Brown, 1977).
5. Robert O. Keohane, *After Hegemony: Cooperation and Discord in the World Political Economy* (Princeton, N.J.: Princeton University Press, 1984).
6. Stephen D. Krasner, ed., *International Regimes* (Ithaca, NY: Cornell University Press, 1983).

7 Leon Gordenker and Thomas G. Weiss, "Pluralizing Global Governance: Analytical Approaches and Dimensions," in *NGOs, The UN, and Global Governance*, eds Thomas G. Weiss and Leon Gordenker (Boulder, Colo.: Lynne Rienner, 1996), 17–47; JoAnn Fagot Aviel, "NGOs and International Affairs," in *Multilateral Diplomacy and the United Nations Today*, 2nd edition, eds James P. Muldoon Jr., JoAnn Fagot Aviel, Richard Reitano and Earl Sullivan (Boulder, Colo.: Westview Press, 2005), 159–172; and Bob Reinalda, ed., *The Ashgate Research Companion to Non-State Actors* (Burlington, Vt.: Ashgate, 2011).
8 John J. Mearsheimer, "The False Promise of International Institutions," *International Security* 19, no. 3 (1994/5): 5–49.
9 Gerry Stoker, "Governance as Theory: Five Propositions," *International Social Science Journal* 50, Issue 155 (1998): 17–28; and Jan Kooiman, *Governing as Governance* (London: Sage, 2003).
10 Commission on Global Governance, *Our Global Neighbourhood: Report of the Commission on Global Governance* (Oxford: Oxford University Press, 1995), 2.
11 James N. Rosenau, "Governance, Order and Change in World Politics," in *Governance Without Government: Order and Change in World Politics*, eds James. N. Rosenau and E. O. Czempiel (Cambridge: Cambridge University Press, 1992), 4.
12 Martin Hewson and Timothy J. Sinclair, eds, *Approaches to Global Governance Theory* (Albany, NY: State University of New York Press, 1999).
13 Klaus Dingwerth and Philipp Pattberg, "Global Governance as a Perspective on World Politics," *Global Governance* 12, no. 2 (2006): 198–199.
14 David Held and Anthony McGrew, "Introduction," in *Governing Globalization: Power, Authority and Global Governance*, eds David Held and Anthony McGrew (Malden, Mass.: Polity, 2002) 9–10; and Jim Whitman, *The Fundamentals of Global Governance* (Basingstoke: Palgrave Macmillan, 2009).
15 Erik Voeten, "The Political Origins of the UN Security Council's Ability to Legitimize the Use of Force," *International Organization* 59, no. 3 (2005): 527–557.
16 Michael Barnett and Martha Finnemore, *Rules for the World. International Organizations in Global Politics* (Ithaca, NY: Cornell University Press, 2004).
17 Daniel W. Drezner, *All Politics Is Global: Explaining International Regulatory Regimes* (Princeton, NJ: Princeton University Press, 2007).
18 Margaret P. Karns and Karen A. Mingst, *International Organization: The Politics and Processes of Global Governance*, 2nd edition (Boulder, Colo.: Lynne Rienner, 2010).
19 Martin Koch, "Non-State and State Actors in Global Governance," in *Ashgate Research Companion to Non-State Actors*, ed. Bob Reinalda (Burlington, Vt.: Ashgate, 2011), 197–208.
20 Margaret E. Keck and Kathryn Sikkink, *Activists beyond Borders: Advocacy Networks in International Politics* (Ithaca, NY: Cornell University Press, 1998), 2.
21 Anna Ohanyan, *NGOs, IGOs, and the Network Mechanisms of Post-Conflict Global Governance of Microfinance* (New York: Palgrave Macmillan, 2008), 3.
22 Anna Ohanyan, this volume, 83.

23 Devesh Kapur, "Processes of Change in International Organizations," in *Governing Globalization: Issues and Institutions*, ed. Deepak Nayyar (New York: Oxford University Press, 2002), 345–346.
24 Drezner, *All Politics Is Global*.
25 Andrew Hurrell, "Power, Institutions, and the Production of Inequality," in *Power in Global Governance*, eds Michael Barnett and Raymond Duvall (Cambridge: Cambridge University Press, 2005), 35.
26 Darren G. Hawkins, David A. Lake, Daniel L. Nielson and Michael J. Tierney, eds, *Delegation and Agency in International Organizations* (Cambridge: Cambridge University Press, 2006).
27 Alexander Cooley and James Ron, "The NGO Scramble: Organizational Insecurity and the Political Economy of Transnational Action," *International Security* 27, no. 1 (2002): 5–39.
28 David A. Lake and Mathew D. McCubbins, "The Logic of Delegation to International Organizations," in *Delegation and Agency in International Organizations*, eds Darren G. Hawkins, David A. Lake, Daniel L. Nielson and Michael J. Tierney (Cambridge: Cambridge University Press, 2006), 341–368.
29 Clifford Bob, *The Marketing of Rebellion: Insurgents, Media, and International Activism* (Cambridge: Cambridge University Press, 2005).
30 Jonathan Goodhand, *Aiding Peace? The Role of NGOs in Armed Conflict* (Boulder, Colo.: Lynne Rienner, 2006), 177.
31 Dorothea Hilhorst, *The Real World of NGOs: Discourses, Diversity and Development* (London: Zed Books, 2003), 6.
32 Michael J. Tierney, Alex Thompson and Catherine Weaver, eds, (manuscript under revision) *The Politics of International Organizations: Bridging the Rationalist–Constructivist Divide*; also see Joel E. Oestreich, ed., *International Organizations as Self-Directed Actors* (New York: Routledge, 2012).
33 Catherine Weaver, "The World's Bank and the Bank's World," *Global Governance* 13, no. 4 (2007): 493–512.
34 Karns and Mingst, *International Organization*, 547–552.
35 Valerie Sperling, *Altered States: The Globalization of Accountability* (Cambridge University Press, 2009), 319.
36 Andreas Kruck and Volker Rittberger, "Multilateralism Today and Its Contribution to Global Governance," in *The New Dynamics of Multilateralism: Diplomacy, International Organizations, and Global Governance*, eds James P. Muldoon, Jr., JoAnn Fagot Aviel, Richard Reitano and Earl Sullivan (Boulder, Colo.: Westview Press, 2010), 51–52.
37 Allen Buchanan and Robert O. Keohane, "The Legitimacy of Global Governance Institutions," *Ethics and International Affairs* 20, no. 4 (2006): 407.
38 Viejo Heiskanen, "Introduction," in *The Legitimacy of International Organizations*, eds Jean-Marc Coicaud and Veijo Heiskanen (New York: UNU Press, 2001), 10–12.
39 Marco Schäferhoff, Sabine Campe and Christopher Kaan, "Transnational Public-Private Partnerships in International Relations: Making Sense of Concepts, Research Frameworks, and Results," *International Studies Review* 11, no. 3 (2009): 465.
40 Kooiman, *Governing as Governance*,183.
41 Thomas G. Weiss and Rorden Wilkinson, "Global Governance to the Rescue: Saving International Relations?" *Global Governance* 20, no. 1 (2014): 19–36.

3 Network institutionalism
A new synthesis for NGO studies

Anna Ohanyan[1]

- **Policy network theories**
- **New institutional theories and NGO studies**
- **Network institutionalism: a new synthesis for NGO studies**
- **Conclusion**

Non-governmental organizations (NGOs) have been relatively neglected in International Relations (IR) theory and now pose a singular challenge to the field. The reasons are many, including the lack of quantitative NGO studies;[2] the heterogeneity of the NGO sector itself; state-centrism within the field of IR; and the multiplicity of ways NGOs both cooperate and conflict with state-centric institutions. Polarization among the main schools of the discipline has also been a major hurdle in developing NGO theories.[3] Paying so little attention to NGOs in world politics, however, has limited the applicability of dominant IR theories to understand and explain the increasingly globalized social realities around the world. Most importantly, IR tends to underappreciate the associative capacities of NGOs, which DeMars and Dijkzeul in this volume describe as "their unremitting and expansive bridging," and the implication that NGOs are ontologically intertwined with other players in world politics. These blind spots are due partly to the dominance within the discipline of methodological individualism, which stems largely from rational choice theories, and holds that individual actors (both state and non-state) are the primary unit of analysis in political science and are mostly driven by utility maximization.[4] This methodological strategy offers very few paths to capture the associative nature and the ontological interdependency of NGOs with other actors. As I argue in this chapter, network-based institutional approaches offer a constructive remedy for the problem.

Explaining the bridging and associative capacities of NGOs may be more effective, I argue, as part of a broader research undertaking that rests on understanding the institutional reality of NGOs in world politics. Studies documenting the quantitative rise of the NGO sector in world politics have done little to assess the qualitative impact of that development, particularly in light of the new links and relationships that NGOs have created with state-centric structures of world politics. While studies in transnational politics have developed theoretical frameworks in which to examine the agency of non-state actors,[5] the specific role and the institutional impact of NGOs on structures of global governance remains a promising and underexplored research area. Greater appreciation of NGO embeddedness in institutional networks is paramount for furthering NGO studies in meaningful ways, which will also serve to expand the analytical scope of the studies in international organizations and global governance.

This chapter calls for nuanced analysis concerning the specific institutional conditions under which NGOs are empowered and/or constrained. It points out that such institutional conditions generally do not map out in terms of simple dichotomies between "state" and "non-state," "domestic" and "international," "public" and "private," and "interests" and "ideas." These conditions are much more complicated, rivaling the intricacy of biological cells and networks. Models that transcend such dichotomies can be more effective in theorizing about NGOs while also advancing and enhancing the explanatory and analytical power of the dominant IR schools of realism, liberalism and constructivism. In the context of this volume, I undertake to further theorize NGO bridging, especially across agency and structure, thereby advancing the project proposed in the Introduction, while also challenging it in some respects.

The associative nature of NGOs must be brought in to make theoretical progress in understanding NGOs. Their tenacious bridging with other actors in world politics generates profound implications for understanding both agency and structure as institutionalized in transnational networks. NGOs exercise *agency* by bridging; and at the same time their bridging creates *structural* effects on NGOs themselves and other actors in the network. By bridging, I argue, particular NGOs and their networks become more firmly embedded in "organizational fields" defined by both issues and regions; in short, over time NGOs *institutionalize* their bridged relationships with donors, host governments, and societal partners.

Specifically, NGO studies can be advanced most effectively if NGOs are analyzed within their immediate and network-based institutional arrangements among which their associative capacities are played out. As I have argued elsewhere, understanding the structural attributes of networks can be a powerful determinant for understanding NGO behavior.[6] The synthesis of policy network theories with new institutionalism, as developed in this chapter, offers concrete methodological and conceptual tools to think about *bridging, power*, and *practice* in NGO politics. NGOs are actors and carriers of bridging practices that occur through network-based institutionalization in world politics. NGOs actively cultivate such networks, but they are also co-opted and brought into networks by other actors—donors, for instance. In these bridging processes NGOs cultivate the institutional fabric of networks but are also shaped by the institutional constraints that such networks generate. Understanding the institutional effects and outcomes of such bridging is one major research direction for NGO studies.

The integrated network approach developed here also captures the power imbalances between NGOs and other actors, and illuminates the impact of such imbalances in world politics. It offers new dimensions of power, such as the structural position of an organization within a network, which becomes consequential as to how well each network member can advance its goals relative to the other actors. In terms of practice (particularly the bridging and power dynamics), this integrated approach raises questions as to what motivational logic informs NGO practice. To explore these issues, the researcher has to transcend methodological individualism, which assumes the NGO imperative to organizational survival as its primary explanation.

Briefly, the complexity of the institutional environment in world politics has significantly evolved since the creation of the United Nations and the Bretton Woods system in the aftermath of World War II. NGOs have risen in parallel to such changes. The new theoretical frameworks, therefore, have to account for both developments. Institutions and organizations in world politics have become larger and more complex, and thereby more important to collective life.[7]

In an effort to develop a theoretical framework that can capture the associative capacities of NGOs and their relationship to their immediate networks, I now turn to provide a brief overview of *policy network theories*, which have evolved separately from institutional theories. This will be followed by a discussion on three strands within the family of *institutionalist theories* that provide the vocabulary and the analytical framework amenable to integration with *network theories* for advancing NGO studies in world politics.

Policy network theories

Networks house a variety of actors—state and non-state, public and private. They are driven by both conflict and cooperation between actors with varied interests, while also carrying, shaping, and framing ideas and identities in world politics. Drawing from sociological institutionalism, networks can also be defined as organizational fields, as they represent a community of organizations that share a meaning system and that interact more frequently with one another than with the outside world.[8]

Networks are by no means entirely cooperative. They are also far from egalitarian. On the contrary, networks are characterized by deep power imbalances between members in terms of their resource endowments and their structural positions in the network. Moreover, the term "network" may also convey a functionality of relationships between the network members, that is, network members come together to purposefully advance their own goals and to maximize their organizational goals. However, the real and messy politics of the NGO sector does not sustain such an understanding of cooperative purposefulness. While functionalism may explain one aspect of the rise of NGOs, it underestimates the forces of institutional isomorphism, politics and path dependencies that have also been important in consolidating the NGO sector in global politics.

I now turn to present a brief overview of the main schools of policy network theories—the American and British interest intermediation and the German governance approaches—before exploring the institutional forces of network politics that are consequential for NGO studies. I argue that the network approach to NGO studies in IR is a useful bridge between NGO studies and dominant IR theories that generally treat NGOs as inconsequential and marginal in world politics.

Network literature is interdisciplinary, drawing from sociology, anthropology, political science, and public administration, among other fields. Research into networks in political science and public administration has been triggered by several factors, including changes in governance structures in industrialized democracies, weakening administrative capacities of a state in the wake of accelerated globalization,[9] and transborder problems. Some argue that network development signals a crisis within the institutions of governance, and networks form to fill a governance vacuum.[10]

Studies in American politics were influential in advancing debates on network operation in the 1950s and 1960s.[11] This literature recognizes the frequent contacts among interest groups, bureaucratic agencies, and the government, all of which interacted to make most of the routine decisions in a given policy area.[12]

As with many other network theories, when applied to the network politics of NGOs, this American school of network research also yields

86 *Theory*

functionalist explanations of network formation and consolidation. Indeed, NGOs are partly sustained by funding they receive from their donors, which are important members of these networks, and by the political clout, leverage, and access these organizations bestow on them. In such functionalist explanations resource interdependencies of network members are essential factors in creating and sustaining networks, and NGOs' relationships with their donors are rather symbiotic. By engaging with NGOs in policy networks, intergovernmental organizations have compensated for the organizational resource shortages they face on the ground. NGOs are known for their responsiveness to the grassroots,[13] and intergovernmental organizations have compensated for their hierarchical nature and their organizational rigidity in crisis situations by forming links with NGOs.[14] Such explanations build on rational choice theories and are primarily focused at the organizational level. Although in some cases such explanations yield thoughtful analysis, they fail to elaborate on cases when NGOs or their donors form networks, even when such partnerships fail to deliver or constrain these organizations. In short, networks are not always more efficient tools of problem solving in world politics, which, however, has not prohibited their formation.

The American sources of policy network theories have greatly influenced the British frameworks of network analysis.[15] Richardson and Jordan even argue that the policy communities, issue networks, and iron triangles observed within American domestic politics are generally representative of policy-making patterns in other stable liberal democracies.[16] They maintain that governments are then disaggregated and society is fragmented, which is reflected by the large number of interest groups. Consequently, the policy-making process becomes a complex game between networks that links particular interests and different sections of the government.

Both the British and American sources of network analysis resonate with the interest intermediation school of network analysis,[17] where networks are considered to be a qualitatively new type of state–society relation. Regardless of the analytical differences within the interest intermediation school of network analysis, most of the researchers concur in placing the networks on a continuum ranging from highly integrated policy communities at one end to loosely integrated issue networks at the other.

In contrast to the American and British literature on networks, which focuses primarily on interest intermediation, the German literature centers on the governance school of network analysis. Although the approaches have marked differences, they are not mutually exclusive. Börzel claims that the interest-intermediation school applies to all kinds of relations between various public and private actors.[18] For the governance school, policy networks are developed to capture only specific forms of public–private interaction in public policy, those characterized by a nonhierarchical coordination, as opposed to hierarchy and market as two distinct modes of governance.[19] The governance school of network analysis considers policy networks to be institutional arrangements that are capable of delivering services and filling governance gaps locally and globally.[20] In this respect, networks are themselves actors engaged in collective action.[21]

The governance school of network analysis best captures the NGO engagement with its transnational donor structures in the area of service delivery in international development. It reflects the thickening and strengthening of interorganizational ties and the institutionalization of governance processes in world politics over the past several decades. A cursory glance at the literature reveals that the NGOs that were the most networked, either in donor structures or among their grassroots stakeholders, have been most effective in scaling up their operation in a shorter period of time.[22]

Table 3.1 provides a comparative overview of the various well established schools in network research. These approaches are compared in terms of the level of institutionalization of networks they assume, the dominant logic of formation and consolidation of networks, and the treatment of power in network arrangements. These three categories correspond to the tripartite concepts of *practice*, *bridging*, and *power* as presented in the Introduction by DeMars and Dijkzeul.

The network mechanism of engagement in global politics by NGOs and international organizations has profound institutional implications for global politics and the actors involved, but network theories fail to fully explore this reality. Network theories offer the language and the framework in which to examine the interface between public and private sectors as well as between the domestic and international domains of politics. However, network theories tell us little about the changes in the institutional environment in global governance. Network theories treat networks as interorganizational coalitions, while institutionalism, as elaborated in the next section, captures their consolidation as institutional arrangements of global governance. The functionalist emphasis of network theories is another limitation when explaining the rise of NGOs in the twentieth century. They explain network formation through utilitarian and rational choice approaches, so that the institutional dynamics of network formation and consolidation are insufficiently treated. These network theories fail to distinguish between

88 *Theory*

Table 3.1 Comparative overview of policy network theories

		Two approaches	
		Interest intermediation approach (American and British schools)	*Governance approach (German school)*
Three dimensions	*Level of institutionalization (Practice)*	Networks as loose and variable relations	Networks as stable structures and continuous institutional relations
	Logic of network formation and consolidation (Bridging)	Functionalist	Functionalist
	Power	Power asymmetries in networks acknowledged	Networks as horizontal and nonhierarchical arrangements

organizations and institutions, thereby unveiling very little of the process of institutionalization in world politics as facilitated by NGOs and networks. The institutional effects of structures of global governance on NGOs and networks are also poorly explored within conventional network theories. Most important, the existing network theories tell us little about the institutional identity of NGOs in global governance.

New institutional theories and NGO studies

The central research direction that I believe will shape further NGO studies is the examination of the effect of the institutional environment of NGOs on their behavior, and an examination of the institutional effects of NGOs on other organizations and structures of global governance. I also argue that theoretical approaches integrating policy network theories with new institutionalism are a useful research strategy to that end. Providing a comprehensive overview of institutionalism is not the purpose in this section. Instead, I will focus on those strands within new institutionalism that are most consequential for building NGO theories that can capture their associative capacities and the implications for agency and structure. In particular, this section will briefly examine rational choice institutionalism, historical institutionalism and sociological institutionalism, and will elaborate as to how these theories relate to policy network theories discussed in the previous section. Overall, the new institutionalism has been effective in generating understanding about how institutions affect organizations, and as early as the 1970s, institutional theories produced research in that direction

Rational choice institutionalism posits the centrality of rational actors with fixed preferences who can promote complementarity and coordination with other actors as they correct collective action problems, including the "tragedy of the commons."[23] This branch of institutionalism is theoretically compatible with the functionalism of both schools of policy network theory reviewed above, which explain network formation through utilitarian, rational choice processes. To clarify, policy network theory has highlighted the added value of network modes of governance, alternative to the hierarchy and market. To a certain extent, such approaches have assigned rationality and functionality to policy networks, which, however, captures only one dimension in the global policy-making process. I have argued elsewhere that the functional capacity of a network is a function of its internal structural attributes: some networks, depending on a range of structural characteristics, are more effective in delivering governance than others.[24]

According to Schmidt, in American politics rational choice institutionalism resonated with principal-agent theories which examined how "principals" (Congress, executive or political parties) maintain control over "agents" to which they delegate, such as bureaucracies, regulatory agencies, courts, etc.[25] In IR, rational choice institutionalism and principal–agent theories have been applied to explain delegation from states to international organizations of authority and responsibility within certain boundaries.[26] However, this application of rational choice theory failed to reach the delegation from various actors to NGOs. In addition, it assumes fixed preferences and rationally calculated behavior. In previous work, I have followed a rational choice approach in defining networks as interorganizational coalitions of state and non-state actors that are formed by resource dependencies between them and are sustained by rationally constructed renegotiations among the actors, the ongoing nature of the relationships, and the organizational inertia of all members.[27] In this approach, networks are understood as structures formed "by design" rather than "by default" and organizational inertia, as is actually often the case.[28] Historical institutionalism, to be discussed next, corrects for this limitation by highlighting the constraining power of structures on individual actors, such as NGOs.

Historical institutionalism in particular has expanded conventional understanding of institutional effects on behavior by including informal institutions and clarifying which institutions matter and how.[29] This approach generated a structuralist understanding of political behavior as it showed how institutional systems structure individual and

90 *Theory*

collective action. Although the original focus of historical institutionalism was on state structures, it later evolved to explain the origins and development of institutional structures in general in explaining political action and the process of governing.[30] This is a significant departure from functionalist or rationalist perspectives of political behavior according to which organizations evolve to develop the particular characteristics needed to advance a particular goal or meet a particular organizational need. Against this institutionalist backdrop, NGOs can be understood as having evolved toward professionalization and greater bureaucracy partly as a way to interact with donor structures more effectively, and partly as a way to emulate these very donor structures and gain legitimacy.[31] For instance, NGOs often complain of the amount of time they spend on reporting to their multiple donors,[32] which often have very specific reporting guidelines, ranging from the frequency of reports to the indicators and conditionalities that must be reported by the NGO.

Historical institutionalism defines institutions as both formal and informal rules and procedures that shape conduct.[33] Most importantly, historical institutionalism views institutions not as reflections of aggregate individual choices but as structures reflecting unanticipated effects that can have an independent influence on social processes.[34] One way to apply historical institutionalism to NGO studies is to distinguish between the organizational changes within NGOs, as effects, which are driven by the causal factors of (1) organizational rationality, in particular efficiency concerns, (2) power politics within networks, and (3) the institutional forces and isomorphism that pressure NGOs from outside. This research strategy continues to acknowledge the agency of NGOs at the organizational level, but expands the scope of analysis to underline the bounded rationality of NGOs and the institutional constraints they face within their networks.

Factoring power into institutional analysis is another major contribution of historical institutionalism, which is particularly consequential for further NGO studies in world politics. In contrast to most policy network theories, historical institutionalism recognizes how institutional structures privilege some social groups at the expense of others. Translating this position for network analysis indicates that the position of an organization, in this case an NGO, within a network can provide it with access to resources (material and other), and that such endowment with power is highly contingent on the network structure. For instance, the degree of power concentration among the network members is one network attribute that is consequential for the organizational autonomy of NGOs.[35] Indeed, this approach affords us great flexibility in capturing the bridging practices that are central to the institutional identity of the NGO sector in world politics. The development of methods to study the institutional effects of networks on NGOs calls for appreciating the complexity that is characteristic of the organizational fabric of global governance.

Sociological institutionalism is the third variant of the new institutionalism that enables researchers to capture the bridging practices characteristic of an NGO's engagement in world politics. This approach maintains that institutionalization constrains organizational rationality.[36] Here the emphasis on the external culture or world polity and their ability to shape the organization and its rules and routines is one of the key characteristics of sociological institutionalism.[37] Changes internal to the organization are largely explained by the transformations in the regulatory and normative patterns in the external world of a given organization. In short, sociological institutionalism treats organizations as socially embedded. This approach contributed to new understandings of organizations as adaptive organic systems shaped and influenced by the social characteristics of their immediate institutional environment rather than as manifestations of rational action.[38]

Depicted as rational actors, NGOs are rather mechanical instruments created to achieve specific goals.[39] Instead, treated within sociological institutionalism, NGOs are adaptive, organic, systems organizations that over time become infused with value "beyond the technical requirements of the task at hand"[40] as they organically adapt to their environment, thereby becoming institutionalized. Particularly relevant for NGO studies is the institutionalist claim that organizations with "unclear technologies and/or difficult to evaluate outputs" are particularly sensitive to the institutional pressures of their environments.[41] In such cases, organizations adapt to their environment by developing features similar to that environment—an important precondition to secure social approval and legitimacy from that environment. NGOs are often examples of organizations with unclear technologies and difficult to evaluate outputs. Indeed, NGOs have been increasingly institutionalized to become more professional and even more bureaucratic in many contexts,[42] clearly mimicking the international organizations and bilateral aid agencies that started to fund them extensively in the 1970s. This approach is structural in its essence and is contrary to the dominant focus on NGO agency within the literature. Many nuances related to institutional effects on NGOs have been under-studied as a result.

Sociological institutionalism, which is essentially an institutional treatment of the organization, has been influenced both by old and new institutionalisms.[43] Here it suffices to highlight that new institutionalism

92 *Theory*

emphasizes interorganizational influences when explaining irrationality, which is yet another tacit endorsement of network-based understandings of NGOs and their behavior in world politics. However, it is the definition of the external environment of an organization within new institutionalism that provides the strongest support for network-based approaches to NGO studies. In particular, new institutionalism defines such environments as "organizational sectors or fields roughly coterminous with the boundaries of industries, professions, or national societies."[44]

NGO research calls for fresh theoretical frameworks that are responsive to the associative capacities and ontological interdependence of NGOs with other state and non-state actors. NGOs are institutionally embedded in networks of various complexity and size, which house public and private donors, as well as other state and non-state actors. Sociological institutionalism can help to address the question: What is the institutional significance of these networks for NGOs, as well as for the structures of global governance? In particular, sociological institutionalism helps to define the key concepts of organizations, networks and institutions.

For sociological institutionalism, NGOs are understood as organizations in general, that is, as collective actors with legal rights, capacities and resources that are independent of other actors.[45] Philip Selznick, a leading scholar of institutional analysis of organization, differentiated between (1) the organization created originally as a rational instrument to achieve specific goals, and (2) the organization as an "adaptive, organic system affected by the social characteristics of its participants as well as by the varied pressures imposed by its environment," which over time may be transformed into institutions.[46]

Networks, similar to organizations, are also collective actors, but they are built on inadequacies of capacities and resource shortages among organizations constituting the network. In a way, networks can be viewed as transitional structures between organizations and institutions. Meyer and Rowan argue that organizations carry the influences of their institutional environments.[47] In a similar vein, others observed that the growth and collaboration of cross-organizational professional networks spread new and varied models of organizing in the latter half of the twentieth century.[48] Here networks are understood as carriers of institutional effects between organizations, which they accomplish by increasing interactions between organizations, enhancing information sharing as well as mutual awareness and responsiveness between them. In this process, networks contribute to the broader institutionalization of organizing modes and authority patterns around the organizations.

Selznick maintains that organizations will either institutionalize themselves or will collapse sooner or later. Specifically, he observes that:

Institutionalization is a process. It is something that happens to an organization over time, reflecting the organization's own distinctive history, the people who have been in it, the groups it embodies and the vested interests they have created, and the way it has adapted to its environment ... In what is perhaps its most significant meaning, "to institutionalize" is to *infuse with value* beyond the technical requirements of the task at hand.[49]

Therefore, while organizations are mechanistic and technical, institutions are infused with value. Sociological institutionalism defines institutions as "taken for granted repetitive social behavior that is underpinned by normative systems and cognitive understandings that give meaning to social exchange and thus enable self-producing social order."[50]

In short, the new institutionalisms can be enormously beneficial for further theories related to NGO studies in IR. However, the familiar criticism that institutionalism faces in regard to its inability to explain social change is also applicable to NGO studies. In addition, in a critique of institutional theories, DiMaggio insisted that they must incorporate "the reality of purposive, interest-driven, and conflictual behavior."[51] Nevertheless, institutional theories, particularly historical institutionalism, still tend to portray politics as rather harmonious and conflict-free, and therefore to theorize poorly on power and authority. Hence, articulating conditions under which agency (i.e., the NGO), relative to structure (networks and organizational fields), takes precedence is an essential prerequisite for building institutional theories of NGOs.[52] Theories built on the institutional effects on the NGO sector do not explain cases when NGOs are agents of social change and transformation; similarly, the initiatives to study NGO bridging practices assume NGO agency, and not the structure. The question at this point is whether the new institutionalism allows us to determine the balance of agency and structure as applied to NGO politics in global governance. If not, what are the alternatives? How effective is network institutionalism (developed in this chapter) in addressing that balance in the context of NGO studies? In short, the institutional contours of bridging need to be specified, and network institutionalism may offer a starting point to do so.

Network institutionalism: a new synthesis for NGO studies

The synthesis of new institutionalism and policy network theories offers a distinct approach to understanding the structure–agency debate in the context of NGO studies, which is rooted in the comparative analysis of authority arrangements in networks where NGOs are embedded. In this integrated approach, which for the purposes of this chapter I will call "network institutionalism," network structure matters in shaping the extent of NGO autonomy and agency, as maintained by policy network theories. At the same time, it transpires from the new institutionalisms that networks are also organizational fields, and as such, are also products of NGO bridging. Network institutionalism focuses on the network position of an NGO as an important variable that can explain the extent of NGO agency in world politics. The immediate question becomes: How can we determine those network attributes within which NGOs are more *empowered* or *constrained* relative to other players in global governance? Network analysis contributes to NGO studies by demonstrating how NGOs can be constituted by their immediate institutional environments and by the complex web of relationships they develop and by which they are sustained throughout their operation.[53] The three new institutionalisms help to understand which of those network ties matter in terms of creating long-term institutional effects within networks of which NGOs are a part. Although their behavior is affected by these structures,[54] NGOs can also be politically proactive in cultivating such networks in the first place, which is particularly the case in advocacy NGOs.[55] Therefore, by attaching themselves to existing coalitions and networks, NGOs complicate such coalitions, cultivate organizational fields and networks, and acquire positions to alter policy outcomes on the ground. Indeed, NGOs have used networks to increase their funding, expand issue areas in which they are involved, enhance their mobility worldwide, and improve their overall performance. Most importantly, by embedding themselves in networks, *NGOs have elevated their institutional position in local and/or global governance structures*, and it is this institutional development that is missed by most literature on NGOs and IR.

Core assumptions of network institutionalism

One of the major shortcomings of NGO research is its conceptualization of civil society as a monolithic entity—a "black box" of sorts. Viewing civil society in such categorical terms prevents one from seeing the institutional diversity of the relationships between NGOs and various structures of authority, state and non-state. Young has underscored the variance of institutional forms supporting NGO relationships with state structures, pointing to NGO independence from the government, as well as the complementarity and competition between the two.[56] Network institutionalism and its core assumptions presented in this section, challenge NGO scholars to specify the institutional conditions under which NGOs move in the triangular space between civil society, the state, and the market,[57] assuming complementary, competitive and confrontational roles relative to structures of governance nationally and globally.[58] In this way, network institutionalism as a research agenda can open the black box of civil society in the same way as liberalism opened the black box of states seeking to identify domestic political determinants for international organizations and foreign policies that states exercise: it can expose the complexity and the nature of relationships within civil society as well as between civil society actors and governments. Several specific core assumptions underpin network institutionalism.

First, network institutionalism acknowledges the mutually constitutive nature of relationships between networks as structures/organizational fields and NGOs as agents. Specifically, it offers a framework in which to study the way NGOs shape the institutional fabric of their immediate organizational coalitions by engaging in the various types of bridging practices discussed earlier. It also delineates network conditions under which NGOs are emboldened by the institutional ties, created by bridging, that bind them into such organizational coalitions; yet, NGOs can also be constrained by these networks in various stages of a policy process in which they take part.

Second, network institutionalism highlights that these relationships can be both cooperative and conflictual, and the particular mode of NGO bridging (mechanistic, regulative, normative, or mimetic, as discussed at the end of this section), is a major consideration here. More research is needed to examine whether networks formed through mechanistic bridging are more likely to be harmonious than, say, networks formed through normative or mimetic bridging.

Third, network institutionalism recognizes the agency of NGOs in these networks, in which NGOs often serve as proxies for ideas and values in international politics. Therefore, network institutionalism can offer novel theoretical approaches in explaining the ascendance of ideas and values in international politics.

Fourth, network institutionalism treats the state itself as disaggregated and networked, echoing observations that the state is just one among other kinds of actors that participate in global governance. NGOs, as associative actors, define their identity and political action relative to various sources of authority, of which the disaggregated state is one among many.

Structure and agency

As stated, network institutionalism allows for approaches that identify when NGOs are either *constrained* by the network or *constituting* it.[59]

96 *Theory*

The first, or *constraining* approach underscores the structural impact of networks on NGOs and highlights the supremacy of networks as *structures*. Networks can constrain NGOs for a variety of reasons, such as when the accountability lines between donors and NGOs are tight; when the NGO operates in a smaller network with few donors, therefore having little bargaining power inside the network; when the network is dominated by states that may need the NGO services in program implementation, but do not hold the values that the NGO may stand for; when the network members do not share similar policy goals; and when the NGO's bargaining power in the network is weak. In similar situations, networks' power can dominate NGO choices and leave very limited room for the NGO to maneuver. Multiple mechanisms are at play to constrain the NGO behavior in these networks. Networks can constrain the NGOs' room to maneuver because they embed the NGOs into structures of dependency and upward accountability toward the donors.[60] It has been acknowledged that NGOs are "structurally dependent on bureaucratic state apparatuses at national as well as international levels."[61] Therefore, being dependent on donors for resources, NGOs have strained to fulfill their proclaimed goal of serving the marginalized and grassroots communities and as a result have undermined their own democratic potential.

In addition, networks can reinforce the existing institutions in global governance because they act to compensate for the shortages these institutions may possess. As a result, they prolong the institutional life of institutions of global governance (even in cases of inefficiencies and organizational pathologies) and produce more stable and coherent social systems in world politics.[62] A related network effect is their promotion of conditions for organizational conformity, standardization, and uniformity within the NGO sector as a whole.[63] This is partly due to the resource shortages NGOs face everywhere and the "survival of the fittest" organizational strategies among NGOs.[64] The growing internationalization of policy-making processes has extended access to NGOs into these international structures and bureaucracies, but has also limited their potential for autonomous and independent action.

The second, or *constitutive* approach underlines the *agency* of the NGOs, illuminating mechanisms through which NGOs shape their immediate network environments and, ultimately, the structures of global governance. Networks can also be constitutive, in which case NGOs can use networks and become tools of institutional change in world politics. Networks can be constitutive for NGOs when they empower NGOs as administratively independent actors of global politics. Such constitutive scenarios are possible under certain network conditions in which the NGO ends up altering the final policy outcomes delivered by the network. Specifically, NGOs are most empowered and likely to exercise their agency in large networks with diverse policy goals among the members and where no single donor provides the bulk of the resources to the NGO. In such networks NGOs are insularly embedded in the networks,[65] which enables them to carve out the most space to maneuver against their multiple donors. Altered policy outcomes as pushed by the NGO are often the result of such institutional conditions in networks.

Through their network-based engagements, NGOs have rather proactively managed to reduce information asymmetries in global governance. They embed themselves into a locality and then transmit lessons learned upward to their donor networks, which are often marginally and indirectly involved in the regions where NGOs work. As such, network-based NGO engagement has enhanced the implementation capacities of bilateral and multilateral institutions.

In terms of these constitutive and constraining dimensions of network institutionalism, Hirsch has suggested that "the decisive question is whether NGOs are mere functional components of the wider regulatory complex, or are they actors with the potential for democratic self-determination and design?"[66] The network approach to the NGO sector, as detailed earlier, posits that NGOs can be both constrained and empowered by the network structures in which they are embedded, but further studies could delineate the network conditions under which each scenario is more likely. Therefore, understanding when networks are constitutive or constraining of NGOs is a fruitful research area as derived from network institutionalism.

Network institutionalism is distinct from historical and sociological institutionalism in several respects. The main distinction is the NGO bridging capacity, which reflects NGO agency and "institutional entrepreneurship."[67] In contrast to historical institutionalism in particular, network institutionalism pays greater attention to the incentives and the ability of NGOs to forge increasingly complex linkages with other actors.[68] To this end, the structural theory of NGOs, as developed by DeMars,[69] provides a very useful adjustment to historical institutionalism and serves as a foundation for the network institutionalism research agenda introduced in this chapter. In the Introduction to this volume, DeMars and Dijkzeul develop this insight to propose that one of the "anchoring practices" of NGOs is that "they link with societal and political partners in at least two countries." Network institutionalism calls for delineating the conditions under which each of these outcomes occur.

Four types of bridging

Lastly, network institutionalism is also helpful in understanding the practice of NGO bridging in world politics as one example of the institutionalization of networks initiated and/or facilitated by NGOs. Bridging practices allow NGOs to institutionalize their position in structures of global governance, but that institutional transformation is intermediated by network-based organizational fields, hence the value of the network approach for theorizing about NGOs in IR. As discussed earlier, organizational fields are network-based because they represent communities and coalitions of organizations with a recognized area of institutional life and with key suppliers, resources, regulatory agencies, and other organizations that produce similar services and products.[70] NGOs have become central to cultivating and institutionalizing organizational fields in world politics. Their unique capacity for bridging is a key organizational asset for NGOs in playing a major role in the institutional life of organizational fields at the global level. In particular, NGO bridging practices within networks and organizational fields are manifested through various mechanisms. For instance, DiMaggio and Powell differentiate between coercive, mimetic, and normative mechanisms of institutionalization within organizational fields.[71] Scott highlights regulative, normative, and cultural–cognitive institutional pillars that are conveyed through symbolic systems, relational systems, routines, and artifacts.[72] The bridging practices of NGOs in networks and organizational fields reflect similar patterns.

I identify four types of NGO bridging practices within networks and organizational fields: *mechanistic, regulative, normative*, and *mimetic*. This typology develops, and also challenges, the categories of bridging identified in the Introduction to this volume. With my first type, *mechanistic bridging*, NGOs often successfully foster networks and partnerships in the developing world because they can do the job, whatever it entails, from microfinance delivery in a financially sustainable manner to building schools or healthcare systems. Mechanistic bridging is clearly characterized by the organizational functionality of NGOs within networks.

With the second type, *regulative bridging*, NGOs are successful in their bridging practices because they have a track record in a given country or an issue area. Therefore, they offer predictability of behavior and capitalize on the donors' need to work within established channels of aid delivery. Donors that opt to work with the same NGOs in every new country where they become involved often cite this very particular reason for having a bias toward the same partner. They often cite fiduciary capacities, which are one example of the need for predictability and certainty that the network mechanism of governance provides to donors and the NGOs alike. This, in a way, is a "path dependency" argument. I describe this as regulative bridging because fiduciary capacities of NGOs and their ability to meet the administrative and regulatory demands of their donors during policy implementation are key mechanisms of bridging in such cases.

The third type, NGO bridging in networks and organizational fields, or *normative bridging*, is facilitated by the "logic of appropriateness" on the side of the donors, who often try to build legitimacy by becoming involved with the NGO sector.[73] It follows from the application of the cultural approach to network politics in institutionalism that networks provide "moral or cognitive templates for interpretation and action."[74]

The fourth type of bridging is *mimetic* because networks and organizational fields are reproduced from one country to the next. A certain level of diffusion and transfer of network-based governance arrangements from one country to another is a dominant pattern of global governance as facilitated by NGOs, donor networks, and organizational fields.[75] For instance, interorganizational networks of NGOs and donors were established in postwar Bosnia and Herzegovina to introduce microfinance into the country. This network mechanism of governance in microfinance was also replicated, with some adjustments, in Kosovo, Afghanistan, and a range of other postwar countries where the main international organizations involved in microfinance had a field presence.[76]

Conclusion

Understanding the institutional reality of NGOs within structures of global governance is the main theme of this chapter. I have argued that studies documenting the quantitative rise of the NGO sector in world politics have largely neglected the qualitative impact of that development. This is particularly important when considering the NGOs in light of the new links and relationships they have created with state-centric structures of world politics. To this end, this chapter offered network institutionalism as a theoretical tool to address that gap and to serve as a bridge between NGO studies and IR. In an effort to develop an institutional perspective on NGO studies, the chapter has integrated network theories with historical and sociological strands of the new institutionalism. Building on this theoretical discussion, and after introducing the key assumptions of network institutionalism, the chapter has offered four types of NGO bridging practices as directions for further research in NGO studies. These offer a way to think about future NGO studies in a more comprehensive manner while also stimulating new research directions that can strengthen the study of NGOs and the study of IR.

A research agenda for network institutionalism explores both actor-centered analysis that emphasizes the agency of NGOs, and network-centered analysis that stresses the structural effects of networks on NGOs.[77] Further research in network institutionalism would also inquire about the specific institutional effects NGOs have on global policy outcomes. Specifically, how has NGO emergence and institutionalization in global politics altered any established organizational patterns of behavior among donor governments and other states? And, has network membership in any way emboldened NGOs in that process? What, if any, are the network effects of promoting learning processes within NGOs? What institutional opportunities do networks present for NGOs in terms of enhancing their public legitimacy and democratic credentials and their effectiveness in transferring policies and lessons learned from region to region? Do networks have any influence over the governance processes internal to the NGO?

One of the crucial questions that network institutionalism research should explore is the role of the state and the way in which the network-based operation of NGOs alters, dilutes, or enhances the power of state actors in processes of global, national, and local governance. Network institutionalism in NGO studies builds on the image of disaggregated statehood, albeit for a variety of reasons, for developed and developing countries. The zero-sum view that any political gains on the side of the NGO translate into losses for the political power of the state misrepresents the complexity of governance processes: NGOs may weaken the state's capacities in some areas but strengthen it in others. The study of NGO operation within their immediate network-based institutional contexts will help to delineate institutional conditions when NGOs overpower a state and/or strengthen state capacities. Hence, network institutionalism offers a framework within which to probe broader questions: What is politics like beyond the state? What role, if any, do networks play in hollowing out the state? How do NGOs factor into that process?

Notes

1 A different version of this chapter was published as Anna Ohanyan, "Network Institutionalism and NGO Studies," *International Studies Perspectives* 13 (2012): 366–389.
2 Leon Gordenker and Thomas G. Weiss, "NGO Participation in the International Policy Process," *Third World Quarterly* 16, no. 3 (1995): 543–555.

3 Steve Smith, "The United States and the Discipline of International Relations: Hegemonic Country, Hegemonic Discipline," *International Studies Review* 4, no. 2 (2002): 67–85.
4 Shu-Yun Ma, "Political Science at the Edge of Chaos? The Paradigmatic Implications of Historical Institutionalism," *International Political Science Review* 28, no. 1 (2007): 57–78; and Richard W. Scott, *Institutions and Organizations: Ideas and Interests* (Los Angeles, Calif.: Sage, 2008).
5 Robert O. Keohane, "Governance in a Partially Globalized World," *American Political Science Review* 95 (2001): 1–13; and Klaus Dingwerth, *The New Transnationalism: Transnational Governance and Democratic Legitimacy* (New York: Palgrave Macmillan, 2007).
6 Anna Ohanyan, "Policy Wars for Peace: Network Model of NGO Behavior," *International Studies Review* 11, no. 3 (2009): 475–501.
7 James G. March and Johan P. Olsen, "The New Institutionalism: Organizational Factors in Political Life," *American Political Science Review* 78 (1983): 734–749.
8 Melissa Wooten and Andrew J. Hoffman, "Organizational Fields: Past, Present and Future," in *The Sage Handbook of Organizational Institutionalism*, eds Royston Greenwood, Christine Oliver, Roy Suddaby and Kerstin Sahlin-Andersson (Los Angeles, Calif.: Sage, 2008).
9 Duane Swank, *Global Capital, Political Institutions, and Policy Change in Developed Welfare States* (Cambridge: Cambridge University Press, 2002).
10 Wolfgang Reinicke and Francis Deng, *Critical Choices: The United Nations, Networks, and the Future of Global Governance* (Ottawa: International Development Research Centre, 2000).
11 David Marsh, "The Development of the Policy Network Approach," in *Comparing Policy Networks*, ed. David Marsh (Philadelphia, Penn.: Open University Press, 1998).
12 Grant A. Jordan, "Sub-Government, Policy Communities and Networks: Refilling the Old Bottles," *Journal of Theoretical Politics* 2, no. 2 (1990): 319–338.
13 Mark Lindenberg and Coralie Bryant, *Going Global: Transforming Relief and Development NGOs* (Bloomfield, Conn.: Kumarian Press, 2001); Mari Fitzduff and Cheyanne Church, "Stepping Up to the Table: NGO Strategies for Influencing Policy in Conflict Issues," in *NGOs at the Table: Strategies for Influencing Policies in Areas of Conflict*, eds Mari Fitzduff and Cheyanne Church (New York: Rowman and Littlefield, 2005); and Alnoor Ebrahim, "Accountability Myopia: Losing Sight of Organizational Learning," *Nonprofit and Voluntary Sector Quarterly* 34, no. 1 (2005): 56–87.
14 Cinnamon Carlarne and John Carlarne, "In-Credible Government: Legitimacy, Democracy, and Non-Governmental Organizations," *Public Organization Review* 6 (2006): 347–371.
15 R. A. W. Rhodes, "Policy Networks: A British Perspective," *Journal of Theoretical Politics* 2, no. 3 (1990): 293–317.
16 Jeremy J. Richardson and Grant Jordan, *Governing Under Pressure: The Policy Process in a Post-Parliamentary Democracy* (Oxford: Martin Robertson, 1979).
17 Anna Ohanyan, *Winning Global Policies: The Network-Based Operation of Microfinance NGOs in Bosnia and Herzegovina, 1996–2002*, Doctoral Dissertation (Syracuse, NY: Political Science Department, Syracuse University,

2003); and Tanja A. Börzel, "Organizing Babylon: On Different Conceptions of Policy Networks," *Public Administration* 76, no. 2 (1998): 253–273.
18 Börzel, "Organizing Babylon," 253–273.
19 The governance school usually casts policy networks as alternative to hierarchy and market. It further highlights that policy networks allow for nonhierarchical coordination, and as such, it is a distinct third model of governance.
20 Reinicke and Deng, *Critical Choices*.
21 Miles Kahler, "Networked Politics: Agency, Power, and Governance," in *Networked Politics: Agency, Power, and Governance*, ed. Miles Kahler (Ithaca, NY: Cornell University Press, 2009).
22 Peter Uvin, Pankaj S. Jain and David L. Brown, "Think Large and Act Small: Toward a New Paradigm for NGO Scaling Up," *World Development* 28, no. 8 (2000): 1409–1419.
23 Jon Elster and Aanund Hayland, *Foundations of Social Choice Theory* (Cambridge: Cambridge University Press, 1986); and Elinor Ostrom, *Governing the Commons* (Cambridge: Cambridge University Press, 1990).
24 Anna Ohanyan, *NGOs, IGOs, and the Network Mechanisms of Post-Conflict Global Governance in Microfinance* (New York: Palgrave Macmillan, 2008); and Ohanyan, "Policy Wars for Peace," 475–501.
25 Vivien Schmidt, "Institutionalism," in *The State: Theories and Issues*, eds Colin Hay, Michael Lister and David Marsh (New York: Palgrave Macmillan, 2006).
26 Lisa Martin, *Democratic Commitments* (Princeton, N.J.: Princeton University Press, 2000).
27 My earlier work emphasized how the internal structure of a network shapes the autonomy and performance of NGOs (Ohanyan, *Winning Global Policies*; Ohanyan, *NGOs, IGOs, and the Network Mechanisms*; and Ohanyan, "Policy Wars for Peace," 475–501). Then I approached networks primarily as inter-organizational coalitions. More recently, my research agenda has evolved towards acknowledging the broader institutional effects of networks in world politics and of networks on NGOs, as explored in other branches of institutionalism. Currently I am exploring the opportunities that networks create for NGO agency, as well as the constraints imposed on NGOs by network structures. In short, my research agenda is to understand the politics of interaction between networks and NGOs.
28 Anna Ohanyan, "The Effects of Global Policy Networks on Peacebuilding: Framework of Evaluation," *Global Society Journal: Journal of Interdisciplinary International Relations* 24, no. 4 (2010): 529–552.
29 Ma, "Political Science at the Edge of Chaos?" 57–78.
30 Schmidt, "Institutionalism."
31 Ebrahim, "Accountability Myopia," 56–87.
32 Sasha Minch, Interview by author (Portland, Ore.: Mercy Corps August 2002); and Paul G. DiMaggio, "Interest and Agency in Institutional Theory," in *Institutional Patterns and Organizations: Culture and Environment*, ed. L. G. Zucker (Cambridge, Mass.: Ballinger, 1988).
33 Kathleen Thelen and Sven Steinmo, "Historical Institutionalism in Comparative Politics," in *Structuring Politics: Historical Institutionalism in Comparative Analysis*, eds Sven Steinmo, Kathlen Thelen and Frank Longstreth (Cambridge: Cambridge University Press, 1992).

34 Scott, *Institutions and Organizations.*
35 Ohanyan, "Policy Wars for Peace," 475–501.
36 Paul G. DiMaggio and Walter W. Powell, "The Iron Cage Revisited: Institutional Isomorphism and Collective Rationality in Organizational Fields," in *The New Institutionalism in Organizational Analysis*, eds Walter W. Powell and Paul G. DiMaggio (Chicago, Ill.: University of Chicago Press, 1991).
37 Michael Barnett and Martha Finnemore, *Rules for the World: International Organizations in Global Politics* (Ithaca, NY: Cornell University Press, 2004).
38 Philip Selznick, "Foundations of the Theory of Organizations," *American Sociological Review* 13 (1948): 25–35.
39 Scott, *Institutions and Organizations.*
40 Philip Selznick, *Leadership in Administration* (New York: Harper and Row, 1957), 17.
41 Royston Greenwood, Christine Oliver, Kerstin Sahlin and Roy Suddaby, "Introduction," in *The Sage Handbook of Organizational Institutionalism*, eds Royston Greenwood, Christine Oliver, Roy Suddaby and Kerstin Sahlin-Andersson (Los Angeles, Calif.: Sage, 2008), 6.
42 Ebrahim, *NGOs and Organizational Change.*
43 DiMaggio and Powell, "The Iron Cage Revisited."
44 Paul G. DiMaggio and Walter W. Powell, "Introduction," in *The New Institutionalism in Organizational Analysis*, eds Walter W. Powell and Paul J. DiMaggio (Chicago, Ill.: University of Chicago Press, 1991), 13.
45 Scott, *Institutions and Organizations*; James Coleman, *Power and the Structure of Society* (New York: Norton, 1974); and James Coleman, *Foundations of Social Theory* (Cambridge, Mass.: Belknap Press, 1990).
46 Selznick, "Foundations of the Theory of Organizations," 25–35.
47 John W. Meyer and Brian Rowan, "Institutional Organizations: Formal Structure as Myth and Ceremony," *American Journal of Sociology* 83 (1977): 340–363.
48 Jason Owen-Smith and Walter W. Powell, "Networks and Institutions," in *The Sage Handbook of Organizational Institutionalism*, eds Greenwood *et al.*
49 Selznick, *Leadership in Administration*,16–17.
50 Greenwood *et al.*, *The Sage Handbook of Organizational Institutionalism*, "Introduction."
51 DiMaggio, "Interest and Agency in Institutional Theory," 5.
52 Ibid.
53 William E. DeMars, *NGOs and Transnational Networks: Wild Cards in World Politics* (London: Pluto Press, 2005).
54 Ohanyan, "Policy Wars for Peace," 475–501.
55 Margaret E. Keck and Kathryn Sikkink, *Activists beyond Borders: Advocacy Networks in International Politics* (Ithaca, NY: Cornell University Press, 1998); and DeMars, *NGOs and Transnational Networks.*
56 Dennis R. Young, "Alternative Models of Government-Nonprofit Sector Relations: Theoretical and International Perspectives," *Nonprofit and Voluntary Sector Quarterly* 29, no. 1 (2000): 149–173.
57 John Cameron, "Development Economics, the New Economics and NGOs," *Third World Quarterly* 21, no. 4 (2000): 627–636.
58 Indeed, the space may be reconceptualized as quadrangular, to include international public institutions along with civil society, state and market.

59 Elisabeth E. Clements and James M. Cook, "Politics and Institutionalism: Explaining Durability and Change," *Annual Review of Sociology* 25 (1999): 441–466.
60 Lindenberg and Bryant, *Going Global*; Jennifer M. Brinkerhoff, "Donor-Funded Government–NGO Partnership for Public Service Improvement: Cases from India and Pakistan," *Voluntas: International Journal of Voluntary and Nonprofit Organizations* 14, no. 1 (2003): 105–122; Shepard Forman and Derk Segaar, "New Coalitions for Global Governance: The Changing Dynamics of Multilateralism," *Global Governance* 12, no. 2 (2006): 205–226; Eoghan Walsh and Helena Lenihan, "Accountability and Effectiveness of NGOs: Adapting Business Tools Successfully," *Development in Practice* 16, no. 5 (2006): 421–424; and Ebrahim, *NGOs and Organizational Change*.
61 Joachim Hirsch, "The Democratic Potential of Non-governmental Organisations," in *Transnational Democracy: Political Spaces and Border Crossings*, ed. James Anderson (New York: Routledge, 2002), 207.
62 Lynne G. Zucker, "Where Do Institutional Patterns Come From? Organizations as Actors in Social Systems," in *Institutional Patterns and Organization: Culture and Environment*, ed. Lynne G. Zucker (Cambridge, Mass.: Ballinger, 1988); and Clements and Cook, "Politics and Institutionalism," 441–466.
63 John W. Meyer, Gili S. Drori and Hokyu Hwang, "World Society and the Proliferation of Formal Organization," in *Globalization and Organization: World Society and Organizational Change*, eds Gili S. Drori, John W. Meyer and Hokyu Hwang (New York: Oxford University Press, 2006).
64 DiMaggio and Powell, "The Iron Cage Revisited."
65 Ohanyan, "Policy Wars for Peace," 475–501.
66 Hirsch, "The Democratic Potential of Non-governmental Organisations," 207.
67 Sushanta Sarma, "NGO Transformation: Institutional Entrepreneurship in Indian Microfinance," *Business Strategy* Series 12, no. 4 (2011): 167–176.
68 William F. Fisher, "Doing Good? The Politics and Antipolitics of NGO Practices," *Annual Review of Anthropology* 26 (1997): 439–464; Leon Gordenker and Thomas G. Weiss, "Developing Responsibilities: A Framework for Analysis. NGOs and Services," *Third World Quarterly* 18, no. 3 (1997): 433–455; Lindenberg and Bryant, *Going Global*; DeMars, *NGOs and Transnational Networks*; Ebrahim,"Accountability Myopia," 56–87; and Ohanyan, *NGOs, IGOs, and the Network Mechanisms*.
69 DeMars, *NGOs and Transnational Networks*.
70 DiMaggio and Powell, "The Iron Cage Revisited."
71 Ibid.
72 Scott, *Institutions and Organizations*, 79.
73 Carlarne and Carlarne, "In-Credible Government," 347–371.
74 Peter A. Hall and Rosemary C. R. Taylor, "Political Science and the Three New Institutionalisms," *Political Studies* 44, no. 5 (1996): 939.
75 Ohanyan, *NGOs, IGOs, and the Network Mechanisms*.
76 Ibid.
77 I have elaborated such a research agenda in Ohanyan, "Network Institutionalism and NGO Studies," 366–389.

Part III
Crosscutting evidence
History, region, accountability

4 The co-evolution of non-governmental and intergovernmental organizations in historical perspective

Bob Reinalda

- The ideal of a democratic state: popular sovereignty and human rights
- Emergence of multilateral conferences and follow-up conferences
- Emergence of private actors and transnational contacts
- Institutionalization and continued existence
- Bureaucratization and professionalization
- Control over NGOs by IGOs
- Conclusion

This chapter traces the emergence of non-governmental organizations and intergovernmental organizations (NGOs and IGOs) as part of wider changes in the international system of states. It does not take the traditional Westphalian state as its point of departure but looks upon the territorial state as a historical process, in which non-governmental actors have achieved their place as well. While most International Relations (IR) theory builds on sovereignty and warfare as the main characteristics of modern state building since 1648, this chapter includes the declaration of new ideas about "popular sovereignty" and "human rights" during the War of American Independence (1776) and the French Revolution (1789), as well as the transformation of these ideas into political reality through political struggle by citizens both nationally and internationally. It discusses the emergence of multi-lateralism at the Congress of Vienna (1814–15), which set in motion a number of innovations, inventions and learning processes, as a new phase of the Westphalian state. It also discusses the rise of private organizations with a public purpose, which were well aware of this new multilateralism and developed transnational networks in order to have a stronger power base within it. The growth of multilateral and follow-up conferences, which proved to be open to NGO influence, resulted in a process of institutionalization, with IGOs based on regular general assemblies, permanent secretariats, a professionalization of its staff and an open stance towards NGOs. The next phase of international organization was characterized by an increase in scale of international bureaucracies, including forms of control over NGOs. This chapter argues that during the last two centuries NGOs and IGOs have co-evolved by constituting networks in which they engaged in a two-way instrumentalization.[1]

The ideal of a democratic state: popular sovereignty and human rights

The decline of the Holy Roman Empire since the end of the Middle Ages impeded the functioning of feudal states and free cities. The end of the Thirty and Eighty Years' Wars in 1648 resulted in the treaty of Westphalia, which put into words the general principles with regard to territorial states and the relations between them. When these principles were gradually transformed into actual states and governments, authorities began to define exact territorial borders and within those borders they started to centralize authority in a national government. This process of state building with borders and capitals was accompanied by a large number of wars between, and within, states. Initially this state building remained restricted to Europe and Northern America, but in the twentieth century it also developed elsewhere.

The foundation of the ideal type of democratic state was laid during the Enlightenment of the eighteenth century, when ideas about mutual equality, individual freedoms and the emancipation of Jews, slaves and women gained weight. Liberal philosophers rejected the fairly undemocratic plea by Thomas Hobbes in his *Leviathan* (1651) to bring an end to the anarchic situation in the "state of nature" between men and between states by setting up a sovereign power to command and protect both. They concurred rather with Jean Bodin, who had argued that even a sovereign is subject to certain rules vis-à-vis citizens and other sovereigns, and with John Locke, who in 1690 had defended a "limited government" based on consent by, and an active role for, its citizens. The creation of "democratic institutions" would allow citizens to accept the curtailment of their various rights and provide them with procedures to, if necessary, correct their government. The model for legitimate government was found in the idea of a "social contract," which regards sovereignty as the result of a contract between the members of a society. Jean-Jacques Rousseau developed this idea more fully in his *Du Contrat Social* (1762). It implies that citizens accept the sovereign power, but are also guaranteed certain inalienable rights and liberties.

The idea of "popular sovereignty" regards the will and consent of the people as the source of all political power and of a state's legitimacy. The foundation of the United States in 1776 made this idea explicit, given the first words of its 1787 Constitution: "We the People of the United States ... do ordain and establish the Constitution." The 1776 *Declaration of Independence* had already stressed that "all men are created equal; that they are endowed by their Creator with certain unalienable rights; that among these are life, liberty, and the pursuit of happiness." In 1791 these ideas were developed further in the *Bill of Rights*. These first ten amendments to the American Constitution limit the powers of the federal government and protect the rights of the citizens. The *Declaration of the Rights of Man and the Citizen*, issued during the French Revolution, became part of the French Constitution of 1791. It regards the people as sovereign and citizens as equal, and recognizes the individual's freedoms, such as those of speech and of the press.

The way to transform the new ideas about popular sovereignty and human rights into political reality was through political struggle by citizens, as the mere proclamation of these declarations did not yet make them effective. This enduring political struggle included the restriction of the monarch's power through a stronger accountability of the executive to the parliamentary representation of the people, the separation of powers between the legislative, the executive and the judiciary in a *trias politica*, and the acquisition of more power by the people through a gradual extension of the popular vote. The aim of this political struggle was to guarantee that in modern democracies citizens are protected against abuses by their governments. From the nineteenth century onwards, and thanks to the ongoing political struggle by citizens, the rights formulated in the American and French human rights declarations became embedded in the constitutions of other states, with national variations depending on national preferences and power relations. The emergence of parliamentary institutions and political associations we now call "parties" as a result of this struggle reflects the change in the relationship between the sovereign and its subjects towards more influence for the citizens.

This new phase in the Westphalian state, and the historical emergence of both transnational NGOs and multilateral IGOs, all share in the universalism of individual rights and popular sovereignty and the new ideal of active citizens in a representative state.

Emergence of multilateral conferences and follow-up conferences

Ideas about an ideal state included international relations as well. Various theorists put forward so-called "peace plans." The peace treaty of Utrecht (1713) inspired the Abbé de Saint-Pierre, who attended the conference, to launch his *Projet pour rendre la paix perpétuelle en Europe*. These plans were important in "their broad intellectual contribution of trying to conceive of ways of giving greater structure to a political system comprising numerous autonomous units."[2] They raised fundamental questions with regard to war and peace, suggested ways of handling problems and outlined many of the major choices. The writings of Jeremy Bentham (*Plan for a Universal and Perpetual Peace*, 1789) and Immanuel Kant (*Perpetual Peace*, 1795) advanced proposals for the creation of IGOs through the designing of structures and the assignment of functions to these structures. They included ideas about permanent international congresses with delegations, courts of international justice and a role for public opinion to enforce obedience.

The first implementation of such a plan was set in motion by the powers at Vienna. Inis Claude argues that in 1814, by the end of the Napoleonic Wars, four prerequisites for the development of international organization were satisfied in sufficient measure and in proper combination: states functioning as independent political units; a substantial measure of contact between them; an awareness of the problems which arose out of their coexistence; and recognition of the need to create institutional devices and systematic methods for regulating their relations with each other.[3] John Ikenberry adds that at historical junctures after major wars, when states are grappling with fundamental questions of order, the hegemon may use a strategy of institutional binding. Instead of keeping the option of disengagement open, states then build long-term security, political and economic commitments that are difficult to retract. Binding mechanisms such as treaties, interlocking organizations, joint management responsibilities and agreed-upon standards and principles raise the "costs of exit" and create "voice opportunities" for smaller states, thereby providing structures to mitigate or resolve conflicts.[4] The hegemon at the time, the United Kingdom, managed to succeed in such institutional binding by making concessions and using its financial resources. This set in motion a series of innovations, shaping the core of what we now call IGOs.

The first innovation of 1815 was *the regulation of diplomatic relations*. Given the inadequacies of traditional bilateral diplomacy, new regulations for diplomatic relations agreed upon at Vienna, such as precedence of states and successive classes of representatives, simplified the functioning of bilateral and multilateral diplomacy. A continuing process of codification of customary diplomatic relations was set in motion by the habits and rules practiced by multilateral conferences and IGOs. The major change by the end of the nineteenth century was in the composition of the diplomatic community, which gradually moved away from its aristocratic base towards being more citizen-based.

The second innovation of 1815 was *the use of multilateral conferences and follow-up conferences, with broad purposes and open agendas, as instruments* in international relations. This resulted in the custom that states, having reached agreement at a conference, would convene a follow-up conference to assess whether all states had actually implemented the agreed-upon decisions and policies. If not, or not completely, as was mostly the case, the situation required new deliberations and decisions at this stage, including a decision about a further follow-up conference. Unlike the pattern before 1815, this resulted in an ongoing cycle of conferences dealing with similar and related issues. Apart from this (still ad hoc) continuity, it produced path dependency with regard to the selected common solutions and efforts.

The third innovation consisted of *institutional experimentation and learning processes*. It took the members of the Central Commission for the Navigation of the Rhine, established in 1815 as the first IGO, 17 years to reach agreement on the functioning of this formal organization and to issue its first act. The representatives, among themselves and in contacting their governments, had to clarify the exact interpretation of all legal clauses and the relationship between articulating interests and reaching agreement. In order to achieve progress the formal rule of unanimity had to be used more flexibly and other institutional procedures and arrangements had to be agreed upon to make the organization function. These years represented a thorny learning process among negotiating and cooperating diplomats, adapting the organization's original setup. The foundation of the private International Committee of the Red Cross (1863) and its responsibility for monitoring the intergovernmental Geneva Convention (1864) was another widely observed experiment in creating new structures.

The fourth innovation was the development of *multilateral treaties and international law*. Path dependency was promoted by the fact that multilateral conferences ended with written documents. States encapsulated everything that had been settled and agreed upon in one complete document (*Acte finale*), which contained a summary of the work done and had annexed to it the various documents which had been signed by the governments, initially by the foreign minister but later (for the first time in 1909) also by ministers of other specific departments. Practice soon revealed that treaties on the same topics concluded at a later date would make use of older ones by building on what the older agreements already contained. Conventions and treaties resulting from multilateral conferences enabled the further development of international law, which in turn was promoted by international law NGOs.

Emergence of private actors and transnational contacts

The creation of issue-oriented societies, now known as NGOs, in the United Kingdom from the mid-eighteenth century began with small groups of citizens becoming aware of ethical and social problems. They combined their critical attitude with the assumption that part of the solution was to form associations aiming to deal with these problems. This engagement resulted in group activities, which often included appeals to public authorities. For example, the British Antislavery Society was formed around the time of the American Revolution in 1776. Thus, Great Britain, the same nation that would emerge as hegemonic after the Napoleonic Wars and call the Congress of Vienna in 1815, had already produced one of the first modern NGOs, which envisioned a worldwide transformation of slaves into citizens.

The antislavery societies also understood the importance of the Congress of Vienna for advancing their cause, at which they were present together with other citizens lobbying the Congress, such as representatives of German printers and Jewish communities, arguing for liberty of the press and democratic rights. The antislavery societies were successful in agenda-setting, by petitioning the British Parliament. As a result, the foreign secretary pressed for action in Vienna by including the issue on the agenda. The societies obtained an international declaration against the slave trade from the Congress. This declaration was the first to contain an internationally agreed-upon socio-economic principle, which was intensively used in further action.

NGO presence at Vienna marked the beginning of NGOs visiting and addressing multilateral conferences. They attended and as far as possible contributed to the solution of problems on the agenda. In his inventory of NGO presence in international relations, Steve Charnovitz has shown that governmental officials displayed little embarrassment at participating alongside NGOs in the multilateral conferences of the nineteenth century, where NGOs discovered their capacity to influence governments with ideas and expertise.[5] Conferences with governments from a variety of countries made NGOs aware of the need to also organize in many countries. In this way, the first modern NGOs and

IGOs co-evolved, reinforcing each other's authority as representative bridges between society and state.

After Vienna, American and British antislavery societies developed transatlantic ties and in 1839 organized an international conference in London. Following the meeting British delegations were sent to Continental states to further encourage citizens to establish societies and to pressure their governments, using "information politics" as a means of public pressure.[6] The resulting transnational advocacy networks encouraged those advocating peace, who found their inspiration both in a critical religious conviction and in a preference for free trade as an economic policy. The peace movement of the 1840s thus built on the older networks of the antislavery movement and would itself inspire women to establish their own organizations and transnational networks (starting in 1868) and to address governments and multilateral conferences (resulting in an international convention against traffic in women in 1904). The peace movement strongly promoted and elaborated the idea of arbitration, which also played a role in intergovernmental politics. The schemes that made it possible to establish the Permanent Court of Arbitration in 1899 were prepared by authoritative law-related NGOs established in 1873.[7]

The system of multilateral conferences thus had an open (network) character from the very beginning, with citizens travelling to conferences initiated by governments and, in turn, governmental representatives attending privately-initiated conferences. No serious obstacles were put in place, although formal procedures gave governments a means of control, and non-governmental attendance was appreciated because of the expertise and understanding these NGOs brought to the debates. In various cases private experts were included in official delegations and often were given the leeway to vote independently. If NGOs were not invited to multilateral conferences they would invite themselves. The first time NGOs were formally invited to present their opinion was at the 1907 Hague Peace Conference, which may be considered the first time "consultative status" was granted. Briefly, IGOs and NGOs evolved in an interactive fashion.

The press also promoted the open character of the conference system. The first multilateral conference after Vienna (Aix-la-Chapelle/Aachen, 1818) attracted many journalists who were eager to report on the event. The conference chair had to think carefully about what exactly he would disclose to them. This is considered the beginning of public international diplomacy, because a press communiqué was released followed by a verbal explanation by the chair. The official policy of not informing the press during the 1899 Hague Peace

Conference, which was a break from the general openness of the nineteenth-century conferences, was greeted with dissatisfaction by the members of the press and resulted in the publication of a regular chronicle by the NGOs. At the second Hague Peace Conference in 1907 this restricted press policy was abandoned and the conference organization even cooperated with the newsletter published by NGOs. The official scenario of observing confidentiality was inexpedient, as it had hampered the general acceptance of what was being discussed during the sessions and so did not help to find public support for the agreed-upon international policies.[8] Other conferences and IGOs had similar experiences with a restricted press policy.

Among the explanatory factors for the successes of the nineteenth-century multilateral conferences and IGOs are the industrial economy and the active role of internationally oriented entrepreneurs. Because the modern Westphalian state allowed for the functioning of an independent commercial class, entrepreneurs had relatively great freedom to develop and implement their own economic strategies. The state profited from the creation of the legal, political and social space for this commercial and entrepreneurial class, as it had an increased resource base and developed a more complex class structure and a more pluralist distribution of power and interest within the state, separate from the traditional dynastic ruling establishment. This strengthening of state and society in turn gave an impetus to free enterprise.[9] Firms began to develop their own legal identity as public limited companies, which gave them permanent existence as regards ownership. This meant that owners had limited liability for the firm's debts and that the shares could be traded on a stock exchange (as public trade). Modern industrial capitalism did not take much notice of national borders and evolved into a worldwide phenomenon, with capitalism and the modern state reinforcing one another and with economic competition between states playing an increasingly important role. Because of this competition, governments of states in which industrial capitalism was developing involved themselves in the industrialization process. Generally speaking they did not meddle with the practice of national commercial classes developing their own international strategies. "They strengthened the structures of the state and imposed reforms designed to remove any remaining obstacles that might impede the release of enterprise, market incentives or scientific and technological learning."[10]

During the nineteenth century, free trade as a principle and as a practical policy was promoted by the UK and its Continental rival Prussia, which set up the *Zollverein* of 1834, as well as by citizens who organized in so-called Cobden Clubs, after the British free trade advocate Richard Cobden, which favored free trade and peace. By the end of the nineteenth century internationally active firms began to organize as well, at first by forming trusts and cartels (which met with antitrust legislation) and since 1904 by establishing international industrial federations and an International Chamber of Commerce in 1919. These business federations are NGOs, despite the fact that they represent profit-driven actors rather than activists with principled ideas and values. They lobby multilateral conferences and IGOs in the same way as other NGOs.

Institutionalization and continued existence

The second phase of international organization, roughly from 1865 until the First World War, was characterized by the building of permanent institutions. The term public international union (PIU) became the overarching term for the IGOs of this period. They supplemented the administrative work of governments and took on many problems which had been outside the scope of traditional diplomacy. Institutionalization did not impede the previous openness of the system, as NGOs continued to attend. Often governments were not the only representatives, as in several countries various national services, such as postal, railway and meteorological services, were in private ownership or private groups had initiated the conferences. This mixed character was reflected in the governance structures of several unions. Eventually, however, the various types of mixed institutions tended to change to an intergovernmental format, without excluding arrangements for influence by actors other than governments. Some private unions later transformed into IGOs; otherwise they could not adopt international treaties. The work of the private International Association for Labour Legislation of 1900, which instigated two labor conventions signed by governments in 1906, was continued in 1919 by the tripartite International Labour Organization (ILO), consisting of governments, workers, and employers.

Various PIUs arose from a series of multilateral conferences, which since the 1850s had proved helpful instruments in regulating common problems. But given the continual character of the issues, the series of conferences were given a permanent character to consolidate and widen the cooperation up to that point and to improve regularity, efficiency and expertise. They went through a process of institutionalization, in which the regular (often annual) "general assembly" meetings replaced the former ad hoc combination of conferences and follow-up conferences. The unions were based on an intergovernmental treaty (constitution), which defined their often "functional" aims.

While the bodies that organized conferences were not continuous in their operation, the staff members engaged by the PIUs became responsible for the day-to-day running of their union, thus taking care of continuity and regularity. The primary function of the "bureau" or "secretariat" was to provide information to the member states, but the secretariats became more and more responsible for preparing the agenda and reports for the periodic conferences. Craig Murphy showed that by 1910 the conferences called by the PIUs began to outnumber those arranged at the invitation of heads of state or government. Ironically, most states were unaware of the effects of this institutional innovation engineered by the unions, because they still saw the periodic conferences as a way to oversee the unions' work, whereas the necessary preparation for the conferences in fact gave the unions' functionaries power over the agenda. By 1910 the PIUs were playing roles that used to be played by the foreign ministry of a hosting country or the monarch's personal attendants.[11] The "institutional memory" related to these roles enhanced the position of the secretariat and the awareness of the path dependency in what the organizations had been undertaking.

Derek Bowett argues that the trend towards permanence showed a degree of practicality which was of the utmost significance for future developments.[12] Many unions invented arrangements for the representation of interests other than those of governments, such as dependent territories, private corporations and NGOs. They made a distinction between *convention* and *règlement*, with the effect that amending the latter allowed the unions to adapt to changing needs and circumstances. Although the principle of unanimity was stressed by the constitution, the departure from the unanimity rule became quite common, as most unions invented techniques of weighted and majority voting. The multilateral conferences and PIUs of the second half of the nineteenth century attracted entrepreneurial types who helped to design public railways, health, relief and many other systems. These "public system builders" valued order and control and tried to make society more structured and predictable, while inspiring trust among states was promoted by the Permanent Court of Arbitration. Its existence and its wide social, political and legal support resulted in the inclusion in treaties of a stipulation that disputes arising out of the particular treaty had to be referred to arbitration and to the Court. Both PIUs and NGOs encouraged such action. The major psychological effect of the availability of arbitration procedures was the facilitation of economic and other relations between states and their citizens, since disputes could be settled in peaceful ways.

The outbreak of the First World War constituted an exogenous shock to the evolutionary development of IGOs. Although some PIUs were not mature enough to survive the war period, most of them and also the arbitration court did. Exogenous shocks such as the two world wars thus did not end the process of international organization, but rather produced continued institutionalization, once again promoted by the hegemon. In 1919 a formal organization—the League of Nations—replaced the previous system of peace conferences, and in 1945 the United Nations was established as an improved and enhanced version of the League.

The League continued the previous open stance towards NGOs. During its creation in 1919 international women's organizations gained "access" by lobbying and inviting themselves to be participants, with as their first success a clause in the League's Covenant stating that all positions in the League should be open to men and women equally. Various kinds of NGOs approached the League and its specialized agency, the ILO, representing their group interests or advocating more general positions. They managed to bring in their expertise and were also appreciated because of their relations with civil society. Private international law associations continued to follow and comment on the developments with regard to international law and the League's process of codification. That non-governmental actors played a role in the political games of influence and power was illustrated by the ILO under an active secretary-general. ILO director Albert Thomas, who had strong feelings about his position and his organization's work, successfully used the support of the trade unions as "a base for initiative in international policy."[13]

The creation of permanent secretariats in IGOs resulted in a new type of professional international actor: permanent international civil servants who would become experts in the fields of their organization. They maintained close ties with their counterparts in national ministries, but focused on the international dimensions rather than the national interests, even if their ministry trained them. The 1919 decision to provide the League of Nations with an "international secretariat," rather than one based on national officials who would be loyal to and paid by the member states, enhanced the position of international civil servants, because they were supposed to represent the interests of the organization and were paid by it.[14] Another type of professional international actor that came into being was based on international NGO staff, specializing in particular fields such as arbitration, wounded soldiers, other humanitarian activities and economic interests. These private experts in the same fields as the PIUs and League had similar expertise to international civil servants, albeit from a field-related rather than a state-related IGO viewpoint. However, what these two groups of international civil servants and private experts had in common was the motivation to build public international systems, the need for general and comparable scientific knowledge and the rise of new academic disciplines, such as statistics, international law and international economics, which allowed them common discourses in addition to traditional diplomatic and political language. Various institutions organized private and public multilateral conferences as ways to share and develop such knowledge. Professionalization of IGO and NGO staff as a combined process had begun.

Bureaucratization and professionalization

While the permanent secretariats of the PIUs started as relatively small entities, often dependent on a few individual experts who were closely connected to the establishment and growth of these unions, a process of large-scale bureaucratization began after 1919. The ILO and the League soon had relatively large secretariats, with several hundreds of staff members and almost immediately a detailed division of labor between various parts and sections of their secretariats. The secretariats of most PIUs, employing up to 100 people, bureaucratized similarly but on a smaller scale. IGO secretariats bureaucratized not only in the sense of larger numbers of international civil servants, but also of organizational growth through internal bureaucratic leadership and management and further decentralization and subdivision. Applying organization theory in his *Beyond the Nation-State* (1964), Ernst Haas described how the ILO under its director Thomas built up its organizational core, involving the choice of personnel motivated by and indoctrinated with the organization's mission and ideology. As the organization grew in size and complexity, internal and external administrative procedures, including the position of NGOs, had to be formalized into legal and constitutional channels. Decentralization of staff and program implementation, as well as permitting subunits of the organization some autonomy to develop specific values and procedures, were part of the process.[15] Survival as an institution during and immediately following the Second World War was the result of attentive leadership, the launch of a bold program with technical assistance as a new field of activities, and a careful use of its political environment, and was followed by an enlargement of the organization.[16]

Overlap between parts of an organization and with other IGOs created a new kind of competition between the organizations, as well as new divisions of labor and a need for coordination. This need grew during the League period. The PIUs had not been invited to the Versailles negotiations and remained outside the League, which apart from the ILO set up three specialized bodies which used the term "organization" in their names and were supported by sections of the League's secretariat. These "organizations" in the fields of economic and financial relations, transport and communication, and health, as well as some other bodies of the League, of which the Advisory Committee on the Traffic in Women and Children was strongly dependent on NGOs, in fact became international actors and as such rivals of some of the PIUs functioning in the same fields. The economic and social activities of these specialized League bodies would form the basis for separate specialized agencies in various fields after 1945. A League committee set up in 1939 assessed the absence of both internal and external coordination and recommended that the League should bring all its economic and social work, including that of the ILO, under the direction of one coordinating body, which would be representative and effective. In 1945 this recommendation contributed to the establishment of the UN Economic and Social Council (ECOSOC) and the invitation to PIUs to become part of the UN system of specialized agencies with ECOSOC coordination.

Although during the League days IGOs and NGOs still had public systems in common as goals, the position of NGOs became more dependent on the institutional structures of IGOs than before. While NGOs continued their advocacy activities within IGOs, their position and expertise increasingly became inputs in the political games that were being played within the widening international bureaucracies and between the various bodies of an IGO, along with the inputs by the secretary-general, departmental heads and chairs of bodies. Although in principle this created room for maneuver by NGOs, the demands put on NGO experts were far heavier. They needed to understand not only their own field but also the functioning of IGO bureaucracies, in order to discover the windows of opportunity in the organizations' decision-making processes and in the relations between IGOs. Furthermore they needed to be trained to a greater extent in international law. To be able to participate, NGOs needed more professionalized personnel, as knowledge about the field itself was no longer sufficient.

The period after 1945 showed even larger IGO bureaucracies, of many hundreds and thousands of international civil servants, with complex divisions of labor within and between organizations. In particular, the so-called UN system of specialized agencies and ECOSOC coordination had many bureaucratic subdivisions, an increased extent of specialization, and a stronger position for economics in addition to more traditional international law. Coordination became truly problematic as a result of strong fragmentation and politicization. Not only did overlapping activities of organizations hamper ECOSOC's coordinating work, but also the creation of UN umbrella organizations other than ECOSOC, such as the UN Development Programme (UNDP), the establishment of numerous programs and funds by the General Assembly, the organization of many "world conferences" with their own secretariats, the growth of regional activities and centers, and the diverging ways of funding activities. Institutional overlap and fragmentation would be increased further by political clashes and politicization as a result of the East–West and North–South divides. Later ECOSOC's coordinating capacity was undermined when the most powerful Western states established an external institution with a conference form and an elitist rather than universal character, the G7 (1975), which did not give access to NGOs.

Professionalization of IGO staff was a matter for national ministries, as these provided personnel that came to work in IGOs, and the IGOs themselves, both in their selection and their training of staff members. NGOs active on the intergovernmental level needed staff members who knew their fields well and were also able to function in large international bureaucracies. Initially their training took place mainly within NGOs, where more experienced colleagues helped and trained younger ones, but to an increasing extent it involved education and taking courses. Professionalization was helped by the fact that NGO experts went to work for IGOs and their projects and, in turn, international civil servants moved from IGOs to NGOs. A distinction should be made between NGO staff working in the agenda-setting or input phase of international decision-making and those working on the implementation phase, for instance in a local development project instigated by an IGO. Working on the latter requires different training from participating in the input phase. Another distinction to be made is between staff employed by "Northern" NGOs and those working for local "Southern" NGOs. Although the two share a common concern over development, there are considerable differences between them, such as the availability of resources and training facilities. While the post-war period made professionalization more necessary, it was initially stronger in IGOs, given the government-supported bureaucratic structures and demands, than in NGOs. However, specific bureaucratic developments and demands, such as revision of IGO rules, pressured NGOs into following suit and professionalizing further.[17]

Control over NGOs by IGOs

The relationship between NGOs and IGOs is a two-way process, with each type of actor using the other instrumentally. The main reason for NGOs to approach multilateral conferences and IGOs has been to influence the process of international standard setting, which allows NGOs and other actors to use international principles, standards and norms in domestic politics and in the best case scenario to simultaneously pressure governments from below (through domestic politics) and from above (internationally, when an IGO "names and shames" a government for not implementing the agreed standards). An additional motive has been that recognition by an IGO adds to an NGO's standing and authority. After the foundation of the League of Nations and the ILO many international NGOs moved their headquarters to Geneva. The major reasons that IGOs cultivate relations with NGOs are to gain NGO expertise and to cultivate NGO support for IGO policies. NGOs thus become brokers between IGOs and citizens within states. NGO representatives know, according to David Mitrany, "what it is all about and can judge whether a policy is valid and whether it has been carried out fairly."[18] In addition to roles in the input phase of the policy cycle, NGOs are active in monitoring implementation, followed by deliberation about violations found. The way Amnesty International has monitored the implementation of certain human rights, i.e. as an independent actor with authoritative critical reports, developed into an ideal type of NGO monitoring that is used by other NGOs, although not always achieving the same level of independence and quality.

Although an open stance on NGOs is an old IGO tradition, there have also been restrictions. Conference and IGO secretariats have at times allowed NGOs more or less room for maneuver, or even refused them access. If allowed access, NGOs were formally given consultative status only and, with the exception of the tripartite ILO, excluded from decision-making. The 1945 UN Charter took "NGO" as a term into use[19] and stated that ECOSOC can arrange consultations with NGOs. This was a codification of the League practice, but also a formal restriction as Article 71 stipulated that NGOs can have a say in economic and social affairs, and hence not in security issues. This restriction was due to some influential diplomats, who referred negatively to the strong influence women's NGOs had had in the League's disarmament debates of the 1930s. Some specialized agencies, such as the Bretton Woods institutions, did not give NGOs access. Organizational control in the UN was extended in 1946, when ECOSOC established a committee to draft regulations on NGOs sending observers to

ECOSOC's public meetings to explain their position. These procedures were formally accepted in 1950 and have been revised a few times (1968, 1996). The degree of participation depended on the category to which the NGO belonged. Stricter regulation also helps to control the increasing numbers of NGOs. In 1948 the UN had 40 NGOs with consultative status. In 1968 there were 180, 4.5 times as many, while the total number increased almost fourfold between 1992 and 2005, from 744 to 2,719. Setting up federations or coalitions of NGOs is another solution, something NGOs have successfully done when promoting bans on the use of landmines, small arms and cluster bombs (see below). Peter Willetts rejects the idea that there is a great difference between "consultation" (resulting from the consultative status of NGOs) and "participation" without vote in the ECOSOC deliberations. "From the very first days of the UN, the distinction has been blurred in practice: NGOs have obtained some participation rights that go beyond consultation." He even argues that these developments can be regarded collectively as "converting the UN system from a world of interstate diplomacy to one of pluralist governance at the policymaking level."[20]

An analysis of women's NGOs in the League and the UN shows that they have brought expertise into the decision-making and implementation processes of these IGOs and have shared responsibilities for their public policies. But it is also true that accommodation and diversion forces inspired by these IGOs played a role, even if these did not stop NGOs being successful as private political actors at the global level. Once NGOs have gained access to an IGO, they have to reckon with existing procedures and mechanisms. IGOs make the rules of the game and procedures allow the secretariat to give NGOs more or less room for maneuver during the various phases of deliberation and decision-making. Also relevant is the larger functioning of the organization. Given the dependence of global IGOs such as the League and the UN on their member states, these IGOs are conservative with respect to changes in power relations and to a radical restructuring of economies and societies. They therefore tend to favor the status quo. This leaves less room for actual change in both the member states and the organization itself (for instance, being slow in appointing more female staff) than would appear to be the case when the effect of NGOs in world politics is discussed only in terms of bold international standards that have been initiated and influenced by NGOs.[21]

When, during the 1960s, NGOs became involved in technical assistance given by IGOs, in particular in development aid, availability of funds from IGOs and greater independence from national governments became new reasons for NGOs to work with IGOs. However, IGOs in this field demanded that the NGOs in turn garner support for the IGOs' policies in developing states by making these policies transparent and legitimate. In fact NGOs are obliged to do this under UN rules: an NGO working in partnership with the UN shall undertake to support the work of the UN and to promote knowledge of its principles and activities.[22] Such an agreement makes it harder to be critical of the IGO and its policies. The establishment of Doctors Without Borders (*Médecins Sans Frontières*, MSF) after the Biafra crisis of 1967–70 can be seen as a radical break from status quo power politics, because the founders prioritized the interests of the victims over those of national and IGO politicians. Doctors Without Borders and similar NGOs went their own way, by refusing to work in a foreign state only if its government consented, a condition accepted by the International Committee of the Red Cross (ICRC). This condition was contrary to their view that all victims in a state should be helped, whether the government or leading power permitted it or not. In this way Doctors Without Borders also distinguished itself from the many NGOs which during the 1980s and 1990s became co-implementers of UN development and aid policies. Another rupture of the two-way instrumentalization of NGOs and IGOs emerged in the 1990s with the rise of the anti-globalization movement, which protested against the consequences of neoliberal policies and the support for these by the major economic IGOs. This movement clearly aimed its fundamental criticism at these IGOs, despite the fact that many of the engaged NGOs were cooperating closely with the same IGOs in programs and projects.

Interest groups representing the business community showed two tendencies. One was to eschew the UN and other IGOs and favor self-regulation. In the 1980s the International Chamber of Commerce (ICC) claimed that many of its activities should be undertaken by itself rather than by IGOs, as the business community is closer to the market. "They cannot afford the unhurried deliberations of an intergovernmental body working on the basis of Conventions that take years to prepare and more years to come into effect."[23] Despite this critical attitude the ICC has developed into an international pressure group that is using its consultative UN position extensively. Transnational corporations and their interest groups were effective in preventing strong IGO codes of conduct regulating their behavior during the 1970s, and in setting up an intellectual property interest group in 1986 during the negotiations over a tougher free trade regime. However, the developments in the 1990s, when corporations enjoyed great freedom but were criticized for their conduct with regard to the environment and human rights, had two results. First, corporations began to take the international forums more seriously. When the Multilateral Agreement on Investments failed—a victory claimed by NGOs—the international business community responded by developing "more sophisticated transnational political capacities" and coordinating their activities at national and international level more effectively.[24] Transnational corporations and their interest organizations changed their strategies on climate change, in line with climate discussions at multilateral conferences. They moved from a defensive, reactive approach towards more proactive tactics, with greater support for international initiatives. Second, interest groups representing the business community became more receptive to the appeals from IGOs, which Kofi Annan, for example, promoted with his Global Compact of 1999.

Changes in the conduct of war and the related peacekeeping operations after the end of the Cold War also had consequences for the functioning of NGOs. With an increasing NGO influence on security issues in the International Court of Justice and the UN Security Council during the 1990s, the original UN restriction on the consultative status of NGOs to economic and social affairs lost some of its meaning. However, the stronger position of NGOs within the UN, actively promoted by secretaries-general such as Boutros Boutros-Ghali and Kofi Annan, also came up against developments that undermined NGO work. The increasing acceptance of military intervention forces undertaking humanitarian activities, which used to be carried out by humanitarian NGOs and IGOs, blurred the roles of armed forces and independent relief workers. The new UN policy of integrated UN operations with military and non-military units implied that NGOs had lost the independent and impartial position they had always claimed and emphasized. Later their independence was undermined even further, when they became involved in political campaigns by states and organizations such as the "war on terror," or were made subordinate to the military forces of states or the UN. The period after the Cold War thus shows two contradictory tendencies: on the one hand an enhancement of NGO positions within the UN system and on the other hand a weakening.

Apart from the UN system, non-violent social movements and NGOs have played roles of their own in protests against dictatorships in Eastern Europe and the Middle East. In 1999 and 2000 *Otpor!* (Resistance!) contributed to deposing President Slobodan Milosevic in Serbia. Similar movements caused changes in Georgia in 2003, where Eduard Shevardnadze was forced to resign from the presidency, and in Ukraine in 2004. These East European lessons were learned by the 6

April Movement in Egypt in 2009, which contributed to the dramatic political changes in early 2011. These movements have been inspired by ideas about non-violence and hard-to-resist means to put dictatorships and their public powers in trouble (hugging the soldiers and praying together), as expressed in Gene Sharp's book *From Dictatorship to Democracy* (1993)[25] and supported by the Centre for Applied Nonviolent Action and Strategies (CANVAS) which was established in Belgrade in 2004.

Although NGOs have often been subordinate to IGOs in the immediate process of policy development, other NGOs have also helped in creating IGOs. As stated, NGOs, with trade unions and women's organizations, helped to form the ILO in 1919. During the early 1960s NGOs, such as Oxfam, raised money for the Food and Agriculture Organization (FAO) and supported the need to establish agencies to better combat hunger and poverty around the world. As such they contributed to the establishment of the World Food Programme (WFP) in 1963 and the International Fund for Agricultural Development (IFAD) in 1974. Similar lobbying from environmental NGOs played a role during the creation of the UN Environment Programme (UNEP) in 1972 and the Commission on Sustainable Development in 1993. NGO influence was most visible during the establishment of the International Criminal Court (ICC) in 1998. The diplomatic conference in Rome, which adopted the Court's Statute, was convened by 148 states, 33 IGOs and 236 NGOs, with the NGOs belonging to the Coalition for an International Criminal Court which had been created by 25 NGOs in 1995. In this case NGOs were not only observers but also participants, with special representation in each of the five regional groups. NGO coalitions have also played roles in the adoption of international conventions, such as the Ottawa Convention on Landmines (1997, the International Campaign to Ban Landmines), the UN Program of Action on Small Arms and Light Weapons (2001, the International Action Network on Small Arms) and the Convention on Cluster Munitions (2008, the Cluster Munition Coalition). According to the *Yearbook of International Organizations*, the total number of NGOs keeps growing: from 832 in 1951 to 2,173 in 1972, 4,620 in 1991 and 7,752 in 2009.

Conclusion

This chapter assumes that the Westphalian state itself is a historical process. The rise of ideas about popular sovereignty and human rights, as elements of an ideal type of democratic state, explains why governments accept that citizens are socially and politically active and organize in political parties, NGOs and as an entrepreneurial class. NGOing in the sense of establishing private organizations with public purposes—the first anchoring practice of DeMars and Dijkzeul—therefore is older than often thought, as in its national form it dates back to the late eighteenth century and in its international form to the early nineteenth century. IR thinking that takes into account both realist and liberal assumptions (power and institutions), as shown by Claude and Ikenberry, explains why the Congress of Vienna of 1815 marks a new phase in international relations, with states engaging in networks of multilateral conferences (later institutionalized in IGOs) which are open to private influence from experts and NGOs. From the very beginning citizens and NGOs have understood the windows of opportunity that multilateral conferences and IGOs offer to domestic actors through international standard setting. NGO attendance at Vienna and later multilateral conferences confirms the "representative" and "secular sanction" claims of DeMars and Dijkzeul, because, when bridging the national and international levels, NGOs speak for the people they claim to represent and invoke international norms. To enhance their representative claim NGOs have set up transnational networks, international NGOs and, more recently, federations of international NGOs, which are more representative and more independent of states than internationally-operating national NGOs. Invoking international norms means influencing governments and other actors to set standards, choose a form (recommendation, treaty, program), define the content of the norms and promote compliance.

Despite this confirmation of the two claims, NGOs are not the only ones forming a bridge between the national and the international level. The open character of the conference and IGO system has also been promoted by the press, which reports international developments but has barely been studied as part of international non-governmental influence, and by internationally active entrepreneurs who eventually established international NGOs as well, in the form of business federations. This variety of NGOs clarifies that private actors with egoistic rather than altruistic motives in mind can also influence international standard setting. There is a continuum, with at one end the "conscience of the world" (abolition of slavery), at the other the interests of specific groups (business sectors) and in between combinations (such as, for instance, women: both emancipation and self-interest). NGOs may also strongly disagree among themselves (for instance, in favor of or against reproductive rights). The outcome thus is a compromise, between NGOs too.

Co-evolution of NGOs and IGOs   127

While the second anchoring practice of DeMars and Dijkzeul focuses on transnational links of NGOs, this chapter has concentrated on their intergovernmental links, by discussing how NGOs and IGOs have co-evolved with motives for working with each other on both sides. The claims of self-appointed "global moral compass" and "modular technique" can be confirmed in this two-way relationship. Many international NGOs approaching IGOs are experts with regard to the problems they are dealing with and have strong ideas about how to solve them, in particular by setting international standards that all countries should respect. Public system building, international law (labor, human rights, health, etc.) with global standards, as well as multilateral programming in order to promote implementation and compliance, are core parts of this global moral compass. Even if the business community may be in favor of self-regulation, this does not stop it discussing international norms and pushing for or against them. Among the modular techniques that NGOs bring to IGOs are mobilization of public opinion, framing (as part of agenda-setting), wording (as part of the deliberation on draft resolutions), monitoring implementation (with the Amnesty International model of independent and authoritative reports as an ideal type), and local operations to implement IGO programs for relief and development (based on technology and economic growth as normative forces).

In the co-evolution of NGOs and IGOs, NGOs are frequently in the more dependent position. Notwithstanding their capacity to influence intergovernmental deliberation with new ideas, NGOs are not the ones who pull the strings, because IGOs and their secretariats are making the rules of the game. IGOs are the forums where international negotiation and standard setting take place, with the IGO staff as an important director of affairs alongside the governments of the (powerful) states. Even if professionalization of IGO and NGO staff has been a combined process, professionalization of IGO staff has been primary. IGOs offer opportunities to NGOs, but also regulate them. NGOs first have to gain access and then often encounter control by IGOs through rules and procedures. Although some private groups have rebelled against this control (business organizations favoring self-regulation, Doctors Without Borders and parts of the anti-globalization movement), most internationally active NGOs have accepted this unequal relationship. Others go their own way, such as the non-violent groupings.

At certain historical junctures, however, a few NGOs have produced far-reaching, transformative impacts on the course of world affairs. In this category would certainly be included the British Antislavery Society, but think also of eugenics NGOs in the early twentieth century and the human rights revolution led by Amnesty International in the late twentieth century.[26] NGOs have also helped to bring down dictators, and have maintained or replaced basic governmental support services in parts of the developing world. More recently, NGOs, often through networks involving middle-power states, have been able to help establish new IGOs and international treaties. Therefore, NGOs have in certain periods and across several issue areas been able to exercise significant transformative power in international politics, without becoming installed as established authorities over states and IGOs.

Notes

1 This chapter is based on Bob Reinalda, *Routledge History of International Organizations: From 1815 to the Present Day* (London: Routledge, 2009), which combines the history of IGOs and international NGOs, and Bob Reinalda, "The Evolution of International Organization as Institutional Forms and Historical Processes to 1945," in *The International Studies Encyclopedia: Volume III*, ed. Robert Denemark (Chichester: Wiley-Blackwell, 2010), 1903–1921.
2 Harold Jacobson, *Networks of Interdependence: International Organizations and the Global Political System* (New York: Knopf, 1979), 30.
3 Inis Claude, Jr., *Swords into Plowshares: The Problems and Progress of International Organization* (London: University of London Press, 1966), 17–18.
4 John Ikenberry, *After Victory: Institutions, Strategic Restraint, and the Rebuilding of Order after Major Wars* (Princeton, N.J.: Princeton University Press, 2001), 41.
5 Steve Charnovitz, "Two Centuries of Participation: NGOs and International Governance," *Michigan Journal of International Law* 18, no. 2 (1997): 212.
6 Margaret Keck and Kathryn Sikkink, *Activists beyond Borders: Advocacy Networks in International Politics* (Ithaca, NY: Cornell University Press, 1998), 18.
7 Reinalda, *Routledge History of International Organizations*, 59–71.
8 Arthur Eyffinger, *The International Court of Justice 1946–1996* (The Hague: Kluwer Law International, 1996), 45.
9 Barry Buzan and Richard Little, *International Systems in World History: Remaking the Study of International Relations* (Oxford: Oxford University Press, 2000), 252.
10 Robin Cohen and Paul Kennedy, *Global Sociology* (Basingstoke: Palgrave, 2000), 79.
11 Craig Murphy, *International Organization and Industrial Change: Global Governance since 1850* (Cambridge: Polity, 1994), 112.
12 Derek Bowett, *The Law of International Institutions* (London: Stevens and Sons, 1982), 8–9.
13 Robert Cox, "ILO: Limited Monarchy," in *The Anatomy of Influence: Decision Making in International Organization*, eds Robert Cox and Harold Jacobson (New Haven, Conn.: Yale University Press, 1973), 103.

14 Martin Dubin, "Transgovernmental Processes in the League of Nations," *International Organization* 37, no. 3 (1983): 471–482.
15 Ernst Haas, *Beyond the Nation-State: Functionalism and International Organization* (Stanford, Calif.: Stanford University Press, 1968), 100–101.
16 Bob Reinalda, "Organization Theory and the Autonomy of the International Labour Organization," in *Autonomous Policy Making by International Organizations*, eds Bob Reinalda and Bertjan Verbeek (London: Routledge, 1998), 52–53.
17 Wolf Eberwein and Sabine Saurugger, "The Professionalization of International Non-Governmental Organizations," in *Routledge Handbook of International Organization*, ed. Bob Reinalda (London: Routledge, 2013), 257–269.
18 David Mitrany, *A Working Peace System* (Chicago, Ill.: Quadrangle, 1966), 206.
19 Norbert Goetz, "Civil Society and NGO: Far from Unproblematic Concepts," in *The Ashgate Research Companion to Non-State Actors*, ed. Bob Reinalda (Farnham: Ashgate, 2011), 185–196.
20 Peter Willetts, "From 'Consultative Arrangements' to 'Partnership': The Changing Status of NGOs in Diplomacy at the UN," *Global Governance* 6, no. 2 (2000): 191–192.
21 Bob Reinalda, "The International Women's Movement as a Private Actor between Change and Accommodation," in *Private Organizations in Global Politics*, eds Karsten Ronit and Volker Schneider (London: Routledge, 2000), 165–186.
22 Peter Uvin, "Scaling Up the Grass Roots and Scaling Down the Summit: The Relations between Third World Nongovernmental Organizations and the United Nations," *Third World Quarterly* 16, no. 3 (1995): 500.
23 *Speaking Up for Free Enterprise All Over the World* (Paris: International Chamber of Commerce, 1981), 4.
24 David Levy and Daniel Egan, "Corporate Political Action in the Global Polity," in *Non-State Actors and Authority in the Global System*, eds Richard Higgott, Geoffrey R. D. Underhill and Andreas Bieler (London: Routledge, 2000), 150.
25 Gene Sharp, *From Dictatorship to Democracy: A Conceptual Framework for Liberation*, 4th edition (Boston, Mass.: Albert Einstein Institution, 2010).
26 William E. DeMars, *NGOs and Transnational Networks: Wild Cards in World Politics* (London: Pluto Press, 2005).

5 Being an NGO in the OECD

Elizabeth A. Bloodgood

- New institutionalism, new economics of organization, and NGOs
- National regulations and NGOing
- Being an NGO in the OECD
- NGOing in the United States
- NGOing in Japan
- NGOing in Poland
- Conclusion

The introductory chapter of this volume argues that international nongovernmental organizations (INGOs) happen when private actors address public purposes and link societal and political partners in at least two countries. In particular, INGOs are constituted by their practices, especially networking within and across states and societies, and the power dynamics that result. In this chapter, I argue that national NGO regulations document the rules for INGO behavior in a given country, providing both constraints on behavior and opportunities for resources and participation in political and social processes. National regulations thus function as structures framing the practice of "NGOing," as INGOs bridge countries and navigate networks of social and political actors.

INGOs as both individual organizations and as the third sector are impacted at the most basic levels by regulations which determine their right to exist and operate in a given national context. Government rules define what an NGO is, what INGOs can do, the size and composition of the third sector, and the access to resources for these organizations, as well as the official and formal roles of these actors in governance at the local and even international levels. Like Reinalda and Verbeek,[1] I argue that national regulations are an important place to begin to examine NGOs. National NGO regulations are also useful objects of study for this volume because they provide concrete illustrations of NGO practices in bridging states and societies and the power dynamics that accompany NGO practices. Although INGOs may be able to maneuver more freely than national NGOs, national regulations also affect INGOs because all INGOs are national NGOs somewhere. Many governments require INGOs to establish national branches within their territory subject to their laws in order to operate in-country.

As scholars we need a better understanding of national regulation of INGOs. To see states as in control of INGOs, or INGOs as subverting state authority, is too simplistic and ultimately unproductive. National regulations are not randomly imposed on INGOs, nor fixed over time, but instead result from the historical evolution of state–society relations within countries. As expected by constructivists, states and INGOs craft institutions which confine behavior, while defining identities, and set the context for their future interactions. National regulations are thus a means for each side to exercise power over the other, but power is exercised by both parties within the relationship. Regulations are not simply enforced by governments on NGOs, nor are INGOs capable of fully circumventing national regulations in even the weakest state (although they may be able to renegotiate them). Indeed, there is clear evidence that INGOs do not gravitate to countries with the fewest regulations; instead INGOs network and participate in the promulgation of national regulations because they provide a clear institutional structure within which they are guaranteed space and resources to operate.[2]

This chapter begins from the position asserted by new institutionalists, and the new economics of organization, that regulations as institutions are designed to channel organizations' development and behavior towards desired goals.[3] While they may have markedly different effects than intended, regulations evolve over time as they establish (or reify) norms and ideas about the appropriate relationship between state and society within a given geographic and temporal context. This begins to shade into constructivism, as actors (both governmental and NGO) define the rules which constitute the actors and their practices, then seek to refine the rules that define them and their relative abilities (power and range of motion).

The basic claim that national regulations are useful reflections of the construction of INGOs and their relationships with government and society is examined empirically in this chapter in two ways. First, I look at comparative statistics across the Organization for Economic Cooperation and Development (OECD), which is the intergovernmental organization of the countries with the most industrialized market economies in the world. I examine several basic indicators, namely the basic definitions of NGOs as a type of actor (the identities that NGOs can adopt), the requirements for INGOs to gain legal personality (and thus the protection of national law), and provisions for government oversight (and thus the control government has over the operation of INGOs). Second, I examine the evolution of national NGO regulations, in particular the process by which regulations are made and the participation of NGOs in the making of national regulations, over time in three archetypal cases of common law (United States), corporatism (Japan), and a recent democratic transition (Poland). These cases are selected because they represent three very different political and social contexts and thus should evince strong differences in the ways in which INGOs and governments constitute their relations, and thus practices of "NGOing," in these countries.

New institutionalism, new economics of organization, and NGOs

The central problem in the relationship between states and NGOs is that each sees the other as a potentially useful partner, but with risks.[4] National regulations create the potential for NGOs and states to establish positive working relationships between legal entities with clearly established rights and responsibilities. But national regulations are also an exercise of power with potentially severe consequences to both parties to the relationship. National regulations often provide states with the power to block or dissolve NGOs which do not meet certain criteria or violate specified provisions. National regulations also commit states to uphold certain protections on NGO activities, which can lead to challenges in court if violated.

In defining their relationship today, governments and NGOs worry about changes in the future that might make the other less willing to abide by their commitments, particularly if their interests diverge over time. NGOs are established according to state laws at a particular point in time. As they grow in power, popularity, and legitimacy, they have a greater ability to pressure the state and/or flout state laws. The state, knowing this, thus wants to bind the NGO today to prevent this from happening in the future. But if the restrictions placed on the NGO are too onerous, then the NGO might not form, or will undertake fewer activities and provide fewer benefits to society and/or the state, or will take its resources and form elsewhere. In any of these scenarios, the state will lose benefits such as information, ties to the grassroots, interest representation, social capital, civic education, and basic service provision. The NGO will then have to undertake different activities with fewer resources (economic and political) than it was initially designed to do.

States have two mechanisms to deal with this problem. First, they can establish different legal identities for NGOs, forcing NGOs to select to register as a certain type, and thus revealing information about their type, including their intentions. Second, states can also try to align NGOs' *a priori* commitments with their *ex ante* behavior by promising them resources (economic or political) contingent upon their keeping their organizational goals and activities within certain bounds. Regulations would thus require NGOs to submit regular reports to the state in order to retain their status and thus their benefits or privileges. This approach is used in countries which differentiate between public benefit organizations/charities and general associations, with different requirements for registration and government approval linked to different benefits in terms of tax breaks and government access. International organizations also use this approach when they allow/require NGOs to gain consultative status to formally participate in return for annual or biennial reports and reviews. ECOSOC, for example adopts this model (Reinalda, this volume).

Literature on the new economics of organization argues that governments can and have adopted regulations (formal institutions) as a means to control organizations via prohibitions on bad behavior and, more importantly given monitoring problems, incentives for good behavior.[5] Institutions, as formal and informal constraints on behavior, including ideas, norms, laws, and practices, shape interactions between agents by providing a complex of opportunities and constraints.[6] While this literature initially focused on corporations and interest groups, the central ideas have increasingly been applied to NGOs as complex structures fighting principle–agent and collective action problems for organizational survival and efficacy.[7]

New economics of organization views institutions as contracts used to align the interests of actors that have different information, incentives, and differential abilities to enforce agreements before and after crucial events.[8] While this might involve a principal and an agent, shading into principal–agent theory, the actors can also be companies involved in a vertical production process, levels of government, or the state and an international organization. The central question is how to commit actors to certain behaviors in the future when there is uncertainty about the ways in which interests and relative power to enforce agreements will change as time goes on. Common mechanisms to resolve this dilemma include the use of regular rewards paid slowly over time, a reputation for honesty which can make future negotiations cheaper and easier, and mechanisms to increase the ability of actors to determine others' types and thus force them to reveal private information.[9]

Formal and informal institutions work together to circumscribe behavior, by encouraging appropriate or desirable behavior and prohibiting inappropriate and undesirable behavior. Often formal laws institutionalize customs and norms.[10] Norms of appropriateness also shape the establishment and operation of NGOs, since NGOs acting in ways deemed inappropriate, or seeking goals viewed by society as inappropriate, will have a difficult time attracting sufficient supporters and resources to continue.[11]

This normative element to the interaction between the state and NGOs resonates with both new institutionalism and constructivism.[12] The identities available to NGOs over time shape their interests as well as their appropriate range of endeavors. Charities (public benefit organizations) must act in the public interest, and the kinds of activities defined to serve the public interest are often enshrined in the law. Over time, however, the list of activities has changed, allowing new groups to achieve charitable status while others lose it. Currently one of the biggest debates within many countries concerns the appropriateness of religiously motivated groups which intend to serve only particular populations (those that self-identify with the religion) obtaining charitable status thus declaring they are serving the public good. Similarly there are struggles between NGOs with charitable status, or those that wish to obtain it, and states over the extent to which certain activities, such as civic education and issue advocacy, are political or public interest, and thus whether this is appropriate behavior for public benefit organizations.

New institutionalists expect to see path dependence to the evolution of national institutions, as these often reify past practices and empower actors which work to maintain institutions even in the face of challenges from others.[13] NGO regulations are generally based on historic relations between state and society and evolving ideas about the appropriate realms of behavior for the state and NGOs. This is particularly true of common law countries which often depend upon custom and past court decisions to clarify and reinforce the bounds to NGO and state behavior over time. The evolution of government structures as a result of democratization and industrialization has shaped the perceived need for and appropriate role of NGOs, as have external events, particularly major wars or global economic recession, which cause states to cut back and thus increase the space available for NGO activities (Reinalda, this volume).

National regulations and NGOing

While the previous section focused on the ability of states to align NGO interests and capacities with states' interests, NGOs are not powerless in this relationship. While some INGOs are working to diffuse best practices in government regulation, others are building an international movement for NGO self-regulation and voluntary codes. The International Center for Not-For-Profit Law (ICNL) along with the Open Society Institute (OSI) and Soros Foundations are developing a set of best practices in NGO regulation as well as monitoring changes in regulation, both positive and negative, around the world.[14] The ICNL has advocated governments adopt their standards for regulation via compacts between the third sector and the state within the United States and Europe. While efforts to sign compacts on NGO–government relations have made some gains, and NGOs have had influence on national legislation in some places (most notably Canada, the United Kingdom, Estonia, and Croatia), not all NGOs are in favor of more formal regulation, and governments tend to adopt or implement only those parts of the compact that interest them. In places where NGOs and governments have good working relationships compacts are common, but provide little value added, while compacts are rare and/or not implemented where they might make the most difference.[15]

International organizations, including the UN and the EU, also play a part in mediating relations between governments and NGOs and in designing appropriate national regulations. The UN, in cooperation with the Johns Hopkins Center on Civil Society, has developed protocols to measure the contribution of nonprofit organizations to national economies and a system of accounting known as the Satellite Account to the National Income Accounts. While not direct regulations on NGOs, the new accounting procedures are likely to affect data reporting requirements for NGOs in the future.[16] European integration and continued expansion into new policy areas has had even more direct effects upon national regulations of NGOs within the EU. Article 11 paragraph 2 of the European Convention for the Protection of Human Rights and Fundamental Freedoms specifies that any association should dissolve if it offends against penal laws, exceeds its statutory sphere of activity, or no longer corresponds to the conditions of its legal existence.[17] EU taxation laws are also changing national regulations on tax exemptions for different categories of NGOs.[18] INGOs which have legal standing in the EU can advocate for adjustments to EU law, which has implications for the nature of national NGO regulations within the EU.

A number of major INGOs have argued for voluntary self-regulation on the part of INGOs rather than national regulations. Several major international initiatives have begun to elaborate voluntary codes. The International Committee of the Red Cross (ICRC) and the International Council of Voluntary Agencies (ICVA) have campaigned to spread a voluntary code of conduct for NGOs. The Code of Conduct for the International Red Cross and Red Crescent Movement and NGOs in Disaster Relief has been endorsed and enacted by more than 500 agencies, including Caritas, Catholic Relief Services, Lutheran World Relief, Oxfam, Save the Children, and the World Council of Churches.[19] A second campaign has been launched by Bill Clinton, Interaction, and the United Nations, called the NGO Impact Initiative, to first evaluate current NGO practices and then develop NGO standards for partnering with local communities, engaging donors and spending donations, and guaranteeing quality in relief and development work. A third initiative, the INGO Accountability Charter, includes voluntary codes of conduct for transparency, accountability, and conflicts of interest, and has been endorsed by INGOs including Greenpeace International, Amnesty International, CIVICUS, Transparency International, the World YMCA, Oxfam, Save the Children, and World Vision International.[20] While there are a number of adherents to voluntary codes of conduct,[21] and some of the language used in these codes might migrate into national regulation texts, governments have not stopped regulating NGO behavior and are unlikely to do so in the near future.

Being an NGO in the OECD

I begin the empirical analysis of this paper with cross-national data on national NGO regulations within the OECD.[22] I argue that national NGO regulations are an important point of contention for NGOs and states, and thus that analyzing these regulations can provide a meaningful window into the construction of NGOs and practices of NGOing. Three overarching findings emerge from this analysis.

First, I demonstrate that national NGO regulations exist in all OECD countries, and that they demonstrate considerable variation in NGOs' legal identities and relationships with government. Table 5.1 lists the types of organizational forms non-state, nonprofit entities are permitted to take in each country within the OECD as well as their relative frequencies.[23] It is clear from Table 5.1 that there is a wide variety of possible identities for NGOs, ranging from nonprofit organization to association to corporation, with association and

Table 5.1 NGO identities across the OECD

	Nonprofit	Association	Charity	CSO	PBO	Corporation	Total
Australia		X	X		X	X	4
Austria		X				X	2
Belgium	X	X				X	3
Canada	X	X	X			X	4
Chile		X	X			X	3
Czech Republic		X			X	X	3
Denmark		X			X		2
Estonia	X	X					2
Finland		X					1
France		X			X		2
Germany	X	X			X	X	4
Greece		X					1
Hungary	X			X	X	X	4
Ireland			X			X	2
Israel	X	X			X	X	4
Italy	X	X			X		3
Japan	X				X	X	3
Korea	X					X	2

	Nonprofit	Association	Charity	CSO	PBO	Corporation	Total
Luxembourg	X	X			X		3
Mexico	X			X			2
Netherlands		X			X		2
New Zealand	X		X			X	3
Norway						X	1
Poland		X			X		2
Portugal		X			X		2
Slovakia	X	X			X		3
Slovenia		X			X		2
Spain	X	X			X		3
Sweden		X			X	X	3
Switzerland		X			X	X	3
Turkey		X			X		2
United Kingdom			X			X	2
United States							0
Total	14 (42.4%)	25 (75.8%)	6 (18.2%)	2 (6.1%)	19 (57.6%)	17 (51.5%)	

corporation being the most common. Furthermore, the vast majority of OECD countries have more than one organizational identity that NGOs can adopt.

The transformation of the negative category of non-governmental organization into a positive legal entity has resulted in a great variety of organizational forms. NGOs as a category are constructed differently in different places because the term NGO itself is a negative residual category lacking clear definition. Only in very rare cases, generally in post-communist transition countries such as Poland, is "NGO" a legally recognized organizational category.[24] NGOs instead assume legal identities as nonprofit corporations, associations, societies, or foundations, with or without associated public benefit, civil society organization, or charitable status.

The attribution of a positive organizational identity to NGOs in their relations with a state defines the rules for both the NGO and for the state and helps to allocate responsibilities and obligations between them. The act of regulating thus amounts to an enabling exercise of power on the part of both parties. In Japan, public interest corporations must be approved by the relevant government ministry with which they will work and must attain a minimum level of funding.[25] Obtaining this status then serves as a marker that an organization has a connection with government and has viable economic resources. 501(c)3 organizations in the United States must incorporate at the state level, giving them a geographic locale, and register with the IRS to obtain necessary tax status.[26] In return, however, 501(c)3 organizations receive tax benefits, can confer tax benefits to individuals and corporations which give them donations, and can draw upon the relevant state and federal courts for legal protection and conflict resolution when necessary.

Second, I find that states care enough about NGOs and their constitution as actors to regulate them. This is not an empty area of law in which NGOs are allowed to be or do whatever they want, which would indicate that states care little about NGOs and their practices. NGOs have available identities which give them legal personality in all countries in the OECD. This signifies recognition by the state that NGOs have power and in turn provides them legitimacy, rights, protections, and responsibilities. In many countries, NGOs do not have to organize themselves in a way that gives them legal personality unless they wish, but their available activities and resources (as well as legal protections) are greatly limited if they do not. France and Switzerland are exceptions, as organizations gain legal personality simply by expressing their desire to organize corporatively.[27] More commonly, NGOs must meet certain standards of democratic governance, accounting, public interest, and information reporting in order to maintain their status. In return they receive legal recourse, liability protection, tax breaks, and formal recognition. Table 5.2 describes the steps NGOs must take to gain legal personality within the countries in the OECD. Notable is the degree of diversity in terms of requirements placed on NGOs. While the government has the ability to block the creation of an NGO in some places, this is only true in half of the countries of the OECD.

It is also interesting to note in Table 5.2 that a number of countries impose additional requirements on INGOs before they can operate within their territorial jurisdiction. In Belgium, permission for foreign organizations must be given by royal decree and in Turkey by the Ministry of Interior and Foreign Affairs.[28] In Spain, INGOs can only gain legal recognition and protection if the INGO founds a local branch within the country.[29] In Poland, the INGO must include nationals who can establish the local office.[30] This is an additional mechanism to ground INGOs in the country's jurisdiction in order to make national laws binding on an organization otherwise able to leave in order to evade legislation.

Third, I find that states' regulations on NGOs are not domineering or highly repressive in any country within the OECD. As Table 5.3 demonstrates, there is a wide range of oversight practices within the OECD.

I use government approval to form and government's ability to dissolve an NGO as indicators of the ultimate authority governments can exercise over NGOs. In only half the countries of the OECD is government approval necessary to establish an NGO. In 29 of the 34 countries government can dissolve an NGO, but in the vast majority of countries in which the government can dissolve an NGO (23 of 29) the decision must be made by, or can be appealed to, a national court. With very few exceptions, governments do not have an unlimited ability to intervene in an NGOs' governance or operations or dissolve them without cause or recourse. Korea and Japan are cases in which a government ministry can dissolve an NGO without recourse to a court. But even in these countries, the reasons for dissolution are circumscribed: "In case a legal person operates such business outside the scope of its creative purpose, violates conditions attached to the permission for its formation, or engages in acts harming public interests, the relevant ministries may cancel the permission."[31] Denmark represents the opposite extreme, in that it is highly favorable to NGOs: "No association shall be dissolved by any government measure; but an association may be temporarily prohibited, provided that immediate proceedings be taken for its dissolution."[32]

Table 5.2 NGO procedures for establishment

	Means to gain legal personality	Government approval required	Local presence requirements
Australia	Registration	No	Yes
Austria	Establishment agreement	No	Yes
Belgium	Royal decree, publication of statute	No	Yes
Canada	Government recognition	No	Yes
Chile	Registration	Yes	Yes
Czech Republic	Registration	Yes	No
Denmark	Establishment	No	Yes
Estonia	Registration	No	Yes
Finland	Registration	Yes	Yes
France	Notification of local government	No	Yes
Germany	Registration	Yes	No
Greece	Registration	Yes	No
Hungary	Registration	Yes	No
Ireland	Registration	Yes	Yes
Israel	Publication in official gazette after registration	Yes	Yes
Italy	Government recognition	Yes	No
Japan	Permission of government agency	Yes	No
Korea	Registration, permission of relevant ministry	Yes	No
Luxembourg	Publication of statutes	No	Yes
Mexico	Association	No	Yes

	Means to gain legal personality	Government approval required	Local presence requirements
Netherlands	Notary	No	Yes
New Zealand	Registration	Yes	No
Norway	Association	No	No
Poland	Registration and official decision on registration	Yes	Yes
Portugal	Depositing constitution with local authorities and publication in daily newspaper	Yes	No
Slovenia	Registration	Yes	No
Slovakia	Registration	Yes	No
Spain	Foundation act and agreed upon constitution	No	Yes
Sweden	Establishment	No	No
Switzerland	Expression within statutes of will to organize corporatively	No	No
Turkey	Establishment	No	Yes
United Kingdom	Registration	Yes	No
United States	Registration with tax authorities at federal level; incorporation at the state level	Yes	No

Table 5.3 Government oversight of NGOs across the OECD

	Government approval for legal personality	Government dissolution	Court appeal on government dissolution
Australia	No	Yes	Yes
Austria	No	Yes	No
Belgium	No	Yes	Yes
Canada	No	Yes	Yes
Chile	Yes	Yes	Yes
Czech Republic	Yes	Yes	Yes
Denmark	No	Yes	Yes
Estonia	No	Yes	Yes
Finland	Yes	Yes	Yes
France	No	Yes	Yes
Germany	Yes	Yes	No
Greece	Yes	Yes	Yes
Hungary	Yes	Yes	Yes
Ireland	Yes	Yes	Yes
Israel	Yes	Yes	Yes
Italy	Yes	Yes	No
Japan	Yes	Yes	No
Korea	Yes	Yes	No
Luxembourg	No	Yes	Yes
Mexico	No	No	State level

	Government approval for legal personality	Government dissolution	Court appeal on government dissolution
Netherlands	No	Yes	Yes
New Zealand	Yes	Yes	No
Norway	No	No	
Poland	Yes	Yes	Yes
Portugal	Yes	Yes	Yes
Slovenia	Yes	Yes	Yes
Slovakia	Yes	Yes	Yes
Spain	No	Yes	Yes
Sweden	No	No	
Switzerland	No	Yes	Yes
Turkey	No	Yes	Yes
United Kingdom	No	Yes	Yes
United States	No	No	Yes

Note:
This assesses the bare minimum requirements for an NGO; in many cases, charities/PBOs are held to higher standards, require government approval, and can be dissolved by government action even if simple associations cannot be (e.g., Australia, Canada, United Kingdom, United States).

Being an NGO in the OECD 145

While the current state of NGO regulations within the OECD reveals much about the nature of NGO–state relations, NGO laws change over time. They do not lock in a particular relationship, but evolve to reflect changing NGO practices and power. NGOs as well as the state play a role in making institutions by constructing, reinforcing, and challenging regulations. The evolution of national NGO regulations reflects a mix of needs and wishes on both sides as well as the impact of external events and path dependence, as is predicted by new institutionalism. I examine three particular cases in more detail to better understand the effect of national regulation in constituting NGOs, but also the role of NGOs in making and remaking national regulations as institutions. In each of the cases, the national constitution provides a basic freedom of association, but this is then clarified and elaborated by specific regulations on nonprofits. Table 5.4 provides an overview of the three cases selected to represent different types of states within the OECD and their different relations with NGOs.

NGOing in the United States

NGOs in the United States can take on a broad range of forms in theory. They are generally classified according to their federal tax status. In order to receive tax benefits, and to also give these to donors, they need to meet conditions that have a significant effect on their organization and operation. The most populous categories are 501(c)(3) organizations and 527 organizations. 501(c)(3) organizations are

> Corporations, and any community chest, fund, or foundation, organized and operated exclusively for religious, charitable, scientific, testing for public safety, literary, or educational purposes, or to foster national or international amateur sports competition ... or for the prevention of cruelty to children or animals, no part of the net earnings of which inures to the benefit of any private shareholder or individual, no substantial part of the activities of which is carrying on propaganda, or otherwise attempting, to influence legislation ... and which does not participate in, or intervene in (including the publishing or distributing of statements), any political campaign on behalf of (or in opposition to) any candidate for public office.[33]

501(c)(4) organizations are social welfare organizations; 501(c)(5) are labor and agricultural groups; and 501(c)(6) are business and labor groups. Of the 1.56 million nonprofit organizations in the United

Table 5.4 Case studies

	Date initial regulation	Location of NGO regulation	Geographic provisions	Date of last NPO legislation	Available organizational forms
United States	1939	Constitution, legislation, agency rules, court decisions	Yes	2011	Unincorporated associations, incorporated organizations (501(c)3 charitable, 501(c)4 social welfare, 527), trusts
Japan	1896	Civil code, legislation	No	2008	Public interest legal persons [*koekihojin*] (incorporated foundations and incorporated associations); special nonprofit corporations [*tokuteihieirikatsudohojin*]; other public interest organizations (social welfare entities, medical organizations, private schools, relief and rehabilitation enterprises, and religious organizations); intermediary legal persons [*chukanhojin*]; charitable trusts [*koekishintaku*]; cooperatives [*kyodokumiai*]; unincorporated organizations [*Nin-i dantai* or *Jinkakunakishadan*]
Poland	1932 1989	Constitution, civil code, associations law	Yes	2010	Associations (unincorporated or incorporated) [*stowarzyszeniazwykle* or *zarejestrowane*], unions of associations [*związkistowarzyszeń*], foundations, church-based corporate entities, social organizations established by special laws (e.g., Polish Red Cross), political parties, trade unions and professional organizations

States registered with the Internal Revenue Service in 2012, 979,901 (64 percent) were 501(c)(3) organizations.[34] Another popular identity for NGOs in the United States are 527 "political organizations," meaning "a party, committee, association, fund, or other organization (whether or not incorporated) organized and operated primarily for the purpose of directly or indirectly accepting contributions or making expenditures, or both, for an exempt function."[35] These organizations maintain tax exemptions for themselves but not for donors. The category 501(c)(4) has grown since the 2010 victory of Citizens United in a US Supreme Court case against the Federal Elections Commission over the ability to protect donors' identities, no matter the size of the donation, even when used for election-related political advocacy.[36]

A second level of regulations also shapes NGOs in the United States, as organizations must incorporate at the state level. This produces diversity within the population of NGOs found within the United States and gives NGOs choice in where they incorporate and thus the statutes they follow. Washington, D.C. and New York are popular choices for INGOs given the proximity to important decision-making forums. Washington, D.C. is home to 14,811 NGOs, Virginia 39,566, and New York 98,566. In order to incorporate in Washington, D.C., nonprofit organizations need a registered agent, a registered office within D.C., governance and dissolution procedures, at least three directors and three incorporators, and to pay a one-time fee of $80 and biennial reporting fees of $80.[37] To incorporate in New York, NGOs need only one incorporator and to specify a county where they are located, but many must have approval from a relevant state agency; agree to maintain accounts, minutes, and membership list; and pay incorporation and annual reporting fees ($75 and $9 respectively).[38] In Virginia, NGOs need a registered agent and office, two incorporators and directors, but relatively little information on governance procedures. NGOs in Virginia must register with the Department of Consumer Services to raise money in the state.[39] All NGOs must have a geographic tie at the state level in the form of an office in the jurisdiction where it will incorporate, thus making the NGO accountable for all laws at the state and federal level. While NGOs can register in many states, including Washington, D.C., New York, and Virginia as "foreign" corporations, meaning they are primarily located elsewhere in the United States, they must still have a "local" office. The United States does not differentiate legally between an NGO and an international NGO.

The last major overhaul of the IRS Tax Code was completed in 1986, but incremental changes in state legislation and national rules regarding incorporation, governance, lobbying, hiring, grants and contracts, and allowable activities mean US NGO regulation has shifted over time. For example, provisions of the US Patriot Act have increased the penalties for NGOs found to have aided a terrorist organization with or without intent or knowledge.[40] Revisions in 2009 on the 990 Form used by NGOs to report their earnings and activities to the IRS have also required more NGOs to maintain and report more detailed financial information.[41] And as of 2011, any organization above a threshold size which does not file a Form 990 on an annual basis will automatically have its tax-exempt status revoked.[42] Federal bureaucracies can also change their rules for procedures for obtaining grants and contracts, which can lead NGOs that need these resources to shift their structures. For example, the US Department of State released a best practices document for NGOs seeking to obtain money from USAID for international relief and development work.[43]

NGOs in the United States can use the court system to clarify NGO law, challenge and change interpretation of laws. For example, *Dartmouth College v. Woodward* (1819) tested the state's ability to change the charter of an NGO without trustee approval, and found in favor of NGOs.[44] The Justice Department has also been called on to settle issues of allowable NGO behavior, for example in the case of whether legal advocacy by the NAACP violated 501(c)(3) status[45] and the extent to which 501(c)(4) organizations can engage in political activities.[46] More recent court cases have tested the federal government's powers to dissolve NGOs, and what information must be revealed to NGOs about the grounds for dissolution.[47]

NGOing in Japan

NGOs in Japan are undergoing a major shift in their identities as a result of dramatic changes in nonprofit law in 2006. From 1896 until the most recent reforms, NGOs were generally either public interest corporations (*koeki hojin*) or educational, medical, welfare, or religious corporations (*gakko hjion, iryo hojin, shakai fukushi hojin,* and *shukya hojin*). As of 2006 there were roughly 25,000 public interest corporations, including the largest and most established NGOs in Japan. INGOs generally took this status. Incorporation required a minimum endowment of $2.7 million dollars.

A new law passed in 1998 enabled the creation of a new group of smaller organizations, incorporated as specified nonprofit corporations (*tokutei hieri hojin*):

> [Specified nonprofit activities are:] 1. Promotion of health, medical treatment, or welfare 2. Promotion of social education 3. Promotion

of community development 4. Promotion of science, culture, the arts, or sports 5. Conservation of the environment 6. Disaster relief 7. Promotion of community safety 8. Protection of human rights or promotion of peace 9. International cooperation 10. Promotion of a society with equal gender participation 11. Sound nurturing of youth 12. Development of information technology 13. Promotion of science and technology 14. Promotion of economic activities 15. Development of vocational expertise or expansion of employment opportunities 16. Protection of consumers 17. Administration of organizations that engage in the above activities or provision of liaison, advice, or assistance in connection with the above activities.[48]

While the range of allowable activities was limited, it was more expansive than basic service provision, and the resource threshold was lower. As of 2012, 45,889 new NGOs formed as a result.[49]

Under the original civil code provisions, NGOs were established with the permission of, and a strong attachment to a relevant bureaucratic agency, which required the organization to meet high standards to form. The bureaucratic agency then assumed responsibility for oversight of the NGO:

> Any association or foundation relating to any academic activities, art, charity, worship, religion, or other public interest which is not for profit may be established as a juridical person with the permission of the competent government agency.[50]

As of 2008, NGOs only need to register with the Prime Minister's Cabinet Office to become general incorporated associations or general incorporated foundations. NGOs that wish to obtain special tax treatment will then apply for public interest status from a newly created Public Interest Corporation Commission.[51] There is some uncertainty over the final effects of these reforms, but the expectation is that the new laws will allow new NGOs to form and operate with greater independence. Between 2008 and 2012, 23,938 organizations registered as General Corporations and 5,466 have obtained public interest status.[52]

NGOs played important roles advocating for changes in Japanese regulations. The 1998 reforms have been attributed to NGOs demands for greater flexibility to form NGOs in order to obtain legal protections while helping victims of earthquakes, like the one that occurred in 1995. Media criticism of the government's lack of responsiveness combined with the government's need to reinforce its electoral position by appealing to NGOs (and those that favored NGOs) for electoral support help drive NGOs' desired regulatory reforms.[53] NGOs also played a role in the 2006 reforms. The government convened a private sector advisory council which included NGO representatives in order to examine the Japanese model of national regulation versus other models for regulating NGOs.[54] Reforms to NGO regulation in 2008 provided even more flexibility to NGO operations, identities, and less bureaucratic oversight of their activities. These reforms were possible, in part, because of political weakness in the Liberal Democratic Party (LDP) and thus a need for electoral support from NGOs and their memberships.[55] New NGO laws in Japan have thus institutionalized a significant shift in power between NGOs and the government. While still highly constraining compared to many other OECD countries, new laws provide greater flexibility in, and fewer restrictions on, NGO formation in Japan.

NGOing in Poland

NGO regulations in Poland are among the most recent and the most rapidly evolving. Traditionally NGOs in Poland were known as social organizations (*organizacje spoleczne*). Association laws in Poland date back to 1932, but for many periods of time these provisions were suspended or rewritten to tighten the government's, or foreign occupier's, control of society. The formation and activities of NGOs were subject to strict political and administrative controls.

Since democratization in 1989, new laws have been passed to regulate all aspects of NGO behavior, including a Law on Associations, Law on Foundations, Law on National Court Register, Law on Economic Activity, Law on Procurement, Budget Law, and Law on Income Tax of Legal Persons. NGOs in Poland can be associations or unions of associations and incorporated or unincorporated. Unincorporated associations need only three members, must notify local supervisory authorities of their existence (said authorities have the right to prohibit the association's formation), and have access to court proceedings, although they lack legal personality. Incorporated associations must have 15 people and register in court, but do not require administrative authority authorization to form and gain legal personality. Self-governing local authorities monitor incorporated associations' activities and have the ability to ask the court to dissolve an incorporated association.[56]

Poland is one of the few countries in the OECD in which "nongovernmental organization" (a term adopted from abroad) has legal status. The Law on Associations (1989) posits that:

A non-governmental organization ... acquire[s] the status of a public benefit organization the moment they are included in the State Court Register.[57]

The ability to create an NGO is limited to Polish citizens. INGOs must be incorporated in Poland by Polish citizens. Article 5(1) of the Associations Law states that "International associations may be founded within the territory of the Republic of Poland according to the principles given in the present law."

The role of Solidarity in challenging Communist Party rule, and subsequent democratization, has given NGOs a fair amount of say in negotiating NGO regulation in post-communist Poland. During communist rule, NGOs were only allowed in limited numbers (for example the Polish Red Cross) and were required to support the political and social objectives of the government. Following the Solidarity movement's success in bringing democracy in 1989, a number of NGOs were created (many with close ties to INGOs).[58] The NGO sector in Poland is thus very strong and politically engaged. National bias provisions in Polish regulations thus help the government maintain control over the finances and political power of foreign organizations. Revisions of the Public Benefit and Volunteerism Law in 2010 have tightened the conditions under which NGOs can receive public benefit status, however, in the wake of concerns about excessive NGO authority and spending. The amended law requires NGOs to continuously demonstrate the public benefit nature of their activities for two years prior to getting such status as well as maintain an authority, separate from the board, to monitor their public benefit activities. The law also restricts the ability of public benefit organizations to engage in commercial activities and limits the use of proceeds from commercial activities to their public benefit activities.[59]

NGOs in Poland benefited from the decentralization of power and governing responsibility from a strong center to local areas and new legal space for public–private partnerships. But, at times, legislation hastily written and passed in the rush to democratize has been too lax, allowing for abuse and corruption by some organizations, casting a pall upon NGOs as a group, and leading to reforms.[60] Calls for greater accountability have led to new national regulations as well as voluntary codes for greater financial disclosure and stronger governance standards.[61] The lack of government control over the emerging NGO sector in a context of rapid political change allowed negative practices to develop, and new regulation demonstrates government efforts to retrieve some authority over NGOs.

Conclusion

It is clear from the three cases, and other examples given above, that NGOs are regulated differently even within the relatively homogeneous OECD. I argue that variations in regulations demonstrate that there are different processes to constitute NGOs in different countries and that these are the result of ongoing interactions between states and NGOs involving both collaboration and contention. National regulations are the primary means at states' disposal to control the creation and activities of NGOs. In no country, however, are NGOs regulated out of existence. This indicates some degree of mutual benefit between states and NGOs. But NGO regulations are constantly being challenged, reinterpreted, and rewritten by both NGOs and states. Regulations are thus a concrete example of power being exerted by both sides, one against another, as regulations constrain NGO behavior, but also give NGOs rights and legal protections within the state. Additional research is needed on legal regulation of NGOs in countries beyond the OECD. The cases sketched here are archetypal within the OECD: common law (United States), corporatism (Japan), and recent democratic transition (Poland). These archetypes can be compared to other cases from countries with colonial legacies, occupying forces, and non-democratic governments in order to see the effects of international relations on the power relations between national governments and NGOs. Recent efforts by international NGOs such as the ICNL Center and the Uniform Law Conference of Canada/National Conference of Commissioners on Uniform State Laws to promote new legal codes to standardize nonprofit law, improve protections for political activity by NGOs, and increase access to economic resources, are likely to have interesting effects on power relations between NGOs and governments in the future.

International Relations (IR) as an academic field, however, needs to adapt its theoretical underpinnings even as NGO scholars need to expand their methodological toolboxes in order to advance research on power relations between governments and NGOs.[62] The new economics of organization and new institutionalism provide much better explanations for the nature of national NGO regulations and the processes by which these change over time than do classic IR theories. New institutionalism and the new economics of organization are specifically focused on explaining the organizational characteristics and behavior likely to emerge within a given set of institutional opportunities and constraints, and why organizations evolve with these institutions in particular ways.[63] To see states as in control of INGOs, or INGOs as efforts to subvert state authority, as is traditionally done within IR, is too simplistic. INGOs are neither epiphenomenal, serving as temporary expedients for states, as is argued by realists, nor subsumed within and beneath intergovernmental organizations, as is assumed by liberals. New institutionalism instead argues that INGOs must engage governments as the object of their activities, but also as partners, obstacles, sources of legitimacy, legal protectors, funders, and arenas for activism. INGOs bridge between the domestic and the international, as even INGOs must locate in national jurisdictions to gain legal personality and organizational identities. But nationally grounded NGOs interact in the international realm by networking between NGOs and states. It is thus more useful to examine the ways in which regulations constitute the appropriate forms and behaviors of INGOs than to argue that INGOs are either state agents or beyond the reach of the state.

Examining the interaction between states and NGOs in the process of reforming national NGO regulations provides a window into their power relationships. The fact that NGOs willingly submit themselves to state power because they desire regulation as a means of obtaining legal rights and protections is a puzzle for traditional IR. New institutionalism not only argues that this is to be expected, but that different international NGOs will find a more natural fit in different national contexts, thus shaping global patterns of INGO location, operation, and power. National regulations not only set the ground for conflict or cooperation between NGOs and states, but they can also create the outlines of conflict between states. Governments partner with NGOs in opposition to positions held by governments and NGOs elsewhere, for instance over government control of foreign aid operations or definitions of human rights.[64] It is impossible to further explore these puzzles without first challenging the ways we see NGO–government relations and NGO power in world politics.

Notes

1 Bob Reinalda and Bertran Verbeek, "Theorizing Power Relations Between NGOs, Inter-Governmental Organisations and States," in *Non-State Actors in International Relations*, eds Bas Arts, Math Noortmann and Bob Reinalda (Aldershot: Ashgate, 2001), 145–58.
2 Elizabeth Bloodgood, "The Diffusion of NGO Regulation and the Decline of Global Democracy?" Presented at the International Society for Third Sector Research Annual Conference in Barcelona, Spain, 9–12 July 2008.
3 Avner Greif, *Institutions and the Path to the Modern Economy* (Cambridge: Cambridge University Press, 2006); Lauren Edelman, C. Uggen and H. Erlanger, "The Endogeneity of Legal Regulation," *American Journal of*

Sociology 105 (1999): 406–54; Elisabeth Clemens and James Cook, "Politics and Institutionalism: Explaining Durability and Change," *Annual Review of Sociology* 25 (1999): 441–466; Paul DiMaggio and Walter Powell, "The Iron Cage Revisited: Institutional Isomorphism and Collective Rationality in Organizational Fields," in *The New Institutionalism in Organizational Analysis*, eds Walter W. Powell and Paul J. DiMaggio (Chicago, Ill.: University of Chicago Press, 1991), 63–82.
4 D. R. Young, "Alternative Models of Government-Nonprofit Sector Relations: Theoretical and International Perspectives," *Nonprofit and Voluntary Sector Quarterly* 29, no. 1 (2000): 149–172; Adil Najam, "The Four C's of Third Sector-Government Relations," *Nonprofit Management and Leadership* 10, no. 4 (2000): 375–396; Julie Fisher, *Non-Governments: NGOs and the Political Development of the Third World* (West Hartford, Conn.: Kumarian Press, 1998).
5 Terry Moe, "The New Economics of Organizations," *American Journal of Political Science* 28 (1984): 739–77; Beth Yarbrough and Robert Yarbrough, "International Institutions and the New Economics of Organization," *International Organization* 44 (1990): 235–59.
6 James March and Johan Olsen, "The New Institutionalism," *American Political Science Review* 78 (1999): 734–49.
7 Elizabeth Bloodgood, "Institutional Environment and the Organization of Advocacy NGOs in the OECD," in *Advocacy Organizations and Collective Action*, eds Aseem Prakash and Mary Kay Gugerty (Cambridge: Cambridge University Press, 2010), 91–130.
8 Moe, "The New Economics of Organizations," 739–77; Douglass North and Barry Weingast, "Constitutions and Commitment: Evolution of Institutions Governing Public Choice," *Journal of Economic History* 49, no. 4 (1989): 803–832; and Yarbrough and Yarbrough, "International Institutions and the New Economics of Organization," 235–59.
9 Oliver Williamson, *The Economic Institutions of Capitalism: Firms, Markets, Relational Contracting* (New York: Free Press, 1985); Yarborough and Yarborough, "International Institutions and the New Economics of Organization," 235–59; Greif, *Institutions and the Path to the Modern Economy*; North and Weingast, "Constitutions and Commitment," 803–832.
10 Douglass North, *Institutions, Institutional Change, and Economic Performance* (Cambridge: Cambridge University Press, 1990); DiMaggio and Powell, "The Iron Cage Revisited," 63–82.
11 John Meyer and David Strang, "Institutional Conditions for Diffusion," *Theory and Society* 22 (1993): 487–512.
12 March and Olsen, "The New Institutionalism," 734–49.
13 Kathleen Thelen, "Historical Institutionalism in Comparative Politics," *Annual Review of Political Science* 2 (1999): 369–404; Ellen Immergut, "The Theoretical Core of the New Institutionalism," *Politics and Society* 26, no. 1 (1998): 5–34.
14 International Center for Not-For-Profit Law, "07-20-2006: ICNL Representatives Participate in Civil G8 Summit in Moscow," (www.icnl.org/news/2006/20-Jul.html); and Leon Irish, Robert Kushen and Karla Simon, *Guidelines for Laws Affecting Civic Organizations*, 2nd edition (New York: Open Society Institute, 2004).

15 Radost Toftisova, "Implementation of NGO-Government Cooperation Policy Documents: Lessons Learned," *International Journal of Not-for-Profit Law* 8, no. 1 (2005): 11–41.
16 *Handbook on Non-Profit Institutions in the System of National Accounts* (United Nations, Department of Economic and Social Affairs, Statistics Division ST/ESA/STAT/SER.F/91), 2003 (http://unstats.un.org/unsd/publication/SeriesF/SeriesF_91E.pdf).
17 Government of Austria, *Vereinsgesetz 2002, BGBl I Nr 66/2002* (2002 Associations Act), Ministry of the Interior (http://cdn1.vol.at/2006/03/vereinsgesetz.pdf).
18 Ole Gjems-Onstad, "The Legal Framework and Taxation of Scandinavian Non-Profit Organisations," *Voluntas* 7, no. 2 (1996): 195–212.
19 International Federation of Red Cross and Red Crescent Societies, "Code of Conduct for The International Red Cross and Red Crescent Movement and NGOs in Disaster Relief" (1994) (www.ifrc.org/en/publications-and-reports/code-of-conduct/); and International Council of Voluntary Agencies, "ICVA's Work on the Code of Conduct and Humanitarian Principles" (www.icva.ch/doc00001245.html).
20 INGO Accountability Charter (Berlin, 2005) (www.ingoaccountabilitycharter.org/).
21 Mary Kay Gugerty and Aseem Prakash, *Voluntary Regulation of NGOs and Nonprofits* (Cambridge: Cambridge University Press, 2010).
22 My data on national NGO regulation shares similarities with the CIVICUS Survey of the State of Civil Society. Variables concerning the legal environment and political context of a country constitute one quarter of their Civil Society Index; see V. Finn Heinrich and Lorenzo Fioramonti, eds, *CIVICUS Global Survey of the State of Civil Society, vol. 2, Comparative Perspectives* (West Hartford, Conn.: Kumarian Press, 2008). The Comparative Nonprofit Sector Project focuses on the economic context and consequences of non-profits; see Lester Salamon, Helmut Anheier, Regina List, Stefan Toepler and S. Wojciech Sokolowski, *Global Civil Society: Dimensions of the Nonprofit Sector* (Baltimore, Md.: Johns Hopkins Center for Civil Society Studies, 1999). My data on national regulation includes more detail on the specifics of a broader set of regulation from a larger sample of countries than the CIVICUS and CNSP datasets.
23 Iceland is omitted for lack of data.
24 Government of Poland, *Parliamentary Act of April 7, 1989: Law on Associations* (1989 LOA) (www.icnl.org/research/library/files/Poland/assoc.pdf).
25 Government of Japan, *Act on Authorization of Public Interest Incorporated Associations and Public Interest Incorporated Foundations (Act No. 49 of 2006)* (2006 Act on Incorporation) (www.cas.go.jp/jp/seisaku/hourei/data/AAPII.pdf).
26 Government of the United States, *U.S. Code, Title 26: Internal Revenue Code, Subtitle A: Income Taxes, Chapter 1: Normal Taxes and Surtaxes* (www.law.cornell.edu/uscode/text/26/subtitle-A/chapter-1).
27 Government of France, *Associations Law (Law no. 5253, Official Gazette No. 25649, 23-11-2004)* (2004 Associations Law), translated by Argus Translation Agency; and Government of Switzerland, *Code Civil Suisse—Livre Premier: Droit des Personnes* (1912 Civil Code), Federal Authorities

of the Swiss Confederation, (www.admin.ch/opc/fr/classified-compilation/ 19070042/index.html).
28 Government of Belgium, *27 Juin 1921.—Loi sur les Associations sans But Lucratif, les Associations Internationales sans But Lucratif et les Fondations* (www.ejustice.just.fgov.be/cgi_loi/change_lg.pl?language=fr&la=F&table_name=loi&cn=1921062701); and Government of Turkey, *Associations Law (Law no. 5253, Official Gazette No. 25649, 23-11-2004)* (2004 Associations Law) (www.icnl.org/research/library/files/Turkey/assocen.pdf).
29 Government of Spain, *Ley Orgánica 1/2002, de 22 de marzo, reguladora del Derecho de Asociación,* Boletín Oficial del Estado, Ministerio de la Presidencia (www.boe.es/buscar/doc.php?id=BOE-A-2002-5852).
30 Government of Poland, 1989 LOA.
31 Government of Korea, *Act Concerning Establishment and Operation of Nonprofit Corporations (Law No. 2814, promulgated on December 31, 1975)* (1975 Nonprofit Act) (http://asianphilanthropy.org/APPC/philanthropy-law-in-Asia-1999.pdf), 230–239.
32 Government of Denmark, *Danmarks Riges Grundlov (Grundloven) (Lov nr. 169 af 05/06/1953)* (1953 Constitution), Retsinformation.dk. (www.retsinformation.dk/Forms/R0710.aspx?id=45902&exp=1).
33 U.S. Code, Title 26, Subtitle A, Chapter 1, Subchapter F, Part 6, Section 501(c)(3).
34 Amy Blackwood, Katie Roeger and Sarah Pettijohn, "The Nonprofit Sector in Brief" (Washington, DC: The Urban Institute, 2012), (www.urban.org/UploadedPDF/412674-The-Nonprofit-Sector-in-Brief.pdf).
35 U.S. Code, Title 26, Subtitle A, Chapter 1, Subchapter F, Part 6, Section 527(e)(1).
36 Independent Sector, "Political Activity of 501(c)(4) Tax Exempt Organizations," Washington, DC (www.independentsector.org/501c4_organizations; Independent Sector); and Independent Sector, "Scope of the Nonprofit Sector," Washington, DC (www.independentsector.org/scope_of_the_sector).
37 District of Columbia, Office of the Deputy Mayor for Planning and Economic Development, "Start a Business, Nonprofit Corporations" (http://dmped.dc.gov/page/nonprofit-organizations).
38 New York State, Division of Corporations, Title 19, Chapter IV (www.dos.ny.gov/corps/nfpcorp.html#certinc).
39 Hurwit & Company, Nonprofit Law Resource Library, "Initial Filings for Virginia Nonprofit Organizations" (www.hurwitassociates.com/l_s_initial_va.php).
40 Government of the United States (2001), "Uniting and Strengthening America by Providing Appropriate Tools Required to Intercept and Obstruct Terrorism (USA Patriot Act) Act," 107–56, U.S. Government Printing Office (http://frwebgate.access.gpo.gov/cgi-bin/getdoc.cgi?dbname=107_cong_bills&docid=f:h3162enr.txt.pdf).
41 U.S. Internal Revenue Service, "Automatic Exemption Revocation for Non-Filing: Frequently Asked Questions" (www.irs.gov/Charities-&-Non-Profits/Automatic-Exemption-Revocation-for-Non-Filing:-Frequently-Asked-Questions-2).
42 U.S. Internal Revenue Service, Tax-Exempt Status for Your Organization, Publication 557, (www.irs.gov/pub/irs-pdf/p557.pdf).

43 U.S. Department of State, "General NGO Guidelines for Overseas Assistance" (www.state.gov/documents/organization/220005.pdf).
44 Peter Dobkin Hall, "A Historical Overview of the Private Nonprofit Sector," in *The Nonprofit Sector: A Research Handbook*, ed. Walter Powell (New Haven, Conn.: Yale University Press, 1987), 5.
45 J. Craig Jenkins, "Nonprofit Organizations and Policy Advocacy," in *The Nonprofit Sector: A Research Handbook*, ed. Walter Powell (New Haven, Conn.: Yale University Press, 1987), 301.
46 Citizens United v. Federal Election Commission, Supreme Court Case no. 08–205, 2010 (www.law.cornell.edu/supct/html/08-205.ZS.html).
47 Humanitarian Law Project, *et al.* vs. Alberto Gonzales, *et al.*, nos. CV98–1971ABCRCX and CV03–6107ABCRCX, United States District Court C. D. California, 2005, (www.uniset.ca/other/cs5/380FSupp2d1134.html); Holder, Attorney General, *et al.* v. Humanitarian Law Project *et al.*, Supreme Court Case no. 08–1498, 2010 (www.supremecourt.gov/opinions/09pdf/08-1498.pdf); KindHearts for Charitable Humanitarian Development, Inc. v. Timothy Geithner, *et al.*, Case no. 3:08CV2400 in the US District Court for the Northern District of Ohio, 2009, (www.charityandsecurity.org/system/files/KindHearts%20order%208.18.09_0.pdf); and Al-Haramain Islamic Foundation, Inc., *et al.* v. Barack Obama, *et al.*, Case no. C 07–0109 VRW in the US District Court for the Northern District of California, 2010, (www.charityandsecurity.org/system/files/Order%20March%202010%20AlHO.pdf).
48 Government of Japan (1998 SNPC Law), E-Gov. Ministry of Internal Affairs and Communications, (http://law.e-gov.go.jp/htmldata/H10/H10HO007.html), Schedule 2, Article 2.
49 The Japan Association of Charitable Organizations (JACO), "Charitable and Non-profit Organizations in Japan Data Book," (www.kohokyo.or.jp/english/Source/Data%20book2012.pdf), 3.
50 Government of Japan (1896 Civil Code), Civil Code Act 89 of 1896, (www.law.tohoku.ac.jp/kokusaiB2C//legislation/pdf/Civil%20Code.pdf), Article 34.
51 Japan Committee for International Exchange (JCIE), "Japan's Nonprofits Prepare for a New Legal System," *Civil Society Monitor* no. 12 (2007), (www.jcie.org/researchpdfs/CSM/CSM_No12.pdf); and Government of Japan, *Act on Authorization of Public Interest Incorporated Associations and Public Interest Incorporated Foundations (Act No. 49 of 2006)* (2006 Act on Incorporation), Cabinet Secretariat, translations of Laws and Regulations (in compliance with Standard Bilingual Dictionary) (www.cas.go.jp/jp/seisaku/hourei/data/AAPII.pdf), Article 2.
52 JACO, "Charitable and Non-profit Organizations in Japan Data Book," 3.
53 Robert Pekkanen, "Japan's New Politics: The Case of the NPO Law," *Journal of Japanese Studies* 26, no. 1 (2000): 111–148.
54 JACO, "Charitable and Non-profit Organizations in Japan Data Book."
55 Yuko Kawato and Robert Pekkanen, "Civil Society and Democracy: Reforming Nonprofit Organization Law," in *Democratic Reform in Japan: Assessing the Impact*, eds Sherry L. Martin and Gill Steel (Boulder, Colo.: Lynne Rienner, 2008), 196–7; and Keiko Hirata, "Civil Society and Japan's Dysfunctional Democracy," *Journal of Developing Societies* 20, nos. 1–2 (2004): 107–235.

56 Ewa Les, Slawomir Nalecz, and Jakub Wygnanski, "Defining the Nonprofit Sector: Poland," *Working Papers of the Johns Hopkins Comparative Nonprofit Sector Project*, no. 36 (Baltimore, Md.: Johns Hopkins Center for Civil Society Studies, 2000), 13.
57 Government of Poland, 1989 LOA, Article 22.2.
58 Patrice McMahon, "International Actors and Women's NGOs in Poland and Hungary," in *The Power and Limits of NGOs*, eds Sarah Mendelson and John Glenn (New York: Columbia University Press, 2002).
59 Government of Poland, *Act of Law of April 24th 2003 on Public Benefit and Volunteer Work*—consolidated text after last amendment on 22 January 2010 (www.pozytek.gov.pl/Public_Benefit_and_Volunteer_Work_Act_567.html).
60 Les *et al.*, "Defining the Nonprofit Sector: Poland."
61 Angela Bies, "Self-regulation in Poland's Non-governmental Sector: Internal and External Dynamics, Mandatory and Discretionary Approaches," Paper presented at the International Society for Third Sector Research Annual Meeting, Cape Town, South Africa, July, 2002.
62 Elizabeth Bloodgood and Hans Peter Schmitz, "The INGO Research Agenda: A Community Approach to Challenges in Method and Theory," in *Routledge Handbook of International Organization*, ed. Bob Reinalda (New York: Routledge, 2013), 67–79.
63 DiMaggio and Powell, "The Iron Cage Revisited," 63–82.
64 Paul Nelson and Ellen Dorsey, *New Rights Advocacy: Changing Strategies of Development and Human Rights NGOs* (Washington, DC: Georgetown University Press, 2008).

6 The accountability and legitimacy of international NGOs

Cristina M. Balboa

- Why the rising calls for NGO accountability?
- Accountability and bridging functions
- What does traditional literature tell us?
- Beyond traditional theories of accountability
- Limits of accountability
- NGO accountability and the New Life Children's Refuge in Haiti
- Conclusion

As I began to write this chapter, challenges to NGO legitimacy competed with demands for NGO action in relief efforts for the Haitian earthquake tragedy—from Rush Limbaugh questioning White House support for United Way efforts,[1] to critics challenging Yele's Haiti fundraising as supporting the rock-star lifestyles of relief workers,[2] to ten members of a US Baptist church, as members of the NGO New Life Children's Refuge, sitting in a Haitian jail awaiting trial for kidnapping 33 Haitian children and attempting to transport them to an orphanage in the Dominican Republic.[3]

These are timely examples of the rising calls for accountability of international non-governmental organizations (NGOs) over the past decade. International environmental NGOs have been asked to account for their financial practices, partnerships, and methods.[4] The NGO Human Rights Watch was accused by its founder of demonizing Israel.[5] Cultural groups like the Kuwait-Cambodia Islamic Cultural Training Center have been accused of providing financial support to terrorist groups like Al-Qaeda.[6]

This chapter examines issues of NGO accountability and legitimacy through a thorough discussion of both scholarly and practitioner literatures.[7] It argues that the complex nature of international NGOs precludes the use of traditional International Relations (IR) theory to explain or even describe NGO accountability and legitimacy. Instead, scholars and practitioners must look beyond the clear but confining typologies of traditional political science to apply other disciplines and approaches and to create more precise—and more complex—portrayals of NGO accountability. First, this chapter discusses why NGO legitimacy and accountability are increasingly important in global governance. Second, it explores how accountability explains and is explained by the bridging concepts of "NGOing" laid out in this volume. Third, the chapter highlights some helpful frameworks for accountability drawn from IR, management, development, public policy and organization theory literatures. It also shows how perhaps the most prominent framework of accountability used in IR—principal–agent theory—is surprisingly inappropriate for discussing international NGOs. Fourth, while this chapter contends that all actors are accountable in some way and to some actors (perhaps solely to their own board or mission), it also argues that our current notions of accountability—especially traditional approaches—are limited. Finally, the New Life Children's Refuge case study illustrates how these different approaches to accountability can both illuminate new facets of NGO accountability and also fall short of fully explaining these complex relationships.

Why the rising calls for NGO accountability?

While NGOs are commonly seen as inherently good—representing the disenfranchised, defending democracy, human rights, the environment and other important causes—NGOs are often less than democratic themselves. Even as NGOs call for increased transparency of corporations, intergovernmental organizations and states, their own transparency is lacking.[8] Recent scandals have the public questioning the integrity and legitimacy of the growing number of NGOs worldwide.[9]

While practitioners are calling for more accountability of transnational NGOs, the academic community is asking why these calls for accountability are increasing in the first place.[10] Part of the answer may be the vast expansion of NGO "bridging" practices as described in this volume. A helpful illustration of NGO bridging can be found in Koppell's hypothesis that increased salience of actors in global governance is due to two variables: (1) power (defined simply as "getting what is wanted"), and (2) "publicness" (central to every NGO's claim to serve some public purpose).[11] The more power an organization exercises over an issue, the more its legitimacy comes into question. Likewise, the more "public" an organization's actions and arenas of influence, the more salient its work becomes to the public eye.

While NGOs have always bridged civil society and the state by being private actors pursuing public goods, both their publicness and power have grown in the past few decades as a result of the globalization of new public management and neoliberal economics—two closely related policy schools that promote smaller government and more participation in policy by non-state actors. In this governance environment, NGOs are acting increasingly like governmental regulatory agencies, but without commensurate accountability mechanisms, thus generating increased concerns about their legitimacy as policy actors.[12]

To make concrete the link between accountability and legitimacy challenges of non-state actors, I borrow a definition from the field of sociology: Legitimacy exists when "the actions of an entity are desirable, proper, or appropriate within some socially constructed system of norms, values, beliefs and definitions."[13] Operationalizing accountability and legitimacy has proven much more difficult because, as relational concepts, they often change depending upon who invokes them.

Because NGOs lack the mechanisms for public voice institutionalized in democratic states, they seek legitimacy through accountability. Accountability has generally been defined as "answerability," with many variations on how this is implemented. One point of agreement is that to be accountable, one must report and be responsible for one's actions and outcomes.[14] Here lies the critical link between accountability and legitimacy: *If legitimacy applies when an actor operates within a socially constructed system of norms, values, beliefs and definitions, then accountability is the way one assures compliance to that system.* From the vantage point of the power-wielder, accountability is viewed as a means to turn its power into legitimate authority; that is, to maintain the current power relationship.[15] At the same time, from the vantage point of those demanding accountability, it is viewed as a means to ensure power is used in a way that reflects their needs and desires; that is, as a tool to curb power. For both the powerful and the weak, therefore, accountability is an instrument of power.

Accountability and bridging functions

As the above discussion indicates, increasing calls for NGO accountability may stem from the rising power and publicness of NGOs in world affairs, and their increased bridging of state and civil society. Two other NGO bridging functions—between conflict and cooperation, and between agent and structure—point to the dynamic nature of NGOing in networks, which confounds the study of NGO accountability.

Even where international NGOs seek cooperation to achieve their mission, they do so in a conflicting environment, especially where NGOs seek to profoundly transform broad social norms and paradigms.[16] If the NGO is powerful enough to change the norms, values and paradigms of civil society, then civil society will converge with the mission of the NGO. Alternatively, demands for legitimacy and accountability may quell NGO power, shifting its mission and actions to converge with the norms of civil society. In either case, the NGO becomes more legitimate by quelling calls for accountability and converting conflict into cooperation.

An additional hurdle to our scholarly study of NGO accountability is that NGOs simultaneously operate as both agents for the actors they represent (e.g., victims of human rights violations, endangered species, disenfranchised citizens) and structure to the networks they create. As both agent and structure in this bridging function, NGOs are at once objects of accountability (when they are being called to account by other actors) and agents of accountability (when they call others—the state, corporations, or other NGOs—to account).[17] This dual role creates a cobweb of relationships that makes the study of NGO legitimacy difficult, but also creates a demand for NGOs to practice what they preach in terms of accountability. This bridging function necessitates an interdisciplinary approach to studying NGO accountability: internal actions and policies of the international NGO can be best explained through organization literature, while relationships between NGOs and other actors in the network (including principals like the funders, victims, species or citizens) can be seen through a combination of organization, sociology, public policy, and IR literatures. One discipline cannot capture the complexity of NGO accountability, and very few scholarly works have attempted to address the issue comprehensively.

Another perplexing factor for the measure and explanation of NGO accountability is the multiple actors to whom they must account. While states are primarily accountable to their constituents, and firms are primarily accountable to their stockholders, the practice of connecting transnational and trans-societal actors also makes the issue of NGO accountability less straightforward. NGO funders demand financial accountability for their resources invested in the NGO cause. States demand accountability in the form of tax laws and regulations.[18] Citizens demand that NGOs act in their best interest. Other NGOs offer voluntary professional standards and processes of collaboration. NGO activists and staff themselves, with their refined expertise and reduced paychecks, are invested enough in the cause to make demands on how programs are implemented and with whom the organization collaborates. As bridges between multiple actors, NGOs have difficulty determining the primary principals to whom they must account. We who study NGOs face the same challenge.

These multiple bridging roles—between state and civil society, between conflict and cooperation, between agency and structure, between transnational and trans-societal actors—make NGOs unique actors on the global policy stage. While using bridging concepts pushes our portrayal of NGOs to a more accurate level, our scholarly tools have not developed enough to offer more than blurry explanations of NGO action and accountability. The next section explores that academic uncertainty and highlights efforts to push the literature to further clarity.

What does traditional literature tell us?

Political scientists, including IR scholars, tend to view accountability in terms of representative democracy, arguing simply that the governed should have a say in their governance.[19] Accountability is the answer to a democratic deficit. The concept is an intuitive one for many. However, operationalizing this concept in a way that it can be described and explained within these complex networks is a difficult task.

Many attempts have been made to operationalize accountability. Directional descriptions abound:[20]

- *Horizontal* systems of accountability among organizational or individual peers.
- *Vertical* accountability where citizens and their associations hold the more powerful accountable through mechanisms like oversight, separation of powers, ombudsperson, conflict management.
- *Internal* or reflexive accountability where NGOs are accountable to their own values, mission and staff.

While these directional theories may be the building blocks for accountability frameworks, each one is limited. Because NGOs serve as bridges between multiple actors, they necessarily are accountable in all three directions at once. The more comprehensive frameworks discussed below incorporate the multiparty and multidirectional nature of NGOs.[21]

To better explain this relatively new concept to IR, it is useful to examine other types of global actors, as well as other disciplines. This next section examines salient descriptions, definitions, and typologies of accountability across sectors.

States and IGOs: principals and agents?

Representative accountability is rooted in the democratic premise that the governors are answerable to the governed for their actions and omissions.[22] Regardless of one's normative approach—libertarian, pluralist, social democrat or deliberative democrat—the consensus in democratic approaches is that the exercise of authority requires the consent of the governed and mechanisms for holding decision-makers accountable between elections.[23] Representative theory focuses on constituents' power to vote state officials out of office, with very few non-electoral mechanisms of redress, thus creating an "accountability as punishment" paradigm.[24]

Traditional public administration, in both theory and practice, assumes that representative accountability can rely on a consistent set of institutions and relationships. However, under new public management (NPM), institutions and relationships are continuously changing form. By emphasizing outcomes over process, and decentralizing or delegating governance to other parties, NPM effectively blurs the lines of accountability. Scholars then turn to principal–agent (PA) theory to find mechanisms to constrain agents' opportunistic actions when they conflict with the goals of the principal.[25]

Similarly to international NGOs, intergovernmental organizations (IGOs) like those of the United Nations system, such as the International Labour Organization (ILO) and the International Atomic Energy Agency (IAEA) are gaining increased power and publicness, and commensurately increased challenges to their legitimacy as policymakers and implementers. Like the democracy literature, the IGO literature grounds accountability on the equivalence principle: the scope of costs and benefits of a good or policy should mirror the scope of jurisdiction in which decisions are taken on that good or policy.[26]

As sketched in Figure 6.1, IGOs operate under the assumed legitimacy of an extended principal–agent model—that they are working with the consent of democratically elected governments and therefore are indirectly democratic.[27] In theory, the governed could exercise their power over IGOs by exerting representative accountability over their elected governments who, in turn, voice their will to the global governance mechanisms. As long as each agent (the state and the global governance mechanism) reflects the preferences of the principal (the elected officials and the state, respectively), they remain in legitimate power.[28]

Even under the best conditions in state bureaucracies, however, principal–agent relationships are not without their problems and constraints, including information asymmetries, hidden actions, shirking,

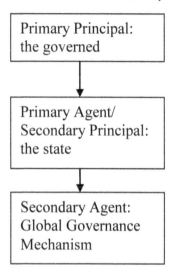

Figure 6.1 Principal–agent relationships of global governance

Madison's dilemma, and multiple principals.[29] The networked forms of governance in which international NGOs operate are even more complex. Many scholars have started their examination of NGO accountability with representative theory or PA theory, only to be quickly discouraged by their inability to explain these NGO complexities.[30] For one, NGOs are not elected, and therefore cannot be unelected as in representative accountability. Also, since NGOs serve as both agent and structure—both principal and agent in PA theory—their cobweb of relationships makes agency theory less instructive.[31]

L. David Brown offers three critiques of representative and PA theory.[32] First, as in representative accountability, PA theory assumes clearly defined, two-party, hierarchical relationships. Second, representative and PA theories assume that expectations and goals of relationships are clearly defined from the earliest stages of the network through clear contracts and mandates. Third, these theories also assume that all actors involved have, from the beginning of the relationship, the capacity needed to fulfill the responsibilities of the network. In practice, however, these three criteria rarely, if ever, are present for NGOs. As bridges between the state and civil society, NGOs normally operate within multiparty initiatives where there is no single, clear line between principal and agent, and no clear division of labor among actors.[33] These factors, combined with changing roles, responsibilities, and goals, make accountability relationships difficult to define *ex ante*. As DeMars and Dijkzeul emphasize in the Introduction, various NGO partners attach a wide range of salient and latent agendas to their partnerships, some of which are not publicly acknowledged. Last, actors in multiparty initiatives very often do not have the needed capacity at the beginning of the initiative, and the capacities required change over the life of the network, demanding learning throughout.

Explaining NGO accountability with traditional theory

While representative and principal–agent accountability cannot capture the complexity of NGO relationships, their scholarly proponents help to operationalize accountability with three driving questions:

Accountability for what?

Robert Behn operationalizes principal–agent relationships with a three-part typology: accountability for finances, fairness and performance. While accountability for finances and fairness involves organizational processes, accountability for performance is solely based on outcomes.[34] This is the crux of Behn's Accountability Dilemma: the constraints put on a process for financial or fairness accountability could adversely affect the efficiency of the policy to produce desired outcomes. He proffers that while traditional public management has had an accountability bias for process over product, NPM has overturned this bias to focus more on outcomes than processes. In contrast to Grant and Keohane,[35] Behn argues that accountability mechanisms not only punish past wrongdoing, but also (by creating standards to which actors must adhere) deter future wrongdoing. Behn's *ex post* and *ex ante* approach agrees with more empirical and NGO-specific discussions and views on accountability, that past performance and sanctions will inform future decisions.

Accountability to whom?

Perhaps the most comprehensive traditional discussion of the accountability of NGOs in policy networks is the work of Robert Keohane with various co-authors,[36] who together promote eight types of accountability:

1 Electoral: where the governors are controlled by those who elected them.

2   Hierarchical: where principals within a bureaucracy can remove non-elected agents from office, and constrain or reward their actions.
3   Supervisory: a form of hierarchical accountability relationship but between organizations in a network rather than individuals within a bureaucracy.
4   Fiscal: where funding agencies can demand reports from, and ultimately sanction, the agencies they fund.
5   Legal: which includes judicial or quasi-judicial processes (e.g., lawsuits, fines, or imprisonment).
6   Reputational: where the sanctions of embarrassment and damage to reputation of the actor are produced, usually through publicity.
7   Market: where the information that markets provide creates rewards and punishments, impacting the business's fiscal security.
8   Peer: includes mutual evaluation of organizations by their counterparts.

Accountability how?

While Behn and Keohane offer insights regarding to whom and for what one must be accountable, Koppell adds a third question to the discussion on accountability: How?[37] He argues that scholars and practitioners often conflate "control" and "accountability." While direct control is one way to ensure that an actor is accountable, it is only one manner of doing so.

These three sets of questions are summarized in Table 6.1. This synthetic framework understands that accountability is not a binary attribute. An actor is always accountable to *someone*, for *something* and in a specific *manner*. The more accurate and helpful question is "Are the NGOs balancing their accountability demands effectively?"[38] The non-traditional forms of accountability highlighted in the next section speak to this question directly.

Beyond traditional theories of accountability

In an effort to more clearly define and explain NGO relationships as they appear in the empirical data, scholars and practitioners have turned to literatures outside of the traditional IR field. This section will highlight and evaluate the more salient theories for NGO accountability, including stakeholder theory, contingency-based, rights-based, and mutual accountabilities.

That NGOs often take on the task of holding corporations accountable makes the stakeholder approach to accountability—one born of the management field and preferred by NGO practitioners—an interesting paradigm. Like NGO accountability, corporate accountability is

168 *Crosscutting evidence: history, region, accountability*

Table 6.1 Three questions of accountability

To whom?	For what?	How? Meaning what?
• Electorate (principal) • Non-electorate governed (principals) • Supervisory (hierarchy) • Peers (horizontal) • Market	• Finances (process): was the money spent and tracked in the way it was intended? • Fairness (process): Were the rules, laws and regulations for these policy arenas followed? • Performance (outcomes): Did the actor accomplish its mandate?	• Transparency: Did the organization reveal the facts of its performance? • Liability: Did the organization face the consequences of its actions? • Controllability: Did the agent do what the principal desired? • Responsibility: Did the actor follow the rules and/or norms of its network? • Responsiveness: Did the actor fulfill a substantive expectation of its non-principal clients?

Source: Based on Robert D. Behn, *Rethinking Democratic Accountability* (Washington DC: Brookings Institution Press, 2001); Jonathan Koppell, *The Politics of Quasi-Governments: Hybrid Organizations and the Dynamics of Bureaucratic Control* (Cambridge: Cambridge University Press, 2003); Jonathan Koppell, "Pathologies of Accountability: ICANN and the Challenge of 'Multiple Accountabilities Disorder,'" *Public Administration Review* 65, no.1 (2005): 94–108; L. David Brown and Mark H. Moore, "Accountability, Strategy, and International Nongovernmental Organizations," *Nonprofit and Voluntary Sector Quarterly* 30, no. 3 (2001): 569–587. Ruth W. Grant and Robert O. Keohane, "Accountabilty and Abuses of Power in World Politics," *American Political Science Review* 99, no. 1 (2004): 29–43.

difficult because of the multiple stakeholders to whom they could be accountable: owners, creditors, employees, customers, other corporations, and the general public through state institutions.[39] Management literature introduced stakeholder theory in the 1980s. Twenty years later the One World Trust based its Global Accountability Project (GAP analysis) on stakeholder accountability, which rejects the hierarchical relationships of traditional theory and is defined as the right to hold an organization or individual to account granted to any group or individuals (both within the organization and external to it) who can affect or are affected by an organization.[40] GAP sees accountability first and foremost as about engaging with and being responsive to stakeholders, and balancing the demands of various stakeholders with the organization's mission.[41] Like other approaches, GAP starts with a stakeholder analysis and prioritization based on the organization's mission and values, and then establishes a process for incorporating stakeholder accountability in operations.[42] While it may be difficult to answer to a diverse set of stakeholders with potentially conflicting demands, accountability mechanisms cannot be fully understood without acknowledging these diverse stakeholders and what they require for the organization to be accountable.

Most important to the GAP framework is another contribution of management theory: organizational learning. In a nutshell, true organizational learning comes not just from determining the strategic changes needed for an organization, but also challenging the assumptions made in creating that strategy in the first place. It is about seeing the dynamic nature of relationships as part of a larger system. Accountability is foremost an opportunity for organizational learning which must be balanced with external demands.[43] It is a process that occurs not only when something goes wrong, but as a proactive part of the daily operations of the organization. By applying both stakeholder theory and organizational learning concepts to NGO accountability, scholars and practitioners have been able to capture a more accurate view of these complicated and dynamic actors. They point to the importance of examining NGOs both as agent and as structure in networks, and necessitate an interdisciplinary approach to their study.

Contingency-based accountability

Responding to the idea that accountability means different things to different actors and in different contexts, some scholars call for a contingency model of accountability.[44] Stakeholders require different information in different forms in order to satisfy their demands. The type of organization also determines specialized types of accountability.[45] For example, accountability timelines, indicators and processes for short-term emergency relief work are different from long-term poverty-reducing work.[46] Even more basic, an NGO's perception of the problem it is addressing impacts how it defines accountability.[47] Implementing accountability frameworks demands a culturally specific knowledge of stakeholders.[48] A one-size-fits-all approach to accountability is just not practical or desirable for the diversity of NGOs and stakeholders. Contingency approaches to accountability acknowledge this and make context-, actor-, and capacity-specific accountability frameworks a priority. This approach can draw from multiple disciplines, including political science, management and anthropology in determining how

Rights-based accountability

The rights-based approach to accountability acts as a justification for accountability that also reframes the process. While other approaches to the issue answer the questions of for what, to whom and how accountability might be implemented, rights-based approaches ask *why one might strive to be accountable in the first place*. NGOs who endeavor to be accountable often do so in order to please their funders and/or avoid sanctions from other actors. In the rights-based approach, NGOs are encouraged to be accountable to walk the talk of their mission. Since they advocate for rights, NGOs need to be accountable to support their constituency's rights and, "clearly articulate to their supporters and to the public who they are, what their role is, where their support comes from, and to whom they are accountable."[49] This variation on stakeholder theory combines a logic of appropriateness (where NGOs become accountable because of some normative need) with a logic of consequences (where an actor becomes accountable in order to avoid sanctions or achieve its mission),[50] requiring an interdisciplinary approach to accountability to address the NGO's functions as both agent and structure, as well as a transnational, trans-societal bridge.

Mutual accountability

The stakeholder approach is not the only framework for accountability to respond to the multiparty and multidirectional nature of NGO accountability. Brown's discussion of mutual accountability is one of the more developed alternatives to representative and agency models.[51] Unlike traditional stakeholder approaches, mutual accountability does not see relationships solely from the vantage point of one NGO. Rather, it strives to see the entire network of actors simultaneously. Mutual accountability addresses the shortcomings of traditional theories by its focus on multiple parties in undefined relationships with undefined capacities and goals, all of which evolve over time. It is grounded in shared values, goals and in relationships of mutual trust between autonomous actors that are negotiated as a prerequisite for cooperation.[52] An actor could lose valued relationships and social status if it does not respect the process of mutual accountability.

While mutual accountability is a true advancement of accountability theory, it does have its limits. Brown's work is particularly suited for multi-party initiatives or campaigns: networks where, while actors may have different visions or strategies, they generally focus on the same issues. As DeMars in this volume indicates, networks often include conflicting and even invisible actors who may work in opposition to the goal of the campaign or initiative. Without seeking out these conflicting or invisible actors, the process may give the false impression that all stakeholders are reaching this consensus of values and goals. While Brown emphasizes that the first step of mutual accountability—negotiating shared values and visions—may take a long time, it still assumes that shared values and visions are achievable. However, while some organizations are open to reassessing their vision and goals in light of other actors, in other more adversarial networks, merely sharing this information with opposing actors represents an unacceptable vulnerability for many actors—especially those whose safety or existence is at risk. An honest broker may be needed to initiate this process which, even still, could require much of the actor's resources.

Limits of accountability

While the above discussion of various accountability frameworks points to some of their limits, there are other broader limits to the concept. First, as the complexity described above demonstrates, the theory and practice of accountability do not always match. Moreover, accountability paradoxically requires both healthy skepticism and a "supportive moral order" to be effective. This section will highlight two other overarching themes limiting our understanding of NGO accountability: the presumed conditions for accountability and the technical and political aspects of accountability.

Conditions for accountability

The assumed pre-existing conditions for accountability pose a problem for implementation. In order for an actor to be an agent or an object of accountability, the network must exhibit *consistent norms of behavior*.[53] Empirical studies illustrate the difficulty of bringing multiple actors to consensus on norms within a single network. As members of several networks at once, international NGOs often find that notions and mechanisms of accountability that might work in one network are completely different in another network.[54] As stated, practitioners of accountability are legitimated by culture, values, or social strictures. To assume that these cultures, values and social strictures are the same world-over directly contradicts the notion that true accountability is context-specific.[55] However, as DeMars and Dijkzeul emphasize in the Introduction (especially Table I.2), to recognize that NGO accountability is particular to each social context conflicts with the universal normative and causal claims that all NGOs must continually claim to participate in the NGO "game." This dynamic implies that NGOs are incentivized to elude the accountability of particular social contexts.[56]

While accountability is often seen as a means to constrain power, most discussions assume a *minimal level of power* on behalf of the agents of accountability.[57] That is, in order to call someone to be accountable, the power disparity between the objects of accountability and the agents of accountability cannot be so great that the objects have no obligation to answer the call. This often causes a skewed approach to accountability where the powerful control the objects (e.g., funders requiring more accountability of NGOs or governments) and the powerless constituents of the objects (e.g., the poor, the disenfranchised) do not have enough power to require accountability on their own and are at the mercy of the objects to respond to their requests.[58] Unless the NGO deliberately designates their primary accountability relationship to their constituents, those constituents could be left out of accountability discussions.

The last limiting prerequisite of accountability is *capacity*. One of the most prevalent complaints of NGOs is that acquiring information for evaluation and accountability can refocus already limited time and resources away from their mission. Thus accountability mechanisms are often the last to be entered into a budget and the first to be cut in light of budget constraints.[59] The different spheres of influence in which an international NGO operates—global, national and multiple local arenas—require different types of capacity for both operations and accountability.[60] Without the proper capacity or accountability mechanisms that contribute to their mission, being accountable could be seen as working against organizational productivity.

Some scholars assert that allowing all those affected by an actor's policy to hold them accountable could conceivably create enough veto points to halt the policy process altogether, rendering the actor ineffective.[61] Koppell demonstrates how by trying to be too accountable—accountable to too many stakeholders about too many issues and in ways the stakeholders have yet to define or agree upon—the object of accountability can become paralyzed in what he calls Multiple Accountabilities Disorder (MAD).[62] My previous work illustrates that actors can overcome MAD by investing in creating the administrative, political, and technical capacities needed to operate in international,

national, and local spheres of influence, and the bridging capacity needed to negotiate between spheres.[63] With these capacities, an NGO can balance participation with achieving its mission.

Technical approaches to a political issue

In addition to limiting preconditions of accountability, operationalizing the concept suffers from using technocratic approaches to what is often (if not always) a political issue. Alnoor Ebrahim calls this set of oversights "myopias."[64]

The first myopia is to emphasize short-term goals and evaluations rather than long-term social change, a result of the norm of not valuing the learning from failed projects and the power imbalance that focuses accountability to funders rather than constituents, clients or mission.[65] This myopia can be traced back to the 1980s when the multilateral development banks began using indicators and logical framework analysis to respond to the calls for accountability, placing the focus on quantifiable and identifiable results at the center of the accountability movement and its associated certification and ratings schemes. While easy to understand, these frameworks cannot capture the diversity of understandings and implementation mechanisms from village to global levels and are not helpful in measuring long-term and immeasurable outcomes like empowerment.[66] This indicator movement has the potential to (1) endanger NGO programs by highlighting (in the name of transparency) its strategic efforts, thus giving opposing groups munitions and targets for reducing the NGO's impact; and (2) encourage abandoning the projects altogether, due to lack of ability to "prove" success to funders due to its inability to quantify long-term impact.[67]

The second myopia concerns participatory processes that are more about the demonstration of participation than about sharing procedural power. While some scholars recommend that actors move from a "logic of compliance" (where an actor is accountable for fear of sanction) toward a "logic of participation" (where an actor is accountable as a result of incorporating stakeholders' voices into their work),[68] participation does not necessarily mean influence. In reality, these processes could amplify the voices of those with more influence while those with less remain silenced.[69] With this myopia, actors go through the motions of participation without any true incorporation of stakeholders' needs and desires into the programmatic agenda.

DeMars (in this volume) adds a third myopia to Ebrahim's list: only engaging actors who are obvious and mutually recognized stakeholders in one's work. It is a facile assumption that the important stakeholders are exclusively those that openly show an interest in network participation. Hidden stakeholders can do great damage to an NGO's work, either acutely by their late involvement and introduction of new NGO accountability demands, or chronically by impairing NGO accountability efforts by setting the policy agenda and creating competing norms for the network.[70] Alternatively, hidden actors like foreign security or intelligence agencies may be instrumental in achieving the network's goals, but only if they remain behind the scenes because their public exposure could delegitimize the entire network.

To avoid these myopias, efforts at NGO accountability must both incorporate a system of relationships beyond the hierarchical, and also focus on long-term impacts.[71] Some scholars (especially those concentrating on rights-based accountability) pose a new question of accountability to counter myopias: Why accountability? or: For what purpose? By asking this question, accountability mechanisms are no longer short-term, or concentrated on controlling relationships. Rather, they begin to focus on how to fulfill the mission of the organization. Instead of performing evaluations and participatory processes in addition to the mission, these processes work towards the mission, under the assumption that dissenting voices will eventually be heard.[72] This approach may cause difficulty for the object of accountability, but should bring about a more authentic legitimacy. Even better, incorporating dissenting voices from the beginning of a process could preempt a stakeholder detour from the mission, allowing the NGOs to achieve more over time.[73]

Ebrahim offers several propositions to overcome these shortcomings based on both empirical data and theoretical background. In a nutshell, he suggests that organizations make their mission their first priority and organizational learning their central means to achieve that mission. By doing this, staff will see accountability and evaluation as central to their work, instead of as an additional burden detracting from their work. They will embrace error as a learning opportunity and create capacity to respond to uncertainty.[74] This affirms the importance of an interdisciplinary approach to accountability—one that incorporates IR and other disciplines for the interactions between actors, as well as organizational theory to explain what pushes actors to balance the calls for accountability between actors.

NGO accountability and the New Life Children's Refuge in Haiti

The case of the New Life Children's Refuge (NLCR)—a young, small international NGO—illustrates how different approaches to accountability can both illuminate new facets of NGO relationships, and also fall short of full descriptions or explanations of their accountability.

The NLCR was legally formed in November 2009 to work in Haiti and the Dominican Republic with the mission "to provide a loving Christian environment for abandoned and unwanted children."[75] The devastating earthquake of 12 January 2010, with its high mortality rate, increased the number of Haitian orphans by an estimated 20,000 over the already staggering number of 300,000.[76] Reflecting a heightened sense of emergency, NLCR refocused its energies to "rescue Haitian Orphans abandoned on the streets, makeshift hospitals or from collapsed orphanages in Port au Prince and surrounding areas, and bring them to New Life Children's Refuge in Cabarete, Dominican Republic."[77] Drawing on donations and volunteers from her local church and community, the NLCR's founder and executive director, Laura Silsby, put together a rescue mission of ten people and boldly revised the organization's programming "to go now [versus] waiting until the permanent facility is built."[78] Just one week after the earthquake the team of volunteers set out to fly to the Dominican Republic, rent a bus to drive to Port-Au-Prince, then "gather 100 orphans from the streets and collapsed orphanages," and finally return by bus to the Dominican Republic.[79]

With very little experience in the international adoption process or working within the Haitian governmental bureaucracy, Laura Silsby was warned that getting permission to take the children out of the country would be time-consuming and difficult. Both Dominican Republic officials and Haitian orphanage officials warned her not to attempt to transport children without contacting the proper authorities and obtaining official permission.[80] Supporters back in Idaho received reports that Silsby was working with Haitian officials to get the proper paperwork. However, on 29 January 2010, she and the nine other volunteers were arrested while trying to cross the border from Haiti to the Dominican Republic with 33 undocumented Haitian children, ranging from age 2 months to 12 years.[81]

Eight of the ten volunteers who were jailed signed a note saying that they were lied to and had nothing to do with securing any documents necessary for their work.[82] These eight were released from jail in Haiti after some of the parents of the 33 children (all of whom had at least one living parent) testified that they had asked for their children to be taken.[83] While orphanages have become a form of respite for some financially desperate Haitian parents, many of these particular parents had means to care for their children, but were told that NLCR could offer them better educational opportunities.[84]

Kidnapping charges for all ten Americans were dropped, but Silsby remained in Haiti weeks longer awaiting trial on charges of arranging irregular travel. In May 2010 she was found guilty, sentenced to time already served, and returned to the United States. The organization's second-in-command, Charisa Coulter, declared that the volunteers were just Christians who were "obeying God's calling" by going to Haiti and helping its children.[85]

The New Life Children's Refuge example embodies all of the bridging functions this book has introduced:

- Since the Haitian state alone had little capacity to address the issues of its quickly rising population of needy children, the NLCR attempted to act as a bridge between the state and civil society.
- As a bridge between conflict and cooperation, the cooperative voices of their financial supporters and the parents who placed their children in NLCR's care pushed the organization to take more action; conflicting voices point out that the organization had neither the local capacity or understanding to find shelter for these children safely or legally.
- NLCR's singular dedication to its mission—regardless or perhaps because of the lack of structure and process in the Haitian state—illustrates its ability to act as agent of accountability (calling for Haitian society and state to care for these children), and object of accountability (being arrested for not following the norms and laws for orphanages in Haiti).
- Last, and perhaps most pronounced, are NLCR efforts to bridge transnational actors who care for needy children, but without the requisite transnational capacity to do so legally, and outside the norms of international children's advocacy programs.

Analyzing this case study through the different approaches to accountability will give some insight into the approaches themselves. Viewed through a principal–agent lens, advocates for orphans might consider that the orphans themselves would be principals. At times, Silsby appears as either principal or agent. However, the language of the mission and volunteers insists, in effect, that "God's will" is the principal and the NLCR volunteers are acting as God's agents.

Using directional and stakeholder models of accountability opens up the field of actors to whom the organization must be accountable, to a broader collection of international actors, including their funders, the Haitian and Dominican Republic states, agencies and institutions, the orphans and their families, other international orphanages in both

Haiti and the Dominican Republic (as well as the field of international orphanages in general), other Haitian relief NGOs, UN agencies, and other principals whose influence and involvement in the network was hidden. Most hidden to the volunteers seemed to be the Haitian bureaucracy and the norms of international orphanage agencies. While NLCR acted in the interest of the stakeholders they felt mattered most, they eventually had to reconcile with overlooked or "hidden" principals and authorities.

A contingency approach to NLCR's relationships would call for types of accountability appropriate for relief in an intercultural, crisis environment. This might mean that the organization would have worked with other relief organizations in Haiti and the Haitian government to determine the best way to operate quickly and legally. It might mean heeding the advice of other international orphanages about the process of finding children in need. It would mean having an understanding that while the bureaucracy of Haiti was in disarray it still did exist, with processes for orphan protection in place. A contingency-based approach would also have given NLCR staff an understanding of the culturally-specific use of orphanages by Haitian parents for respite or educational purposes without intention of fully divesting their rights as parents. Being more context-oriented might have taken more time than NLCR felt it should spend, but the end result could have meant they could be serving needy children today instead of being distracted by its leadership spending more than three months in jail.

A mutual accountability approach may have been the most challenging for NLCR, since it would build on the contingency approach in order to create a network of actors with shared values, goals and relationships *over time*. NLCR was a young NGO, incorporated just months before the earthquake. Haiti was a country in crisis, trying to recover from an estimated 250,000 deaths and aid over 1 million homeless people.[86] Building mutual accountability would have taken more time than was available to stem the crisis. Therefore, while mutual accountability is a desirable state for long-term relationships, it does not seem plausible for organizations that are new to the network and must quickly deliver some results in order to maintain funding and gain legitimacy. It also seems implausible for relief organizations who might have the capacity and flexibility to act and move from one crisis to another, since these organizations cannot predict where the next crisis will occur and develop the mutual values, goals and relationships required for mutual accountability.

Perhaps a rights-based approach might have helped NLCR the most in its accountability relationships, as it would have required the NLCR to examine not just their role but also their responsibilities to each actor. Since orphanages are advocates for children, they must consider the children's rights before acting. Would trafficking undocumented children work to the children's advantage in the long term? Would placing children with adoptive families (when their own families expect them to return) be in their and their families' interests? The rights-based approach's first requirement (an examination of political context) would have revealed any hidden network actors and given NLCR the bureaucratic and legal understanding to create an orphanage for Haitian children without the predicament they experienced.

This extreme case, in which a severe breakdown of accountability destroyed the NGO itself, points to a larger truth: any NGO that endures over time has successfully managed its accountability challenges to the extent of retaining those partners essential for its survival.

Conclusion

Whether or not one believes they should take on this role, NGOs are providing more and more public goods around the globe.[87] As increasingly powerful players in the public arena, NGOs pose a new challenge for the democratic principle that those who are governed should have a say in their governance. Accountability is a means for closing that democratic gap, as well as a tool for NGOs to become more legitimate providers of public goods. This volume provides a uniquely accurate description of NGOs in the global sphere through its discussion of NGOs as bridges. These bridging roles create distinctive opportunities and challenges to the study of NGO accountability, especially for IR scholars.

Because NGOs act as a bridge between state and civil society, any study of NGO accountability must acknowledge the increasing power of NGOs in international relations and policy arenas. While much IR literature reserves discussion of power and legitimacy to the state, scholars must now apply these concepts to NGOs and discern which IR theories and concepts are helpful in the description and explanation of NGOs and which are not. This bridging function also means that no NGO operates in isolation; they inherently operate within a network of actors with varying degrees of interaction (including instances where some actors remain hidden from the NGO) and varying transparency in their goals for participation. Accountability literature (including IR theory) does not adequately address the issues of NGO networks, the presence of concealed actors and their agendas, and the power relationships they create.

Accountability and legitimacy 179

Because NGOs move between conflict and cooperation, and aim to convert conflict to collaboration, any study of NGO accountability must acknowledge and attempt to capture the dynamic nature of their relationships. Discussions of NGOs must recognize their role as change agents. This change takes place not only within both the networks and material environments in which they work, but also within the NGO itself. As the NGO achieves its goals (or learns from failure), it must adapt its goals and strategies. As actors within the network, political environments, material environments, and social norms change, so too must the NGO. In order for NGOs to be accountable (or for scholars to offer an accurate portrayal of NGO accountability relationships), they must incorporate change into analytical frameworks.

Because NGOs are both agency and structure, any study of accountability must include interdisciplinary approaches in order to capture their multiple roles as object and agent of accountability. An NGO's internal structure, capacity and management affect how it can manage its relationships within the network. These internal attributes are also affected by the NGO's power within the network. With multiple actors in multiple networks and cultures, NGOs and NGO scholars must consider context-specific ideas of accountability in order to respond earnestly to calls for accountability. These context-driven approaches to accountability will also require an interdisciplinary approach (such as anthropological methods to describe the context in which they operate, and organizational literature to explain NGO internal dynamics).

Because NGOs act as transnational and trans-societal bridges, studies of NGO accountability must incorporate more detailed empirical research to move from description to explanation of these complex actors. The idiosyncrasies of NGOs on the global policy stage make applying traditional IR theories a challenge. In order to make these theories more appropriate—or make new theories altogether—to explain NGO relationships, scholars must work with practitioners and scholars of other disciplines to create accurate case studies of NGOs, both as organizations (focusing on their internal workings) and as actors within networks (focusing on their relationships with other actors). Without an iterative process that closes the gap between empirical work and theoretical scholarship, and the related gap between weak NGO accountability on the ground and soaring NGO normative aspirations, our understanding of these growing players in international relations will remain stunted.

All actors are accountable in some way to some actor or another. Portrayals of international NGO accountability must therefore look beyond bilateral relations to incorporate more systemic network views of power and practice. With these bridging functions in mind, the NGO accountability challenge to IR theory will result in scholarship that not only reflects the changing actors on the global stage, but that also pushes scholars to incorporate new fields of study into IR and to innovate new and imaginative theory.

Notes

1 Rush Limbaugh, "How Obama and Democrats Have Politicized the Earthquake in Haiti," Transcript, 18 January 2010 (www.rushlimbaugh.com/daily/2010/01/18/how_obama_and_democrats_have_politicized_the_earthquake_in_haiti).
2 Stephanie Strom, "Haitian Quake Brings More Money and Scrutiny to a Charity," *New York Times*, 4 February 2010.
3 Marc Lacey, "Haiti Charges Americans with Child Abduction," *New York Times*, 4 February 2010.
4 Christine MacDonald, *Green, Inc.: An Environmental Insider Reveals How a Good Cause has Gone Bad* (Guilford, Conn.: The Lyons Press, 2008); David B. Ottaway and Joe Stephens, "Nonprofit Land Bank Amasses Billions," *Washington Post*, 4 May 2003; and Mark Dowie, *Conservation Refugees: The Hundred-Year Conflict between Global Conservation and Native Peoples* (Cambridge, Mass.: MIT Press, 2008).
5 David Bernstein, "Human Rights Watch Goes to Saudi Arabia: Seeking Money to Counterbalance 'Pro-Israel Pressure Groups,'" *Wall Street Journal*, 15 July 2009.
6 Sebastian Strangio and Khouth Sophak Chakrya, "NGO holds alleged link to terrorism: Kuwaiti charity's local operations reignite concerns of extremism," *Phnom Penh Post*, 25 February 2010.
7 Several arguments in this chapter are developed from Cristina M. Balboa, "When Non-governmental Organizations Govern: Accountability in Private Conservation Networks," Ph.D. dissertation in Environmental Governance, Yale University, 2009.
8 Hetty Kovach, Caroline Neligan and Simon Burall, *The Global Accountability Report 1: Power Without Accountability?* (London: One World Trust, 2003) (www.wto.org/english/news_e/news03_e/gar2003_e.pdf); Jan A. Scholte, "Civil Society and Democratically Accountable Global Governance," *Government and Opposition* 39, no. 2 (2004): 211–233; and Miles Kahler and David A. Lake, eds, *Governance in a Global Economy: Political Authority in Transition* (Princeton, N.J.: Princeton University Press, 2003).
9 Sasha Courville, "Understanding NGO-based Social and Environmental Regulatory Systems: Why We Need New Models of Accountability," in *Public Accountability: Designs, Dilemmas and Experiences*, ed. Michael W. Dowdle (Cambridge: Cambridge University Press, 2006), 271–300; Edward Weisband and Alnoor Ebrahim, "Introduction: Forging Global Accountabilities," in *Global Accountabilities: Participation, Pluralism, and Public Ethics*, eds Alnoor Ebrahim and Edward Weisband (Cambridge: Cambridge University Press, 2007), 1–24; and Lisa Jordan, "A Rights-based Approach to Accountability," in *Global Accountabilities*, eds Ebrahim and Wiseband, 151–167.

10 Thorston Benner, Wolfgang H. Reinicke and Jan M. Witte, "Multisectoral Networks in Global Governance: Towards a Pluralistic System of Accountability," *Government and Opposition* 39, no. 2 (2004): 191–210.
11 An actor's power is a function of (1) the size and number of spheres of influence in which it operates, (2) the level of constraint placed on it by other actors, and (3) the concentration of authority. An actor's publicness can be measured by the extent to which it: (1) wields exclusive authority of sanction, (2) pursues the common or public good, and (3) affects the "public" side of the individual. See Jonathan G. S. Koppell, "The Legitimacy–Accountability Connection and Transnational Governance Organization," Paper presented at the Annual Conference of the American Political Science Association, Washington, DC, 1–4 September 2005; and Jonathan G. S. Koppell, *World Rule: Accountability, Legitimacy, and the Design of Global Governance* (Chicago, Ill.: University of Chicago Press, 2010).
12 Ngaire Woods, "Multilateralism and building stronger international institutions," in *Global Accountabilities*, eds Ebrahim and Weisband, 27–44; Monica Blagescu, Lucy de Las Casas and Robert Lloyd, *Pathways to Accountability: The GAP Framework* (London: One World Trust, 2005); and Brijesh Nalinakumari and Richard MacLean, "NGOs: A Primer on the Evolution of the Organizations That Are Setting the Next Generation of 'Regulations,'" *Environmental Quality Management* 14, no. 4 (2005): 1–21.
13 Mark C. Suchman, "Managing Legitimacy: Strategic and Institutional Approaches," *Academy of Management Review* 20, no. 3 (1995): 574.
14 Robert D. Behn, *Rethinking Democratic Accountability* (Washington, DC: Brookings Institution Press, 2001); Blagescu, de Las Casas, and Lloyd, *Pathways to Accountability*; Coralie Bryant, "Evaluation and Accountability in Emergency Relief," in *Global Accountabilities*, eds Ebrahim and Weisband, 168–192; Lisa Jordan, "Political Responsability in Transnational NGO Advocacy," *World Development* 28, no. 12 (2000): 2051–2065; Robert O. Keohane and Joseph S. Nye, "Redefining Accountability for Global Governance," in *Governance in a Global Economy: Political Authority in Transition*, eds Miles Kahler and David A. Lake (Princeton, N.J.: Princeton University Press, 2003), 386–411; Kovach et al., *The Global Accountability Report 1*; Jonathan Koppell, *The Politics of Quasi-Governments: Hybrid Organizations and the Dynamics of Bureaucratic Control* (Cambridge: Cambridge University Press, 2003); Jonathan Koppell, "Pathologies of Accountability: ICANN and the Challenge of 'Multiple Accountabilities Disorder,'" *Public Administration Review* 65, no. 1 (2005): 94–108; and L. David Brown and Mark H. Moore, "Accountability, Strategy, and International Nongovernmental Organizations," *Nonprofit and Voluntary Sector Quarterly* 30, no. 3 (2001): 569–587.
15 Koppell, "The Legitimacy-Accountability Connection."
16 Paul Wapner, "Governance in Global Civil Society," in *Global Governance: Drawing Insights from the Environmental Experience*, ed. Oran Young (Cambridge, Mass.: MIT Press, 1997), 65–84.
17 Weisband and Ebrahim, "Introduction: Forging Global Accountabilities," 1–24; and Alnoor Ebrahim, "Toward a Reflective Accountability in NGOs," in *Global Accountabilities*, eds Ebrahim and Weisband, 193–224.
18 Elizabeth Bloodgood, this volume.

19 Kahler and Lake, *Governance in a Global Economy*; and Matthias Koenig-Archibugi, "Transnational Corporations and Public Accountability," *Government and Opposition* 39, no. 2 (2004): 234–259.
20 Alnoor Ebrahim, "Making Sense of Accountability: Conceptual Perspectives for Northern and Southern Nonprofits," *Nonprofit Management and Leadership* 14, no. 2 (2003): 191–212; Weisband and Ebrahim, "Introduction: Forging Global Accountabilities," 1–24; Anne Marie Goetz and Rob Jenkins, "Citizen Activism and Public Accountability: Lessons from Case Studies in India," in *Global Accountabilities*, eds Ebrahim and Weisband, 65–86; Nalinakumari and MacLean, "NGOs: A Primer on the Evolution of the Organizations That Are Setting the Next Generation of 'Regulations'"; and Blagescu, de Las Casas and Lloyd, *Pathways to Accountability*.
21 David Lewis, "Bringing in Society, Culture and Politics: Values and Accountability in a Bangladeshi NGO," in *Global Accountabilities*, eds Ebrahim and Weisband, 131–148.
22 Scholte, "Civil Society and Democratically Accountable Global Governance," 211–233.
23 David Held and Matthias Koenig-Archibugi, "Introduction," *Government and Opposition* 39, no. 2 (2004): 125–131.
24 Behn, *Rethinking Democratic Accountability*.
25 Ibid.; and L. David Brown, "Multiparty Social Action and Mutual Accountability," in *Global Accountabilities*, eds Ebrahim and Weisband, 89–111.
26 David Held, "Democratic Accountability and Political Effectiveness from a Cosmopolitan Perspective," *Government and Opposition* 39, no. 2 (2004): 364–391; and Michael Mason, *The New Accountability: Environmental Responsibility across Borders* (London: Earthscan, 2005).
27 Keohane and Nye, "Redefining Accountability for Global Governance," 386–411.
28 Held and Koenig-Archibugi, "Introduction," 125–131.
29 D. Roderick Kiewiet and Matthew D. McCubbins, *The Logic of Delegation: Congressional Parties and the Appropriations Process* (Chicago, Ill.: University of Chicago Press, 1991), 22–39; and Terry M. Moe, "The New Economics of Organization," *American Journal of Political Science* 28, no. 4 (1984): 739–777.
30 The use of voluntary regulation to form accountability "clubs" is a recent advancement to principal-agent theory. Club membership signals to the NGO's various principals that it is working to address multiple demands by adhering to club standards, thus reducing the need for multiple monitoring and evaluation efforts and offering an alternative to detailed "contracts" between multiple principals and the NGO. See Mary Kay Gugerty and Aseem Prakash, eds, *Voluntary Regulation of NGOs and Nonprofits: An Accountability Club Framework* (Cambridge: Cambridge University Press, 2010).
31 Ebrahim, "Toward a Reflective Accountability in NGOs," 193–224.
32 Brown, "Multiparty Social Action and Mutual Accountability," 89–111.
33 Held, "Democratic Accountability," 364–391; and Held and Koenig-Archibugi, "Introduction," 125–131.
34 Behn, *Rethinking Democratic Accountability*.
35 Ruth W. Grant and Robert O. Keohane, "Accountabilty and Abuses of Power in World Politics," *American Political Science Review* 99, no. 1 (2004): 29–43.

36 Ibid.; and Keohane and Nye, "Redefining Accountability for Global Governance," 386–411.
37 Koppell, *The Politics of Quasi-Governments*.
38 Balboa, "When Non-governmental Organizations Govern."
39 Koenig-Archibugi, "Transnational Corporations and Public Accountability," 234–259; and Lewis, "Bringing in Society, Culture and Politics," 131–148.
40 Kovach et al., *The Global Accountability Report 1*; and Weisband and Ebrahim, "Introduction: Forging Global Accountabilities," 1–24.
41 Blagescu et al., *Pathways to Accountability*.
42 Hugo Slim, "By What Authority? The Legitimacy and Accountability of Non-governmental Organizations," Paper Presented to the International Council on Human Rights, Geneva, Switzerland, 10–12 January 2002.
43 Peter M. Senge, *The Fifth Discipline: The Art and Practice of the Learning Organization* (New York: Doubleday Currency 1990); Lewis, "Bringing in Society, Culture and Politics," 131–148; Blagescu et al., *Pathways to Accountability*; Alnoor Ebrahim, *NGOs and Organizational Change: Discourse, Reporting, and Learning* (Cambridge: Cambridge University Press, 2003); and Chris Argyris, *Reasons and Rationalizations: The Limits to Organizational Knowledge* (Oxford: Oxford University Press, 2004).
44 Bryant, "Evaluation and Accountability in Emergency Relief," 168–192; Maryam Zarnegar Deloffre, "Doing Good: Social Accountability in Humanitarianism," Ph.D. dissertation, George Washington University, 2011; and Derick W. Brinkerhoff, "Taking Account of Accountability: A Conceptual Overview and Strategic Options," Draft Report to U.S. Agency for International Development, Center for Democracy and Governance, Implementing Policy Change Project, Phase 2, Abt Associates (Washington, DC: 2001).
45 Brown and Moore, "Accountability, Strategy, and International Non-governmental Organizations," 569–587.
46 Ebrahim, "Toward a Reflective Accountability in NGOs," 193–224.
47 Deloffre, "Doing Good: Social Accountability in Humanitarianism."
48 Lewis, "Bringing in Society, Culture and Politics," 131–148.
49 Jordan, "A Rights-based Approach to Accountability," 156–7.
50 James G. March and Johan P. Olsen, "The Institutional Dynamics of International Political Orders," *International Organization* 52, issue 4 (1998): 943–69; and Balboa, "When Non-governmental Organizations Govern."
51 Brown, "Multiparty Social Action and Mutual Accountability," 89–111.
52 Margaret Henderson, Gordon P. Whitaker and Lydian Altman-Sauer, "Establishing Mutual Accountability in Nonprofit-Government Relationships," *Popular Government* 69, no. 1 (2003): 18–29.
53 Weisband and Ebrahim, "Introduction: Forging Global Accountabilities," 1–24.
54 Edward Weisband, "Conclusion: Prolegomena to a Postmodern Public Ethics: Images of Accountability in Global Frames," in *Global Accountabilities*, eds Ebrahim and Weisband, 307–339.
55 Benner et al., "Multisectoral Networks in Global Governance," 191–210.
56 Cristina M. Balboa, "How Successful Transnational Nongovernmental Organizations Set Themselves Up for Failure on the Ground," *World Development* 54 (2014): 273–287.

57 Weisband and Ebrahim, "Introduction: Forging Global Accountabilities," 1–24; and Woods, "Multilateralism and Building Stronger International Institutions," 27–44.
58 Jordan, "A Rights-based Approach to Accountability," 151–167; and Blagescu et al., *Pathways to Accountability*.
59 Bryant, "Evaluation and Accountability in Emergency Relief," 168–192; and Kovach et al., *The Global Accountability Report 1*.
60 Balboa, "When Non-governmental Organizations Govern."
61 Keohane and Nye, "Redefining Accountability for Global Governance," 386–411; and Woods, "Multilateralism and Building Stronger International Institututions," 27–44.
62 Koppell, "Pathologies of Accountability," 94–108.
63 Balboa, "How Successful Transnational Nongovernmental Organizations Set Themselves Up for Failure on the Ground," 273–287.
64 Ebrahim, "Toward a Reflective Accountability in NGOs," 193–224.
65 Hans Peter Schmitz, Paloma Raggo and Tosca Bruno-van Vijfeijken, "Accountability of Transnational NGOs: Aspirations vs. Practice," *Nonprofit and Voluntary Sector Quarterly* 41, no. 6 (2012): 1175–1194.
66 Jordan, "A Rights-based Approach to Accountability," 151–167; Alan Fowler, *Striking a Balance: A Guide to Enhancing the Effectiveness of Non-Governmental Organisations in International Development* (London: Earthscan, 1997); and Lewis, "Bringing in Society, Culture and Politics," 131–148.
67 Bryant, "Evaluation and Accountability in Emergency Relief," 168–192.
68 Weisband and Ebrahim, "Introduction: Forging Global Accountabilities," 1–24.
69 Woods, "Multilateralism and Building Stronger International Institutions," 27–44.
70 Balboa, "When Non-governmental Organizations Govern."
71 Ebrahim, "Toward a Reflective Accountability in NGOs," 193–224.
72 Bryant, "Evaluation and Accountability in Emergency Relief," 168–192.
73 Balboa, "When Non-governmental Organizations Govern."
74 Ebrahim, *NGOs and Organizational Change*.
75 Katy Moeller, "Grand Ambitions: Laura Silsby Has Tackled Life with Faith in God and Herself," *Idaho Statesman*, 13 February 2010.
76 Audrey Barrick, "U.S. Christian Testifies in Haitian Court," *Christian Post*, 14 May 2010; and Bethanne Stewart and Katy Moeller, "Laura Silsby has arrived back in Idaho from Haiti," *Idaho Statesman*, 18 May 2010.
77 New Life Children's Refuge, *New Life Children's Refuge: Haitian Orphan Rescue Mission* (www.esbctwinfalls.com/clientimages/24453/pdffiles/haiti/nlcrhaitianorphanrescuemission.pdf).
78 Ibid.
79 Ibid.
80 Moeller, "Grand Ambitions."
81 Barrick, "U.S. Christian Testifies in Haitian Court."
82 Marc Lacey and Ian Urbina, "Americans Held in Haiti Are Divided Over Leader," *New York Times*, 8 February 2010.
83 Simon Romero and Ian Urbina, "Judge Releases Eight Americans Jailed in Haiti," *New York Times*, 18 February 2010.
84 Ginger Thompson and Shaila Dewan, "Parents Tell of Children They Entrusted to Detained Americans," *New York Times*, 3 February 2010; and

Ginger Thompson, "Bleak Portrait of Haiti Orphanages Raises Fears," *New York Times*, 7 February 2010.
85 Barrick, "U.S. Christian Testifies in Haitian Court."
86 Ibid.
87 Balboa, "When Nongovernmental Organizations Govern"; and Jessica F. Green, *Rethinking Private Authority: Agents and Entrepreneurs in Global Environmental Governance* (Princeton, N.J.: Princeton University Press, 2013).

Part IV
Case evidence
NGOs and networks

7 Theoretical and practical implications of public–private partnerships for labor rights advocacy

Shareen Hertel[1]

- Definitional issues
- The contemporary context
- Exploring the paradoxes of PPPs
- The challenges of governance
- Conclusion

On 24 April 2013, an eight-story building near Dhaka, Bangladesh collapsed, killing more than 1,100 garment workers.[2] The deadliest clothing factory disaster in history has ignited far reaching financial and reputational consequences for apparel companies in Bangladesh and globally, dramatizing the need for transnational institutions to create bridges of responsibility between workers, corporations and consumers.[3]

In their introduction, DeMars and Dijkzeul argue that standard liberal institutionalist conceptions of institutions and cooperation are "far too narrow and static to encompass the complex bridging institutionalism of nongovernmental organizations." Non-governmental organizations (NGOs) *anchor* their work in the act of *bridging* divides, and in doing so they "generate myriad transnational encounters where *power* is at play." The "most important activity" that NGOs carry out, they argue, "is not making or enforcement of rules" but instead their "imperative to affiliate with far flung societal and political partners."[4]

Yet an important sub-set of NGOs focuses their efforts explicitly on rule-making, while at the same time engaging in the bridging activity that the contributors to this volume so richly illustrate across a range of cases. This chapter focuses on groups involved in such rule-making activities, specifically in relation to the protection and promotion of labor rights. NGOs involved in rule-making on labor rights share a willingness to work astride a series of divides: a divide separating the for-profit and non-profit sectors; another separating governmental and non-governmental entities; and yet another separating the production of goods with "public" characteristics (such as environmental protection or public health, which all enjoy in common without reducing utility for another) from the production of private goods (such as consumer products).

Labor rights NGOs straddle these numerous divides because the problems they seek to address are intrinsically multidimensional. They craft their missions and organizational structures distinctly. Some groups leave the NGO sector entirely, forgoing the traditional 501(c)(3) non-profit tax status under US law in order to be able to gain revenue from the promotion of strategies to enhance corporate responsibility.[5] Others have hybrid forms of organizing that defy traditional categorization, such as labor unions involved in "social movement unionism"—a form of grassroots organizing involving dues-paying members alongside community residents[6]—or the creation of "worker centers," which function as nodes of organizing and community service provision.[7]

One common trend among labor rights NGOs is the emergence of public–private partnerships (PPPs), defined here as relationships that groups in the non-governmental/nonprofit sector establish with groups in the private, for-profit sector in the interest of promoting labor rights. Most such relationships are collegial, although some evolve only after pitched confrontation. This chapter explains the contemporary context in which labor rights PPPs have arisen, explores the domains in which they are prevalent, and analyzes several of the governance challenges typical of rule-making arrangements of this type. It does so with the intent of demonstrating how a fuller engagement with NGOs enriches IR theory—not only by deepening the analysis of power intrinsic to realism and liberal institutionalism, but also by illustrating the role of NGOs as brokers of new normative understandings that may alter concrete policy outcomes, in the vein of constructivist theory.

The bridging activity carried out by NGOs in the labor rights arena challenges not only our empirical categorizations but also central theoretical frameworks in both International Relations (IR) and Comparative Politics theory, which tend to arrogate NGOs to the highly normative space occupied by altruistic "norms entrepreneurs."[8] The willingness of NGOs to engage in PPPs on labor rights also challenges our notions of how power is generated and transacted within networks. At present, labor rights PPPs generally fail to transform fundamentally the system of production they seek to redress; some risk being used instrumentally by business for reputational reasons. Yet they are integral to a dynamic new form of rule-making in international relations and are an increasingly common mechanism of corporate governance that merits close attention.

Labor rights advocacy 191

It is precisely this type of unconventional NGO-driven interaction that this volume invites us to explore as we seek to challenge more traditional IR theory through a rigorous encounter with NGOs. Here as elsewhere in this volume, we find that practice is once again outstripping theory as it relates to NGOs. This chapter thus aims to situate NGOs involved in public–private partnerships on labor rights within the book's broader endeavor of challenging conventional interpretations of international relations.

Definitional issues

Marco Schaferhoff, Sabine Campe and Christopher Kaan have recently written a masterful survey of the IR literature on what they term "public–private partnerships." They define PPPs as "institutionalized transboundary interactions between public and private actors, which aim at the provision of collective goods."[9] They then outline a research agenda for scholarship on PPPs, calling specifically for more research on the conditions under which partnerships are "effective and legitimate governance tools,"[10] as well as research on situations under which they fail[11] or present negative unintended side effects.[12]

This chapter takes up their call for more research on PPPs. I do so mindful of the benefits as well as risks inherent in this new form of partnership. I also push beyond the definition of PPPs presented by Schaferhoff *et al.* because I argue that they focus too narrowly only on PPPs involved in provision of "public goods" (i.e., goods that are non-rival and non-excludable in nature).[13] In so doing, they miss a slice of reality-on-the-ground that we cannot afford to ignore: namely, those NGOs involved in PPPs that focus on the production of private goods (i.e., goods that are excludable and rival), specifically labor rights monitoring. Public goods theory is indeed suited for analyzing the provision of solutions to environmental problems, and a sizeable group of NGOs involved in PPPs focus their energies on rule-making in connection with environmental governance. (There are generalized and non-restrictive benefits to all citizens when companies are restricted from polluting watersheds through inappropriate waste disposal, for example, or when they have incentives to reduce environmentally harmful waste creation in product manufacturing or packaging.)

But labor rights complicate the streamlined definition of PPPs laid out by Schaferhoff *et al.* because PPPs involved in rule-setting on labor rights have a hybrid character: they engage in activities with joint benefits to the public sector (i.e., government and members of civil society, more generally) and to the private sector (i.e., the for-profit sector). Labor rights PPPs thus better fit the subcategory of "joint-product" or "club" goods because they generate uneven benefits to participating companies and have some exclusionary characteristics.[14] The reputational benefits that accrue to individual corporations from participation in voluntary labor rights PPPs are indeed rival. In the marketplace, consumer and investor perceptions of corporate reputation are explicitly competitively based. Companies involved in voluntary labor rights monitoring initiatives seek to "out-perform" one another in terms of social responsibility in the interest of increasing market share. Labor rights monitoring thus enhances corporate reputation as much if not more so than it enhances the welfare of actual workers or their societies, more broadly.

Similarly, the benefits to consumers of being able to consume "sweatshop-free" garments may seem on the surface to be non-rival (i.e., if we raise labor standards in a market-based system of production and consumption, the good becomes available to any consumer with the resources to purchase it). But even this type of arrangement creates the potential for some market stratification by income and hence, is not as truly "public" as is enhanced corporate environmental regulation through PPPs. Moreover, current labor rights monitoring programs have inherently restrictive characteristics. For example, a labor rights monitoring program for producers of logo-bearing apparel sold by colleges and universities, such as the Fair Labor Association (FLA) or the Worker Rights Consortium (WRC), naturally excludes from its monitoring those producers which are not making products for the collegiate market.[15]

The hybrid character and practice of labor rights PPPs thus complicates Schaferhoff *et al.*'s work—and also usefully complicates DeMars and Dijkzeul's depiction of the anchoring practices of NGOs as "private actors" that "address public purposes." NGOs involved in labor rights monitoring can step in to fill a vacuum left by inefficient state regulation of workers' rights and labor standards. Or they can help create a competitive advantage for companies which are willing to engage in voluntary monitoring initiatives that go "above and beyond" the existing minimum floor of official government labor regulation. Or they may engage in both types of bridging simultaneously or sequentially. They do so in response to the varied challenges they face in an increasingly complex policy context.

The contemporary context

One of the overarching features of contemporary labor rights regulation is its heterogeneity. Labor rights are officially regulated at varying levels: national, regional, and international. There is a wide range of national regulations covering multiple aspects of workers' rights and labor standards (e.g., wages, working hours, health and safety, freedom of association and collective bargaining, etc.). But national regulations differ significantly by country in terms of scope and content, and they can vary within countries by geographic sub-region or industry sector.

Regional mechanisms exist for regulating labor rights as well. One example is the North American Agreement on Labor Cooperation (NAALC)—colloquially referred to as the "labor side accord" to the North American Free Trade Agreement. The European Union's Community Charter of Fundamental Social Rights of Workers—colloquially referred to as the European "social charter"—is another. But not all regions of the world have such agreements, and their impact in policy terms is highly debated. At the international level, the mandate of the World Trade Organization (WTO) does not allow for the explicit integration of labor rights within global trade rules,[16] and the global labor standards promulgated by the International Labour Organization (ILO) are difficult to enforce. Individual states ratify ILO conventions and in so doing, agree to uphold these principles through robust enforcement of national law. But if they fall short, the ILO has limited sanctioning powers at its disposal.[17]

As a consequence not only of the heterogeneity of "official" (i.e., state-led) mechanisms but also of concerns over their effectiveness, there has been an increasing trend over the decade toward "voluntary" enforcement of labor standards through PPPs.[18] Many voluntary initiatives are sector-specific. Examples include the above-referenced standards developed by the FLA and WRC for monitoring labor rights in collegiate apparel manufacturing; or soccer ball production standards aimed at eliminating the use of child labor in that sector, developed by the International Federation of Football Associations (FIFA).[19] Other voluntary initiatives involve more broadly-based management systems audit approaches, such as those pioneered by the International Standards Organization (ISO) through its ISO 9000 quality standard and ISO 14000 environmental standard as well as the more recent SA8000 human rights auditing standard developed by Social Accountability International.[20]

In part, as noted earlier, the trend toward voluntary standards stems from a concern on the part of corporations that bottom line profits can be harmed by public relations scandals related to labor rights problems—particularly in a media environment in which problems in factories thousands of miles away become the evening feature news of potential consumers who heretofore would have remained unaware of such situations. Private corporations have thus been willing to enter into labor rights PPPs with NGOs because they wager that the risk of not doing so outweighs the cost.[21]

Exploring the paradoxes of PPPs

But why do NGOs engage in PPPs? In part, they do so because of what the literature has long recognized as the principled interest the staff and supporters of NGOs have in creating a "better world" through often incremental efforts. Labor rights PPPs often involve people on the NGO side who view their victories in incremental terms—factory by factory, firm by firm, sector by sector, country by country. Paradoxically, however, they are engaged in a struggle against what could be considered a natural product of contemporary capitalism, namely the "race to the bottom" in labor standards as capital seeks out cheaper labor in a highly internationalized global marketplace.[22]

Equally paradoxically, the relationships among groups involved in labor rights PPPs could be argued to reflect the broader structural inequalities of the global economic system: manufacturers or retailers based in industrialized countries negotiate codes that will govern how manufacturing takes place in sites within the developing countries. The lead NGOs involved in brokering PPPs are disproportionately based in industrialized countries. In most cases, workers themselves are not centrally involved in these discussions—unless represented by unions, and unions are not the drivers in many PPPs.[23]

The cynic could thus dismiss the NGOs involved in such collaborative monitoring ventures with corporations as either naïve or complicit in the very problem they are ostensibly seeking to solve. Yet NGOs may be working for transformation from within by invoking a practice that DeMars and Dijkzeul identify as integral to the "anchoring" work NGOs do: namely, by invoking "the claim of circumscribed causality—that the NGO's operations or presence will have no side effects on the target country's politics or society."[24] In the case of PPPs, this claim of circumscribed causality applies less to countries than to companies. Many of the NGOs involved in PPPs push for improved labor standards without threatening the profit-making raison d'être of the company itself.

NGOs have limited leverage over the system-wide imbalances inherent in the current global trade regime that generate the very types of abuse they seek to monitor. Yet those involved in PPPs are willing to engage in an incrementalist approach because they are motivated by the immediacy of worker rights abuses. They cannot wait for the global trade system to be altered; they want to address the problems workers

Labor rights advocacy 195

face now. NGOs choose to engage in PPPs because they can leverage corporate sensitivity to reputational risk. Corporations, in turn, engage in a process of brokering voluntary monitoring standards because of the potential benefits of risk mitigation and the potential gains to corporate reputation.

Let me be clear: PPPs are not a panacea for labor rights enforcement by either states or multilateral institutions such as the ILO. Even the parties involved in contemporary voluntary monitoring arrangements recognize that the inherently imperfect nature of monitoring itself means there is a perennial risk of missing key infractions—and following therefrom, the risk of consumer backlash. Others caution against a "lowest common denominator" effect of setting labor rights standards when a large number of actors within a given economic sector are involved (a classic collective action problem).[25] Still others caution against the unintended consequences of blunt instruments, such as product boycotts, which can ensue once monitoring data become public.[26]

In addition, PPPs are often the target of criticism from activists and scholars based in developing countries who argue that labor standards impose an undue burden on poor countries.[27] The Southern argument runs: Britain, the United States, and other advanced industrial countries developed two centuries ago during the Industrial Revolution without labor standards. Why should developing countries today face such standards? Southern governments argue that calls for labor rights standards in international trade agreements ignore the persistence of structural barriers to trade (e.g., US and European trade subsidies to agriculture, steel and other strategically important sectors), which successive multilateral trade reform efforts have failed to address. And they argue that current institutional frameworks—particularly the WTO, but often PPPs as well—favor the interests of actors based in industrialized countries.

Southerners also argue that calls for labor standards ignore the structural changes in key industries brought about by late twentieth-century technological advances such as the advent of the bar-code inventory, real-time communications and financial technologies, and containerized shipping. All of these factors increase competitive pressures within low-wage manufacturing industries, which can literally "move overnight" if manufacturers find it "uncompetitive" to work in a particular country (read: if workers or governments demand too much of them in terms of labor or environmental standards). Southerners argue as well that calls for labor rights ignore the nature of the contemporary global trade in cheaply produced goods, which undergirds Northern consumer spending.[28] Consumers in the North are always hunting for bargains, and this comes at a human cost. Until

196 *Case evidence: NGOs and networks*

they are willing to pay what labor is worth, the argument runs, exploitation will continue. (Notably, this argument generally glosses over the weakness of existing national legislation on labor rights in many countries and corresponding governmental monitoring systems—which are often stretched to the breaking point in terms of human resources and capacity, and are prone to corruption.)

At a more abstract level, Schaferhoff *et al.* warn that:

> research should keep an eye on the complex performance of PPPs, as the rise of PPPs has led to a more fragmented and uncoordinated global arena, wherein authority is exerted by a multitude of state and nonstate actors. Although PPPs are intended to supplement rather than replace traditional intergovernmental organizations, and although some of them have proven to be effective governance instruments, PPPs may have unintended side effects that could distort (inter-)state policies.[29]

The authors were prescient in this observation, because a central critique of voluntary labor rights monitoring is that it has led to a surfeit of rules which ultimately confuse more than enlighten at the factory level, diminishing willingness to do anything more than observe the minimum, at best, and increasing incentives to shirk.[30]

Factories based in developing countries often act as suppliers of goods produced for export under contract with European, American, and other manufacturers and retailers. Each manufacturer or retailer, in turn, may have its own corporate code of conduct. For developing country suppliers, adherence to a manufacturer or retailer's code of conduct is a condition of doing business. Suppliers often juggle multiple contracts with multiple manufacturers, and thus must adhere to multiple codes, regardless of potential conflicts among the actual requirements of the codes. For example, corporate codes of conduct differ widely on how "child labor" is defined.[31] There are varying benchmarks in international law on child labor: ILO Convention 138 on Minimum Age stipulates three different possible minimum ages—12, 14, and 15 years—which a ratifying country can choose from to set national law, based on the country's own level of development. Particular types of work, in turn, are classified as the "worst forms" of child labor and are entirely prohibited under ILO Convention 182 on Worst Forms of Child Labour (that is, child slavery, illicit work, prostitution/sale of children, and hazardous work).

Corporate codes thus include a confusing array of benchmarks. They can prohibit work at various ages and/or they can prohibit different forms of work. Presented with complex and conflicting regulations, the

Labor rights advocacy 197

factory manager in Bangladesh or Honduras or China will often become confused. The manager will post the codes received from manufacturers and retailers on the factory wall, but they are frequently printed in English and often include little to no clear language on how workers can report violations. In the end, this diminishes a company's willingness to do anything more than observe the minimum floor, at best. At worst, the proliferation of standards increases the incentive for local factories to shirk by rigging monitoring, coaching employees to lie about their ages, or to hide when manufacturers' representatives make factory visits to assess compliance with a code of conduct.

Yet despite all these caveats, labor rights PPPs are here to stay. Data show that an increasing number of US-based business schools are incorporating corporate social responsibility into undergraduate and graduate curricula, and the number of NGOs involved in PPPs in the areas of monitoring, information-sharing, and direct advocacy is growing. Rather than duplicate the existing research on corporate social responsibility,[32] this chapter explores how analysis of labor rights PPPs can enrich our understanding of IR theory by bringing to light new forms of rule-making.

Domains of PPPs

In order to illustrate how NGOs contribute to rule-making in international relations, I have developed an original three-part typology of the domains in which labor rights PPPs exist. In each of them, NGOs are involved in *bridging* among a range of actors who are differentially located in terms of *power* (classically understood in economic terms) and in bridging different normative understandings of "appropriate" conduct in terms of labor rights. Briefly, the three domains can be summarized as follows:

- The first domain involves NGOs in direct rule-making and enforcement of worker rights and labor standards through voluntary monitoring initiatives aimed at enhancing corporate compliance with such norms.
- The second domain involves NGOs in activities aimed at indirectly influencing rule-making through the creation of information on corporate compliance with related standards.
- The third domain involves NGOs in activities aimed at indirectly influencing compliance through protest and other forms of action involving confrontation with companies.

Non-governmental groups involved in the first and second domains are typically involved in relatively collegial interactions with business, whereas groups in the third domain often engage in sharp confrontation. Conflict in the third domain can lead to the forging of working relationships over time, but this is by no means a given.

The first domain involves NGOs in directly crafting with corporations a list of acceptable as well as unacceptable forms of conduct that may take the form of a company-specific "code of conduct," a sector-wide code or industry standard, or an auditing standard. NGOs thus engage in the practice of bridging between workers on the ground and corporate decisionmakers. NGOs in this domain are ever mindful of the difference in power separating workers and management: although unionized workers do have collective forms of representation, NGOs in the first domain can serve as strategic interlocutors with management by helping to forge the corporate codes of conduct or auditing standards that will be used to independently gauge corporate performance on labor rights. This role is even more crucial when workers are not unionized. Bridging between people with vastly differing levels of power is thus integral to the rule-making function of NGOs involved in PPPs in this first domain.

The baselines for different types of action specified within such codes or standards may vary, but certain tendencies are clear. Typically, companies agree to default to the national law of the countries in which they do business or to international labor standards, "whichever is higher." ILO conventions offer a set of internationally negotiated thresholds for conduct, as do major UN conventions such as the UN Convention on the Rights of the Child (CRC), the International Covenant on Economic, Social and Cultural Rights (ICESCR), and the International Covenant on Civil and Political Rights (ICCPR).[33] Corporate codes of conduct often refer to these documents as justifying the specific metrics included in the code. Moreover, the comprehensive UN Guiding Principles on Business and Human Rights developed through a consultative process spearheaded by John G. Ruggie are now routinely invoked by companies as they benchmark their own practices against international norms.[34]

The very fact that companies willingly evoke United Nations treaty language in their codes could be an indication of the belief that the standards will ultimately have little "bite." Indeed, there is a vast literature that demonstrates empirically the lack of state enforcement of UN treaties[35]—so why should it be any different for corporations? This opens up the possibility that the NGOs involved in brokering such arrangements are simply being instrumentalized. As DeMars and Dijkzeul point out: "It is important for scholars to recognize that powerful actors may seek to instrumentalize international organizations in several different and contradictory ways: as agents to accomplish an explicit goal; or as impotent sham agents to create the illusion of effective action; or for some extraneous purpose apart from either success or failure in its explicit goal."[36] NGOs too are vulnerable to such instrumentalization, but they also resist it.

The non-governmental organizations involved in PPPs in the first domain willingly act in a mediating role, engaging companies in the process of developing voluntary rules that often echo international law—regardless of the level of credibility of the latter. The rationale for the NGOs which take part is that in the absence of formal laws at the national level (or because of inadequate enforcement thereof), an imperfect voluntary monitoring standard may be better than the status quo. NGOs in the first domain engage in the practice of rule-making mindful of the gulf between what different parties at the table consider the minimum acceptable standards; their strategy is often to broker a series of relative optimums, forging consensus piecemeal by essentially integrating key aspects of each of the negotiating parties' preferred solutions into the final agreements. As DeMars and Dijkzeul observe, NGOs play a central role within networks in bridging and institutionalizing both cooperation and conflict: "This occurs as a normal and routine, if mostly hidden, part of an NGO through the latent agendas that societal and political partners"—including the corporations involved in PPPs—"attempt to attach to the NGO operations. Successful NGO professionals learn complex scripts to keep their partners in the game by not totally discouraging partners' hopes for attaining latent agendas."[37]

The NGOs involved in crafting and monitoring labor rights through PPPs in the first domain thus walk a fine line between principle and pragmatism. They are willing to partner with corporations in the interest of controlling the most notorious of human rights abuses such as forced disappearances, forced labor, and extrajudicial killings—all of which are violations of clearly defined non-derogable human rights.[38] Examples of PPPs developed to address violations of this type include the Kimberley Process Certification Scheme for diamond production, and the Extractive Industries Transparency Initiative involving companies in the oil, gas and mining industries.[39] NGOs are also willing to engage in PPPs even when the human rights benchmarks at stake are less clearly defined—precisely because they want a stake in specifying acceptable terms of conduct. For example, the issue of "living wage" is fiercely debated among NGOs and businesses, with little agreement on how to set comparable baselines for wages across countries at varying levels of development. Yet NGOs involved in PPPs continue to raise the subject in negotiations of individual corporate codes and industry standards.

The second domain involves NGOs in efforts to influence corporate conduct indirectly, by making data on labor rights performance available to the general public and to members of the investment community, in particular. NGOs involved in PPPs in this domain leverage information as power. They bridge information gaps by relaying information on corporate conduct to the consumers and investors who want to purchase ethically. The primary mission of NGOs involved in PPPs in the second domain is public outreach and education; the indirect effects of their bridging efforts are shifts in corporate performance. The power of NGOs in this second domain is thus rooted in the quality of the information they produce (or relay) about corporate conduct. They risk compromising their ability to influence corporate conduct if the quality of their information is compromised. A central challenge for NGOs involved in this second domain is to maintain a level of objectivity regarding the data they elicit from companies; this is necessary in order for NGOs to preserve the validity of their assessments. Creating a transparent and robust assessment methodology is one step. Carefully controlling the release of corporate performance assessments is another. Targeting the information to maximally influence corporate practice is yet another challenge.

The advent of "socially responsible investing" over the past three decades has led to a growth industry among NGOs involved in producing data on corporate performance in a wide range of areas—including labor rights.[40] NGOs may release data in a range of forms, including: detailed corporate case studies; ordinal performance rankings against standardized benchmarks; and indexed corporate performance. There is a range of rubrics for evaluating corporate performance in relation to substantive norms on labor rights: some involve self-reporting by companies and others involve NGOs ferreting out data on their own and producing reports. There is also a range of indicators associated with corporate social responsibility. Some are produced by for-profit or quasi-private entities (such as money management firms or consulting groups) and are only available for purchase.[41] Others are produced for public consumption, by NGOs dedicated to making their rubrics and rankings widely available at little to no cost to the public. Examples of NGOs which produce publicly available data include the Global Reporting Initiative and the Business and Human Rights Resource Centre,[42] both of which are involved in assessing various aspects of corporate accountability—the former by developing standardized performance indices across a wide range of categories (including but not restricted to labor rights), the latter by compiling news and information on violations as well as examples of corporate best practice on environmental management and human rights, including labor rights.

The third domain involves NGOs that seek to influence corporate conduct through protest and other forms of direct action. This is by far the most radical form of NGO engagement with rule-making. In contrast to the other two domains, NGOs in the third domain aggressively seek to force a change in corporate conduct. Their power comes from their ability to shock the public with revelations of instances in which corporations fail to uphold either national law or voluntary standards governing labor rights. NGOs then use the knowledge they have mobilized concerning such infractions as leverage in order to negotiate higher labor standard-setting. NGOs in the third domain do not typically negotiate the standards themselves; rather, the information they mobilize is strategically relayed to groups in the first domain. In this sense, then, NGOs in the third domain bridge the gap between consumers (i.e., those who want information on corporate conduct for the purpose of purchasing ethically) and companies (i.e., those which may not disclose such information until prompted by the incentives of groups in the second domain). They also bridge gaps between NGOs themselves, which need varying types of information to carry out their functions in distinct domains.

NGOs in the third domain function less as collaborative partners than as members of a "fire brigade."[43] They are the radical flank that makes negotiation possible in the first domain, and that enhances the likelihood of corporations releasing information to ratings groups in the second domain. Far from making claims of "circumscribed causality," NGOs in the third domain challenge both the profit-making imperative of business and the proprietary nature of corporate information. They tend to straddle the North/South divide more easily than their counterparts in the other two domains, because they embrace a wider critique of contemporary forms of capitalism. The International Labor Rights Fund (ILRF) and United Students Against Sweatshops (USAS) are both examples of "fire brigade" types of NGOs based in the United States. Examples from other regions include the Netherlands-based Clean Clothes Campaign (CCC)—a network of over 250 affiliated NGOs worldwide which spurs consumer activism on labor rights issues—and the Third World Network (TWN), a Malaysia-based policy advocacy organization with a long history of activism on multinational corporate conduct.[44]

Another form of NGO activity typical of this domain is shareholder activism, a process through which NGOs mobilize institutions with large holdings of corporate stock to pressure corporations for reforms of key business practices.[45] The annual shareholders meeting is thus an arena for struggle: NGOs work well in advance to influence the content of the proxy voting process. They may also stage the involvement of representatives of institutions, such as religious denominations or unions, which hold considerable amounts of stock in pension and/or investment funds. Or they may invite people adversely affected by the corporation's practices to be present during such meetings.

The US-based Interfaith Center for Corporate Responsibility (ICCR)[46] has been involved in shareholder activism for four decades, and is credited with influencing corporate policy shifts on issues as wide-ranging as divestiture from South Africa during apartheid[47] and the adoption of standards for infant formula marketing in the developing world.[48] Shareholder activism has also been critical to the unionization of manufacturing plants in challenging contexts, such as along the US-Mexico border.[49] For example, institutional investors and religious organizations (such as the American Friends Service Committee) have partnered with Mexican grassroots organizations such as the Comité Fronterizo de Obreras (CFO) to bring the voices of workers into shareholders' meetings in order to advocate for independent unionization of an Alcoa factory in the Mexican state of Coahuila.[50]

This account of three separate domains of labor rights advocacy admittedly builds a stylized typology. There are undoubtedly groups that have moved from one domain to the other over the course of their institutional lifetimes. For example, the Council on Economic Priorities (CEP) was founded in 1969 as a 501(c)(3) nonprofit organization with the mission of rating the corporate responsibility of the Fortune 500 (the largest publicly traded companies in the United States), along with selected companies that are not publicly traded. CEP produced *Shopping for a Better World*, its hallmark guide, which cross-referenced retail brands with their parent companies and offered consumers a report card on individual corporate practices. The goal was to encourage responsible shopping by consumers empowered through enhanced access to information—a classic example of an NGO involved in the second domain.

Over time, however, CEP began to grapple with the need to assess how US companies were managing their supply chains—that is, the contracting of production through suppliers in far-flung locales across the developing world. Though CEP integrated information on codes of conduct into its ratings criteria in the late 1990s, its founders opted to influence corporate conduct by moving out of the second domain and into the first: they created a standard for use in auditing human rights practices in actual factories, to be used by companies in supply chain management. A separate nonprofit entity, Social Accountability International (SAI), was thus created in 1997, which developed the SA8000 standard for assessing human rights in the workplace. SAI now accredits auditors to monitor workplaces against the criteria of the SA8000 standard; other NGOs as well as some private consulting firms have taken up the mantle of doing the actual in-plant monitoring using the rubric of the SA8000 standard, in a classic example of first domain activity. Eventually, the original CEP shuttered its doors, shifting several of its key information-generating projects to other NGOs which work in the second domain.[51]

As this vignette demonstrates, the three domains are illustrative of the range of activities NGOs can undertake to promote and protect labor rights through PPPs. The bridging involved is fluid: NGOs can opt to participate in PPPs focused on direct rule-making and standards enforcement, or they can seek to influence corporate activity indirectly through the creation of information on corporate compliance with related standards. They can also opt for protest and other forms of action involving confrontation with companies, or for some combination of activity across the three domains as the NGO itself evolves over time. The decision to operate in one domain or another depends upon the NGO's mission, political orientation, skills, and strategic opportunities. What is far more complex is gauging whether PPPs in any of these domains ultimately effect change in the nature of the global economic relationships that give rise to labor rights violations.

The challenges of governance

In a very general sense, NGOs—regardless of whether they focus on labor rights or not—face the perennial challenge of negotiating power. They do so among their own staff members and vis-à-vis counterpart organizations within the NGO sector. A recent large-scale survey of the leaders of over 150 transnational US-based NGOs found that their leaders distinguish between "networks and partnerships" by characterizing the former as loose affiliations principally focused on information-sharing, and the latter as "formalized, usually based on a binding or contractual relationship." When asked to identify problems typical of each sector, NGO leaders replied that networks often suffer from "lack of commitment and waste of resources" whereas the "*primary challenges in partnerships are unequal power relations and other forms of inequality* ... "[52]

NGOs negotiate power at multiple levels. They negotiate the distribution of resources they control as well as agenda-setting power vis-à-vis the local populations on whose behalf they advocate or which they serve directly. They negotiate with the governments, businesses, or other social forces targeted in pursuit of their goals. NGOs operate in a realm in which norms are their principal currency. For those NGOs involved in PPPs on labor rights, the appeal to norms is central to their efforts to constrain corporate action through rule-making, information generation, or protest.

But the paradox of labor rights PPPs is that corporations are not directly bound by the human rights norms so routinely invoked in the context of rule-making on labor rights. Instead, they are indirectly bound: states are the parties to human rights treaties, not corporations. States sign and ratify treaties, and in so doing commit themselves to respect, protect, and fulfill the rights included therein. Corporations are bound principally by national regulations in the countries in which they are chartered and in which they carry out their business activities. States create and enforce those regulations in the interest of protecting human rights—that is, in the interest of ensuring that non-state actors (such as corporations) do not violate rights. States also create an enabling environment for the fulfillment of rights by setting tax policies that directly affect how businesses operate.[53]

But states can and often do trade away rights in the interest of encouraging economic growth. States routinely fail to adequately enforce labor rights regulation, either because of lack of capacity or of political will. They often set tax policies that benefit corporations at the expense of workers. Ironically, the NGOs involved in PPPs disproportionately focus their efforts on pressuring companies—not states—for reform.[54] In doing so, they direct their energies toward remedies for harm without addressing the root causes of labor rights violations: the economic and political structures that shape the governance of labor rights more broadly.

NGOs involved in the first domain of labor rights PPPs illustrate this dilemma of "constrained governance" most clearly. These NGOs typically help forge the voluntary standards that govern labor rights, but generally not the formal legal rules—laws. The risk of setting the bar too low is ever present precisely because NGOs are not "inside" a corporation and thus suffer from information shortfalls regarding the true scope of what the corporation could concede in terms of wages, hours, etc. Corporations also maintain the power of exit: they can simply move production from one location to another.[55] Hence, NGOs involved in direct negotiations may be forced to make concessions on benchmarks simply in the interest of maintaining production in a given locale, region, or sector. These are settings in which the paradox of power is clearest: NGOs get to help forge the rules governing labor rights, but not at the expense of corporations doing business. From a classical realist position in IR theory, the power of NGOs is thus trumped by states and/or corporate interests (which are closely aligned with those of states).

NGOs involved in the second domain face other challenges. Those involved in generating information on corporate conduct cannot entirely control the final use of the data they produce. If investors choose to dump stocks of a company charged with using child labor, for example, the NGOs which produced the rating may deem it better for the children involved if the company stays and works out a program of reform and remediation. But investor pressure may result in a decision to "cut and run" on the part of the company concerned. The unintended consequence may thus be to worsen the livelihood prospects of the communities at the local level in the country where manufacturing actually happens.[56] Liberal institutionalists, then, could argue that despite the creation of institutional mechanisms through which NGOs transact in the power of norms, the real currency in the context of labor rights PPPs is economic power.

Those NGOs involved in "fire brigade" activities in the third domain risk yet another challenge: that of being dismissed by their targets as simply too extreme to be taken seriously. This is not surprising, because these are the groups that most forcefully challenge the structural underpinnings of labor rights abuse. Their willingness to speak truth to power is why they opt for action in the third domain, on the radical flank of the PPP spectrum. Their outsider status is simultaneously their principal tool and their greatest limitation: they create the pressure that makes possible negotiation over rules in the first domain and information generation in the second one, but they often do so at great cost institutionally.

They may face threats of lawsuits for libel by corporations they "name and shame"; their members and supporters may risk arrest for unauthorized protests on private property, such as in front of factories or corporate headquarters; or their staff may risk arrest for trespassing in their efforts to gather data on behind-the-scenes factory practices. NGOs in this third domain must grapple constantly with the question of whether the risks they take are commensurate with the costs when achieving their goals is such a long-term prospect. Though they emphasize a language of "right" conduct (the central organizing principle of constructivist theory), NGOs in the third domain may literally be silenced by states (through the police, military or courts) or by non-state actors which illegitimately use force with the acquiescence of the state. The silencing of labor rights advocates and unionists by state and paramilitary forces throughout Latin America during the "dirty war" years of dictatorship from the 1970s through the late 1980s gives chilling testimony to the risks of actors in the third domain.

Conclusion

At first glance, the prospects for labor rights PPPs may seem gloomy. The constraints on NGOs operating in all three domains are significant. Many of the NGOs involved in labor rights advocacy are so busy with their ongoing activities or face such uphill battles that they have yet to make the shift toward greater engagement with the states that set and implement the formal rules of the national, regional, and international labor rights and trade regimes. Consequently, their influence over structural conditions that give rise to abuse in the first place remains limited. The realist could argue, "Why bother with PPPs, then, if states hold all the power?"

This chapter takes PPPs seriously because their presence is transforming the nature of rule-making on labor rights, albeit incrementally. By analyzing the governance implications of PPPs involved in labor rights monitoring using the concepts of anchoring, bridging and power that animate this volume, this chapter has illustrated how NGOs involved in all three domains are altering the way labor rights are framed (to employ the constructivist term), whether through voluntary standard-setting or in terms of public notions of "right" conduct. Though the odds may be stacked against easy victories for NGOs in this sector, labor rights activists are among the most determined people in the non-governmental arena. The challenges created by proliferating standards are not lost on them. Nor are the challenges created by the threat of corporate exit from a given country, or by the risks to NGO staff and the workers who report abuses, attempt to unionize, or engage in protest. Nor are they unaware of the hierarchies that persist among groups engaged in advocacy themselves.

Despite all of these challenges, these NGOs take on corporate targets thousands of times their size, and through their efforts at rule-making, information-sharing, and protest, they force the world to "see" the people who make the products and deliver the services—often under poor conditions—that we consume on a daily basis. The success of labor rights PPPs rests, in large part, on making visible these largely "invisible" people. Casting light on abuse is central to shifting the terms of debate over how and under what conditions globalized trade and commerce will continue to unfold. Labor rights PPPs thus continue to prick the consciences of business leaders and to shame the comfortable into action by insisting that decent working conditions become part of the price of doing business in the twenty-first century.

Notes

1 This chapter has been adapted with permission from: Shareen Hertel, "The Paradox of Partnership: Assessing New Forms of NGO Advocacy on Labor Rights," *Ethics and International Affairs* 24, no. 2 (2010): 171–189.
2 "Death Toll in Bangladesh Passes 1,100," *New York Times*, 11 May 2013.
3 Steven Greenhouse, "Retailers Are Pressed on Safety at Factories," *New York Times*, 10 May 2013.
4 William E. DeMars and Dennis Dijkzeul, "Introduction," this volume.
5 There is a whole universe of fee-for-service-type organizations that conduct research on corporate social responsibility. Examples include Ethical Consumer, Accountability, and Maplecroft, as well as mainstream consulting organizations, such as KPMG (Klynveld Peat Marwick Goerdeler) and Deloitte, Touche, Tohmatsu Limited, which have developed business auditing practices around corporate responsibility principles.
6 Dan Clawson, *The Next Upsurge: Labor and the New Social Movements* (Ithaca, NY: Cornell University Press, 2003); and Bill Fletcher, Jr. and Fernando Gapasin, *Solidarity Divided* (Berkeley, Calif.: University of California Press, 2008).
7 Janice Fine, *Worker Centers: Organizing Communities on the Edge of a Dream* (Ithaca, NY: Cornell University Press, 2006); and Michelle Camou, "Synchronizing Meanings and Other Day Laborer Organizing Strategies: Lessons from Denver," *Labor Studies Journal* 34, no. 1 (2009): 39–64.
8 Margaret E. Keck and Kathryn Sikkink, *Activists beyond Borders: Advocacy Networks in Transnational Politics* (Ithaca, NY: Cornell University Press, 1998).
9 Marco Schaferhoff, Sabine Campe and Christopher Kaan, "Transnational Public-Private Partnerships in International Relations: Making Sense of Concepts, Research Frameworks, and Results," *International Studies Review* 11, no. 3 (2009): 455.
10 Ibid., 452.
11 Ibid., 459.
12 Ibid., 464.
13 Paul A. Samuelson, "The Pure Theory of Public Expenditure," *Review of Economics and Statistics* 36, no. 4 (1954): 387–89.
14 For more on "joint-product" or "club" goods, see Todd Sandler and Keith Hartley, "Economics of Alliances: Lessons for Collective Action," *Journal of Economic Literature* 39, no. 3 (2001): 869–96.
15 On the mandate, history, and membership of the Fair Labor Association (FLA) see www.fairlabor.org/. On the Worker Rights Consortium (WRC) see www.workersrights.org/about/; and Julie Elkins and Shareen Hertel, "Sweatshirts and Sweatshops: Labor Rights, Student Activism, and the Challenges of Collegiate Apparel Manufacturing," in *Human Rights in Our Own Backyard: Injustice and Resistance in the United States*, eds William T.

Armaline, Davita Silfen Glasberg and Bandana Purkayastha (Philadelphia, Penn.: University of Pennsylvania Press, 2011).
16 Susan Ariel Aaronson and Jamie Zimmerman, *Trade Imbalance: The Struggle to Weigh Human Rights Concerns in Trade Policymaking* (Cambridge: Cambridge University Press, 2007), 35.
17 For an impassioned response to charges that the ILO lacks enforcement power, see remarks by Juan Somavia (then director-general, ILO) excerpted in James Atleson, Lance Compa, Kerry Rittich, Calvin William Sharpe and Marley S. Weiss, *International Labor Law: Cases and Materials on Workers' Rights in the Global Economy* (St. Paul, Minn.: Thompson West, The Labor Law Group American Casebook Series, 2008), 88–90.
18 Shareen Hertel, "Human Rights and the Global Economy: Bringing Labor Rights Back In," *Maryland Journal of International Law* 24 (2009): 283–95; and Simon Zadek and Alex McGillivray, "Responsible Competitiveness: Making Sustainability Count in Global Markets," *Harvard International Review* 30, no. 2 (2008): 72–77.
19 United Nations Global Compact, Human Rights and Business Dilemmas Forum, "Combating Child Labour in Football Production" (http://human-rights.unglobalcompact.org/case_studies/child-labour/child_labour/combating_child_labour_in_football_production.html#.U7w3svk7uSp).
20 Deborah Leipziger, ed., *SA8000: The First Decade: Implementation, Influence, and Impact* (Sheffield: Greenleaf, 2009).
21 David Vogel points out that the empirical evidence on the relationship between corporate social responsibility and profit is actually inconclusive, in *The Market for Virtue: The Potential and Limits of Corporate Social Responsibility* (Washington, DC: Brookings Institution Press, 2006), xvi–xvii, 13, 28–33.
22 Ken Silverstein, "Shopping for Sweat: The Human Cost of a Two-dollar T-shirt," *Harpers* 320, no. 1916 (2010): 36–44.
23 Rainer Braun and Judy Gearhart, "Who Should Code Your Conduct? Trade Union and NGO Differences in the Fight for Workers' Rights," *Development in Practice* 14, nos. 1–2 (2004): 183–96.
24 DeMars and Dijkzeul, "Introduction."
25 Mancur Olson, *The Logic of Collective Action: Public Goods and the Theory of Groups* (Cambridge, Mass.: Harvard University Press, 1965).
26 Gay Seidman, *Beyond the Boycott: Labor Rights, Human Rights, and Transnational Activism* (New York: American Sociological Association/ Russell Sage Foundation, 2007); Shareen Hertel, *Unexpected Power: Conflict and Change Among Transnational Activists* (Ithaca, NY: Cornell University Press, 2006); and Marc Ellenbogen, "Can the Tariff Act Combat Endemic Child Labor Abuses? The Case of Côte d'Ivoire," *Texas Law Review* 82, no. 5 (2004): 1315–1347.
27 Martin Kohr, "How the South Is Getting a Raw Deal at the WTO," in *Views from the South: The Effects of Globalization and the WTO on Third World Countries*, ed. Sarah Anderson (Chicago, Ill.: LPC Group, 2000), 7–53.
28 Robert Reich, *Supercapitalism: The Transformation of Business, Democracy, and Everyday Life* (New York: Alfred A. Knopf, 2007); and Ellen Ruppel Shell, *Cheap: The High Cost of Discount Culture* (New York: Penguin Press, 2009).

29 Schaferhoff et al., "Transnational Public-Private Partnerships in International Relations," 465.
30 Seidman, *Beyond the Boycott*, 3.
31 Aaron Berstein and Christopher Greenwald, "Benchmarking Corporate Policies on Labor and Human Rights in Global Supply Chains," *Capital Matters Occasional Paper Series* 5 (Cambridge, Mass.: Pensions and Capital Stewardship Project, Labor and Worklife Program, Harvard Law School, November 2009), 3.
32 Vogel, *Market for Virtue*; Roseann Casey, "Meaningful Change: Raising the Bar in Supply Chain Workplace Standards," Corporate Social Responsibility Initiative, Working Paper no. 29 (Cambridge, Mass.: John F. Kennedy School of Government, Harvard University, November 2006); Marsha A. Dickson, Suzanne Loker and Molly Eckman, *Social Responsibility in the Global Apparel Industry* (New York: Fairchild Books, 2009); Rory Sullivan, ed., *Business and Human Rights: Dilemmas and Solutions* (Sheffield: Greenleaf Publishing, 2003); Simon Zadek, *Doing Good and Doing Well: Making the Business Case for Corporate Citizenship* (New York: The Conference Board, 2000); and Jeffrey Barber, "Mapping the Movement to Achieve Sustainable Production and Consumption in North America," *Journal of Cleaner Production* 15, no. 6 (2007): 499–512.
33 Full text for these and other UN human rights treaties at www2.ohchr.org/english/law/.
34 For analysis of current benchmarks included in codes globally, see John G. Ruggie, the UN Special Representative of the Secretary-General on the Issue of Human Rights and Transnational Corporations and Other Business Enterprises, via the Business and Human Rights Resource Centre portal: www.business-humanrights.org/SpecialRepPortal/Home; and John Ruggie, *Just Business: Multinational Corporations and Human Rights* (New York: W. W. Norton and Company, 2013).
35 Todd Landman, *Protecting Human Rights* (Washington, DC: Georgetown University Press, 2005); and Oona Hathaway, "Why Do Nations Join Human Rights Treaties?" *Journal of Conflict Resolution* 51, no. 4 (2007): 588–621.
36 DeMars and Dijkzeul, "Introduction"; and Daniel W. Drezner, *All Politics Is Global: Explaining International Regulatory Regimes* (Princeton, N.J.: Princeton University Press, 2007).
37 DeMars and Dijkzeul, "Introduction," 29.
38 UN Declaration on the Protection of all Persons from Enforced Disappearances; ILO Conventions 129 and 105 (regarding forced labor); International Covenant on Civil and Political Rights, Article 8 (regarding forced labor); and ICCPR Article 6, 14 and 15 (regarding extrajudicial killing), available at www.ohchr.org/.
39 Cynthia A. Williams, "Civil Society Initiatives and 'Soft Law' in the Oil and Gas Industry," *Journal of International Law and Politics* 36, nos. 2/3 (2004): 457–502; and Carola Kantz, "The Power of Socialization: Engaging the Diamond Industry in the Kimberley Process," *Business and Politics* 9, no. 3 (2007): 1–20.
40 Vogel, *Market for Virtue*.
41 Examples of private indices of corporate social responsibility have included ratings of corporate performance such as the FTSE KLD 400 Social Index

(i.e., Financial Times Stock Exchange/Kinder Lydenberg and Domini), colloquially referred to as the "Domini Social Index" (www.msci.com/products/esg/ and www.domini.org).
42 Detailed information on the mandate of each organization at: Global Reporting Initiative (https://www.globalreporting.org) and the Business and Human Rights Resource Centre (http://business-humanrights.org/en).
43 Mathew D. McCubbins and Thomas Schwartz developed the concept of "fire brigade" monitoring to explain third-party monitoring as a means of Congressional oversight in their article, "Congressional Oversight Overlooked: Police Patrol Versus Fire Alarms," *American Journal of Political Science* 28, no. 1 (February 1984): 165–179.
44 International Labor Rights Forum (www.laborrights.org/about); United Students Against Sweatshops (http://usas.org/); Clean Clothes Campaign (www.cleanclothes.org/); Third World Network (www.twnside.org.sg/); and Matthew Hilton, *Prosperity for All: Consumer Activism in an Era of Globalization* (Ithaca, NY: Cornell University Press, 2009).
45 Xiaohua Yang and Cheryl Rivers, "Antecedents of CSR Practices in MNCs' Subsidiaries: A Stakeholder and Institutional Perspective," *Journal of Business Ethics* 86, issue 2 supplement (2009): 155–69, see especially page 163.
46 Interfaith Center for Corporate Responsibility (www.iccr.org/).
47 Seidman, *Beyond the Boycott*.
48 Kathryn Sikkink, "Codes of Conduct for Transnational Corporations: The Case of the WHO/UNICEF Code," *International Organization* 40, no. 4 (1986): 815–40.
49 Joe Bandy, "Paradoxes of Transnational Civil Societies Under Neoliberalism: The Coalition for Justice in the Maquiladoras," *Social Problems* 51, no. 3 (2004): 410–31.
50 Greg Norman, "Maquila Workers Celebrate Victory in Struggle for Freedom of Association," Comité Fronterizo de Obreras (March 2002) (www.cfomaquiladoras.org/maquilaworkerscelebratevictory.en.html); and Hertel, *Unexpected Power*, for a broader treatment of the work of CFO.
51 This institutional history is related in Leipziger, *SA8000: The First Decade*.
52 Margaret G. Hermann, Jesse D. Lecy, George E. Mitchell, Christiane Pagé, Paloma Raggo, Hans Peter Schmitz and Lorena Viñuela, "Transnational NGOs: A Cross-Sectoral Analysis of Leadership Perspectives," Moynihan Institute of Global Affairs, Syracuse University, 19 April 2010 (www.maxwell.syr.edu/uploadedFiles/moynihan/tngo/Abridged_white_paper_19_APR_2010.pdf), 24, emphasis added.
53 Hertel, "Human Rights and the Global Economy," 287–88.
54 Vogel, *Market for Virtue*; and Seidman, *Beyond the Boycott*.
55 Albert O. Hirschman, *Exit, Voice, and Loyalty: Responses to Decline in Firms, Organizations, and States* (Cambridge, Mass.: Harvard University Press, 1970).
56 Hertel, *Unexpected Power*.

8 NGOs in peacebuilding
High expectations, mixed results
Patrice C. McMahon[1]

- NGOs and peacebuilding in Bosnia
- The difficult truths
- Unfulfilled expectations
- An analysis of multiple NGO realities
- Conclusion

Peacebuilding has become a booming business, but not just for governments and international organizations.[2] Increasingly, non-governmental organizations (NGOs) are regarded as important partners in peacebuilding, defined by Boutros-Ghali as all actions to identify and support structures which will strengthen and solidify peace.[3] Although policymakers readily acknowledge the role of NGOs in peacebuilding exercises, academics often do not, as the introductory chapter by William DeMars and Dennis Dijkzeul makes clear. Most International Relations (IR) research overlooks or discounts NGOs, and this is true not just of realist scholarship, but also applies to most studies of peacebuilding. Scholars writing from a liberal or global governance perspective tend to see NGO involvement as unequivocally positive, as a sign of "better global governance."[4] Recent studies in peace and security cast doubt on the virtues and power of these non-state organizations.[5] However, here too much is assumed or asserted about NGOs, and there is little empirical research that focuses squarely on NGOs in peacebuilding.

Using Bosnia and Herzegovina (BiH) as an in-depth case study, this chapter argues that contemporary peacebuilding has been guided by the conviction that NGOs—both international and national—are essential players in building peace and stability. Policymakers believe that NGOs provide a range of essential services in post-conflict settings, NGOs bridge important gaps, particularly between national actors and international organizations, and serve as cost-effective and relatively efficient mechanisms for transforming societal relations and empowering locals.

212 *Case evidence: NGOs and networks*

This chapter examines how international actors have tried to establish and strengthen national NGOs in Bosnia as a way to promote stability, peace and democracy. It also assesses to what degree, and with what limitations, international actors can promote the domestic NGO sector.

The first section provides evidence of the important role of NGOs in peacebuilding in BiH from 1996 to 2009. It argues that although the categories of *NGOs* and *civil society* are conceptually distinct and may comprise different actors, international peacebuilders in BiH, including the European Union, the US government, and the Organization for Security and Cooperation in Europe (OSCE), often mistook one for the other. Thus, the existence of national NGOs was regarded as evidence of a vibrant civil society; NGOs were assumed to serve as bridges between Bosnian society and the reconstituted state, and to link international ambitions to local realities. The second section of the chapter considers how this effort to build national NGOs impacted outcomes in BiH. It suggests that although members of the international community spent a lot of money and time establishing and supporting NGO development, the outcomes were mixed. The third section offers an explanation for why national NGOs have often failed to produce intended effects, using principal–agent theory and elaborating on the structural environment associated with peacebuilding. The fourth section examines some conceptual and policy approaches for understanding and improving the performance of NGOs in peacebuilding.

To be clear, I do not suggest that NGOs working in BiH have failed completely, or that they have undermined peacebuilding efforts. Instead, the chapter points to certain structural factors that influence and constrain peacebuilding efforts and specifically the work of NGOs. The thick, descriptive analysis relies on primary and secondary sources, as well as insights gleaned from semi-structured interviews with Bosnian policymakers, academics and civil society representatives, as well as internationals working in Bosnia over a ten-year period.[6] I corroborate my findings with the research of numerous Balkan scholars.[7] The paper ends not with the conclusion that NGOs matter little to peacebuilding efforts in this country, but with a brief discussion of the multifaceted realities of NGOs in peacebuilding.

NGOs and peacebuilding in Bosnia

The strife that enveloped the former Yugoslav republic from 1992 to 1995 and resulted in ethnic cleansing, concentration camps, and some 100,000 deaths prompted a significant multilateral response from the international community. Western governments, regional organizations, and international NGOs all became deeply involved in stitching Bosnia back together. For this reason, this Balkan country is often heralded as one of the most positive examples of the international community's concern, commitment, and delivery of assistance for post-conflict reconstruction.[8] From 1996 to 2007 some $14 billion flooded into this country of about 4 million people; between 1995 and 2005 the US government alone provided $1.3 billion of bilateral assistance.[9] From 2001 to 2006, the European Union (EU) provided €2.5 billion of assistance, with annual budgets exceeding €60 million from 2007 to 2009.[10] International involvement included many other public and private actors, and by 1999 over 170 international and some 360 local NGOs were involved in what they themselves defined as "civil society development."[11]

Given the large number of organizations and their involvement in so many different sectors, it is impossible to quantify and examine all of the activities of the "international community." Some trends are, nonetheless, clear from examining the priorities, policies, and statements of the most important international actors; the trend that I focus on here is the international community's desire to establish national NGOs as a way of strengthening civil society and building peace. Certainly, the first task of the international community when it arrived in Bosnia in 1996 was to consolidate the peace with a large foreign military presence. The second, equally important task was to manage the country's ethnic dilemmas in the long term with the creation of a federal state that both divided the country and kept it together. Given the military realities on the ground, the Dayton Peace Agreement divided the country into the Federation and the Republika Srbska. At the same time, the constitution included provisions for joint political institutions, power-sharing practices, and the right of return for refugees. In practice, this left the country separated into two mono-ethnic units while numerous top-down and bottom-up mechanisms were established to reunify the country and the population.

Despite the importance of an international military presence and complex power-sharing arrangements, a durable peace ultimately depended on the existence of a society committed to democratic pluralism and reconciliation. In this task too, the international community became intricately involved. Preparing, holding, and monitoring national and local elections was only a starting point because democratic consolidation and a self-sustaining Bosnia necessitated the creation of a vibrant civil society. The international community's involvement throughout post-communist Europe in the 1990s was informed, if not co-opted, by those who tied the international community's post-Cold War mission to promoting democracy and strengthening civil society.[12] Support for the associational sphere of interest groups which stands between the private sphere of the family and the public sphere of the state, in fact, became a hallmark of assistance to post-communist countries because of its perceived ability to challenge the state's power while it simultaneously fosters democracy from below.

Imperceptibly, however, international efforts to foster democracy and strengthen civil society from the bottom up led to focusing on a very narrow set of organizations, namely NGOs.[13] International peacebuilding strategies went in two directions: "bottom-up" assistance to establish national NGOs that would help develop a democratic political culture worked in tandem with "top-down" efforts to organize elections and political parties, and both kinds of assistance were deemed crucial for peacebuilding.[14] Over time, strengthening Bosnia's civil society became the leading hallmark of successful state building. Developing a vibrant civil society was singled out as important because without it, "the Dayton Accords ... and the hope of a united Bosnia and Herzegovina will be lost."[15] Thus, what started as an interest in peace, stability and democracy morphed into an extensive and intensive effort to engage international NGOs and establish national NGOs.

International investment in civil society development was only a small fraction of the international community's overall budget in BiH, but almost all of it was channeled through and to NGOs.[16] Precise figures do not exist on how much was spent to support NGOs in Bosnia, but it is clear that developing NGOs and civil society featured prominently in the agendas of governments, multilateral agencies, and international NGOs operating in BiH.[17]

The OSCE and the US Agency for International Development (USAID) led the international community's efforts to strengthen Bosnia's civil society, and both emphasized establishing national NGOs as a primary way of achieving this objective. In 1996, the OSCE's mission to BiH was restructured to focus on democratization and civil society with the goal of bringing the "international community into a closer relationship with grassroots groups and associations which could provide a counterpoint to the politics of the governing authorities and nationalist parties."[18] Over time, the OSCE's work evolved into an expansive civil society agenda, with two of its departments focused on enhancing civil involvement and social activism.[19] The OSCE has remained committed to "the creation of an active and engaged civil society able to act as an equal partner to the government and to take action on its own behalf."[20]

USAID similarly relied on international and national NGOs to strengthen civil society, reorienting its funding priorities and programs throughout the 1990s.[21] During the Bosnia war, the majority of USAID funding went to international NGOs to implement the government's program and further its goals. Once the conflict ended, the United States turned to domestic NGOs because "in the long term, a pluralistic civil society will be essential and thus the role of nongovernmental organizations, as advocates for citizen interests and avenues for citizen participation, must be strengthened."[22] By this point in time, USAID had already established both the Center for Democracy and Governance (to support American NGOs working with NGOs in Eastern Europe) and its New Partnerships Initiative, which focused "significant resources on strengthening civil society and helping to restructure the relationships between states and civil societies."[23] By 2000, USAID had developed a comprehensive democratic agenda in Bosnia, encouraging a pro-democratic political leadership and a vibrant civil society.[24]

By the end of the 1990s, the EU was the single largest contributor to Bosnia's reconstruction, and it too claimed that the "voices of the people" were important vehicles for promoting good governance and peace.[25] Although the EU never developed a civil society agenda comparable to OSCE or USAID, it emphasized NGOs as important agents of peacebuilding in BiH.[26] The EU, in fact, linked civil society to NGOs, and the existence of both in Bosnia to the country's future membership of the EU: "A strong civil society in BiH is an EU priority: building democracy from grassroots level, to eradicate discrimination, reconcile ethnic tensions, and improve human and civil rights, is critical to fulfilling the Copenhagen political criteria for EU Membership."[27]

Beyond these three major donors—USAID, OSCE and the EU— several other organizations have invested heavily in Bosnian peacebuilding. Both the World Bank and NATO have directed increasing levels of aid to Bosnia through international and national NGOs.[28] Three of the largest international NGOs—Catholic Relief Services, the International Rescue Committee, and CARE—started to work in BiH during the war and stayed after, explicitly focused on creating and supporting national NGOs.[29]

This international interest in developing and strengthening national NGOs was neither limited to peacebuilding nor confined to Bosnia. In other parts of Central and Eastern Europe, and in post-conflict countries like Rwanda and Afghanistan, the international community regularly promoted the creation of national NGOs as partners and

The difficult truths

The arrival of NATO-led troops in Bosnia in early 1996 ended the bloodshed overnight, and within a few years, reconstruction efforts were deemed "remarkably successful."[31] Despite good news on many fronts, Bosnia continues to be riddled with economic, political and ethnic challenges and the country's future remains at risk.[32] Official unemployment is more than 25 percent.[33] In 2007, almost 20 percent of the country lived in poverty, and another 30 percent was in danger of falling into poverty.[34] The 2006 elections—the most important since the war's end because of the scheduled departure of the UN's high representative—were fraught with nationalist rhetoric.[35] In the years since, Bosnian leaders have threatened to split the country further into ethnic enclaves. It is hard to call Bosnia a success story; yet, it would be equally unfair to say that international efforts have failed.

What has been the effect of international support and investment in national NGOs? Have NGOs become the intended bridge between different groups and international ambitions and local realities? The following examines this impact by looking at *micro, meso*, and *macro* outcomes.[36] Given the country's dearth of independent organizations during the communist period, a good deal can be said about the micro level impact on individuals and certain groups in society. However, it is more challenging to verify the impact of these international investments on meso- or macro-level outcomes, that is, on government policies or broader processes related to peace, democratization and reconciliation.

At the *micro level*, international support for NGOs has had an obvious and direct effect on the number of national NGOs in Bosnia and on the landscape of society. After having a few independent organizations, by 1997, 130 national NGOs were registered at the state level.[37] Within a decade, the EU reported that there were over 3,000 domestic and international "non-state" actors registered at the state and entity levels and in the Brcko District.[38] A 2008 survey found that there were 9,095 registered NGOs in BiH, but only 4,629 were estimated to be active.[39] The different terms used, as well as the varied numbers, illuminate some of the problems of measuring both impact and the growth of the NGO sector. Yet, regardless of the term used or the number estimated, all of the national NGOs relied heavily, if not exclusively, on international support.⁴⁰ At least in numerical terms, international interest in NGOs has had a positive impact on micro-level outputs, and investments in this sector have indeed yielded a significant number of national NGOs.

Fieldwork, government and foundation evaluations, and secondary sources attest to a more complicated picture of outcomes at the meso level, especially if one accepts that the number of NGOs says little about their role in shaping policy or political change. In fact, many of Bosnia's national NGOs are not active and exist only on paper.⁴¹ For the most part, national NGOs play only a small role in shaping policy. Some issues, like those related to women and economic development, have been "well covered and appear to be the strongest organizationally and financially."⁴² Women in Bosnia have certainly benefited from international attention and support for national NGOs, but complications and problems are also evident. For example, in the late 1990s, Bosnia was home to about 100 national and international NGOs focused on women's issues; they provided counseling and support for rape victims, trained unemployed women, promoted women's rights, and assisted men and women with reintegration.⁴³ However, most of these NGOs disappeared when international funds dried up, failing to become embedded in domestic society.⁴⁴ This rare evaluation of women's NGOs may help explain why other NGOs in Bosnia remain weak and ineffectual.

Existing assessments of Bosnian NGOs conclude that despite improvements in certain areas, Bosnia's NGO sector remains relatively unchanged since the late 1990s.⁴⁵ USAID evaluates NGOs according to seven criteria; of these, only advocacy and public image have improved markedly. In 2005, the European Commission reported that while the situation for NGOs was improving in BiH, there was little evidence to conclude that with more time and less funding, NGOs would become important civil society actors. "Non-state actors continue to face substantial difficulties in guaranteeing their long-term sustainability ... They exist as long as the projects exist which means they advocate issues as long as they are paid to."⁴⁶ A USAID evaluation highlights some achievements of the NGO sector in 2008, including signs of cooperation and networking among NGOs and more government interest in and reliance on NGOs; yet, it concludes that the NGO sector still remains in "mid-transition"—as it was in 1999—with NGOs only beginning to play a role in policy issues.⁴⁷

Some evaluations discuss these negative and unintended outcomes, seeing them as a direct consequence of international support for NGOs.⁴⁸ One evaluation of NGOs in the Balkans indicates that throughout the region, national NGOs do not enjoy the trust of the people; they often lack experience and are widely perceived as income generators for those who are lucky enough to be employed by them.[49] Other reports and interviews regularly note that Bosnian NGOs are neither effective nor genuinely representative of "the people."

Given their limited success at the meso level, it would be quite a stretch to suggest that NGOs—either international or national—have had any impact whatsoever on macro level outcomes. Yet, it is important to remember how much has been written on NGOs and civil society and their assumed and tight link to democracy, ethnic reconciliation and peace.[50] This research suggests that these relationships are exaggerated and poorly understood. An international official in Brcko, a town in eastern Bosnia that experienced a great deal of ethnic violence but has since been held up as a model of ethnic cooperation, explained that neither international nor domestic NGOs had played an important role in the city's development.[51] OSCE officials in Brcko concurred, admitting that while the OSCE has worked hard to make NGOs both self-sustaining and interethnic, they were neither.[52] In fact, Bosnians remain skeptical of the sway of NGOs in everyday life and decision-making, but many believe that the explosion of NGOs—funded by the international community—has produced unintended and negative consequences for the NGO sector and for Bosnian society. As one Bosnian scholar put it, "civil society development is 'mission impossible'; despite large doses of international assistance being injected into Bosnian society, only a few hundred NGOs are active in the country, and far fewer have succeeded in playing any role in promoting good governance."[53]

There are notable success stories in places like Sarajevo and Tuzla, where the NGO community is more active and has coordinated on specific projects, but there are far more examples of bad practices, corruption, and NGOs that exist only to receive international funds. The reality is that most Bosnian NGOs were created because of international funding and they lack domestic roots and local legitimacy; thus, they were unable to engage in effective advocacy or outreach.[54] Even Bosnians who have been involved in the NGO sector have a hard time listing their concrete achievements or concluding that they have strengthened civil society or contributed significantly to peacebuilding.[55] As one NGO official admitted, international involvement in this area has produced an unfortunate dynamic: Westerners come to Bosnia wanting to make a difference, but what has happened is that NGOs, both international and national, have kidnapped civil society and instead pursued their own interests.[56] Local knowledge and experiences are regularly discounted by internationals because Bosnians have grown up in a communist society, plagued with ethnic hatreds. The international community feels that it must teach, rather than partner with, the "natives."[57]

The main justification for supporting the creation of NGOs in BiH was clear and perhaps unassailable; NGOs bridge many gaps, between society and the state, between antagonistic elements of society, and between domestic and international groups. The hope was that the existence of national NGOs, often funded and trained by international NGOs, would transform civil society and strengthen the Bosnian state. The outcome would be democracy, ethnic moderation, and stability. It does take a long time for these changes to occur, but fieldwork and research have not generated convincing evidence that Bosnian NGOs are "kicking in," proving important to these outcomes, or even that NGOs are modestly improving everyday life for Bosnians. One cannot ignore the fact that Bosnia's future is still in question, because ethnic nationalists—voted into office by the Bosnian people—threaten to undermine more than a dozen years of peacebuilding activities.[58]

Unfulfilled expectations

Scholars have done a good job examining what the international community got right in Bosnia, and there is some consensus on this. Explaining why BiH has not been transformed into a democratic state, despite the generous support of the international community, is more difficult but has been addressed.[59] This section explains why international support and reliance on NGOs may have yielded so few positive, measurable effects on policymaking and domestic change. It argues that the failures are due, in part, to the number of actors involved in peacebuilding and the environment itself, which brings together diverse organizations with competing agendas and financial constraints. Consequently, there are few incentives and many constraints on NGOs to become genuine partners in peacebuilding. Put differently, as much as international actors might see NGOs as bridging several divides, there are structural, material and practical reasons that stand in their way.

The actors involved

It is well known that organizations with a common interest do not always act to further common goals.[60] This failure to cooperate is more likely when there is a large number of actors working on the same issue, the absence of positive inducements, or no ways to sanction members.[61] Cooperation among states is even more difficult when the goals of these actors are unclear, contradictory, or poorly specified.[62] This makes it easier for organizations to shirk their responsibilities and pursue private, rather than public, goals. One way to respond to the problem of too many actors is to create an institution that can provide "the rules of thumb" and a framework that will "diminish transaction and information costs and sanction and enforce behavior."[63]

International peacebuilding is best conceptualized as a collective action problem writ large.[64] As such, in peacebuilding there is no such thing as a unitary "international community." At best, it is a conglomeration of somewhat like-minded organizations. It might be tempting to think that more is better but this is certainly not the case for peacebuilding in BiH.[65] Within a year of the war's end, some 200 international NGOs, 18 UN agencies, and 27 intergovernmental organizations, as well as 17 different foreign governments, were actively involved in the country's reconstruction.[66] Although this significant presence declined in the subsequent years, in 2007 BiH was still home to nine major bilateral donors, five multilateral donors, and numerous international NGOs.[67] Nonetheless, scholars continue to refer to the "international community" as if this were a single actor or even a cohesive group that acts in unison to achieve a common goal. Nothing, in fact, could be further from the truth, and this was even true when the Dayton Peace Accords were signed in 1996.[68] In BiH, the international community has always been a heterogeneous, even unwieldy group that includes three categories of actors: national governments (primarily those on the Steering Board of the Peace Implementing Council), intergovernmental organizations, and international non-governmental organizations.[69] The latter group itself is "an untidy community," encompassing philanthropic organizations, relief agencies, and private sector firms.[70]

The collective action problem is even more significant when international actors are not clear about what they want to accomplish, when they are competing with each other, or hold conflicting objectives. The 1996 peace agreement attempted to unify the international community's mission in Bosnia; in reality, it left the international community's objectives and strategies intentionally vague.[71] Critics point out that the peace agreement is a complex, even inconsistent document plagued by ambiguity.[72] Its annexes specified what international bodies were tasked to do, but they did not explain what would happen if these organizations failed to carry out their responsibilities. Despite important accomplishments, much was left up in the air, without any reasonable framework to sanction or to force outcomes;

from the outset, Dayton suffered from an "enforcement gap" if promises were not kept.[73]

The Office of the High Representative (OHR) was created in 1996 to provide "rules of thumb" and a framework to coordinate, oversee, and implement the so-called "will of the international community." Yet, this office, which was set up by the UN and officially represented all of the members of the Peace Implementing Council, was actually the voice for 55 countries and international agencies, all of which had their own and sometimes conflicting priorities.[74] Because of its obvious shortcomings, in 1997 the powers of the high representative were broadened; the "Bonn powers" provide the OHR with nearly unchecked authority, including the authority to impose legislation and dismiss any public official from office who stands in the way of the implementation of Dayton and the promotion of tolerance and interethnic cooperation.

Frustrated by local obstructions, the OHR has increasingly implemented a "trusteeship model" of imposing peace from above. Since 2002, the OHR has also acted as the EU's representative. Nonetheless, the office was never given the authority or the resources required to manage such a complex or contentious task. Moreover, early on the Americans stressed their desire to implement only the military aspects of the peace treaty, rejecting efforts to empower the OHR with civilian or political authority. Later, when the Americans wanted to broaden the OHR's responsibilities and strengthen its civilian powers, the Europeans resisted.[75] Over time, the OHR's responsibilities grew and its staff and budget ballooned and then shrunk, but its authority has remained ill-defined, subordinated to NATO and the military mission and vulnerable to the personality and leadership style of the high representative.[76]

The existence of so many international actors has, undoubtedly, had a positive effect on the establishment of Bosnian NGOs, but this overwhelming presence has also contributed to the creation of a disembedded civil society, or a situation where domestic organizations look outside their country, rather than inside, for support, direction, and legitimacy.[77] The sudden explosion of so many internationally-financed NGOs has also contributed to information failures, with Bosnian organizations knowing little about what is happening within their own country, and this is even true of organizations with a similar mandate. In 1996, an international NGO established a Bosnian NGO (ICVA BiH) to encourage communication among the growing NGO community and to serve as an interface between domestic and international organizations involved in peacebuilding.[78]

One of ICVA's achievements, at least from the perspective of those outside of Bosnia, has been the publication of regular reports of organizations working in BiH. Although these publications are used by members of the international community in Bosnia and Western academics, many NGO activists in Bosnia are still unaware of these publications and are unclear about what this organization does. Indeed, in visiting ICVA's Sarajevo office in 2007, it was apparent that this organization's activities are limited and oriented toward a foreign, rather than domestic, audience. In 2008 a Department for Cooperation with NGOs was created to address this ongoing problem, though it is still not functional.[79]

The environment

The number of groups working in a specific area indeed affects their willingness to provide "an optimal amount of a collective good."[80] It is also true that these organizations are embedded in a unique social setting characterized by uncertainty.[81] These problems can lead individuals working within organizations to behave in a myopic, but reasonably adaptive manner. NGOs are generally considered to be altruistic agents, but they are still rational, self-interested actors that may need to focus on their own organization's survival as well as broader, public goals.[82] Peacebuilding inherently involves a great deal of uncertainty, from the nature of aid itself, to budgetary constraints, to how states and international organizations inevitably engage in this complex undertaking. It is, thus, a precarious environment for both international donors, who face competing international crises and domestic demands, and domestic NGOs that depend on international support for their existence.

"Aid policies, like any policies, do not exist in a vacuum," and while altruism is part of the reason that donors fund peacebuilding, foreign aid simultaneously serves other important domestic purposes."[83] Like elsewhere in the world, aid to Bosnia created numerous and lucrative opportunities for a range of public and private actors. Rarely did international funds go to the region directly but were instead channeled through intermediaries, to international NGOs or to other Western organizations that were expected to carry out the will of governments.[84] Both USAID and the EU supported American and European NGOs respectively to work in the Balkans because, after all, these government agencies must reflect the interests and needs of their domestic constituencies.[85] The business of aid had the unintended effect of creating a richly endowed international community that appeared almost overnight in Bosnia. Instead of strengthening civil society and "capacity building," these actions had the effect of "capacity sucking," especially for NGOs that so desperately relied on money for infrastructural development and to foster a domestic constituency.[86]

NGOs benefit from international involvement and resources, but the tendency for international donors to spend money quickly and evaluate "success" in terms of money spent on inputs rather than on sustainable long-term results, inevitably shaped the calculus and priorities of NGOs.[87] After inundating Bosnia with money in the mid-1990s, assistance declined precipitously; in 1996, the EU spent over €440 million in BiH; by 2000 this figure fell to €100 million, and by 2006 it was down to €64 million.[88] US assistance similarly dropped off, from a high of $300 million in 1998 to $72 million in 2006.[89] In 1997 the World Bank spent some $200 million on projects in BiH; by 2007 its budget was about $40 million.[90] Declining interest in Bosnia meant that for NGOs to stay afloat they needed to be sure their organization's goals were in line with international (rather than domestic) priorities, which rarely included money for institutional development. Forced to provide quantitative evidence of their achievements, NGOs increasingly worked on projects that coincided with the international community's goals and could be measured, rather than responding to local needs.[91]

As the director of a Sarajevo-based NGO put it, "the international community made a big mistake in Bosnia; it basically threw a lot of money at the country's problems without agreeing on the solution."[92] Almost overnight, hundreds of NGOs were established, but with little thought for their long-term development or regard for their survival. Budgetary concerns and the absence of a coherent strategy resulted in a high mortality rate for NGOs. This may also help explain the gap between registered NGOs and those that are considered genuinely active. For most NGOs, staying active requires some injection of external funds but sometimes it can be difficult to know what international organizations want, as their priorities change from year to year, making it difficult for NGOs to become experts in one area. Too often international organizations ended up funding high profile issues rather than putting money in existing NGOs that were trying to develop institutional capacity.[93] All of this ambiguity and insecurity only intensified competition among NGOs that were competing for the attention and funding of the same international donors, preventing them from developing into a stable, well-connected group inclined to coordination and cooperation.

An official from the OSCE remarked that when he arrived in Bosnia (after working in Kosovo) he was surprised that the international community's approach to Bosnia was still so "up in the air" and that there were so few mechanisms in place to connect different organizations, both international and domestic, and assess NGO achievements.[94] Even the OSCE, which has worked continuously with NGOs since 1996, does not have a "global approach" to working with NGOs. In fact, it has no comprehensive list of all of its NGO partners; it has no way of knowing what NGOs are doing, and no mechanism of evaluation, making it impossible to take stock of lessons learned or to avoid duplication in certain issue areas.

The incentives and constraints

Underpinning many of the problems associated with NGO development in Bosnia are characteristics associated with problems of delegated discretion, or what is known as "principal–agent relationships." This is an analytical expression of what results from differing interpretations of how organizations should best achieve common goals. Inevitably, the principal, the actor with the highest authority, delegates agents to help carry out the principal's goals; although efficiency requires handing over some decisions and authority, the very act of delegation creates problems of control and supervision.[95] In all principal–agent relationships, there is no guarantee that agents will pursue the principal's goals, especially when it is difficult to monitor behavior, measure achievements, or punish agents for pursuing their own private interests.[96] The incentives and constraints that both principals and agents face help explain why actors with a common goal often fail to reach it and why they do not behave in predictable or intended ways.

The peacebuilding process creates numerous incentives for international actors—as principals—to emphasize quick solutions to getting the job done while it simultaneously constrains local NGOs—as agents—from becoming independent, indigenous organizations. In total, the peacebuilding enterprise fails to create the necessary incentives to allow both sets of organizations to adopt long-term solutions for developing domestic capacity. Governments and international organizations were certainly inspired by the horror that befell Bosnia between 1993 and 1995, but they had other, more selfish reasons for coming to Bosnia's rescue, like containing the conflict and preventing any more refugees from spilling into Europe.[97] From the very beginning, international organizations promoted and promised a quick solution to the Bosnian problem.[98] For some members of the international community, investments in NGOs were merely a substitute for real political action, providing little reason for them to develop a long-term NGO strategy.[99] At least according to some, NGOs were merely supposed to be inexpensive and quick solutions to complex problems.[100] However, since the investments in NGOs and civil society were so small, compared to the hefty investments being made in economic development and security, the international community had little incentive to monitor NGOs or punish those that failed to implement their programs or follow through on their promises. At the same time, governments and other donors were pressured to provide tangible proof of their investments, encouraging them to use short-term contracts, or engage agents that agreed to certain "deliverables" rather than "cooperative" agreements premised on cultivating relationships with organizations that strive for long-term, but less tangible and measurable outcomes. The EU, for example, stresses that NGOs should develop indigenous support, yet it continues to change its priorities, giving small, short-term grants that prevent NGOs from developing and implementing a long-term plan.[101]

Some argue that domestic NGOs, like large international NGOs, are more interested in self-promotion and increasing their own budgets than in advancing broader public goals like peacebuilding.[102] In the Bosnian context, this does not necessarily ring true and most NGOs I have interviewed or have knowledge of appear to be committed to advancing public and progressive goals, though their staffs are also, not surprisingly, motivated to keep their jobs and organizations afloat. There are, however, many good reasons why Bosnian NGOs have failed to become important partners in peacebuilding. Changing international priorities place enormous constraints on what NGOs do in the short term while making it almost impossible for them to reach out to the local population or plan for the future.[103] For an NGO that wants to stay in business, its top priority is considering and responding to the priorities of those who fund them. As rational, self-interested actors, NGOs have a strong incentive to hire staff members with fluent English and develop assessment techniques to ensure that they have a track record that they can show to future potential funders, displacing other priorities, like fostering a domestic constituency or education system, that are undeniably slower and incremental. These same incentives present NGOs with little reason to communicate with other domestic actors. Even in late 2008, international officials remarked that despite years of encouragement and admonishment, NGOs still work in a "silo mentality."[104] Thus, despite monthly donor meetings most international organizations work alone, in the way they have for years, with little coordination and cooperation with other actors.

If these incentives and constraints were not enough, most NGOs usually have more than one funding source, producing the so-called "multiple principals problem," which makes it even more difficult for NGOs to align their interests with those who provide their funding. It also makes it nearly impossible for governments and international organizations to monitor their behavior. Delegation is even more complex because of the involvement of international NGOs. International NGOs receive money from governments and they, in turn, provide grants to Bosnian NGOs, making the chain of delegation even longer and outcomes more difficult to monitor, measure, and evaluate.

Peacebuilding in Bosnia is influenced by a range of organizations, but these organizations and their behavior are shaped by the structural environment that they inhabit. This setting and the incentives and constraints it produces mean that there is much uncertainty and room for dysfunctional behavior. There are, thus, many reasons why NGOs cannot make local needs a priority and why they often find themselves merely implementing the goals of the international community or doing only what is necessary to keep their organization afloat.

An analysis of multiple NGO realities

This research does not suggest that international investment in NGOs to bridge several divides is necessarily a bad strategy, but it does provide ample evidence that, at least in Bosnia, this strategy has failed to produce intended outcomes. NGOs are an obvious part of the country's social landscape, providing numerous services and many jobs; at present, however, there is little evidence to conclude that they are either bridging different communities of people within Bosnia or effectively translating international ambitions into local change. NGOs do not always represent the voices of the Bosnian people, nor do they play a significant role in promoting democracy, interethnic tolerance, or peace. Like other chapters in this book, this research offers a structural explanation for the behavior of international and domestic actors and it demonstrates the conflictive power relationships associated with NGOs. That is, although NGOs are working hard and accomplishing certain objectives, their work is simultaneously impeded by structural constraints and incentives.

There are advantages and disadvantages to using the principal–agent (PA) theoretical framework to assess the broader role of NGOs in peacebuilding. PA can help explain unintended behaviors and explain why NGOs are sometimes unable to achieve their goals, despite good intentions and hard work. Yet, the framework also has notable drawbacks; it streamlines too much of what has happened in BiH; its assumptions about NGO behavior undeniably simplify the more complex motivations of these heterogeneous organizations. Moreover, PA assumes that NGOs have the same goals as the governments and intergovernmental organizations that support them; and the approach does not accommodate well the dynamic process of change in NGO–donor networks.

This empirical field research explains the complexity of post-war peacebuilding. It suggests that NGOs have many agendas, some which are obvious but others which are latent and perhaps even unknown. For example, perhaps it is enough that NGOs are providing jobs and skills for individuals—even if the organizations are not sustained or their objectives achieved. In time, perhaps these individuals will use their skills in other ways, ideally, helping to build democracy and peace from the bottom up. It is almost impossible, however, to track individuals and their trajectory without highlighting a skewed sample. Principal–agent theory neither illuminates the different motivations of NGO officials, nor does it capture change well. In contrast, fieldwork and interviews over time can demonstrate that institutional behavior, actors, setting, and incentive structure are all constantly evolving and adapting.

The disappointing performance of certain NGOs in specific sectors, combined with the reality of Bosnian society after more than a dozen years of investment and changing international conditions, have pushed international actors to acknowledge their errors, and they are regularly restructuring institutions and incentives to better monitor behavior and improve outcomes. International actors and NGOs are, thus, more likely to emphasize strengthening domestic capacity instead of identifying a specific agenda or specific benchmarks. For the US government, disappointment with the development of Bosnian NGOs and the NGO sector has resulted in a number of changes. There is, for example, some backlash against NGOs and the US government is working more with contractors that agree to specific, tangible outcomes, even though they have no evidence that this approach will produce better results.[105] Like other international actors, the US government is also giving more attention to strengthening state institutions, and making assistance to NGOs conditional on cooperation with the Bosnian government or other NGOs.[106] Similarly, EU members have shifted to helping Bosnian government institutions prepare for eventual accession while the European Commission has focused its efforts on strengthening government institutions, the rule of law, and economic development, making funding for NGOs contingent on their cooperation with other NGOs and with government.[107]

Some international donors, like the Swedish government, continue to invest in Bosnian NGOs, encouraging them to develop an indigenous capacity by building networks, creating umbrella organizations, or conducting research that takes stock of the lessons learned.[108] The Swedish International Development Agency is known as one of the very few international donors that conducts thorough evaluations of its work. Although its methodology is highly regarded and its efforts applauded, this practice is still not generally repeated by other donors. Its evaluation of its refugee return programs, women's issues, and peacebuilding all recognize the perverse dynamic created in the mid-1990s by the international community's zeal to create NGOs. Catholic Relief Services (CRS) has similarly overhauled its international assistance programs, making capacity building a priority and undertaking specific steps to empower local people and NGOs, rather than just giving jobs to international employees.[109]

The failure of many NGOs in Bosnia to become self-sustaining or more active in shaping policies is indeed unfortunate, but it is not permanent and the situation is not without hope. Elsewhere in the region there has been a similar, though less pronounced, trend in the early 1990s, fueled by international support for NGOs. Disappointing returns and unintended consequences have, however, resulted in significant shifts in funding strategies, and have created situations where local actors have sacrificed international support to accomplish domestically-driven agendas and encourage the development of a local constituency.[110] In the last few years, the inability of Bosnia's NGO sector to become self-sustaining or to become genuine representatives of civil society, along with the contradictory belief that the work has been done in the Balkans and it is time for international actors to move on to other pressing crises, have contributed to frustration among locals. However, and importantly, it has also fueled a distinct sense of liberation, as Bosnians have started to admit that their society has become overly dependent on the international community and that domestic solutions, and thus genuine domestic NGOs, are crucial to the country's stability and independence. Bosnian NGOs may remain dependent on the international community and other challenges are likely to remain. However, Bosnian NGOs are starting to find their voice, and since 2008 have started to work together to affect government policies.[111] They are only slowly becoming their own principals.

Conclusion

This volume is explicitly interested in how NGOs challenge IR theory. They do so in many ways that are often difficult to capture empirically, in part because the NGOs are so diverse, their work divided into so many sectors, and their effects so diffuse. Given the dearth of research on NGOs in peacebuilding, the goal here has been to demonstrate the importance of NGOs to policymakers, to assess the success and failure of the NGO peacebuilding strategy in Bosnia, and to explore the usefulness of both PA theory and this volume's analysis of NGO bridging to explain the complexities of peacebuilding NGOs. This chapter makes at least four contributions to the questions raised by DeMars and Dijkzeul in the introduction.

First, while academics may debate the role of NGOs in international relations, this research provides clear empirical evidence that at least in post-conflict peacebuilding settings like Bosnia, NGOs matter a great deal. They matter especially to Western policymakers, the goals they identify, and the policies and strategies they develop to foster peace. Put differently, in the day-to-day practice of building peace, governments and international organizations clearly and readily look to NGOs.

Second, NGOs are assumed to matter in peacebuilding because they are perceived as bridges; they are deployed with the purpose of bridging different groups within post-conflict societies, to bridge civil society and the reconstituted state, and to bridge international ambitions and local realities. The existence and growth of local NGOs is therefore regarded as an important indicator of stability, reconciliation and peace, and also as a force to promote them. With this said, these variables and processes are difficult to track. Ideally, NGOs will help bring people of different ethnic groups together and help transform relations and attitudes, but this, arguably, takes a while to occur. This means that new methods and approaches are needed to better understand when and where NGOs are best able to bridge actors and issues, and where and when they fail to achieve these goals. It is possible that too much donor influence may actually hamper their ability to bridge successfully between societal partners.

Third, this research highlights *how* NGOs bridge the material–normative divide and, although many NGOs are committed to positive change, these actors—like other organizations—face a series of material and organizational incentives and constraints that affect their behavior. The theoretical emphasis in this volume on the bridging roles of NGOs highlights this empirical dynamic in peacebuilding NGO networks. However, it is not clear to what extent the theory of bridging can explain the failure of peacebuilding NGOs to "bridge" (in the sense of reduce and ameliorate) the ethnic divides in Bosnia. It may be, because peacebuilding is so deeply intertwined with larger security issues, that actors such as ethnic leaders, donor governments and the military play a larger role than they do in other issue areas. As a consequence, these

230 *Case evidence: NGOs and networks*

political actors may seek to manipulate NGOs to such an extent that they become ineffective in achieving their mandates.

Finally, the principal–agent framework provides a useful, but incomplete way to explain complex and multi-layered outcomes with multiple causes, especially in vertical relations between donors and NGOs in the field. It also demonstrates conflictive power relationships, and why and how NGOs can have both positive and negative, unintended consequences. This is because NGOs always exist within a larger context and are dependent upon their relationships with other actors. Yet, PA theory captures neither change nor nuances well, especially beyond those vertical donor–NGO relationships. This is problematic because, in addition to NGOs' other qualities, they are defined and distinguished by change, their ability to respond, their capacity to adapt, and their willingness to restructure. At the same time, as much as we try to generalize about NGOs and their behavior, their greatest strength lies in their diversity and distinctiveness. The NGO challenge to IR theory, thus, becomes an even greater challenge for empirical research to track and demonstrate the practice and the power of NGOs.

Notes

1 I would like to thank the following for their comments on earlier drafts: Dennis Dijkzeul, William DeMars, David Forsythe, Paula Pickering, and Jon Western. I also thank Aaron Hansen and Kristen Broyhill for their research assistance.
2 James Dobbins, *America's Role in Nation-Building: From Germany to Iraq* (Santa Monica, Calif: RAND, 2003); Michael Ignatieff, *Empire Lite: Nation Building in Bosnia, Kosovo, and Afghanistan* (London: Vintage, 2003); Michael W. Doyle and Nicholas Sambanis, *Making War and Building Peace: United Nations Peace Operations* (Princeton, N.J.: Princeton University Press, 2006); Virginia Page Fortna, *Does Peacekeeping Work? Shaping Belligerents' Choices after Civil War* (Princeton, N.J.: Princeton University Press, 2008); and Robert Ricigliano, *Making Peace Last: A Toolbox for Sustainable Peacebuilding* (Boulder, Colo.: Paradigm, 2012).
3 *An Agenda for Peace*, Report of the Secretary-General of the United Nations (A/47/277—S/24111), 17 June 1992.
4 Thomas G. Weiss, *International NGOs, Global Governance, and Social Policy in the UN System*, Occasional Papers no. 3, Helsinki, Finland: STAKES, National Research and Development Centre for Welfare and Health (1999): 6.
5 Alexander Cooley and James Ron, "The NGO Scramble: Organizational Insecurity and the Political Economy of Transnational Action," *International Security* 27, no. 1 (2001): 5–39; Sarah Mendelson and John Glenn, eds, *The Power and Limits of NGOs* (New York: Columbia University Press, 2002); A. Lawrence Chickering, Isobel Coleman, P. Edward Haley

and Emily Vargas-Baron, *Strategic Foreign Assistance: Civil Society and International Security* (Stanford, Calif: Hoover Institution Press, 2006); and William Easterly, *The White Man's Burden: Why the West's Efforts to Aid the Rest Have Done So Much Ill and So Little Good* (New York: Penguin, 2006).

6 I began fieldwork in Bosnia in September 2000 and returned for several weeks at a time in 2001, 2003, 2005, 2007, 2008, and 2010. In total, I conducted more than 150 interviews in Bosnia, in the Federation cities of Sarajevo, Mostar, Zenica, Travnik and Brcko. Interviews were conducted alone or in a group, in English or with a Bosnian translator.

7 David Chandler, *Bosnia: Faking Democracy After Dayton* (London: Pluto Press, 2000); Roberto Belloni, "Civil Society and Peacebuilding in Bosnia and Herzegovina," *Journal of Peace Research* 38, no. 2 (2001): 163–180; Florian Bieber, "Bosnia-Herzegovina: Developments towards a More Integrated State?" *Journal of Muslim Minority Affairs* 22, no. 1 (2002): 205–218; V. P. Gagnon, "International NGOs in Bosnia-Herzegovina: Attempting to Build Civil Society," in *The Power and Limits of NGOs*, eds Sarah Mendelson and John Glenn (New York: Columbia University Press, 2002), 207–231; Timothy Donais, "A Tale of Two Towns: Human Security and the Limits of Post-War Normalization in Bosnia-Herzegovina," *Journal of Southern Europe and the Balkans* 7, no. 1 (2005): 19–33; Keith Brown, ed., *Transacting Transition: The Micropolitics of Democracy Assistance in the Former Yugoslavia* (Bloomfield, Conn.: Kumarian Press, 2006); Adam Fagan, "Civil Society in Bosnia Ten Years after Dayton," *International Peacekeeping* 12, no. 3 (2005): 406–419; Adam Fagan, "Neither 'North' nor 'South': The Environment and Civil Society in Post-conflict Bosnia-Herzegovina," *Environmental Politics* 15, no. 5 (2006): 787–802; and Dina Francesca Haynes, ed., *Deconstructing the Reconstruction: Human Rights and the Rule of Law in Postwar Bosnia and Herzegovina* (Burlington, Vt.: Ashgate, 2008).

8 Zlatko Hertic, Amela Spacanin and Susan Woodward, "Bosnia and Herzegovina," in *Good Intentions: Pledges of Aid for Postconflict Recovery*, eds Shepard Forman and Stewart Patrick (Boulder, Colo.: Lynne Rienner, 2000), 315.

9 Steven Woehrel, *CRS Report for Congress. Bosnia and Herzegovina: Issues for American Policy* (www.au.af.mil/au/awc/awcgate/crs/rl32392. pdf), 10 February 2005. For US bilateral assistance, US Department of State, "U.S. Foreign Policy and Foreign Assistance Objectives and Priorities," *FY 2007 U.S. Government Assistance to and Cooperative Activities with Central and Eastern Europe* (www.state.gov/p/eur/rls/rpt/seedfy07/116196.htm).

10 "EU Assistance to BiH," Delegation of the European Union to Bosnia and Herzegovina (2007), (www.europa.ba/?akcija=clanak&CID=22&jezik=2&LID=32).

11 *The ICVA Directory of Humanitarian and Development Agencies Operating in Bosnia and Herzegovina* (Sarajevo: International Council of Voluntary Agencies, 2000).

12 Thomas Carothers, *Aiding Democracy Abroad: The Learning Curve* (Washington, DC: Carnegie Endowment for International Peace, 1999); Larry Diamond, *Developing Democracy: Toward Consolidation*

(Baltimore, Md.: Johns Hopkins University Press, 1999); Marina Ottaway and Thomas Carothers, eds, *Funding Virtue: Civil Society Aid and Democracy Promotion* (Washington, DC: Carnegie Endowment for International Peace, 2000); Karen E. Smith, "Western Actors and the Promotion of Democracy," in *Democratic Consolidation in Eastern Europe*, eds Jan Zielonka and Alex Pravda (Oxford: Oxford University Press, 2001), 31–57; Sharon L. Wolchik and Jane L. Curry, eds, *Central and East European Politics: From Communism to Democracy* (Lanham, Md.: Rowman & Littlefield, 2007); and Paula Pickering, "Peacebuilding in the Balkans: The View from the Ground Floor" (Ithaca, NY: Cornell University Press, 2007).
13 Ottaway and Carothers, *Funding Virtue*, 11; Brown, *Transacting Transition*.
14 Belloni, "Civil Society and Peacebuilding," 163–180.
15 Chandler, *Bosnia*, 88.
16 Brown, *Transacting Transition*, 10.
17 Ian Smillie and Goran Todorovic, "Reconstructing Bosnia, Constructing Civil Society: Disjuncture and Convergence," in *Patronage or Partnership: Local Capacity Building in Humanitarian Crises*, ed. Ian Smillie (Bloomfield, Conn.: Kumarian, 2001); and Jeroen de Zeeuw and Krishna Kumar, eds, *Promoting Democracy in Postconflict Societies* (Boulder, Colo.: Lynne Rienner, 2006).
18 Chandler, *Bosnia*, 138.
19 Belloni, "Civil Society and Peacebuilding," 163–180.
20 Organization for Security and Co-operation in Europe, *OSCE Annual Report 2008*, Office of the Secretary General, Vienna 2009 (www.osce.org/secretariat/36699).
21 David Chandler, "Democratization in Bosnia: The Limits of Civil Society Building Strategies," *Democratization* 5, no. 4 (1998): 78–102; and Jude Howell and Jenny Pearce, *Civil Society and Development: A Critical Exploration* (Boulder, Colo.: Lynne Rienner, 2001).
22 USAID, FY 1998 Congressional Presentation.
23 USAID, "Core Report of the New Partnerships Initiative," 1995. After November 2001, the Center became the Office of Democracy and Governance.
24 USAID, FY 2000 Congressional Presentation.
25 Fagan, "Civil Society in Bosnia," 13.
26 Smillie and Todorovic, "Reconstructing Bosnia."
27 "Democracy and Human Rights," Delegation of the European Union to Bosnia and Herzegovina, 2008 (www.delbih.ec.europa.eu/Default.aspx?id=116&lang=EN).
28 Ann C. Hudock, *NGOs and Civil Society. Democracy by Proxy?* (Malden, Mass.: Blackwell, 2001), 50; Alcira Kreimer, John Eriksson, Robert Muscat, Colin Scott and Margaret Arnold, *The World Bank's Experience with Post-Conflict Reconstruction* (Washington, DC: World Bank, 1998); "History of the NATO-led Stabilisation Force (SFOR) in Bosnia and Herzegovina," NATO, 2001 (www.nato.int/sfor/docu/d981116a.htm); and Linton Wells and Charles Hauss, "Odd Couples: The DoD and NGOs," *PS* (July 2007): 485–487.

29 Chip Gagnon, "Catholic Relief Services, USAID, and Authentic Partnership in Serbia," in *Transacting Transition: The Micropolitics of Democracy Assistance in the Former Yugoslavia*, ed. Keith Brown (Bloomfield, Conn.: Kumarian Press, 2006). The author also interviewed several CRS representatives in 2007, 2001, and 2000 in Sarajevo, Bosnia. On the International Rescue Committee, see "The IRC in Bosnia & Herzegovina," (www.rescue.org/where/bosnia_herzegovina). On CARE International see Smillie and Todorovic, "Reconstructing Bosnia."
30 Sarah Chayes, *The Punishment of Virtue Inside Afghanistan After the Taliban* (New York: Penguin, 2006); Chickering et al., *Strategic Foreign Assistance*; Sarah Henderson, "Selling Civil Society," *Comparative Political Studies* 35 (March 2002): 139–167; Mendelson and Glenn, *The Power and Limits of NGOs*; and Peter Uvin, *Aiding Violence: The Development Enterprise in Rwanda* (West Hartford, Conn.: Kumarian Press, 1998).
31 "Reshaping International Priorities in Bosnia and Herzegovina," Berlin: European Stability Initiative, 2001.
32 Patrice McMahon and Jon Western, "The Death of Dayton," *Foreign Affairs* (September/October 2009): 69–83; and "Bosnia's Gordian Knot: Constitutional Reform," International Crisis Group, *Europe Briefing* no. 6812 (July 2012) (www.crisisgroup.org/en/regions/europe/balkans/bosnia-herzegovina/b068-bosnias-gordian-knot-constitutional-reform.aspx).
33 "Bosnia and Herzegovina Gap Analysis, USAID Strategic Planning Division Report," January 2011 (www.usaid.gov/sites/default/files/documents/1863/Bosnia%20and%20Herzegovina%2001-2011.pdf).
34 *Bosnia and Herzegovina Country Partnership Strategy for FY08–FY11*, World Bank Report CAS Completion Report, January 2011 (http://siteresources.worldbank.org/BOSNIAHERZEXTN/Resources/362025-1240235526234/CPS_BH_completion.pdf).
35 Peter Lippman, "Bosnia's 'Historic' Elections: The Usual Tensions, Plus a Seed of Hope," *Washington Report on Middle East Affairs* (December 2006) (www.wrmea.com/archives/December_2006/0612032.html), 32–33.
36 Imco Brouwer, "Weak Democracy and Civil Society Promotion: The Case of Egypt and Palestine," in *Funding Virtue: Civil Society Aid and Democracy Promotion*, eds Marina Ottaway and Thomas Carothers (Washington, DC: Carnegie Endowment for International Peace, 2000), 21–48.
37 *The NGO Directory* (Sarejevo: International Council of Voluntary Agencies, 1998).
38 "Mapping Study of Non-State Actors (NSA) in Bosnia-Herzegovina," Delegation of the European Union to Bosnia and Herzegovina, 2005.
39 USAID, *2008 NGO Sustainability Index for Central and Eastern Europe and Eurasia*, June 2009, (www.csogeorgia.org/uploads/developmentTrends/11/sustainability_index-2008.pdf).
40 USAID Mission Profile, "Bosnia and Herzegovina: The Challenge," 2007, photocopy.
41 Bieber, "Bosnia-Herzegovina," 205–218; Fagan, "Neither 'North' nor 'South,'" 787–802; and Pickering, *Peacebuilding in the Balkans*, 124.
42 "Mapping Study of Non-State Actors (NSA) in Bosnia-Herzegovina," 75.
43 Martha Walsh, "Aftermath: The Role of Women's Organizations in Postconflict Bosnia and Herzegovina," Working Paper no. 308 (July 2000), Center for Development Information and Evaluation, U.S.

Agency for International Development (http://pdf.usaid.gov/pdf_docs/PNACJ946.pdf), 11.
44 Ristin Thomasson, *To Make Room for Changes: Peace Strategies from Women Organisations in Bosnia and Herzegovina* (Sweden: The Kvinna till Kvinna Foundation, 2006), 35–37.
45 USAID, *NGO Sustainability Index*, Reports 2006, 2007, 2008.
46 "Mapping Study of Non-State Actors (NSA) in Bosnia-Herzegovina," 74.
47 USAID, *NGO Sustainability Index*, 2008.
48 "Evaluation of the Olof Palme International Center Western Balkans Program, Strategy for South East Europe Program, Albania, Bosnia and Herzegovina, Serbia, and Kosovo" (www.palmecenter.se/en), March 2006.
49 "Evaluation of the Olof Palme International Center Western Balkans Program."
50 Camilla Orjuela, "Building Peace in Sri Lanka? A Role for Civil Society?" *Journal of Peace Research* 40, no. 2 (2003): 195–212.
51 Interview with Judith Jones, Brcko, Bosnia, 2003.
52 Interview with Tadeusz Kazimierz, Brcko, 2003.
53 Miroslav Zivanovic, "Civil Society in Bosnia and Herzegovina: Lost in Transition," in *Civil Society and Good Governance in Societies in Transition*, ed. Wolfgang Benedek (Vienna: Neuer Wissenschäftlicher Verlag GmBh, 2006), 39.
54 Zivanovic, "Civil Society," 39–53; Pickering, *Peacebuilding in the Balkans*, 124; and Gagnon, "Catholic Relief Services."
55 Confidential interview with representative of International Council of Voluntary Agency, Sarajevo, October 2008.
56 Confidential interview with representative of the Center for Human Rights, Sarajevo, October 2008.
57 Gagnon, "Catholic Relief Services," 173.
58 McMahon and Western, "The Death of Dayton," 69–83.
59 Ibid.
60 Mancur Olson, *The Logic of Collective Action: Public Goods and the Theory of Groups*, 2nd edition (Cambridge, Mass.: Harvard University Press, 1971), 2.
61 Ibid., 53–65.
62 Fukuyama, *State Building*, 50–51.
63 Kenneth A. Oye, "Explaining Cooperation Under Anarchy: Hypotheses and Strategies," in *Cooperation Under Anarchy*, ed. Kenneth A. Oye (Princeton, N.J.: Princeton University Press, 1986), 20–22.
64 Henderson, "Selling Civil Society," 139–167.
65 Fukuyama, *State Building*.
66 ICVA Directory, Sarajevo, 1997.
67 "Bosnia and Herzegovina: The Challenge," 2007.
68 Richard Holbrooke, *To End a War* (New York: Random House, 1998); and Ivo Daalder, *Getting to Dayton* (Washington, DC: Brookings Institution Press, 2000).
69 The Peace Implementing Council was created in 1995 to represent the fifty-five countries and various international agencies that were involved in helping to implement the Dayton Peace Accords.

70 Mari Fitzduff and Cheyanne Church, *NGOs at the Table: Strategies for Influencing Policy in Areas of Conflict* (New York: Rowman & Littlefield, 2004), 3.
71 Holbrooke, *To End a War*; and Bose, *Bosnia after Dayton*.
72 Holbrooke, *To End a War*; and Chandler, *Bosnia*.
73 Daalder, *Getting to Dayton*, 174.
74 Anna Jarstad, "International Assistance to Democratization in Bosnia and Herzegovina, Kosovo and Macedonia," *Synthesis Report* 1, Swedish Emergency Management Agency, 2005: 31.
75 Holbrooke, *To End a War*, 364.
76 Jarstad, "International Assistance to Democratization," 31.
77 Zivanovic, "Civil Society," 39–53; and Pickering, *Peacebuilding in the Balkans*, 124.
78 Smillie and Todorovic, "Reconstructing Bosnia."
79 USAID, *NGO Sustainability Index*, 2008.
80 Olson, *The Logic of Collective Action*, 35.
81 Terry M. Moe, "The New Economics of Organization," *American Journal of Political Science* 28, no. 4 (1984): 739–77.
82 Ibid., 744; and Cooley and Ron, "The NGO Scramble," 5–39.
83 Janine R. Wedel, "U.S. Foreign Aid and Foreign Policy: Building Strong Relationships by Doing It Right!" *International Studies Perspectives* 6, no. 1 (2005): 36.
84 Janine R. Wedel, *Collision and Collusion: The Strange Case of Western Aid to Eastern Europe* (New York: Palgrave Macmillan, 2001), 27.
85 Brown, *Transacting Transition*; and Fagan, "Neither 'North' nor 'South,'" 787–802.
86 Fukuyama, *State Building*, 39–40.
87 Henderson, "Selling Civil Society," 139–167.
88 EU assistance to BiH, 2007.
89 Curt Tarnoff and Marian Leonardo Lawson, "Foreign Aid: An Introduction to U.S. Programs and Policy," *CRS Report*, 29 April 2009 (research.policyarchive.org/19806.pdf).
90 The World Bank, "Bosnia and Herzegovina" (www.worldbank.org/en/country/bosniaandherzegovina).
91 Gagnon, "Catholic Relief Services."
92 Interview with Mirsad Tokaca, Sarajevo, 2008.
93 Fagan, "Neither 'North' nor 'South,'" 787–802.
94 Interview with James Rodehaver, Sarajevo, 2008.
95 Fukuyama, *State Building*, 47.
96 Moe, "The New Economics of Organization," 756.
97 Steven Burg and Paul Shoup, *The War in Bosnia-Herzegovina: Ethnic Conflict and International Intervention* (New York: M. E. Sharpe 1999), 521–522.
98 Belloni, "Civil Society and Peacebuilding," 167.
99 Fitzduff and Church, *NGOs at the Table*.
100 Michael Edwards and David Hulme, *Beyond the Magic Bullet: NGO Performance and Accountability in the Post-Cold War World* (West Hartford, Conn.: Kumarian, 1996).
101 Fagan, "Neither 'North' nor 'South,'" 787–802.

102 P. J. Simmons, "Learning to Live with NGOs," *Foreign Policy* 112 (1998): 82–96.
103 Bieber, "Bosnia-Herzegovina," 205–218; and Fagan, "Neither 'North' nor 'South,'" 787–802.
104 Interview with Katica Hajrulahovic, Sarajevo, October 2008.
105 Interview with Mark Ellingstadt, Sarajevo, 2007.
106 Brown, *Transacting Transition*.
107 Fagan, "Neither 'North' nor 'South,'" 787–802.
108 Interview with Lejla Hadzic, Sarajevo, 2008.
109 Gagnon, "Catholic Relief Services."
110 Mendelson and Glenn, *The Power and Limits of NGOs*.
111 USAID, *NGO Sustainability Index*, 2008.

9 Follow the partners

Agency and explanation in the color revolutions

William E. DeMars

- Color revolutions and the democracy network
- Network analysis in international relations
- Hidden partners—turning the security actors
- NATO's weak agency but strong structure
- The counter-network
- Conclusion: agency and explanation

In the wake of the Euromaidan revolution of 2014, the Arab uprisings of 2011, and earlier color revolutions, it is clear that mass nonviolent democracy movements against authoritarian rule are no panacea. Even when they succeed in bringing down a dictator, they may initiate a protracted period of internal and regional conflict as seen in Ukraine and Egypt. Or they may descend into civil war and de facto state partition as in Syria and Libya.

Whatever the long-term consequences, the mobilization of nonviolent democracy movements has proven to be a resilient political formation, capable of crossing regional and cultural boundaries and structuring national and international political conflict.[1] As revolutionary tactics spread through a growing transnational network, the prospect of where the next one will strike instills both hope and fear.

For both scholars and policymakers, each new mass movement to "overthrow a dictator" heightens the urgency to address a set of thorny questions about the mix of internal and international factors needed to explain such events, and about the agency of democracy activists and their various international political and societal partners.

Agency is a complex concept that includes initiative in pursuing goals, originality in tactics, personal commitment, leadership on behalf of a larger community, and credit for success.[2] The agency of democracy activists in every democracy revolution has been challenged by their political critics, who have branded them as stooges of Western governments and foreign agents acting under the cover of NGOs. For these critics, the mere affiliation with a transnational network is *prima facie* evidence that democracy activists lack initiative, originality, and commitment, do not represent a national base, and do not deserve credit for their success.

However, the agency of democracy activists is also challenged—obliquely and inadvertently—by many political scientists who have attempted to explain the revolutions. As discussed below, their explanations have tended either to narrate the agency of activists in isolation from broader structural factors, or to privilege structural explanations at the expense of agency. Both alternatives, I argue, are based on a false dichotomy between agency and structure. In this chapter I work out a solution that recognizes agency and structure as not merely compatible but mutually constitutive—each is integral to the other and organically interwoven with the other.

This theoretical resolution is pursued through empirical investigation of the roles of NGOs and all their politically relevant "partners" in the spread of the color revolutions. Like many other scholars who not only study but also admire transnational NGOs (democracy activists in this case), I am troubled by a question: How can I explain or narrate their revolutions, including the transnational network linkages, without playing into the hands of those who would delegitimize them as imperialist intrusions—those who would, in effect, impugn the agency of the activists? Some scholars solve this problem by limiting the scope of their empirical investigations exclusively to those actors in the network who share a common discourse, who believe in common norms, and who display explicit visible ties with the NGO activists. Instead, this chapter will show that by following *all* the relevant societal and political partners, even if they are hidden or deviate from the dominant norms of the network, the agency of the activists is recovered and even reaffirmed in a thicker and more vivid portrayal.

In short, the methodological imperative to relentlessly *follow the partners* is the key to both ontological comprehensiveness and epistemological clarity in understanding NGOs and transnational networks.

This chapter first describes the color revolutions and the transnational democracy network in a journalistic manner that is purposely under-theorized (or *implicitly* theorized). The second section presents and critiques an influential IR theory of transnational advocacy networks that emphasizes the agency of activists. The third section explores a category of hidden (or at least veiled) partners that has been essential in all the color revolutions: the security actors in the governments that activists seek to democratize. The fourth section addresses

NGO agency in the color revolutions 239

largely hidden security actors in the transnational structure of the democracy networks. The fifth section brings in the elaborate counter-network created to freeze the democratic revolutions and promote instead an alternative model of "sovereign democracy." The final section proposes broader conclusions on the interplay of agency and structure in the democracy networks, including how transnational democracy activists defend their own agency against critics, and the structural power of the democracy network.

Color revolutions and the democracy network

From 2000 to 2005, a series of mass, non-violent movements successfully overthrew authoritarian leaders in four post-communist countries, and rebuked foreign hegemony in one Arab country (Lebanon). These "color revolutions" resembled in some respects previous waves of democratization, and in particular the 1989 peaceful transitions in Eastern Europe, but they also shared distinctive features and mutual links sufficient to constitute a new pattern, and perhaps a new wave.[3] In the most typical case:

- the entrenched leader of a post-communist country;
- who had routinely manipulated elections to stay in power;
- was ousted by a peaceful majority mobilized by a charismatic youth movement; and
- with foreign training and assistance from a constantly changing transnational network of democracy promoters, including NGOs and governments.

These movements and revolutions surprised even seasoned observers.[4] In most accounts, this wave of color revolutions began with the overthrow of President Slobodan Milosevic in the Bulldozer Revolution in Serbia (2000). Similar movements succeeded to some degree in the Rose Revolution in Georgia (2003), the Orange Revolution in Ukraine (2004), the Cedar Revolution in Lebanon (2005), and the Tulip Revolution in Kyrgyzstan (2005).[5]

Then, quite suddenly, the method stopped working. Nonviolent movements supported by transnational networks continued to replicate and diffuse to other countries through the transnational network, but they no longer succeeded in their goals. In 2005, movements failed in Belarus, Uzbekistan and Azerbaijan. Spreading beyond post-communist states, the Saffron Revolution failed in Myanmar in 2007, and the

Green Revolution in Iran continues to press unsuccessfully for change. Then in 2011, just as suddenly as the revolutions had stopped in 2005, they seemed to reemerge in the Arab world, with the "Dignity Revolution" in Tunisia and the "Lotus Revolution" in Egypt as the most successful examples.[6]

By most accounts, Serbia in the year 2000 created the template for the strategic approach that other color revolutions later adapted.[7] While the 1999 NATO bombing of Serbia had cost a billion dollars, killed thousands of people, and left Milosevic in power, the Otpor October Revolution cost some tens of millions of dollars of Western aid, killed no-one, and got rid of Milosevic.

Not only did NGOs provide Otpor with nonviolence training and supplies, but NGOs also documented the experience and strategy of Otpor, and took it on the road to democratize other countries. Peter Ackerman and Jack Duvall had already produced a series of six historical films on successful nonviolent struggles in the twentieth century.[8] While that film series aired on public television in the United States in 2000, Ackerman and Duvall helped a film team enter Serbia during the Otpor revolution. The project gained support from American GONGOs (government organized NGOs), such as the International Republican Institute, the National Democratic Institute, and the United States Institute of Peace, that were already aiding Otpor.

The result was the film *Bringing Down a Dictator*, which aired on PBS Frontline in March 2002. The film has since been translated into Arabic, Burmese, English, Farsi, French, Indonesian, Mandarin, Russian, Spanish, Uzbek and Vietnamese.[9] From the beginning, it was packaged for export.[10] Ackerman and Duvall formed their own NGO in 2002, The International Center on Nonviolent Conflict (ICNC), to promote the film and other tools for spreading the ideas of nonviolent conflict.[11]

The film itself played a critical role in catalyzing the 2003 Rose Revolution in the former Soviet republic of Georgia. It was shown every Saturday for months on an independent television channel, followed by discussions among Georgians on how to adapt the tactics for their situation.[12] The same film was shown before and during the electoral revolution in Ukraine in 2004.[13] Some activists from Serbia's Otpor and Georgia's Kmara youth movements joined the transnational network, with aid from Western NGOs and governments, to provide training and advice for Ukraine's Pora.[14]

This description reflects a conventional, journalistic account of the color revolutions, implicitly theorized to emphasize the agency of the transnational actors and to some extent the agency of the cosmopolitan youth activists in each country who eagerly import transnational

NGO agency in the color revolutions 241

tactics. It is a pluralist narrative of global civil society rising up against the authoritarian state, and secondarily a globalist story of spreading global norms of democracy. The account underplays social structure and the complexity of agency. The following sections excavate additional layers of the reality of the color revolutions.

Network analysis in international relations

All these color revolutions actively participated in, and helped to replicate and spread, complex transnational networks that featured NGOs in leading roles while including a wide range of other types of actors. The core group in each national movement—such as Otpor, Pora, and Kmara—functioned as, and assumed the institutional shape of, a transnational NGO.

These patterns, and empirical details that will emerge below, raise theoretical questions about NGOs, network replication and change across three categories (see Table 9.1): ontological (what sorts of relevant entities are out there?), methodological (how do we go about finding and investigating them?), and epistemological (how can we understand and give an intelligible account of them?).

Table 9.1 Theoretical questions on replication and change in NGOs and networks

Ontological questions	• What is a network? • In what respects do NGOs lead networks? • Must transnational organizations or institutions be autonomous from state influence to be considered important in their own right?
Methodological questions	• How can an observer identify the actors that are members of a network? • How does an observer know when to stop looking for additional members of a network?
Epistemological questions	• Can members of a network be hidden from outside observers, or even hidden from some other members of the network? • How can the replication and spread of similar networks be explained? • Can both traditional power resources and transnational norms and institutions coexist and play significant causal roles together? • If so, how can we give a coherent account of this complex causality?

242 *Case evidence: NGOs and networks*

The questions in Table 9.1 have been addressed by political scientists for some time, but the academic Balkanization of the discipline has hampered understanding. The phenomena of the color revolutions illustrate the extent to which the subfields of both Comparative Politics and International Relations have failed to cross the boundary between the domestic and the international realms.

From the study of human rights networks and the NGOs that generate them, general network theory can be applied to the democracy networks. Margaret Keck and Kathryn Sikkink have elaborated very clearly a set of premises about networks and NGOs that many other IR scholars share, explicitly or implicitly.[15] Five premises are crucial in shaping what observers and scholars can or cannot see:

1 Keck and Sikkink limit their purview to "transnational advocacy networks" (TANs), thereby excluding from empirical scrutiny those networks, NGOs, and any other types of actors that do not undertake explicit, public, advocacy roles.[16]
2 They affirm that "international and domestic NGOs play a central role in all advocacy networks."[17] They argue both that "activists act on behalf of networks," but also that "The agency of a network usually cannot be reduced to the agency even of its leading members."[18]
3 They acknowledge that networks, while usually led by NGOs, often include a wide range of other types of actors, which may include but are not limited to social movements, foundations, media, "churches, trade unions, consumer organizations, and intellectuals," parts of intergovernmental organizations (IGOs), and parts of governments.[19]
4 They understand and define (transnational advocacy) networks as including "those relevant actors working internationally on an issue, who are bound together by shared values, a common discourse, and dense exchanges of information and services."[20]
5 Crucially, they study and examine networks by analyzing *campaigns*, which they define as "sets of strategically linked activities in which members of a diffuse principled network ... develop explicit, visible ties and mutually recognized roles in pursuit of a common goal (and generally a common target) .... They must also consciously seek to develop a 'common frame of meaning' ... "[21]

These five premises also underlie conventional, journalistic accounts of the color revolutions. In fact, each color revolution has reflected some of Keck and Sikkink's model of transnational advocacy networks. They are led by activists who work through NGOs to publicly advocate shared discourse and norms. The networks include other kinds of members, notably the US Department of State and the foreign ministries of European governments. Members of the networks display explicit, visible ties and mutually recognized roles. Indeed, they recognize each other by observing who engages in public advocacy of the network's common values, norms, and discourse in service of the common goal of "bringing down a dictator."

However, this approach is theoretically problematic in that it simultaneously (1) privileges the agency of the activists, who lead the NGOs, that lead the network, (2) causally attributes the success of the network to the agency of the activists, and (3) guards the first two assumptions by conceptually confining the extent of the network exclusively to those visible actors who openly engage in public advocacy while sharing common discourse, values and goals. In short, for Keck and Sikkink the network and the public advocacy campaign are the same thing, and both are defined to comprise only those actors that share the norms articulated by the activists.

Early on, Keck and Sikkink express the penetrating observation that, "Part of what is so elusive about networks is how they seem to embody elements of agent and structure simultaneously."[22] In this chapter, I attempt to follow this insight, while challenging other aspects of their network theory. By focusing so tightly on the values and norms, or "principled ideas," that are declared by activists on behalf of the whole network, Keck and Sikkink simply reaffirm the agency that activists claim for themselves. In the "boomerang pattern" of transnational campaigns, "domestic NGOs bypass their state and directly search out international allies to try to bring pressure on their states from outside," by throwing boomerangs of information, symbolism, leverage and accountability.[23]

Keck and Sikkink reflect a broad trend within the IR subfield of International Organization to overemphasize the agency of international organizations at the expense of recognizing the structural influence of states.[24] We need conceptual alternatives, I would argue, to the false dichotomy of either affirming the agency of international organizations as autonomous from states, or else denying their agency as the witting or unwitting tools of states. The politics of international organizations is more subtle and interesting than those dichotomous extremes would allow.

Having attributed agency to the activists and the network, Keck and Sikkink can pursue a simple policy analysis to assess the effectiveness and causality of the network. However, by limiting the conceptual and empirical scope of the network exclusively to those actors linked by common norms and public advocacy, this approach fails to consider alternative causal explanations of policy success.

To modify Keck and Sikkink's conception of NGOs and networks, I affirm two of their five premises: that NGOs are the central actors in transnational networks (#2), and that such networks nevertheless include a wide variety of other types of actors (#3). However, in my view, the other three premises work together to obscure from the researcher's gaze critical aspects of the politics of transnational networks. In effect, this approach conflates campaigns and networks, misleading the observer to stop looking for network members too soon. This happens in three ways. First, limiting one's empirical purview to *advocacy* networks, in which the activity of public advocacy defines the networks, reinforces an assumption that non-advocacy NGOs that may share some links with members of the network, and actors that play non-public (hidden) roles in the network, either do not exist as part of the network or are not important. Second, the definition of a campaign reinforces the same blind spot by insisting that network members must "develop explicit, visible ties and mutually recognized roles." Finally, networks and campaigns are effectively conflated as both are defined by their members' "shared values," "common discourse," "common goal," and "common frame of meaning." In effect, they are advising researchers: To find a network, look for a campaign. Keck and Sikkink attempt to avoid this conflation of networks and campaigns by their strategy to "consider non-campaigns—issues that activists identified as problematic, but around which networks did not campaign."[25] However, this strategy does not succeed—networks and campaigns remain effectively conflated in their theory—because these "noncampaigns" are issues on which a group of activists, who had worked together on previous campaigns, already shared common values, discourses, and frames of meaning, and were only seeking new goals and targets.

An alternative approach is to consider as members of a transnational network (not limited to public advocacy) all those actors that share any common partners with the skein of NGOs that is the starting point. NGOs retain their central roles in this conception of network because NGOs are the most prolific partnering actors in world politics. This activity of linking, or partnering, or bridging across types of actors that otherwise would not have anything to do with each other, is one of the "anchoring practices" of NGOs, as suggested in the Introduction to this volume. This point of departure can make a profound difference, not only theoretically but also methodologically, as scholars conduct empirical research in the field. Following this alternative approach, the researcher does not stop looking for partners, or members of the network, when all the public advocacy actors who share visible ties and mutual recognition have been exhausted. Quite often, this is precisely where the more interesting politics of the network really begins. We can test this alternative view of networks by returning to the color revolutions, and "following the partners" to discover additional partners hidden in plain sight.

Hidden partners—turning the security actors

In the film *Bringing Down a Dictator*, Velimir Ilic, the mayor of Cacak, is interviewed saying, "Special units for anti-terrorist actions were expecting us in Belgrade. They'd been cooperating with us closely. We made radio contact with them every ten minutes. I would then give the information to my fellow citizens. We have the police. They are taking our side any minute now." Zoran Dindic, one of the top politicians in the opposition electoral coalition, states in the film, "We didn't know how police would react. We knew that some part of police will not react against the people, but we didn't know about all parts of police. And the police were very, very confused."[26] To this degree, the leaders of Otpor and the electoral coalition against Milosevic, as well as the American activists who made the film, are quite open about the contacts that were sought and achieved with the Serb security forces. In fact, these contacts were much more extensive than the film shows, some of them were partly or fully covert at the time, and not all of them have yet been made public.

In any government, and particularly an authoritarian or semi-authoritarian government, the president or strong man will have at his disposal multiple units of police, military forces, security and intelligence agencies, and elite special forces attached to these various agencies. The literature on the color revolutions is very clear that a central strategic goal of the mass, nonviolent struggle is to induce defections by individual members, or whole organizations, within the security bureaucracies of the dictator who is the target of the revolution. The dictator falls when his security forces disobey his orders to suppress the opposition. This point is most clearly articulated in pieces authored by participants in the color revolutions themselves, or professionals affiliated with the transnational NGOs that aid them.[27]

In the case of Serbia, there is considerable evidence that Otpor and the opposition electoral coalition had developed extensive contacts with the police as part of their purposeful, long-term strategy. The evidence is less clear over what contacts they had with the Serb army

246 *Case evidence: NGOs and networks*

and intelligence agencies. According to Zoran Zivkovic, mayor of Nils and considered an Otpor ally, "We had secret talks with the army and police, the units we knew would be drafted to intervene. And the deal was that they would not disobey, but neither would they execute."[28] According to Binnendijk and Marovic, while the opposition coalition included two retired army generals in its political leadership, "despite these connections, the opposition never established communication with the Army generals, and never received any guarantees that the military would not intervene in the case of a mass protest. In the end, although the Serbian army mobilized troops into the outskirts of Belgrade, there was never a serious attempt to reach the city centre."[29] The army in Serbia may have been deterred by the size of the crowd from intervening, may have had important contacts with other less-noticed network partners, or may have been persuaded that Milosevic was on his way out and decided not to go down with him.

In contrast to Serbia, for the case of Ukraine's Orange Revolution in 2004 there is considerable evidence of strong contacts by the opposition with not only the police, but also the military and the main intelligence agency. According to Binnendijk and Marovic, in Ukraine, beginning two years before the revolution, "opposition elites made direct communication with military officers a central—if covert—objective."[30] Thus, there are limits to the transparency of contacts between the nonviolent revolutionaries and security forces, and covert contacts are a tactical option. In Ukraine there was a dramatic confrontation behind the scenes. Certain special forces units attached to the Interior Ministry were still loyal to President Leonid Kuchma, and it was feared that they would obey orders to use force against the demonstrators in Kiev. In the event, elements in the military and the intelligence agency threatened and persuaded the Interior Ministry to back off, effectively deterring them by the threat of facing a superior force.[31]

What are the theoretical implications of bringing into the story these security actors, who are linked to the principled actors in the network, but "hidden" in plain sight? Are they "partners" in the network? Or are they, rather, "targets" of the network? By the conventional view of partners as actors that share normative commitments and display explicit, visible ties, this is a difficult question. Certainly the security people who retire and join the democracy movement are partners. But what about the covert contacts within the security bureaucracies? If we knew their motives were pure, could we forgive their nonpublic cooperation? In the Ukraine case, one could categorize the military and intelligence elements who assisted the democracy movement as authentic partners in the network, while placing outside the network

NGO agency in the color revolutions 247

the special forces units attached to the Interior Ministry that were deterred from attacking the demonstrators. However, this distinction is untenable because (1) in the end all those units disobeyed orders to attack the democracy activists, and (2) we know very little about the motives of either group.

Indeed, these conceptual distinctions between believers and unbelievers in the norms of the network, and between public and covert ties, are themselves untenable. From the point of view of the activists themselves, these distinctions break down. The strategy of nonviolent resistance is precisely to induce broad cooperation in the campaign from people with a very wide range of motives, and not to demand that they declare their deep personal beliefs. Even the distinction between partners and targets breaks down, because the most successful democracy revolutions *target* the security forces precisely in order to turn them into functional *partners*. It may make more sense to conceptualize the network from the start as including all those actors that share any common ties. Maybe the activists have partners that they do not know about, and that do not share their values.

Perhaps the assumption of shared norms in the network is carrying too much explanatory weight. It distracts from the more complex relationship between social structure and actor agency. For the activists in a democracy network, the overarching structure, the social fact, is the stubborn support of the security bureaucracies for a dictator who keeps stealing elections from a dysfunctional political opposition. If you are, for example, a college student in this society, you can easily exercise agency by finding a place in the corrupt system. Or you can fashion, perhaps with some foreign friends, a form of agency that promises to transform the structure itself. In either case, the given social structure not only constrains your agency, but simultaneously actualizes it. You have no agency without the structure.

It is beyond the scope of this study to review in detail the ways that scholars of comparative politics tend to privilege structural explanations for the color revolutions, in a mirror image of the way IR scholars privilege agentic explanations. Comparativists have never ignored NGOs. However, while they increasingly acknowledge "outside-in" international factors, such as the transnational democracy network in the color revolutions, they still tend to view them as external, exogenous factors that do not have to be explained.[32]

Ironically, both comparativists who study postcommunist revolutions and IR scholars who study the transnational democracy network share the same blind spot. Both largely ignore NATO.

NATO's weak agency but strong structure

It is well documented that the governments of the United States and several European countries provided foreign aid funding to the oppositions in Serbia and Ukraine. And it is known that some of the contacts by the national movements with their national security forces remained covert during some period of the nonviolent struggle. Much less is known about any direct contacts between the diplomatic, military and intelligence agencies in the United States and Europe and the security agencies of the governments of Serbia and Ukraine, or other countries that faced a possible revolution. But there is some evidence.

For Madeleine Albright, the American secretary of state in 2000, getting Milosevic out of power was a very significant goal of American foreign policy. According to William D. Montgomery, who was then based in the US Embassy in Budapest and who had contacts with Otpor leaders during that period:

> Milosevic was personal for Madeleine Albright, a very high priority. She wanted him gone, and Otpor was ready to stand up to the regime with a vigor and in a way that others were not. Seldom has so much fire, energy, enthusiasm, money—everything—gone into anything as into Serbia in the months before Milosevic went.[33]

What else, besides send money, did US and European governments actually do?

Tim Marshall, a veteran television reporter for Britain's Sky News, spent most of 1999 and 2000 reporting from in and around Serbia, covering the lead up to the 1999 NATO bombing of Kosovo and Serbia, the war itself, and also the aftermath, including Otpor's Bulldozer revolution.[34] Rarely is this entire period covered by a single person or narrated as a single story. Instead, most observers are interested primarily in the NATO bombing campaign of 1999, or else in the nonviolent revolution of 2000.[35] Marshall's broader scope allows him to portray the growing attention by NATO member states toward the growing list of transnational threats from former Yugoslavia: humanitarian, human rights, economic, and security threats, in the form of ethnic cleansing, genocide, mass rape, refugees and internally displaced persons, concentration camps, warlords, transnational organized crime, and arms smuggling.[36]

Slobodan Milosevic, the "Butcher of the Balkans," had been the single person most responsible for transnational threats emanating from the former Yugoslavia since it began to break up. Yet for a few years after 1995, Milosevic was considered the solution for the Balkans, rather than the problem, because his adherence to the Dayton Accords held back the region's characteristic chaos. And then during 1998 the Kosovo Liberation Army (KLA) began mobilizing in Kosovo (still part of Serbia), and the Serb police responded to their provocations. As in the early 1990s, the most powerful NATO member states had every reason to train their "eyes" on Milosevic and Serbia, including diplomatic reporting, military intelligence, human intelligence (spies), technical intelligence (signals and imagery), and "open source" intelligence (reporting by journalists and NGOs).[37] Now Milosevic was becoming the problem again, and NATO members were losing their patience with him.

While many of his sources are not named, Marshall obtained a statement on the record from Mark Kirk, who served with US Naval Intelligence during the Kosovo war. Kirk portrayed NATO strategic intentions candidly:

> Through the 90's everyone felt we could work with Milosevic. His mastery of the English language stood him in good stead. But eventually we opened up a huge operation against him, both secret and open. We felt that if we don't get rid of him he's going to start a war in Montenegro and Macedonia, and this not only risked a humanitarian crisis, it also risked our NATO allies Greece and Turkey being dragged in.[38]

In short, beyond humanitarian threats, Milosevic also threatened the unity of NATO itself as he continued to provoke wars. All means, "both secret and open," were on the table.

To keep their eyes on Milosevic, British and American special forces military personnel were inserted in two civilian observer missions sent to Kosovo in 1998 and 1999 by the Organization for Security and Cooperation in Europe (OSCE).[39]

After the breakdown of negotiations in 1999, NATO bombed the Serbian Army in Kosovo, and civilian targets in Belgrade, from March to June 1999.[40] In the lead up to the war and the war itself, the United States and other NATO powers spied on Serbia to identify targets, Serb spies inside NATO reported NATO's target lists and bombing schedules to the Serbian military, and Serb agents fed misinformation to NATO.[41] By June, 50,000 NATO troops were in Kosovo, and Slobodan Milosevic was indicted for war crimes by the UN Special Tribunal, *yet Milosevic was still in power in Belgrade.*

No wonder Madeleine Albright was angry. So were many senior American, British and other European officials. And so were many ordinary

Serbs, and many Serb military, police and government officials. NATO's collective military "agency"—taking the form of thousands of bombs dropped on Serb military targets—had failed to dislodge Milosevic. NATO's military agency was weak.

After what Milosevic had put NATO through during the decade of the 1990s, no one should be surprised that in the year 2000 American and British intelligence capabilities remained focused on Serbian government and society. Spies were engaged in parallel with diplomats and NGO activists from the same countries, whether known or unknown by each other. They were partners, willy nilly. Ironically, in this case, the spooks shared the same target and the same goal of "bringing down a dictator," even if they did not share the values, discourse, common frame of meaning—and especially the visible ties—with the NGO advocacy network.

After the bombing stopped in June 2000, British diplomats in the Foreign Office, military staffers in the Ministry of Defence, and spies in MI6 acted in concert. They were all, in the words of a British ambassador in the region, "talent spotting" (each with their somewhat distinct sets of contacts) for people in Serbia who could help bring down Milosevic.[42] British military and intelligence people made face-to-face contacts with Serb military and intelligence people in London, Belgrade, Montenegro, and Bosnia.[43] The British Foreign Office, for their part, escalated support for independent media, and reached out to members of the political opposition. They promised opposition figures that the West would never again deal with Milosevic.[44]

In short, the central strategic task of the Serb opposition in the upcoming political season—to contact, persuade, and recruit elements of the government, and especially the security forces, to abandon the dictator—was actively aided by the various contacts of British spies, soldiers and diplomats.

Otpor enters Marshall's narrative in October 1999, when the International Republican Institute (an American GONGO) organized a meeting at the Budapest Marriott Hotel for retired US Colonel Robert Helvey to teach Otpor activists Gene Sharp's theory of nonviolence. This scene is familiar from *Bringing Down a Dictator*. However, Marshall adds many more NATO government links to Otpor and the political opposition: German money and training helped support opposition politicians; satellite and mobile phones, faxes and computers came in through the embassy of a Scandinavian country; political technicians came in on diplomatic passports. Some Serb intelligence officials knew about the opposition's foreign government contacts, but neglected to pass the information to other Serbian government agencies that might act on it. The CIA helped identify and freeze out a mole in opposition circles who was passing their tactics to the government.[45]

Marshall's account brings in something that scholars ignore. The elephant in the room is NATO. The politics of the democracy network is not fully intelligible without bringing in the multiple roles of NATO governments.

Does the mere invocation of NATO attention really annihilate the agency and legitimacy of the students in Otpor, as the enemies of Otpor believe and some NGO scholars fear? I would argue no, authentic political agency need not be incompatible with a complex political environment. Ironically, with all of NATO's military and intelligence power, its agency was relatively weak. NATO failed to dislodge Milosevic by bombing in 1999. And NATO spies and military advisors did not overthrow him in a nonviolent revolution in 2000. Instead, a majority of Serbs voted against him, and turned out in the streets to persuade the security forces that they were the majority.

If NATO agency is weak, what of NATO as social structure for the agency of other actors, in particular the democracy activists? What is the secret of structural power? We will need to excavate another layer of the story to understand it.

Bringing NATO into the story clarifies what is at stake at a macro level in the color revolutions. They are part of a larger struggle to transform and reconstitute the dominant political and normative structures of Europe itself. And NATO is not the only alternative on the scene. We need to follow the partners one more significant step.

The counter-network

Some observers argue that the transnational democracy network influences particular revolutions only at the margins.[46] Nevertheless, the surviving dictatorships in regions where revolutions have already succeeded are less complacent about the network's potency to metastasize into their countries. The scale, sophistication and sheer elaborateness of the counter-network against the democracy network is the strongest testimony to the latter's power and appeal.

Russia and Iran have led the way to cooperate with other threatened autocracies to create multifaceted, transnational campaigns to counter the democracy networks across the entire range of their diplomatic, political, military, intelligence, economic, and NGO/civil society dimensions.[47] Vladimir Putin became president of Russia in 2000, the year of the Bulldozer Revolution. His government acquiesced in the transition in Serbia. But it viewed the 2003 Rose Revolution in Georgia with shock and alarm, because it revealed Russia's loss of influence in its vital "near abroad." Then the 2004 Orange Revolution in Ukraine generated real hysteria over the humiliation of losing influence in such a large and important neighbor, and fear of a wave of "colored revolutions" engineered by the West that could sweep the entire region including Russia itself.[48]

The very term, "color (or colored) revolutions," which is repeated without attribution by hundreds of journalists and scholars, emerges at this particular moment. Sergey Ivanov, the Russian minister of defense, coined the phrase in a speech at the Council on Foreign Relations in New York in January 2005. Ivanov asserted that Russia would react strongly "to exports of revolutions to the CIS states, no matter and what color—pink, blue, you name it."[49] Thus, the phrase originated as a *political* claim that the democratic revolutions are a strategy aimed by the West at the entire Commonwealth of Independent States (former Soviet Union). It is ironic that the phrase "color revolution" points to a high-stakes struggle for regional hegemony when it is used by analysts who ignore that struggle.

In 2005 Russia began to mount an elaborate national and international campaign to counter the democracy network. This effort included:

- overhauling Russian electoral laws and targeting independent media and NGOs;
- Creating and funding new GONGOs and civil society organizations loyal to the regimes;
- creating new pro-government youth movements;
- regulating access to and content on the internet;
- exporting similar regulations and practices to other CIS states;
- organizing friendly and pliable election monitoring efforts through regional organizations such as the CIS, Shanghai Cooperation Organization, and the African Union;
- integrating internationally with China and other Asian governments through the Shanghai Cooperation Organization to assert an alternative ideology based on the principles of multipolarity, sovereignty, and stability;
- working with China to use or threaten vetoes in the UN Security Council to defend the principle of sovereignty; and
- creating an international NGO, the Institute of Democracy and Cooperation, with offices in Paris and New York City, to monitor and criticize human rights practices in the West.[50]

The scale and range of these efforts constitute powerful, backhanded testimony to the force of the transnational democracy network. The mounting of the counter-network is also is the most plausible explanation for the freezing of democracy revolutions in post-communist states from 2005 to the Ukraine Euromaidan revolution in 2014.

The stakes in the regional power struggle are significant.[51] The risk of war with Russia is not negligible. The cyber-attack on Estonia in 2007—when the country was already a full member of NATO—certainly originated in Russia, and may have been launched with the collaboration or acquiescence of the Russian government. Russia subsequently fought a combination kinetic and cyber war with Georgia in 2008 after the latter was promised eventual membership in NATO, and then cut off natural gas flows to Ukraine to punish it for political waywardness in 2009. And Russia's 2014 annexation of Crimea, and military influence in eastern Ukraine, creates a new level of insecurity throughout the region.

The stakes of the color revolutions include what power relations will be embedded in the regional social structure of Europe and Central Asia, and perhaps beyond. Once the transnational democracy network exists, and begins to succeed, it becomes part of the given social structure for the agency of the authoritarian governments. Their agency is precisely to assert an alternative structure, but they are forced to do something new because the democracy network has increasingly rendered impotent the authoritarian practices that had worked since 1991.

By acknowledging these regional political stakes, and the structural dimension of the democracy network, this analysis runs the risk of reducing the NGOs and network activists to the level of mere tools in a great power rivalry. Such a conclusion, however, would accept the false dichotomy between agency and structure in explaining social phenomena, by assuming that the structural power of the democracy network (itself constituted by the agency of the NGOs and activists) must be conflated with, and reduced to, the imperialist agency of NATO. Such a conclusion would also misunderstand the reality of power, and the role of international organizations and institutions, and how states and regions are reconstructed in world politics. In other words, it would be simultaneously bad Realism, bad Liberalism, and bad Constructivism.

The alternative to such a comedy of errors will not be found by following deductively some preordained theory. But it just may be realized by thinking through what we have actually discovered empirically by following the partners in the color revolutions.

Conclusion: agency and explanation

There are four challenges at stake in this chapter. The first is the question of how to affirm the authentic political agency of national

254 Case evidence: NGOs and networks

democracy activists, who are denounced by their enemies as merely puppets of the West. The second challenge is to illustrate the methodological benefits of following the partners when studying NGOs, in order to discover all the layers of politics in the network. This challenge complicates the first by illuminating several additional sets of political actors, whose political agency is often misunderstood as a threat to affirming the agency of national democracy activists. Third is a challenge of explanation: for observers to incorporate and assess the relative weights of all the relevant categories of actors: including the national democracy activists, the national security and intelligence elites whose loyalty to the dictator must be undermined, the transnational democracy activists, the international military and intelligence actors in Western governments, and finally the counter-network actors sponsored by Russia and others. The final challenge is also one of explanation: for scholars to overcome the false dichotomy between agency and structure in order to tell the whole story of the color revolutions.

Let us begin by listening to the voices of democracy activists—both transnational and national—defending the authenticity of their own agency.

Peter Ackerman and Jack Duvall have powerfully facilitated the transnational dissemination of the tactics and lessons of mass nonviolent conflict. Their NGO, the International Center on Nonviolent Conflict (ICNC), sets aside a section of its website for "Setting the Record Straight" in response to criticisms. In a representative entry, Jack Duvall argues that the Center is an educational foundation that provides information about how civilian-based movements and campaigns have used civil resistance, but, "We have never taught anyone how 'to overthrow governments.'"[52] The ICNC manages a delicate balance, maintaining that it has never taught anyone how to overthrow governments, while also disseminating hundreds of resources including the video *Bringing Down a Dictator* in ten languages, and Gene Sharp's book, *From Dictatorship to Democracy,* downloadable free of charge in 22 languages.[53]

Duvall is hypersensitive to publicity on the role of transnational democracy activists (like himself and the ICNC), because enemies of democracy routinely use it to discredit local democracy activists. In response, the ICNC frequently distinguishes its own transnational agency from the truly heroic agency of local people responding directly to oppression.

This emphasis on local agency echoes the view of Sonja Licht, herself the director of the Soros Open Society Institute in Serbia during the Bulldozer Revolution. Licht, who occupied the position of a local activist openly allied with outside activists, told Tim Marshall, "We were not helping foreigners, foreigners were helping us. I am Serbian and I am part of the culture. There are people who will never understand."[54] Licht's insistence that "foreigners were helping us," affirms her local agency while acknowledging collaboration with outsiders. It is reasonable to affirm that local democracy activists exercise a kind of "originating agency," proven by their intelligence in adapting general nonviolent strategy to local realities, their success in persuading their countrymen to turn out on the street in massive demonstrations, and their courage in asserting a new kind of citizenship and patriotism. Nevertheless, the influence of outside forces and actors should not be underestimated, whether their role is characterized as inspiration, as direct training and recruitment, or more academically as "diffusion and demonstration."[55]

How can we—outside scholars or journalists—ascertain the relative influence of the transnational activists like Duvall of ICNC, and the national activists like Sonja Licht and the students of Otpor in Serbia? The fairest assessment is probably that the transnational partners and the domestic partners are each a necessary, but not sufficient, condition to explain the successful democratic revolutions, and that there are other structural factors that are also necessary conditions. McFaul and Spector conclude that "Without knowledge and financial resources, the opposition could not have induced change. Yet these resources alone could not have caused the revolutions; a whole host of other conditions were necessary."[56]

The case for the necessary influence of the transnational democracy network can be made more systematically. I would suggest that the influence has four crucial dimensions.

First, the partnering *contact* between transnational actors and domestic activists often becomes direct, personal, longstanding, and serial. It is serial in the sense that some of the activists from each successive revolution go "on the road" to promote the model for adaptation in several other countries.[57] And the series did not start only with Serbia in 2000; activists from previous successful electoral revolutions in Bulgaria, Romania, Croatia and Slovakia in the 1990s advised or provided lessons for the Serbs.[58] Some veterans from each revolution exercise continuing agency by becoming part of the international structure of the democracy network.

Second, successful national democracy activists freely give *credit* to the transnational network for teaching them how to be successful.[59]

Third, the revolutions are *isomorphic* with each other in several crucial respects: in discourse, symbols, tactical borrowing and adaptation, organizational forms, and—most critically—in the strategic logic of how they win, which is drawn (directly or indirectly) from the theories of Gene Sharp.

Fourth, activists in each successful revolution have received indispensable *inspiration* from veterans of previous democracy movements. New activists not only imitate the tactics of their forebears, but also admire and emulate their personal commitment and heroism, even to the point of risking or giving their lives.

To acknowledge in a theoretically systematic way the causal role of both national and transnational activists requires getting beyond the false choice of agency versus agency. The crucial step is to incorporate structural argument, but in a way that also overcomes the misleading dichotomy between agency and structure. This is the fourth challenge of the chapter.

Concerning the color revolutions, I would argue that all these patterns of transnational diffusion and inspiration represent various species of structural power. After certain watershed events, the structure of the international system (or international society) becomes inhabited by new historical possibilities, as well as the institutional infrastructure for cosmopolitan elites to import them into their own countries. The revolutions of 1991 in Eastern Europe, and 2000 in post-communist Serbia, probably count as such watershed events. Crucially, NGOs and their networks have become leading actors in the institutional *infrastructure* of international society for democratization. As a consequence of this structural shift, authoritarian governmental elites find that some of their tested tactics of rule no longer work, or even backfire. In their agency, these elites face new structural realities.

To recover the agency of the nonviolent activists, the theoretical key is to distinguish the *agentic weakness* of NATO military and intelligence power to directly manipulate Serbia, from the *structural strength* of the democratic societies of NATO countries to inspire and diffuse democratic activism.

The secret of structural power is social rather than material. Democratic values and practices that may have originated in the West have shown in the color revolutions the capacity to inspire hope, which, as Václav Havel has said, "is not the same as joy that things are going well, or willingness to invest in enterprises that are obviously heading for success, but rather an ability to work for something because it is good."[60] The secret of structural strength is precisely, if paradoxically, the power to generate resilient free agency—people aspiring to become citizens of a new kind, and institutions that adapt, spread and attract support.

We could push the structural argument again by comparing, *as social structure*, the US-led transnational democracy network and the

Russian-led counter-network. This would offer another glimpse of the secret of structural power. Are the network and the counter-network functionally and morally equivalent? Is the counter-network a broadly decentralized *network*, or rather a *hierarchy* with relatively centralized control and funding located in the governments of Russia, China, or other authoritarian states? The activists of which network exhibit greater personal commitment, moral and physical courage? Which are more inspired and inspiring? This is both a decisive empirical observation and a central theoretical point. The key to structural strength is the power to generate true agency, to create firmer social facts.

In sum, agency and structure are *mutually* constitutive; they are not in competition with each other as alternate explanations for one phenomenon. All agency is socially situated and is discernible by the observer only by looking from the point of view of a particular actor in a particular time and social location. Structural power is as real as agentic power, but is harder to characterize and narrate in a causal explanation. Power relations—often asymmetric, sometimes stable and sometimes rapidly changing—are embedded in every formation of structure and agency. What is structural about social structure? Structure reveals itself as institutionalized practices, that is, practices that are deeply embedded in time and space, in human relationships and groups.[61]

In conclusion, I have suggested that relentlessly following the partners is the methodological key to achieving both ontological unity (integrating agency and structure) and epistemological clarity (affirming activist agency in a politically complex environment) in this case study of NGOs and the color revolutions.

A better understanding of the mutuality of structure and agency also helps to prevent the theoretical homogenization of actors, issues, or norms, which tends to hide the actual politics of particular networks (as argued in the Introduction). Comparison of the color revolutions—broadly conceived from 1989 through the Arab Spring—clearly shows that actors involved in the networks often do not share the same interests or norms. Indeed, they may not want to know about each other's activities. With their variety of actors, interests and norms, the color revolutions do not neatly confine themselves to one issue area, such as security, democratization or human rights. The empirical diversity of actors in these networks challenges the proclivity of IR theory to homogenize them. In this sense, a better theoretical understanding of structure and agency, combined with a methodological and empirical commitment to follow the partners, can make IR theory more fruitful, and our accounts of world politics more accurate and colorful.

Notes

1. The "Arab Spring" protests overthrew dictators in Tunisia, Egypt, Libya and Yemen, who had ruled for an average of 30 years: Marc Lynch, *The Arab Uprising: The Unfinished Revolutions of the New Middle East* (New York: Public Affairs, 2012); Roger Owen, *The Rise and Fall of Arab Presidents for Life* (Cambridge, Mass.: Harvard University Press, 2012); Tariq Ramadan, *Islam and the Arab Awakening* (Oxford: Oxford University Press, 2012); and Fawaz A. Gerges, ed., *The New Middle East: Protest and Revolution in the Arab World* (Cambridge: Cambridge University Press, 2013).
2. Adrian Leftwich, "Bringing Agency Back In: Politics and Human Agency in Building Institutions and States, Synthesis and Overview Report," Research Paper 06: Politics and Human Agency in Building Institutions and States, Developmental Leadership Program, Hawthorne, Australia (June 2009) (www.dlprog.org); and Anthony F. Lang, Jr, *Agency and Ethics: The Politics of Military Intervention* (Albany, NY: SUNY Press, 2002).
3. Samuel P. Huntington, *The Third Wave: Democratization in the Late Twentieth Century* (Norman: University of Oklahoma Press, 1991).
4. F. Gregory Gause, III, "Why Middle East Studies Missed the Arab Spring," *Foreign Affairs* 90, no. 4 (2011): 81–90.
5. Michael McFaul, "Transitions from Postcommunism," *Journal of Democracy* 16, no. 3 (2005): 5–19; Graeme P. Herd, "Colorful Revolutions and the CIS: 'Manufactured' versus 'Managed' Democracy?" *Problems of Post-Communism* 52, no. 2 (2005): 3–18; and Valerie J. Bunce and Sharon L. Wolchik, "Favorable Conditions and Electoral Revolutions," *Journal of Democracy* 17, no. 4 (2006): 5–18.
6. On the transnational links between democracy activists in Tunisia and Egypt and previous color revolutions: David D. Kirkpatrick and David E. Sanger, "A Tunisian–Egyptian Link That Shook Arab History,"*New York Times*, 13 February 2011; and John Pollock, "Streetbook: How Egyptian and Tunisian Youth Hacked the Arab Spring," *Technology Review*, September-October 2011 (www.technologyreview.com/featured-story/425137/streetbook/).
7. Peter Ackerman and Jack Duvall, *A Force More Powerful: A Century of Nonviolent Conflict* (New York: Palgrave, 2000), 478–89; and Michael A. Cohen and Maria Figueroa Küpçü, "Privatizing Foreign Policy," *World Policy Journal* (Fall 2005): 34–52.
8. Ackerman and Duvall, *A Force More Powerful*; and York Zimmerman Inc., "A Force More Powerful: A Century of Nonviolent Conflict," six part film series companion to the book (Princeton, N.J.: Films for the Humanities, 2000).
9. York Zimmerman Inc. website, "Language Versions, Bringing Down a Dictator," (www.yorkzim.com/new/language-versions/#bringingdownadictator).
10. In 2014, English, Russian, Arabic and Mandarin versions were available to view free on YouTube.
11. International Center on Nonviolent Conflict (www.nonviolent-conflict.org).
12. Franklin Foer, "Regime Change, Inc.: Peter Ackerman's Quest to Topple Tyranny," *New Republic*, 25 April 2005.

13 Maria J. Stephan and Erica Chenoweth, "Why Civil Resistance Works: The Strategic Logic of Nonviolent Conflict," *International Security* 33, no. 1 (2008): 43.
14 Oleksandr Sushko and Olena Prystayko, "Western Influence," in *Revolution in Orange: The Origins of Ukraine's Democratic Breakthrough*, eds Anders Aslund and Michael McFaul (Washington, DC: Carnegie Endowment for International Peace, 2006); Andrew Wilson, *Ukraine's Orange Revolution* (New Haven, Conn.: Yale University Press, 2005), 183–92; and Joel Brinkley, "Dollars for Democracy?: U.S. Aid to Ukraine Challenged," *New York Times*, 21 December 2004.
15 Margaret E. Keck and Kathryn Sikkink, *Activists beyond Borders: Advocacy Networks in International Politics* (Ithaca, NY: Cornell University Press, 1998).
16 Ibid., 1–38.
17 Ibid., 9.
18 Ibid., 5 and 216.
19 Ibid., 9.
20 Ibid., 2.
21 Ibid., 7.
22 Ibid., 5. Keck and Sikkink address agency and structure at the beginning and the very end of *Activists beyond Borders*, but do not interrogate the concepts in between.
23 Ibid., 12.
24 The central argument of a leading IO text is to affirm the authority of IGOs understood as autonomous from state power. Michael Barnett and Martha Finnemore, *Rules for the World: International Organizations in Global Politics* (Ithaca, NY: Cornell University Press, 2004).
25 Keck and Sikkink, *Activists beyond Borders*, 7.
26 Steve York, "Bringing Down a Dictator," York Zimmerman, Inc. (Washington, DC, 2001), quotations from the film's closed captions.
27 Srdja Popovic, Andrej Milivojevic and Slobodan Djinovic, *Nonviolent Struggle: 50 Crucial Points* (Belgrade, Yugoslavia: Centre for Applied NonViolent Action and Strategies, CANVAS, 2006), (www.usip.org/sites/default/files/nonviolent_eng.pdf); Stephan and Chenoweth, "Why Civil Resistance Works," 7–44; Anika Locke Binnendijk and Ivan Marovic, "Power and Persuasion: Nonviolent Strategies to Influence State Security Forces in Serbia (2000) and Ukraine (2004)," *Communist and Post-Communist Studies* 39, Issue 3 (2006): 411–429; and Adrian Karatnycky and Peter Ackerman, "How Freedom Is Won: From Civic Resistance to Durable Democracy," *The International Journal of Not-for-Profit Law* 7, Issue 3 (2005) (www.icnl.org/research/journal/vol7iss3/special_3.htm#_ednref1).
28 Quoted in Roger Cohen, "Who Really Brought Down Milosevic?" *New York Times Magazine*, 26 November 2000.
29 Binnendijk and Marovic, "Power and Persuasion," 411–429.
30 Ibid. Also C. J. Chivers, "How Top Spies in Ukraine Changed the Nation's Path," *New York Times*, 7 January 2005.
31 Binnendijk and Marovic, "Power and Persuasion," 411–429; and Anika Locke Binnendijk, "Holding Fire: Security Force Allegiance during Nonviolent Uprisings," Doctoral dissertation, Fletcher School of Law and Diplomacy, Medford, Mass., August 2009.

260 *Case evidence: NGOs and networks*

32 Michael McFaul, "Ukraine Imports Democracy: External Influences on the Orange Revolution," *International Security* 32, no. 2 (2007): 45–83; Mark Beissinger, "Structure and Example in Modular Political Phenomena: The Diffusion of the Bulldozer/Rose/Orange/Tulip Revolutions," *Perspectives on Politics* (June 2007): 259–276; Valerie J. Bunce and Sharon L. Wolchik, *Defeating Authoritarian Leaders in Postcommunist Countries* (Cambridge: Cambridge University Press, 2011); Lucan Way, "The Real Causes of the Color Revolutions," *Journal of Democracy* 19, no. 3 (2008): 55–69; Menno Fenger, "The Diffusion of Revolutions: Comparing Recent Regime Turnovers in Five Post-Communist Countries," *Demokratizatsiya: The Journal of Post-Soviet Democratization* 15, no. 1 (2007): 5–28.
33 Cohen, "Who Really Brought Down Milosevic?"
34 Tim Marshall, *Shadowplay* (Belgrade: Samizdat B92, 2003).
35 Benjamin S. Lambeth, *NATO's Air War For Kosovo: A Strategic and Operational Assessment* (Santa Monica, Calif.: RAND, 2001); Ivo H. Daalder and Michael E. O'Hanlon, *Winning Ugly: NATO's War to Save Kosovo* (Washington, DC: Brookings Institution Press, 2001).
36 Mary Kaldor, *New and Old Wars: Organized Violence in a Global Era* (Stanford, Calif.: Stanford University Press, 1999).
37 William E. DeMars, "Hazardous Partnership: NGOs and American Intelligence in Small Wars," *International Journal of Intelligence and Counter Intelligence* 14, no. 2 (2001): 193–222.
38 Quoted in Marshall, *Shadowplay*, 36. Mark Kirk served in the U.S. House of Representatives from 2001 to 2010, and won Barack Obama's former Illinois Senate seat in November, 2010.
39 Kosovo Verification Mission, Organization for Security and Cooperation in Europe (www.osce.org/node/44552); and Marshall, *Shadowplay*, 39–43 and 49–51.
40 Tim Judah, *Kosovo: War and Revenge*, 2nd edition (New Haven, Conn.: Yale University Press, 2002); and Daalder and O'Hanlon, *Winning Ugly*.
41 Marshall, *Shadowplay*, 87–134.
42 Ibid.
43 Ibid.
44 Ibid., 177.
45 Ibid., 187–204.
46 Way, "The Real Causes of the Color Revolutions," 55–69.
47 Regine A. Spector and Andrej Krickovic, "Authoritarianism 2.0: Non-Democratic Regimes are Upgrading and Integrating Globally," Paper presented at the Annual Meeting of the International Studies Association, 26 March 2008 in San Francisco.
48 Michael McFaul and Regine A. Spector, "External Sources and Consequences of Russia's 'Sovereign Democracy,'" in *New Challenges to Democratization*, eds Peter Nurnell and Richard Youngs (New York: Routledge, 2010), 119–125.
49 Sergey B. Ivanov, Minister of Defense of the Russian Federation, at the Council on Foreign Relations, New York, "The World in the 21st Century: Addressing New Threats and Challenges," 13 January 2005 (www.cfr.org/russian-federation/world-21st-century-addressing-new-threats-challenges/p 7611), quoted in Graeme P. Herd, "Russia and the 'Orange Revolution':

Response, Rhetoric, Reality?" *Connections: The Quarterly Journal* IV, no. 2 (2005): 19.
50 McFaul and. Spector, "External Sources and Consequences," 119–125; Spector and Krickovic, "Authoritarianism 2.0"; Thomas Ambrosio, *Authoritarian Backlash: Russian Resistance to Democratization in the Former Soviet Union* (Burlington, Vt.: Ashgate, 2009); and Rachel Vanderhill, *Promoting Authoritarianism Abroad* (Boulder, Colo.: Lynne Rienner, 2012).
51 Ariel Cohen and Robert E. Hamilton, *The Russian Military and the Georgia War: Lessons and Implications* (Carlisle, Penn.: U.S. Army War College, Strategic Studies Institute, June 2011) (www.strategicstudiesinstitute.army.mil/pdffiles/PUB1069.pdf); Gadi Evron, "Battling Botnets and Online Mobs: Estonia's Defense Efforts during the Internet War," *Georgetown Journal of International Affairs* 9, Issue 1 (2008): 121–125; Simon Pirani, Margarita Balmaceda and Kirsten Westphal, "The Russian–Ukrainian Gas Conflict," *Russian Analytical Digest*, Issue 53 (Zurich: Center for Security Studies, January 2009), (www.css.ethz.ch/publications/pdfs/RAD-53.pdf); and David Bosold, Petr Drulák, and Nik Hynek, eds, *Democratization and Security in Central and Eastern Europe and the Post-Soviet States* (Baden-Baden, Germany: Nomos Publishers, 2012).
52 International Center on Nonviolent Conflict (http://nonviolent-conflict.org/index.php/about-icnc/setting-the-record-straight/1447).
53 International Center on Nonviolent Conflict (http://nonviolent-conflict.org/index.php/learning-and-resources/resources-on-nonviolent-conflict).
54 Marshall, *Shadowplay*, 182.
55 Jillian Swedler, "Spatial Dynamics of the Arab Uprisings," *PS* 46, no. 2 (2013): 230–234; David Patel, Valerie J. Bunce and Sharon L. Wolchik, "Diffusion and Demonstration," in *The Arab Uprisings Explained: New Contentious Politics in the Middle East*, ed. Marc Lynch (New York: Columbia University Press, 2014); and Beissinger, "Structure and Example in Modular Political Phenomena," 259–276.
56 McFaul and Spector, "External Sources and Consequences," 118.
57 Ray Jennings, "Serbia's Bulldozer Revolution: Evaluating Internal and External Factors in Successful Democratic Breakthrough in Serbia," Center on Democracy, Development, and the Rule of Law, CDDRL Working Paper, 2009 (http://iis-db.stanford.edu/pubs/22465/CDDRL_Working_Paper_105_Ray_Salvatore_Jennings.pdf).
58 Jennings, "Serbia's Bulldozer Revolution," 16.
59 Centre for Applied Non Violent Actions and Strategies, CANVAS (www.canvasopedia.org/); Tina Rosenberg, "Revolution U—What Egypt Learned from the Students Who Overthrew Milosevic," *Foreign Policy*, 16 February 2011 (www.foreignpolicy.com/articles/2011/02/16/revolution_u).
60 Václav Havel, *Disturbing the Peace: A Conversation with Karel Huizdala*, translated by Paul Wilson (New York: Vintage Books, 1991), 181.
61 Anthony Giddens, *The Constitution of Society: Outline of the Theory of Structuration* (Berkeley, Calif.: University of California Press, 1986), 13.

10 Heart of paradox
War, rape and NGOs in the DR Congo

Dennis Dijkzeul[1]

- Humanitarian critique
- The trouble in the DR Congo
- The International Rescue Committee (2000–2004)
- Malteser International (2000–2004)
- Women for Women International (2004)
- Partners, colleagues or competitors? NGO debates in 2004
- More partners and hidden networks (2005–2013)
- Conclusion: beyond instrumentalization

In the Democratic Republic of the Congo (DRC), through the violent and protracted aftermath of "Africa's World War," the paradoxical role of NGOs in world politics is acutely clear. Wave after innovative wave of NGOs and UN peacekeepers are thrown at the country, penetrating, monitoring and shaping it, but without sufficiently ameliorating its wounds. This chapter illuminates this paradox through the microcosm of three NGOs—the International Rescue Committee (IRC), Women for Women International (WfWI) and Malteser International—all addressing gender-based violence (GBV) in the Kivu provinces on the DRC's eastern flank. Rape and other forms of GBV are appallingly common in this region. Originally, GBV was closely linked to insecurity, but it has spread throughout society. It is both a weapon of war and a consequence of a severe breakdown of social norms and values. The NGOs' pioneering innovations to address GBV, their similarities and differences with each other, their blind spots, and their chains of societal and political partners, all reveal the structural ability of NGOs to both embody and conceal profound power relationships.[2]

Applying this volume's methodological imperative to "follow the partners," this chapter examines the everyday political aspects of humanitarian action since 2000. The first section explains the political aspects of the networks in which humanitarian NGOs engage and what this means in terms of instrumentalization and inadvertent consequences of humanitarian action. The subsequent section explains the history of the conflicts in the DRC. Each of the following three sections studies one NGO in detail for the period 2000 to 2004, when GBV became an international and organizational humanitarian issue. The next two sections focus on the other "partners" and explain how the broader networks of NGOs, as well as the NGOs' GBV approaches, have evolved since 2005. The concluding section indicates how to understand NGO instrumentalization and inadvertent consequences theoretically.

Humanitarian critique

The theme of inadvertent consequences dominated Humanitarian Studies in the late 1990s and early 2000s, when scholars were trying to come to terms with the horrifying crises after the end of the Cold War, especially in Somalia, Rwanda, and the former Yugoslavia. A broad literature critically demonstrated how the good intentions of humanitarian actors are often diverted to serve other purposes and trigger inadvertent consequences.[3] And yet, with all these documented problems, there has been no sign of decline in the resort to humanitarian aid as a central response by the international community to unstable areas. The critiques fit into the social science tradition of showing a (preferably counterintuitive) underlying pattern of human behavior. Although they were far reaching in seeing the broader context, they were not systematic in terms of explaining these patterns.

In recent years, several scholars have broadened their analysis to discuss the origins,[4] diversity,[5] principles, and execution[6] of humanitarian action. This closer scrutiny of the history and variety of humanitarian action shows that many of the problems identified above have accompanied modern humanitarianism since it was first instituted in the nineteenth century. Although the more historical, ethical and anthropological literature has helped structure the debate on humanitarianism, it has not yet penetrated to the heart of this paradox to explain how humanitarian agencies (mostly NGOs) navigate this treacherous terrain, simultaneously embodying and resisting such instrumentalization.

The fact that so much humanitarian action is carried out by NGOs—or more precisely through networks in which NGOs often play lead roles—accounts for the affinity of the critiques of humanitarianism with our analysis of NGOs in this volume. The humanitarian critique judges organizations for not living up to their own normative goals, while taking those goals for granted. It assumes that humanitarian organizations can and should be reformed or protected so that they become immune from instrumentalization. In contrast, our point of departure is the understanding that transnational NGOs always seek to accommodate their societal and political partners enough to stay in the game, while simultaneously resisting and transforming those partners' parasitical agendas. We start from the assumption that NGO outcomes are shaped by struggles to capture, deploy against others, or neutralize the political impact of NGO operations. In world politics, NGOs are sent or allowed into precisely those situations that most resist straightforward policy responses. In this respect, normative critiques based on assumptions or experiences in Western societies are anachronistic for countries in chronic crisis, because these societies function differently politically and organizationally.[7] If a conventional state organized as a rational Weberian bureaucracy were in place, the special genius of transnational NGOs would be much less necessary.

The interesting thing about NGOs in world politics, therefore, is not that their partners are constantly attempting to instrumentalize them by attaching latent agendas or even taking over their salient agendas. Instead, the interesting thing is how NGOs manage to elude becoming completely instrumentalized, or even instrumentalize others.

These questions are intensified for the eastern DRC, which has been one of the most hazardous environments in the world for both local victims of violence and also national and expatriate humanitarian workers.[8] How did humanitarian NGOs gain and maintain access to the victims of GBV over many years while the conflict actors and perpetrators of violence remained endemic? How did they build a multifaceted and growing global network concerned with GBV? Why do we in the outside world know anything at all about GBV in the eastern DRC? In short, the puzzle is not the impotence of the network, but its access and existence in the first place.

The trouble in the DR Congo

When at the end of the Rwandan genocide in 1994 about 1 million Rwandan Hutu refugees entered the eastern DRC (Zaire at the time), the state and society were already in a deep crisis after three decades of misrule by President Mobutu Sese Seko.[9] The presence of the refugees worsened the dire economic situation and ethnic tensions. The Hutu

Interahamwe—known as the Rwandan *génocidaires*—used the refugee camps as bases to regroup, rearm, and carry out attacks on Tutsis in Rwanda. In response, the Tutsi-dominated Rwandan government together with its Ugandan allies helped set up a rebel group and intervened in Zaire in 1996, ostensibly to foster the return of the refugees and attack the *génocidaires* in the camps. Many refugees indeed returned home, but the intervention also left tens of thousands of refugees and Zairian citizens dead, while the Interahamwe fled into the rainforests from which it preyed on the local population. The rebels, officially led by Laurent Kabila but secretly backed by the governments of Rwanda and Uganda, made rapid progress and overthrew Mobutu in May 1997. Kabila promptly renamed Zaire as the Democratic Republic of Congo.

Over the next one and a half years, the alliance between Kabila and his foreign backers unraveled. In August 1998 ethnic militias with support from the armies of Rwanda, Uganda, and Burundi started another war to replace Kabila's regime. Kabila, however, received unexpected support from Angola, Zimbabwe, Chad, and Namibia, while Uganda and Rwanda grew apart over their differing economic interests and began supporting different rebel groups. As a result, "Africa's First World War" divided the country into a Uganda-dominated North, a Rwanda-dominated East, and a western/southern part where the Kinshasa government was in charge. In the meantime, the Interahamwe continued to destabilize and loot parts of eastern DRC, while various Mai-Mai—originally local self-defense groups that increasingly turned into armed bandits—were also active in the North and East.[10] Over time, the different warring factions and their international supporters became more interested in economic exploitation—for example diamonds and coltan—than in ending the war.[11] Hence, at the local level, the Congolese war broke down into an ever-changing pattern of overlapping micro-wars in which almost all the victims were civilians. One of the most interesting aspects of these wars is that the actual powers behind each major shift, as well as their economic interests, were covert or veiled for months or years, until they were exposed by the reports of transnational NGOs and the United Nations (UN).

At the national and international political levels, peacemaking progressed at a snail's pace. In 1999 the UN established what would become its largest peacekeeping force, the UN Mission in the DR Congo (MONUC). After Laurent Kabila was killed by a bodyguard in 2001, his son, Joseph Kabila, succeeded him as president. He pushed the peace process forward, so that the DRC was reunified, a peace treaty was signed in 2003, and in 2006 he became the first officially elected president. Foreign armies withdrew with the peace treaty, but maintained shadowy involvement in exploiting minerals and sponsoring militias. Violence has never ceased, especially in the east. The national army is underpaid and although it has officially incorporated most rebel factions and militia, it does not function in a unified manner. It actually has incorporated and transmuted the micro wars, and has become one of the main human rights violators in the country. Moreover, regular political killings and widespread impunity persist, while rebel forces and other armed groups continue pillaging and raping.

In 2011, the UN peacekeeping force was renamed the United Nations Stabilization Mission in the DR Congo (MONUSCO), but so far it has been unable to live up to its new name. The rigged elections of 2011 led to protests and localized violence. The Kabila regime has become increasingly authoritarian and the eastern DRC suffers recurrent bouts of violence.[12]

In sum, the security vacuum in the eastern DRC has been filled since 1994 with a mutating brew of *génocidaires*, neighboring armies, criminal gangs, Congolese soldiers, and ethnic militias, all engaged in shifting patterns of predatory rule, generating humanitarian victims and sometimes threatening to destabilize the whole of central Africa. In general, the endemic violence facilitated sexual violence. As one former fighter explained, "If you are allowed to kill, what does rape matter?"[13] At the same time, poverty, malnutrition, and general vulnerability grew. In some places, the conflict totally disrupted communities and families.

Institutions to address the violence barely functioned. The weakened health system could not address epidemics and the consequences of GBV without international support. "The underpaid, poorly trained, and demoralized staff ... are incapable of operating their under-equipped, neglected, and often pillaged or damaged [health] facilities in a manner that responds to the needs of the populations they serve."[14] In addition, people frequently lack the economic means to buy its remaining services, or they have access problems due to the insecurity and long distances involved.

The underpaid and ill-equipped police, who should have played a key role in ensuring security and protection, were often corrupt and violent. Similarly, the legal system almost ceased to function in many areas and was greatly affected by the—sometimes corrupt—influence of local elites, leaving many, especially the poor, more disadvantaged than protected in legal processes. Raped women often did not dare to seek redress either out of fear for social stigma, or further violence at the hands of the police, or they felt too vulnerable to openly confront their perpetrators.

The overarching reality of the eastern DRC since 1994, has been a profound crisis of governance, which remains unresolved today. The DRC, though badly governed, is not politically unoccupied—instead it is filled with weak governmental institutions, traditional leaders, warlord formations of self-financing armies, meddling neighbors, a large UN presence, and NGOs.

Some traditional humanitarian NGOs have provided aid by their usual approach of negotiation with warring groups and other local actors in a clear effort to distinguish themselves as neutral, impartial and independent of UN-led coordination efforts or donor governments, in the hope of preventing instrumentalization. By strictly respecting these principles, Médecins sans Frontières (MSF) is often one of the first NGOs to access such malgoverned space. This was also the case with GBV victims, whom MSF has medically assisted since the peak of the civil war in 2000. Other aid NGOs, such as IRC, generally worked closer with the UN system, including MONUC/MONUSCO, as well as with other NGOs in humanitarian coordination bodies.

The International Rescue Committee (2000–2004)

At one level, IRC can claim a major success by having identified the issue of gender-based violence. It helped frame and convey the victims' suffering to what became an astonishingly extensive web of global health, human rights, feminist, and peace networks. At another level, IRC was in the vanguard of an international community extending governance into the region. It did so, not covertly or on the side, but precisely through its activities of framing humanitarian issues and serving victims.

In the late 1990s, few expatriates stayed in eastern DRC. Nairobi in neighboring Kenya served as the rear base for humanitarian and diplomatic access to the region. Various NGOs, UN agencies, embassies and religious communities would fly staff from Nairobi into eastern DRC for day trips to drop off food or medical supplies, and regularly fly back before dark. The organizations present on the ground would retreat at night to their guarded compounds in the big cities, such as Bukavu and Goma.

Within these severe constraints, IRC conducted an innovative and influential mortality survey to estimate how many people had died as a result of the conflict in the DRC. To count the dead in such a comprehensive manner, as states do, was an innovative extension of NGO governance into the DRC.

The first mortality survey (2000) showed that the conflicts had caused an additional 1.7 million deaths in the DRC, from both disease and direct violence.[15] Suddenly, the DRC gained strong media attention and became a higher priority for the US government and other donors. IRC published five mortality surveys between 2000 and 2007. Although their accuracy has been disputed, their effect in mobilizing international attention and assistance was dramatic.[16] Looking back, the *Christian Science Monitor* reported in 2010 that, "After the International Rescue Committee published its early findings of the DRC death toll, humanitarian aid increased 500 percent. Peacekeeping assistance followed, and today the DRC hosts the world's largest peacekeeping mission, with more than 20,000 members."[17] The surveys allowed many NGOs to extend their physical presence and a growing array of services into the DRC.[18]

After the first mortality survey in 2000, IRC received an invitation from the United States to submit proposals to respond to the crisis. With funding from the US Office of Foreign Disaster Assistance, IRC created a participatory program called Ushirika, a Swahili word for partnership, which aimed to strengthen local associations active in such areas as health and food security in the South Kivu, North Kivu, and (North) Katanga provinces. When Ushirika was in full motion in early 2002, the eastern IRC country director, Michael Despines, heard of a USAID proposal offering up to $500,000 for a strong project to serve victims of torture in the DRC.

Despines was receiving information from IRC-supported health centers on the serious problem of sexual violence, which he knew that no international organization or state donor was systematically addressing. He asked USAID whether GBV survivors could also be considered as "torture victims," because rape was commonly practiced as a weapon of war. Given the severity of the problem, USAID decided to support this idea. Once again, IRC had reframed a humanitarian problem in such a way that a donor could respond. Framing GBV as a form of torture integrated the issue-areas of health, women's rights, and human rights.

Although humanitarian organizations, like IRC, had experience of GBV problems in refugee camps, they had less experience of addressing sexual violence in large, insecure areas with limited access like the DRC. In addition, open discussion of GBV and its consequences could put survivors—as well as service providers/humanitarian actors—at greater risk of reprisals. Moreover, husbands and communities often rejected raped women as impure or (implicit) adulteresses, who might be HIV-infected.[19] This made it challenging to define a strategy and determine what services IRC and other NGOs would be able to provide.

Using its experiences from the Ushirika program, IRC decided to build capacity within local organizations to provide essential services, because these would have access in insecure areas to population groups that international NGOs could not reach. Already many local NGOs, originally created for other purposes, had begun GBV activities with little or no skills or money. IRC partnered with local organizations whose grassroots counselors and community activists could move throughout their geographic areas to link survivors with the necessary services and refer them, when necessary, to hospitals or specialized NGOs.

IRC recruited new staff members with proven experience in the field. This team established a confidential approach to working with rape survivors that was adapted to the Congolese cultural context. It developed a framework to address eight key needs of survivors: primary health care, specialized gynecological surgery, psychosocial counseling, family and community mediation, food and non-food assistance, economic integration, legal assistance, and HIV/STI testing.

In all, 102 local NGOs responded to a call for proposals, from which the team selected eight organizations that showed the most potential to grow and provide quality survivor-centered services. IRC also began strengthening small, informal associations, for example local women's groups; these were called community-based organizations (CBOs). From the UN, the World Food Program, the Food and Agricultural Organization and UNICEF supported the program with basic assistance for daily survival. Delivering this aid was extremely challenging because the perpetrators of sexual violence often pillaged too.

IRC trained and networked the selected organizations, creating a referral system among its partners. In this way, survivors were able to access psychosocial, medical, and legal assistance through the network. The most severe cases were ultimately referred through this system to either Panzi Hospital in Bukavu or DOCS hospital in Goma for specialized care such as reconstructive surgery.

When IRC's GBV phase I closed in November 2003, partner NGOs had served 4,606 survivors, more than initially planned. Since then, partner organizations have extended their reach to people in other regions. In addition, IRC has documented significant gains in partner organizational capacities, including management and project activities. Finally, IRC's GBV activities showed that it is possible to build technical, project management, and administrative capacities in service delivery in a relatively short period of time in situations of chronic crisis, when alternative government services do not exist.

The analysis above shows that IRC overcame considerable obstacles to steadily improve its practice and the lives of the GBV survivors. Yet,

270 Case evidence: NGOs and networks

it is much more difficult to assess the whole GBV network's impact in relation to the overall prevalence of GBV, especially given the rate at which endemic violence continues to generate new victims. IRC preparatory reports had documented severe humanitarian needs, but no exact studies on the prevalence of GBV could be carried out due to the level of insecurity and taboos surrounding GBV. However, the physical presence of IRC and the growing network of international and local NGOs in the DRC did allow the network to document the ongoing violence around them: warriors and humanitarians coexisted in the same space. Security problems caused delays and added to project costs. At times, new waves of pillaging and rape eliminated project gains and projects had to restart or operate at a lower level of activity.

In sum, IRC first provided general health services and capacity building for the Congolese, then created mortality surveys, and then reframed for donors the possibility of addressing GBV in a large, inaccessible area with ongoing violence. Ironically, that framing success set the stage for its greatest trial—to help the victims of GBV in the midst of unchecked, fresh GBV. Generally, the NGO extension of international governance in a partial and incomplete way served to highlight the ongoing insecurity and absence of a responsible national government.

Malteser International (2000–2004)

Malteser International,[20] the relief agency of the Sovereign Order of Malta, has been active in eastern DRC with health and nutrition activities since the influx of Rwandan refugees in 1994. In October 2003 it instituted a mobile clinic, as regular health centers had been looted and destroyed. With this mobile clinic, Malteser observed that many patients had suffered from GBV. In its initial response, it established medical assistance for GBV survivors in 28 selected health centers in South Kivu and Ituri. However an evaluation revealed that this assistance did not suffice to improve the lives of GBV victims. Malteser identified three main components of its response: medical, psychosocial, and economic. The integration of medical assistance for survivors in the overall primary health care support became a principal element of its interventions. In addition, medical assistance reduces the risk of "fake" cases as medical diagnosis can help indicate rape.[21] Other components depend on a verbal presentation, which became problematic as a growing number of women wanted to profit from assistance even if they had not been raped. The number of faked cases also increased when other international and local NGOs provided psychosocial care and economic assistance independently from medical assistance. Yet medical assistance only represents a short-term approach to improve the well-being of the victims. In the end, Malteser strongly linked the three components within an integrated approach.

In contrast to the health sector, no psychosocial or economic government agencies existed that could be reinforced through a partnership. Malteser therefore identified community structures, for example local NGOs, to train them in basic methodologies of psychosocial assistance. It established partnerships with 16 local NGOs, located close to the supported health centers, to address the medical and psychosocial GBV problems in an integrated manner. Malteser trained the selected organizations, and created a referral system among its partners, so that the survivors could access psychosocial and medical assistance. The most severe cases were referred through this system to either Panzi Hospital or Centre Sosame (a psychiatric clinic) in Bukavu for specialized care. Qualified Malteser staff supported these local structures and also took care of specific complicated cases. Malteser also helped improve the working procedures (registering patients, monthly reporting, and interview reports) of its partner NGOs.

Once these structures had been strengthened to provide psychosocial assistance, Malteser began to support them in setting up income-generating activities for women. On the one hand, these activities facilitate the self-reliance and economic reintegration of GBV victims, as well as the economic position of women, who have not been raped but are also vulnerable economically. Malteser's extension of the target group for economic assistance aimed to prevent stigmatization of survivors and the exclusion of other vulnerable groups. However, Malteser did not want to organize distribution of relief items, because these were often pillaged. The income-generating activities provided a safer alternative. Yet it was difficult to resist pressure from the UN agencies that wanted to show their response to GBV through large distributions via partner NGOs. Initially, this constituted a significant difference between Malteser and IRC. Malteser also negotiated directly with the rebels to enhance access and reduce pillaging. Based on its local contact network with all actors and its mandate of neutrality and impartiality, as well as intensive context analysis, Malteser's activities were rarely affected by pillaging.

During implementation, Malteser became increasingly concerned that many local NGOs perceived the issue of GBV as a growth market, although the actual outcomes of their work were weak. Many of these NGOs had good intentions, but lacked the skills to work with GBV survivors. Malteser was also concerned that some heads of local organizations gave the impression that they were more concerned with their own status and financial interests than with the welfare of the survivors.

In July 2004 the GBV project team carried out a mid-term evaluation of the project, also assessing the existing local partnerships. Many partner NGO staff members had received too little training in psychosocial support, medical treatment and referral, and community education. Malteser also noted that many partner organizations stressed the economic needs of the survivors, but paid insufficient attention to their overall well-being. The danger of focusing too much on economic benefits is that people feign being a victim or that it fosters corruption among partner NGOs, for example, with handing out food. Malteser realized that only those organizations that could show results for the survivors should remain. Six partners left the program and a new one was added. Malteser also emphasized the survivors' integration into local communities through education or liaison with organizations that specialized in economic support to the whole community.

In 2004, Malteser and the Provincial Health Inspectorate of the local government carried out a six-month awareness-raising campaign against GBV among the population, police, and military. The campaign indirectly supported the psychosocial work.

When some intervention zones became more stable and numbers of GBV victims fell significantly in 2004, Malteser handed over its GBV activities to local partners, and expanded into more insecure and affected zones, where no other international actors were operating.

As a result, many survivors were able to function better again in society. Communities and husbands had gained a better awareness of the problems associated with GBV and ways to address them. Local partners and the health system gradually improved their functioning.

A comparison of Malteser with the other two NGOs further illuminates the reality of the DRC in 2004. Compared to IRC and WfWI (see below), Malteser worked more directly with survivors through local health structures. Although it helped build the capacity of partner organizations, this was initially not the primary focus of its activities. Malteser is perhaps most interesting in its stubborn attempt to pay attention to its local societal partners and context, challenging the assumption of magic bullet causality. At the risk of delegitimizing its own work and that of other GBV organizations, Malteser directly addressed the problem of soft corruption among its own local NGO partners early on, to the point of dropping six local NGOs. Like both WfWI and IRC, Malteser attempted to change the attitudes and behavior of local leaders—in this case in the police and the military. Finally, it negotiated frequently with the armed groups for access and to explain its humanitarian mission and credentials.

Women for Women International (2004)

WfWI arrived in Bukavu in April 2004, as part of the wave of NGOs that came in after the 2003 peace accord. Shortly after its arrival renewed fighting broke out, so that it had to delay activities until August. Three months later, it was working with over 600 women in Bukavu and planned to expand to at least 1,500 women in 2005. Although it cooperated with local organizations, it did not provide them with financial support. Instead, it partnered with individual women and provided them with tools and resources to move out of crisis and poverty into stability and self-sufficiency. The Wellspring Foundation provided a grant to start up the WfWI DRC office. An estimated 80 percent of WfWI's resources came directly from individual sponsors and institutions.

WfWI operates sponsorship programs for women, similar to well-known systems of child sponsorship. Women donate money and establish direct contact with their "sisters," who receive support through letters and sometimes visits. For some women, this becomes an important source of emotional support. The sponsorship provides immediate, direct financial aid and bridges the gap between relief and development at the individual level. The supporting sister donates $25 every month. This sum is divided into office expenses, vocational skills training, $5 to a savings account that is given as a lump sum to the woman after a year, and $10 given immediately to the sponsored woman for her basic necessities or to invest in income-generating activities.

Upon arrival, the WfWI representative visited most international organizations in Bukavu to see what they were doing for women. While setting up her office, she also worked with local leaders as "the gatekeepers of norms." In collaboration with local leaders, other members of the local community, and other NGOs, WfWI conducted a poverty assessment to identify the most socially excluded women who could benefit from the program.

WfWI selected the women who participated in a one-year training program. Sponsored women formed groups of not more than 20 members to share ideas and support. In addition to identifying women through the poverty assessment, the WfWI DRC office worked in collaboration with other organizations to provide medical and psychosocial assistance to survivors of rape and other forms of sexual violence. In this sense, WfWI filled gaps that other organizations could not address.

WfWI also implemented a unique program to train traditional leaders: "Men's Leadership Training/Addressing the Communal Impact of Violence against Women in Eastern DRC." The training aimed to help community leaders better understand that GBV is not the woman's fault, so that they recognize the community's responsibility to reach out and help women become active participants in community processes.

In its initial assessment in 2004, WfWI found that survivors of rape who participated in the rights awareness and empowerment program started to regain self-confidence and began to recognize their human value as important members of society. WfWI's emphasis on local leaders and communities, as well as its poverty assessments, ensured the participation of the most marginalized women. No other international organization covered by this research worked as directly with local women in such an individualized way. However, it also partnered with other actors quite easily.

WfWI provides an illuminating comparison with IRC and Malteser in its approach to GBV in Congo. With respect to its focus on the individual woman in its signature program, WfWI was more micro in its approach, implicitly endorsing an assumption of "magic bullet causality"— that an international NGO can improve one thing in the DRC without affecting or being affected by the local social or political contexts. In contrast, IRC and Malteser sought to network and build the capacity of local NGOs, explicitly seeking to change the social context. However, WfWI also addressed the social, and even political, context by attempting to educate local leaders, hoping to change their level of knowledge, normative attitudes, and even their behavior. IRC had not yet attempted to address local leadership in a structured training program, perhaps revealing its own assumption of magic bullet causality.

Partners, colleagues or competitors? NGO debates in 2004

With their distinct GBV activities in the period 2003–2004, the three NGOs espoused different norms about the utility of capacity building, which led to different assessments of their impact. As a result, they cooperated on the basis of their public purpose of addressing GBV, but competitive tensions became visible among them in 2004 as they worked on different assumptions about society and insecurity.[22]

Six operational issues stood out:

1 The relative emphasis on either capacity building for local organizations (IRC), or the individual needs of the survivors (Malteser).
2 The advisability of working through community leaders to reach the survivors with more speed and less expense.
3 The dilemma of addressing urgent population needs through food and non-food assistance, or avoiding such assistance because it

fostered corruption, attracted pillaging, and provided incentives to pose as a survivor.
4 The importance of observing and adjusting to shifting needs over time.
5 The judgment of when to be satisfied with the results of capacity building to improve the skills of national project staff.
6 The determination of the actual prevalence of GBV, especially in areas opening up.

Except for the last question, which can in principle be answered in a factual manner, the other five issues depend on NGO mandate and preference. As a consequence, the three NGOs also networked with different, only partly overlapping network "partners." WfWI did not directly support organizations, although it cooperated with them. IRC strongly promoted capacity building for local organizations, NGOs and CBOs, to support their service delivery to GBV survivors. Malteser focused more on serving directly survivors' individual needs through supporting local structures, either NGOs or the local health system.

The questions above highlight the importance of understanding different causal assumptions behind the NGOs' approaches. If an organization emphasizes immediate health and psychological aspects, it is less likely to favor long-term (multi-sectoral) capacity building, and it will define effectiveness and assess impact accordingly. If an organization assumes that the war is going to intensify or last for a long time, it may focus on immediate benefits rather than on building long-term local capacity. Such different causal assumptions and concomitant impact assessments also play a role in the competition for donor funding.

Overall, the multiplicity of operational NGO approaches is vulnerable to the perennial criticism that health NGOs fragment the overall referral and health systems. This is a serious problem—although the individual NGOs may carry out programs that are optimal on the basis of their own mandate, the sum of all NGOs' actions may be suboptimal. However, if the solution of a well-functioning local health system operating in a context of peace and the rule of law already existed, these NGOs would not be there at all.

A political observer must also ask certain questions of all three NGOs: Which local leaders, who have participated in their training programs or who tolerated or encouraged the existence of partner NGOs, were also implicated in local networks of corruption or even violence? Could a completely uncorrupted local leader have any power or personal security in the DRC? The involvement of local leaders has been a principal element of the NGOs' assistance. From the beginning of the project cycle, starting with needs assessment and context/stakeholder analysis, the functioning of the local leadership was an important criteria for project design. Good leaders became important partners of the projects; in the case of bad leaders the NGOs often looked for alternative ways of working with reliable local structures. Comparative research has seldom been carried out on the quality and consequences of networking with and the involvement of these leaders and armed groups, and the NGO assessments of them, in humanitarian action in the DRC.

Ideally, the state would address fragmentation, corruption, and bad governance, but Congolese institutions were so weak that they could not play such a role. Instead, all three NGOs, starting with IRC, have taken over state functions by compiling statistics on mortality, providing health and other services, and protecting vulnerable populations of raped women. It is possible to infer that the three NGOs were more than they seemed. They were creatively extending services—and thereby a kind of governance—into the eastern DRC, potentially competing with or bypassing or transforming the local government.

This is approaching the heart of the paradox—NGOs can only extend international governance so far in a context of endemic violence, and over time they increasingly run up against the limits and contradictions of this larger, unspoken strategy in which they are embedded. The famous tendency of NGOs to fail to assess this long-term or broader impact is not lost on donors. Sometimes donor governments throw NGOs at a problem, not because they expect a total solution, but precisely because they have no better response. The NGOs struggle, innovate, negotiate, serve more victims, report increasingly penetrating analysis of the local context, and buy time until a better response emerges.

More partners and hidden networks (2005–2013)

In addition to the three international NGOs examined above, an array of other network "partners" has become active in the eastern DRC. Their roles and interests help explain how the normative and causal claims cannot be, or can only partially be, fulfilled. These other actors co-determine the impact of the three NGOs and cause various unintended consequences that become clearer from a longitudinal perspective. These include three particular categories of actors, namely human rights organizations, security actors, and coordination bodies. Together with the humanitarian and development actors they involuntarily contributed to the political economy of war, in which some international and local actors gained from armed violence and attempted to instrumentalize these interventions to their own benefit.

Human rights organizations

In 2002, a few months after the eastern IRC director decided to undertake a project on rape, Human Rights Watch detailed egregious GBV in *The War Within the War: Sexual Violence against Women and Girls in Eastern Congo*.[23] It had done research in the eastern DRC, including Bukavu, and met with NGOs, but did not report which ones. The report marked the beginning of a cottage industry of reports on GBV, the judicial system, and impunity.[24] It also provided another justification for local human rights NGOs, such as *Heritiers de la Justice*, to intensify their work. Yet, operational problems plague the human rights issue-area too: How to deal with the ill-functioning justice system? Is it wise to encourage survivors to seek justice when the organizations cannot ensure their protection against reprisals from the perpetrators? Or should human rights organizations just focus on advocacy? Where and how can they cooperate with other types of NGOs? Human Rights Watch highlighted the lack of prosecutions in a 2005 report.[25] Although the DRC government introduced a national law punishing perpetrators of sexual violence in 2006 and has strengthened its Ministry of Gender, Family and Children, which issued a national GBV policy in 2009, practical legal assistance remains a challenge.[26]

Disturbingly and increasingly, people end up in prison after being falsely accused of perpetrating GBV. The weak legal system has a dual use: it can be used to do justice, but it can also be abused by either accused or the accuser.[27]

In sum, human rights organizations have helped ensure that GBV has remained on the international political agenda, but their influence on international military and Congolese actors has been much smaller. Their main modular technique (reporting with naming and shaming) differs strongly from carrying out GBV activities in the field, so that direct synergies with humanitarian and development NGOs are difficult to achieve. Their normative claims also look more compelling than their actual causal effects.

Security actors

The perpetrators of GBV were keenly aware that local staff-members of international NGOs knew about their misdeeds. As a consequence, they tracked the vehicles and activities of the NGOs, caused problems at roadblocks, and threatened local staff members. Understanding the interests and strategy of these perpetrators was necessary to safeguard staff security, obtain access to survivors, and to work towards prevention. Yet, the NGOs possess neither the skills nor the resources to create incentives for these actors to fundamentally change their behavior.

Neither the human rights organizations nor the humanitarian organizations were able to change the political economy of war, improve the functioning of the armed forces, or stem the rise in GBV after the late 1990s. This is something only the security actors and a change in norms could do. Unfortunately, social norms opposing rape have lost influence, so that rape became less associated with insecurity and was increasingly being perpetrated by family and community members. Nevertheless, the NGOs, including IRC's mortality surveys, have played a role in showing the need to strengthen the UN peacekeeping force, MONUSCO. As the *New York Times* reported in 2010:

> Despite more than 10 years of experience and billions of dollars, the peacekeeping force still seems to be failing at its most elemental task: protecting civilians. The United Nations' blue-helmets are considered the last line of defense in eastern Congo, given that the nation's own army has a long history of abuses, that the police are often invisible or drunk and that the hills are teeming with rebels.[28]

Hence, the investments in peacekeeping bore little fruit for a long time, demonstrating that MONUSCO was simply unable to address the insecurity at the root of GBV. Put differently, the UN Security Council, the UN member states, and their peacekeeping troops were also having a hard time realizing their normative goals.

The political economy of GBV aid

The fact that humanitarian aid is a renewable resource caused problems for all NGOs. It turned out that food and non-food distributions fostered corruption among some partners and employees. Congolese staff members from local and international NGOs received pressure from their own extended family members to share part of their income or even to help family members or acquaintances "obtain aid" that they would otherwise not have received.

As stated, NGO support also provides an economic incentive for some women to pose as GBV victims, so that they can benefit from aid. Whereas it is certain that GBV is a horrendous and widespread problem in the eastern DRC, the number may at times be inflated for economic gain by so-called victims.[29] Although the food agencies put pressure on the NGOs to help with food and non-food items, Malteser and WfWI did not provide such aid and IRC stopped providing it.

Similarly, when GBV became a growth market, other international and local organizations entered to gain funding. Some of the "new" organizations did not notice that several organizational networks already existed. Several local organizations without appropriate skills or motives attempted to gain more funding by sending out lists of (supposed) survivors to international NGOs, thus making a mockery of confidentiality, which is often crucial to the survivors. At the same time, these lists also contributed to inflating the number of victims of GBV through double reporting, and reporting of non-cases or ghost cases. Simultaneously, more international NGOs became active. When World Vision, for example, began setting up a GBV program in the autumn of 2004, a representative of one of the three NGOs decided to visit its office. She found out that its staff members did not yet know much about the other ongoing GBV programs. She urged them not to duplicate the work of the other NGOs. After this meeting, she expressed concern about the possibility of misunderstanding and competition by newly arriving international NGOs.

It is not clear how to ensure that opportunistic or less competent actors—international or local—do not disrupt or instrumentalize the work of NGOs. Barriers to entry are low and such organizations can intensify the already existing problems in addressing GBV. As indicated above, current coordination mechanisms address such problems only partially.

Another paradoxical side effect is becoming visible from a longer-term perspective. In 2011–2012, the security situation in South Kivu seemed to stabilize a little, although many risks remain, such as meddling by neighboring countries, ongoing violence by militias and the army, pervasive corruption, and in particular large mutinies in North Kivu. The root causes of generalized violence are still unaddressed.

Nevertheless, several staff members of well-established NGOs argue that the numbers of new GBV victims are declining slowly with the decrease in violence in South Kivu. However, donors are now under pressure to distribute funds from GBV budgets they have created over the last decade. Of course, some organizations, varying from local hospitals to international and local NGOs, as well as their staff members, actually benefit from the current funding levels and the international recognition of mass rape in the DRC. Their positions would be threatened by a decline in funding and they thus have an incentive to

280 *Case evidence: NGOs and networks*

downplay the decline in numbers of victims. GBV funding and activities have thus become institutionalized as an aid industry; another form of everyday instrumentalization of aid that causes inadvertent consequences. Consequently, history will repeat itself in a slightly different fashion. At the start of the last decade, NGOs were late with addressing GBV. Currently, GBV activities take resources away from development and security initiatives that may stem violence and address the root causes of GBV. Over time, even some of the good guys— i.e., some local and international humanitarian and human rights actors—have their own organizational interests and instrumentalize GBV activities for their own purposes.

NGO responses from a longitudinal perspective (2005–2012)

The three NGOs have continued to develop their approaches in response to the trends mentioned above. They all expanded their services deeper into rural and forested areas, and constantly attempted to improve them.

Cumulatively IRC has helped more than 40,000 survivors of sexual violence in the DRC.[30] It integrated its health GBV activities more closely with its general health program. A 2009 USAID evaluation noted about its capacity building: "IRC has greatly tightened the management and technical supervision of its partners. There is more direction and standardization of service provision. [Since 2006] IRC has reduced the number of local ... partners ... At the same time it has deepened the technical support and monitoring of partner performance."[31] IRC also began working closely with scholars from Johns Hopkins University to evaluate its psychosocial work and its recently established Village Savings and Loans Association programs. The latter provides a system of community savings for people who cannot access banks or microfinance institutions. All in all, IRC has increasingly integrated humanitarian and development activities.

WfWI expanded into rural areas with its signature program, offering direct financial assistance, rights education, vocational skills training, and income-generating opportunities. It also successfully expanded its Men's Leadership Program. Over 2,000 men participated. WfWI claims that these activities help build the informal support networks that poor women and GBV survivors need. The DRC office has become WfWI's largest program, and is now under full Congolese leadership.

Malteser has become more holistic. From September 2003 to July 2012, 57,783 GBV survivors received assistance from health structures and local NGOs supported by Malteser in the Kivus. It built further on its medical core competencies and integrated PHC with psychosocial support, family and community mediation, and economic reintegration. It also carried out several awareness-raising campaigns with local institutions. As a result, it has built new competencies. Medical aid, however, remained its entry point for assistance, as it attempts to separate the real victims from those that pose in order to obtain material benefits. Malteser also carried out income-generating projects for whole communities, so that GBV survivors could not be singled out and stigmatized and other vulnerable groups were not excluded.

Although the three NGOs have retained most of their initial differences, they have converged in their responses to the local and international actors that want to benefit from the GBV aid industry in four ways: (1) reduction of local partner-NGOs to help standardize and improve outcomes; (2) strengthening linkages with the existing health services; (3) reducing or stopping food and non-food relief, while working more with communities or women associations; and (4) participating in the cluster approach of NGO and UN coordination.

All in all, the NGOs that enter the violent and chaotic DRC must be recognized as doing much more than identifying particular populations of humanitarian victims and "framing" them to international donors to gain financing for services. By coming to aid, NGOs become in fact the advance guard of an international community seeking to extend some governance, or at least the illusion of governance, into this region. Yet, large problems remain that the NGOs cannot address fully. Instability and the political economy of war only improve marginally, and unwittingly the NGOs have helped create the GBV aid industry/network. The paradox is stark and hidden in plain sight: NGOs are *non*-governments extending incomplete governance/stateness/governmentality into malgoverned space.

Conclusion: beyond instrumentalization

I originally conceived this chapter sitting on the bank of Lake Kivu, reading a book about international NGO politics. A few days later, a friend in Goma pointed out the huge mansion of a warlord. I wanted to push beyond usual NGO evaluations, trip reports, and management studies, and even beyond the conventional critiques of NGOs, which focus more on NGO activities and the concomitant normative claims than on the complicated politics of the networks in which they voluntarily or involuntarily become enmeshed. I have not followed the network of "partners" all the way to the warlord's mansion, but this chapter has explored several analytical approaches that get at the heart of the paradox of humanitarian action in the eastern DRC. In acknowledging the indispensible reality of NGO relations with both societal and political partners in the field, as scholars and practitioners we need to move beyond the somewhat simplistic critique of NGO instrumentalization. Only in so doing will we be able to appreciate the full complexity of the challenges NGOs face, and the true amplitude of their creativity and achievement.

IRC, WfWI, and Malteser all carry out essential GBV work. They save lives, they accompany women who have suffered horrendous personal violation, they provide medical support, facilitate family reunification, carry out community education, and they give an account of the violence to the world. They encounter and work with international donors, local NGOs, local leaders, government institutions including the police and military, local health actors, and finally the target groups: survivors, their families and communities. These NGOs also encounter armed actors, suffering their threats or negotiating access to victims. By cultivating these relationships, in other words by partnering, they place themselves in the field and then attempt to broaden their activities to create the conditions for more successful GBV activities. Acknowledging the reality of this partnering already goes well beyond NGO official goals, normative claims, or signature programs.

The first layer of humanitarian critique, already well established in the literature, is the mutual instrumentalization of NGOs and all the actors to which they are linked, in relations both open and unacknowledged. The humanitarian critique judges organizations for not living up to their own normative goals, but it takes those goals for granted. It assumes that humanitarian organizations can and should become immune from instrumentalization. Without renouncing respect and admiration for the NGO staff I have met in the field, both international and local, there may be a more fruitful way to view the overall problematic.

NGOs are not hard-shelled rational organizations but permeable parts of networks, in which they have to live with and be affected by actors with highly diverse economic and political interests whose agendas, and actual linkages, are rarely clear. They influence and are influenced by the complicated political economy of war and the dynamics of the aid industry. NGO staff never fully comprehend the agency of *all* "partners" in these networks, but they are not passive themselves: they attempt to improve their work over time. Therefore, ultimately a theory of instrumentalization and inadvertent consequences should be a theory of dynamic adaptation and evolving dual use by both NGOs and other actors in their broader environment.

In another analytical step, we can get beyond being scandalized by the instrumentalization of NGOs to notice that many of them negotiate this inevitable challenge with a multilayered creativity that does not show up on their websites. In the eastern DRC, all the international and local NGOs—even the opportunistic latecomers and the softly corrupt and the least responsible—are embedded in a larger international strategy of which they may not be aware. They are extending some degree of transnational governance or stateness into a large, ill-governed space pervaded by ongoing violence, and they are documenting the limitations of that very strategy. Such a task could not be accomplished by a disciplined, centrally coordinated organizational machine. Instead, it is perfect for the special genius of NGOs—that "partner" with whomever or whatever they find before them.

In the process of partnering into the eastern DRC, NGOs are going to get their hands dirty. Let's acknowledge that and ask ourselves: Would we rather have them there with all their flaws, or leave the eastern DRC to the warlords, armies from neighboring countries, and rebels?

It is refreshing to find a few NGOs with savvy staff who can navigate treacherous terrain—physically, morally and politically—with some grace. The three NGOs profiled here have done that. They have networked, and served the GBV victims; each has pushed the envelope of conventional humanitarianism in some way. If and when there is something more constructive to be done in the eastern DRC, who will discover it but someone who is there, African or expatriate, on the ground, with dirty hands, and open eyes?

Notes

1 The author thanks Bill DeMars, Christof Ruhmich, Alfred Kinzelbach, and Karin Wachter for their comments on earlier drafts of this chapter.
2 Research was carried out from September to December 2004 with a field study in the DRC and desk research in Germany. Later field visits, including surveys, qualitative interviews and participant observation in 2006, 2007, 2009, and 2011 provided longitudinal understanding of ongoing developments.
3 Alex de Waal, *Famine Crimes: Politics and the Disaster Relief Industry in Africa* (Oxford: James Currey, 1997); Fiona Terry, *Condemned to Repeat? The Paradox of Humanitarian Action* (Ithaca, NY: Cornell University Press, 2002); David Rieff, *A Bed for the Night: Humanitarianism in Crisis* (New York: Simon & Schuster, 2002); Alexander Cooley and James Ron, "The NGO Scramble: Organizational Insecurity and the Political Economy of Transnational Action," *International Security* 27, no. 1 (2002): 5–39; Antonio Donini, *The Policies of Mercy: UN Coordination in Afghanistan, Mozambique and Rwanda*, Occasional Paper no. 22, Thomas J. Watson Jr.

Institute for International Studies, Brown University, Providence, RI, 1996; Marc Sommers, *The Dynamics of Coordination*, Occasional Paper no. 40, Thomas J. Watson Jr Institute for International Studies, Brown University, Providence, R.I., 2000; and Joanna Macrae, *Aiding Recovery: The Crisis of Aid in Chronic Political Emergencies* (London: Zed Books, 2001).

4 Michael Barnett, *Empire of Humanity: A History of Humanitarianism* (Ithaca, NY: Cornell University Press, 2011); and Peter Walker and Daniel G. Maxwell, *Shaping the Humanitarian World* (London: Routledge, 2009).

5 Joanna Macrae, ed., *The New Humanitarianisms: A Review of Trends in Global Humanitarian Action* (London: Overseas Development Institute, 2002); and Dennis Dijkzeul and William E. DeMars, "Organizaciones Humanitarias Transnacionales: Balance y Alternativas (Transnational Humanitarian Organizations: Taking Stock and Formulating Alternatives)", in *La Transnacionalización, Enfoques Teóricos y Empíricos*, eds Gustavo Ernesto Emmerich and Ludger Pries (Mexico City: Universidad Autónoma Metropolitana, 2011), 101–134.

6 Dennis Dijkzeul and Joost Herman, eds, *Humanitaire Ruimte: Tussen Onpartijdigheid en Politiek (Humanitarian Space: Between Impartiality and Politics)*(Ghent, Belgium: Academia Press, 2010); Dorothea Hilhorst and Maliana Serrano, "The Humanitarian Arena in Angola, 1975–2008," *Disasters* 34, no. S2 (2010): S183–S201; and I. Christoplos, T. Rodríguez, E. L. Schipper, E. A. Narvaez, K. M. Bayres Mejia, R. Buitrago, L. Gómez and F. J. Pérez, "Learning from Recovery after Hurricane Mitch," *Disasters* 34, no. S2 (2010): S202–S219.

7 William Reno, *Warlord Politics and African States* (Boulder, Colo.: Lynne Rienner, 1999).

8 "The Aid Worker Security Database," Humanitarian Outcomes, London and New York (https://aidworkersecurity.org and www.humanitarianoutcomes.org).

9 Koen Vlassenroot, Hans Romkema and Dennis Dijkzeul, "Humanitaire Ruimte Scheppen in de Democratische Republiek Congo [Creating Humanitarian Space in the DRC]" in *Humanitaire Ruimte*, eds Dijkzeul and Herman, 161–65.

10 For exhaustive accounts, see Gerard Prunier, *Africa's World War* (Oxford University Press, 2009), and Filip Reyntjens, *The Great African War* (Cambridge: Cambridge University Press, 2009).

11 *Report of the Panel of Experts on the Illegal Exploitation of Natural Resources and Other Forms of Wealth of the DRC* (Report to the United Nations Security Council, S/2001/357), 12 April 2001.

12 International Crisis Group, "Eastern Congo: Why Stabilisation Failed," *Policy Briefing*, Africa Briefing no. 91, Kinshasa/Nairobi/Brussels, 4 October 2012.

13 David Van Reybrouck, *Congo: Een Geschiedenis* (Amsterdam: De Bezige Bij, 2010), 485 (my own translation).

14 International Rescue Committee DRC, "Application for the Management of Survivors of Torture and Sexual and Gender-Based Violence Umbrella Grant Project for Eastern DRC" (Bukavu, DRC: 2002, mimeo), 4.

15 The final IRC mortality survey estimated that from 1998 to 2007 the DRC has had an excess mortality of 5.4 million people. See Benjamin Coghlan, Valerie Nkamgang Bemo, Pascal Ngoy, Tony Stewart, Flavien Mulumba,

Jennifer Lewis, Colleen Hardy and Richard Brennan, *Mortality in the Democratic Republic of Congo: An Ongoing Crisis* (International Rescue Committee/Burnett Institute, 2008) (www.rescue.org/sites/default/files/resource-file/2006-7_congoMortalitySurvey.pdf).

16 Jina Moore, "New Study Argues War Deaths Are Often Overestimated," *Christian Science Monitor*, 22 January 2010; and Health and Nutrition Tracking Service (HNTS) Peer Review Report, *Re-examining Mortality from the Conflict in the Democratic Republic of Congo, 1998–2006* (Geneva: HNTS hosted by WHO, 15 May 2009, mimeo).

17 In fact, MONUC had already begun its operations before IRC carried out its mortality surveys. In addition to the surveys, geopolitical considerations also played a role in attracting attention and aid, in particular economic interests of the permanent Security Council members. International engagement further increased with the 2003 peace agreement, the 2006 elections, and growing NGO involvement. See Dennis Dijkzeul, "Developing Security in the Eastern Democratic Republic of the Congo: MONUC as a Practical Example of (Failing) Collective Security," in *United Nations Reform and the New Collective Security*, eds Peter G. Danchin and Horst Fischer (Cambridge: Cambridge University Press, 2010), 313–42.

18 Dennis Dijkzeul and Caroline Lynch, eds, *Supporting Local Health Care in a Chronic Crisis: Management and Financing Approaches in the Eastern Democratic Republic of the Congo* (Washington, DC: National Academies Press, 2006).

19 This still occurs: J. E. Trenholm, P. Olsson and B. M. Ahlberg, "Battles on Women's Bodies: War, Rape, and Traumatisation in Eastern Democratic Republic of Congo," *Global Public Health* 6, no. 2 (2009): 139–52.

20 Malteser Hilfsdienst, a German NGO, was transformed into Malteser International in 2005.

21 A medical exam cannot always prove rape. The delay before which some women and girls seek services further reduces the chance of a medical exam verifying claims.

22 Dennis Dijkzeul, *Models for Service Delivery in Conflict-affected Environments: Drawing Lessons from the Experience of the USHIRIKA/GBV Partnerships Programmes in the Eastern DRC*, funded by the Poverty Reduction in Difficult Environment Team of the UK Department for International Development (London, 2005) (www.gsdrc.org/docs/open/CON8.pdf).

23 *The War Within the War: Sexual Violence Against Women and Girls in Eastern Congo* (New York: Human Rights Watch, 2002) (www.hrw.org/legacy/reports/2002/drc/Congo0602.pdf).

24 For example, Global Rights/S.O.S. Justice, *What Justice Is There for Vulnerable Groups in Eastern DRC?* (Washington, DC: Global Rights, 2005) (www.globalrights.org/sites/default/files/docs/SOS_ExecutiveSummary_ENG_FIN.pdf); Action Contre l'Impunité pour les Droits Humains, "Une loi sur la répression des violences sexuelles: De quoi s'agit-il?" (Kinshasa, DRC: ACIDH, 2006) (http://acidhcd.org/Publish/Details/17); and Amnesty International, *Democratic Republic of Congo: Mass Rape: Time for Remedies* (London: Amnesty International, 25 October 2004) (www.amnesty.org/en/library/asset/AFR62/018/2004/en/618e1ff2-d57f-11dd-bb24-1fb85fe8fa05/%20afr620182004en.pdf).

25 Human Rights Watch, "Seeking Justice: The Prosecution of Sexual Violence in the Congo War," *Human Rights Watch* 17, no. 1(A) (2005) (www.hrw.org/sites/default/files/reports/drc0305.pdf).
26 *Loi no 6/018 du 20 juillet 2006 modifiant et complétant le Décret du 30 janvier 1940 portant code pénal congolais,* Journal officiel de la République Démocratique du Congo, 47ème année, no. 15 (1er août 2006); and République Démocratique du Congo, Ministre de la Famille, du Genre et de l'Enfant, *Strategie Nationale de la Lutte contre les Violences Basées sur le Genre* (Kinshasa, November 2009).
27 Nynke Douma and Dorothea Hilhorst, "Fond de Commerce? Sexual Violence Assistance in the Democratic Republic of Congo," Disaster Studies Occasional Paper 02 (Wageningen, Netherlands: Wageningen University, 2012), 51–60.
28 Jeffrey Gettleman, "Mass Rapes in Congo Reveals U.N. Weakness," *New York Times*, 4 October 2010.
29 For a discussion of this problem, see Dorothea Hilhorst, "Hoeveel vrouwen zijn er nu echt verkracht in Congo? [How many women have really been raped in the DRC?]," *Joop*, 31 August 2010 (www.joop.nl/opinies/detail/artikel/4716_hoeveel_vrouwen_zijn_er_nu_echt_verkracht_in_congo/).
30 "IRC in Congo," International Rescue Committee (2007) (www.rescue.org/sites/default/files/migrated/resources/2007/congo_onesheet.pdf).
31 Danuta Lockett and Paul Bolton, *Victims of Torture Fund Evaluation of the IRC Gender Based Violence Program in the Democratic Republic of Congo* (Washington, DC: USAID, 8 May 2009), (http://pdf.usaid.gov/pdf_docs/pdacn138.pdf), 5.

Part V
Conclusions and implications

11 Conclusion
NGO research and International Relations theory

William E. DeMars and Dennis Dijkzeul

- Theory hides politics
- Findings: bridging institutions
- Findings: practice as constructive power
- Findings: power in relationships
- Conclusion: risks of following the partners

The contributors to this book share a common experience of observing real NGOs in the field, and then discovering that the politics they have seen are simply unintelligible for the central debates of International Relations theory. This book renews IR theory by turning it toward the reality of NGOs. Seeking neither to discredit nor reform NGOs, we take them as they are in each particular time and place. We do not, however, take IR theory as it is. Instead, we aim to articulate a radical NGO challenge for IR theory, to reform theory where it conceals world politics.

The real politics of NGOs is doubly veiled, as we argue in the Introduction, by NGOs themselves, and even more thickly by the structure of theoretical debate within IR. The contributors to this book challenge those constraints and blind spots and propose a deeper ontological grounding.

Theory hides politics

Throughout this book we have approached NGOs with three problems in mind. The *problem of power*, embedded in realist theory, asks how NGOs and networks seek to wield power and how other actors attempt to instrumentalize their operations. The *problem of institutions*, linked to liberal theory, asks how NGOs and networks institutionalize world politics, and with what consequences. The *problem of actors*, implicated in constructivist theory, asks how actors in world politics are stabilized or

290 *Conclusions and implications*

transformed, and how NGOs both shape other kinds of actors and are shaped by them. The three problems are intertwined, but conceptualizing NGOs and networks as institutions has proven the most challenging.

IR theory hides NGO politics in several ways. The resulting blind spots can best be illuminated by a closer look at NGO normative claims. The constitutive structure of "NGOing"—of participating in the NGO game—requires that all NGOs articulate four normative claims. NGOs claim the capacity to go anywhere in the world and accurately assess the needs (global moral compass), and to deploy a portable package of tactics in response to those needs (modular technique). They also claim to act with the top-down authority of a universal, normative mandate from a realm above states (secular sanction), and with the bottom-up authority of speaking for, or empowering, the people whose needs are being addressed (representative claim).

Scholarly accounts from globalist and pluralist schools echo these official NGO normative claims, while simultaneously hiding the politics. The veiling begins when NGO *normative claims*—embodied in a charismatic NGO leader, a noble mandate, and an inspiring origin story—hold the attention of observers so intensely that few make the effort to really think through the implicit *causal claims*.

Two causal claims are crucial. NGOs implicitly claim that their interventions will effectively ameliorate identified needs (*magic bullet causality*), yet will produce no significant side effects on local or national society or politics (*circumscribed causality*). Using standardized, modular tactics, NGOs transfer people, resources, norms and information into many different societies, collectively on a very large scale, and claim that they generate no side effects. By these claims, NGOs assert their status as operating "above politics," that is, causally autonomous from all political and societal power struggles.

One consequence is to bolster a blind spot that is pervasive among both IR scholars and activists—the illusion that issue domains, articulated vividly at NGO headquarters and on their websites, stay neatly isolated from one another in the field. The assumption of *exclusive vertical political causality* (bottom-up representation, or top-down enforcement) is logically conjoined to this assumption of *null horizontal political causality* between NGOs working on different issues in the same society. Both claims become progressively less credible as NGOs spread, increase in number, and innovate into new issue areas. For researchers, the theoretical assumption of pristine issue domains conceals real politics by misleading observers to stop looking for partners and politics at the edge of the issue domain. Most of the interesting politics lies just beyond that edge. Of course, savvy and competent

NGO field staffers know quite well that they must attend to and manage very real side effects that overflow the issue domain, but they are also politically astute enough to keep this management in the background, out of the news and off the website. At the same time, staff at headquarters cannot know all the details in the field, and even the most experienced NGO field managers have a hard time discerning all partners and their latent agendas.

In their cosmopolitan, normative universality, therefore, NGOs abstract from the particular political formations and social institutions of their host communities and nations. If observers remain focused on the NGO normative claims, they rarely examine the implausibility of NGO causal claims to perform almost "surgical" operations of altruism. If ideas and norms were really tantamount to institutions, then idealist constructivism would capture more of the institutional phenomena of NGOs and networks than it does.

The next stratum of ideas covering NGO politics is a composite of several ways in which IR theories homogenize the actors in world politics to be more amenable to theoretical manipulation. This is important because the matrix for politics in the network is constituted by NGO societal and political partners, precisely in the heterogeneity (not presumed homogeneity) of their multiple and often conflicting latent agendas. Such NGO politics takes three overlapping forms: institutional bridging by NGOs (liberal politics), power-laced encounters between partners in the network (realist politics), and transformational interactions that reshape the actors themselves, including states (constructivist politics). Theories that conceptually homogenize actors in the network enjoin researchers—implicitly but powerfully—to stop looking for partners and politics when they run out of apparently homogeneous actors. It is ironic and surprising that the three theoretical schools of realism, liberalism and constructivism—which IR scholars are trained to view as locked in battle through a series of "great debates" lasting generations—are quietly, if inadvertently, complicit with each other in obscuring world politics by homogenizing the actors.

The form of actor homogenization easiest to excavate is laid down by pluralist and globalist accounts of NGOs, which confine themselves within the normative mandates and issue areas recognized by donors, recipients and host governments. As idealist constructivists, pluralists and globalists stop looking for partners in the network when they run out of actors that mutually recognize each other as publicly advocating the network's common norms. Their accounts fail to discover hidden or covert partners, partners that are normatively deviant, or the latent agendas of visible partners.

Another form of actor homogenization is deeply buried in several decades of IR theory debates. To accuse neorealism and neoliberalism of state-centrism is a commonplace. In another respect, however, the "neos" are *insufficiently state-centric* to notice that the most powerful states compete with each other, not only militarily and economically, but also by projecting their respective models of liberal state–society relations onto other states. For the historically most successful of the Western major powers—Great Britain and the United States—NGOs have served as privileged transnational carriers of various ideals of state–society relations at least since the British Antislavery Society in 1777. Ironically, these NGOs have been all the more powerful when they have operated independently of, or even in opposition to, their home governments. The accelerating global proliferation of NGOs today is *prima facie* evidence of the successful inscription of Western pluralism on the world, as much by attraction as by projection.

By conceptual borrowing from economics and the natural sciences, rationalism and positivism together reinforced a methodological individualism that assumes actors to be autonomous and unaffected by interactions with other actors with respect to their conceptions of interests, their rationality for calculating how to achieve their interests, and their capabilities for pursuing them. This methodological individualism means that states can be treated analytically as "black boxes" whose internal politics and standards of justice can be assumed and therefore ignored. Hence, it is not merely by their state-centrism that neorealism and neoliberalism have veiled world politics, but even more by their assumption of the common and homogeneous rationality of all states. This abstraction enabled theoretical parsimony, but at the cost of hiding real politics.

The effects of this rationalism and positivism spill over into studies of NGOs in two ways. First, any serious "strategic" analysis of other actors, including NGOs, is expected to adopt a similar methodological individualism and assume the common, homogeneous rationality of all the actors.[1] These approaches move in the right direction when exposing some of the politics of NGOs, particularly internecine NGO competition for scarce resources from political partners, including donor resources, public attention and credibility, and influencing government regulatory policies. However, such strategic analyses remain one-dimensional by reinforcing an assumption of actor homogeneity, and largely ignoring hidden negotiations and power struggles involving various societal partners in the network.

The second spill-over into NGO studies is the surprising commonality between rationalist (or rational choice) and sociological approaches, which are sharply contrasted with each other in conventional accounts.

Both approaches conceptually homogenize actors, but by different theoretical paths. Rationalist approaches assume that actors share a common rationality, on the basis of *methodological individualism*. But sociological approaches tend to assume that actors share common norms, and arrive at actor homogenization by the opposite path of *methodological collectivism*.[2] This overlooked convergence of rationalist and sociological approaches has muddied previous efforts by IR theorists to import ideas from economics, sociology and history (dubbed "new institutionalisms" for the last 30 years).

Finally, the deepest stratum concealing NGO politics is the way that IR theories, and theoretical debates, police and reinforce the boundaries of international relations as an academic discipline. IR theory has effectively detached the study of international politics from comparative politics, from political philosophy, and from American politics as a force shaping the world. Real NGOs relentlessly transgress these abstract boundaries between subfields. For political theory, NGOs propagate universal normative mandates into transnational popular and political culture, along with conflicting ideas about rights and legitimate political authority. NGOs operate in each country, but maintain constitutive links with political and societal partners in other countries, overloading both "outside-in" and "inside-out" causal paths between comparative politics and IR. And the public purposes pursued by NGOs are so universalistic as to obscure their origins in Western political ideas and institutions, particularly as filtered through Anglo-American political culture.

In sum, we have identified several broad paths by which IR theory hides NGO politics:

1. Realism, despite its preoccupation with states and power, is insufficiently state-centric to notice two centuries of transnational power projection through NGOs by the societies of liberal major power states.
2. Idealist constructivists echo NGOs themselves in recognizing exclusively vertical axes of political causality—either norm enforcement from above or societal representation from below. They thereby rule out of consideration horizontal causal interactions of NGO operations with local politics and society, or with NGOs in other issue domains.
3. All three schools of IR theory inadvertently homogenize the actors in world politics, and thereby hide the politics, in three related but distinct ways:
    a idealist constructivists delimit their scope of research to only those actors that mutually recognize each other as publicly

articulating common norms and operating within issue-area boundaries;
b   rationalists attribute a single, common, strategic rationality to all NGOs, and portray them as autonomous and unaffected by interactions with other actors; and
c   both liberals and sociological institutionalists assume that actors in networks share common norms.
4   IR theory systematically overlooks how real NGOs transgress the conceptual boundaries between comparative politics, international relations, American hegemony, and normative political theory that are reinforced by the subfield divisions of political science.

NGOs routinely traverse these dead zones ignored by much of IR theory. Their apolitical universalism eases their importation into other countries and regions, whose domestic politics and society are purportedly left unscathed, but which in reality host multiple, ongoing negotiations and power struggles between transnational societal and political partners in the NGO network. Each chapter of this book sheds light on neglected aspects of NGO politics. To assess these findings, and address the problem of institutions, we first turn to the chapters that address NGOs and networks as institutions.

Findings: bridging institutions

Our approach can bring to liberal IR theory a much broader conception of *international institutions* by illuminating how NGOs bridge between partners and build transnational networks. Political institutions are theoretically elusive and conceptually problematic not only for IR, but also for the broader discipline of political science. Despite the lack of a singular definition of institutions, we propose that NGO network relations are international institutions for three reasons.

First, there is a narrow liberal institutionalist reason for conceptualizing NGOs and networks as international institutions. All international institutions as conventionally understood—intergovernmental organizations (IGOs), treaties and even diplomacy—already and increasingly function in practical relations to NGO networks. This pattern has burgeoned particularly since 1990, but the coevolution of NGOs and IGOs goes back two centuries. All arenas of world politics are increasingly permeated by NGOs and networks, which clearly form a kind of "institutional" arrangement.

Second, there is a path-dependent constructivist reason. Many international issues and functions that today are addressed primarily through NGO networks might otherwise have been ignored entirely or addressed primarily through other kinds of international institutions. Instead, since 1945 there has been a complex movement from other institutional forms and toward NGO networks. NGOs are more flexible, decentralized and adaptive than the historical alternatives, but also more easily coopted, marginalized, or instrumentalized by powerful actors. At the same time, NGO networks "institutionalize" the environment within which other actors in world politics operate, to the point that today states, multinational corporations, insurgent groups, and warlords are all forced to develop an NGO strategy. These institutional phenomena demand constructivist interpretation.

Third, there is a realist power reason for thinking about NGOs and networks in terms of international institutions. For over two centuries, the two countries whose governments at critical junctures fostered the creation of intergovernmental organizations and multilateral diplomacy, whose economies led the expansion of international capitalism, and whose militaries led the defense against a series of totalitarian challenges, were the same countries whose societies catalyzed the creation and global diffusion of NGO networks as a pervasive institutional form—Great Britain and the United States.

Calling attention to this stark, historical convergence of power may indeed offend and repel liberal-minded scholars. At the same time, within IR theory it is precisely the unwillingness of most realists, liberals and constructivists to face these historical facts in their various implications that makes this book necessary.

The contributors to this volume have taken on the challenge of understanding NGOs as institutions. Indeed, of all the concepts proposed in our Introduction, NGO bridging is the one most enthusiastically embraced by all our contributors. Five chapters theorize NGOs by drawing upon a particular body of institutional theory: McMahon on principal–agent theory, Mingst and Muldoon on global governance, Balboa on accountability theory, Ohanyan on new institutional theories, and Andersen on practice theory. The fact that these contributors chose to address NGO institutional theory from a wide range of points of view forcefully places on the table the problem of institutions.

Themes of NGO responsibility, accountability and hypocrisy are pervasive in this book. Who is watching the watchers? NGOs are revered globally as a trusted institution. However, at the same time more scholars are questioning the presumptive legitimacy accorded to NGOs.

296 Conclusions and implications

Patrice McMahon reports that international donors supported NGOs for peacebuilding in Bosnia, while considerable evidence showed that NGOs failed to bridge interethnic divides at the societal level. She utilizes principal–agent (PA) theory—a form of economic institutionalism—to scrutinize the accountability of the NGOs (agents) to their government and IGO donors (principals), and then to explain the apparent lack of impact and failure of accountability by the NGOs in Bosnia. In the end, however, she faults PA theory, which mistakenly "assumes that NGOs have the same goals as the governments and intergovernmental organizations that support them." In our terminology, PA theory fails to explain the lapse of NGO accountability because it conceptually homogenizes the norms or rationalities of NGO partners in the network. As *institutional theory*, the PA approach accounts for the links between NGOs and their donor partners, but not for the links between NGOs and their societal partners—in this case, the mutually hostile ethnic communities of Bosnia.

International NGOs effectively elude all attempts at tight accountability, both in theory and in practice, according to Cristina Balboa's wide-ranging assessment. For major theorists, full accountability would demand no less than eight distinct criteria and institutional enforcement mechanisms. Even nontraditional theories of accountability (such as stakeholder, contingency, rights, and mutuality theories) cannot be fully applied to international NGOs because NGO networks lack all three necessary requirements for them to work: (1) consistent norms of behavior, (2) sufficiently powerful agents of accountability, and (3) sufficient NGO organizational capacity to account in all directions and to all criteria. The first requirement, consistent norms of behavior, turns out to be decisively significant. The finding that such consistent norms are missing, even when NGOs operate in the same issue area and network, falsifies both pluralist and globalist versions of idealist constructivism, as well as most applications of sociological institutionalism. Despite the appearance that common norms function as the glue unifying all the actors in a network, in practice actual norms are too heterogeneous to provide the basis for actor accountability.

In principle, an NGO could learn to respond accountably to all of its partners by undertaking a thorough stakeholder analysis. However, to attempt to hold NGOs fully accountable, Balboa argues, could, "conceivably create enough veto points in the policy process to halt the process altogether." Indeed, the fully accountable NGO would simply perish of "Multiple Accountabilities Disorder" (MAD)! In addition, a thorough stakeholder analysis could reveal any hidden partners and agendas, whose public acknowledgement could be fatal to the legitimacy and sustainability of the NGO network.

Balboa draws a startling conclusion: the "larger truth" is that "any NGO that endures over time has successfully managed its accountability challenges to the extent of retaining those partners essential for its survival." The implication, we would argue, is that the mere continuing existence of an NGO from day to day provides sufficient evidence that an NGO is accountable to its stakeholders; that is, the NGO is accountable enough that crucial partners at least suspend disbelief in the NGOs' constitutive normative claims, and maintain their partnership. Therefore, the only accountability that is possible is already guaranteed by the existential requirement that the NGO maintain bridges to essential partners.

PA theory is often applied to intergovernmental organizations (IGOs) in a similar way. The conceptual premise of PA theory is that IGO/NGO effectiveness results from subjecting the organization to strict accountability under its state donors. However, another influential approach, drawn from closely related fields of organizational and bureaucratic theory, takes precisely the opposite tack. Michael Barnett and Martha Finnemore, for example, conceptualize IGO effectiveness as rooted in organizational autonomy from state interests, allowing the organization to independently pursue its principled mandate as understood by its own experts and officials. The IR literature, therefore, is split between two views: that the effectiveness of international organizations is enhanced by strict accountability to donors, or that effectiveness is threatened by such accountability.

This polarization in the literature offers a clue to deeper processes of agency and structure. It is difficult to theorize both structure and agency at the same time, and to keep them in dynamic balance. In this case, PA theory privileges structure (the constraints of donor relations), while bureaucratic theory privileges agency (organizational autonomy to pursue a principled mission). Our theoretical device of partner latent agendas, embedded in the two anchoring practices of NGOing, shows its utility at precisely this point. The network of partners, with all their open and latent agendas, not only constrains the NGO as structure, it also, and simultaneously, constitutes the NGO as a relatively autonomous agent.

Both McMahon's and Balboa's chapters point in the same direction: While NGOs hold other actors accountable, the accountability of NGOs themselves is stubbornly elusive, both in theory and practice. This is essential to consider today, as NGOs take on more responsibility and gain more influence, to the point of participating in the "global governance" architecture of the world.

As Karen Mingst and James Muldoon show, the literature on global governance is increasingly probing the accountability and legitimacy of global actors, including NGOs. In the 1990s, this literature was among the first to recognize that NGO networks were becoming part of governance institutions with growing scope and influence. Yet there are normative and conceptual tensions built into some of the global governance literature. One problem is that any arrangements that do not have the consent of the governed cannot fall under the definition of legitimate global governance. How is it possible to know from the outside which arrangements are more or less consensual, and therefore more or less legitimate as governance? Ironically, the world relies heavily on NGOs to monitor and critique governance arrangements. But given the difficulties with holding NGOs themselves accountable, does the mere presence of NGOs guarantee that local people consent to particular governance arrangements? Are NGOs being deployed to lend the presumption of legitimacy to arrangements that, in some cases, may not have the full consent of the governed? Until recently, the literature on NGOs in global governance has not aggressively probed these tensions and questions.

Transparency is another central issue for both accountability and global governance. As we proposed in the Introduction, all NGOs veil the terms of their embeddedness in networks with social and political partners. They do so structurally, not necessarily through the purposive agency of NGO staff. We have incorporated Brian H. Smith's theoretical insight that the partners of NGOs pursue multiple "latent" agendas that are often in tension with each other, and may be hidden from public view. Indeed, as Smith argues, "Too much disclosure or evaluation of actual project performance could be frustrating to subgroups for whom the myths are important and could create serious obstacles for their continuing commitments to make the system work."[3] Therefore, transparency is a dangerous ideal for NGOs, not necessarily because NGO officials wish to mislead or hide anything, but because keeping some things latent or below the surface is part of the constitutive structure of NGOing across any broad transnational network.

The theoretical problem of modeling NGOs as bridging institutions in world politics overlaps with the normative problem of establishing a basis for NGO accountability. NGO accountability is elusive for the same reasons that theorizing NGO networks as international institutions is elusive. To reveal more than it conceals, an adequate institutional theory of NGOs must account for the latent agendas of NGO partners, the interwoven conflict and cooperation that NGO networks institutionalize, and the reality of hidden or normatively deviant partners.

The academic discipline of management studies, Cristina Balboa reminds us, is the source of several of the theoretical and practical strategies for providing accountability in international NGOs, including principle–agent theory, stakeholder theory, and organizational learning approaches. These strategies reflect the overlap between the literatures on global governance, NGO accountability, and international public administration.[4] However, we suggest that the very structure of international NGOs and their networks will frustrate virtually all attempts to incorporate tight management, accountability or transparency.

Is the consistent pattern of NGO unaccountability entirely inadvertent? Is it a pathology to be cured? Or is NGO unaccountability, at least to some degree and in some respects, designed into the institutional form of NGOs? Is the popularity of the NGO organizational form due in part precisely to its inherent unaccountability? And why is the question of NGO accountability emerging with such force now?

We can chip away at these questions of engineered unaccountability in three ways. First, NGO accountability is enhanced if powerful states make it a priority. Since 9/11, the United States and its allies have shut down an array of Islamic welfare NGOs that were alleged to be funding branches of Al Qaeda and other jihadists.[5] The governments of Russia and Egypt have clamped down heavily on foreign NGOs within their borders, claiming the NGOs were agents of foreign powers seeking to destabilize the government.[6] However, these examples also show that strict accountability can kill NGOs. When governments want NGOs to survive, they do not over-regulate them.

Second, according to our approach, the constitutive structure of NGOs, encoded in their anchoring practices, entails links with political and societal "partners" in several countries. Many large NGOs are active in scores of countries—with both political and societal partners in each one. This far-flung organizational network structure virtually guarantees diffuse accountability.

Third, it is commonplace for NGO professionals, both in the field and at headquarters, not to know who all their partners are, and not to divulge to donors everything they know. Nor do they always know—or want to know—their partners' latent agendas. In addition, it is commonplace for donors to purposefully deploy NGOs with loose accountability. For example, in the Great Lakes region of Africa in the 1990s, every major branch of humanitarian NGOs failed to achieve its mission: international development, early warning and conflict prevention, human rights, humanitarian relief, peacemaking and peacebuilding, and refugees.[7] Yet, taken together, they have not suffered any dearth of donor support as a result of their collective failure.[8]

As the evidence mounts, is there any responsible alternative to acknowledging that something else must be going on in NGO networks, something in addition to the pursuit of official mandates? As scholars we cannot fully acknowledge something until we can theorize it, in this case in institutional terms.

Anna Ohanyan theorizes the remarkable bridging, or "associative capacities," of NGOs by incorporating insights from three major branches of the "new institutionalisms": rational choice institutionalism, historical institutionalism, and sociological institutionalism.[9] We share Ohanyan's intuition that all three new institutionalisms are needed to fully explicate NGOs and their networks. Each approach can bring a distinctive central insight and explanatory style to social analysis. Rational choice knows that human actors, individually and in groups, are capable of long-term, strategic rationality to create and sustain their interests, including mutually beneficial institutions. Sociology knows that human actors swim in a sea of culture and institutions that shape persons and organizations as much as persons and organizations shape culture. And historical institutionalism knows that rational strategies and cultural dynamics both play out in path-dependent, historical processes.

However, we also pose some questions for this integrative approach. First, is it necessary or possible to integrate the three new institutionalisms into a single theory? If NGOs are indeed "multiple realities," then they may require multiple perspectives to discern and recognize all their facets. In addition, how can institutional theory borrow from rational choice and sociological institutionalisms while avoiding the pitfalls that both tend to "homogenize the actors" to overlook divergent rationalities and norms among NGO partners? As Hall and Taylor observe, sociological approaches have emphasized macro-level cultural and institutional influence to the degree that actors "seem to drop from sight," and the scene looks like "action without agents." Similarly, rational choice approaches stress so much the collective benefits recognized by a shared rationality that they mask the institutional reality of "a struggle for power and resources."[10]

Based on the Introduction and on Morten Andersen's proposal of a practice approach to understanding the processes of NGOing, we now tie practice theory back in.

A practice approach to NGO institutional theory

A practice approach to NGOs would seek to achieve four goals: to provide a coherent institutional account of NGOs and networks; to cut through the fog of theory concealing the politics of NGOs; to endow researchers with permission to follow NGO societal and political partners beyond their common norms; and to construct a framework that invites dialogue and cross-fertilization between any relevant academic disciplines.

Practice theory has emerged in a useful form in the social science discipline of anthropology, which may fit the study of NGOs quite well. Anthropology is more attuned to unique and variegated normative differences among smaller social communities, and less ready to generalize across large social groups. It can also handle the multiple realities and intermingled ontologies presented by real NGOs. The research method of ethnography—immersion and participant observation through field work—lends itself to discerning the divergent norms and rationalities of various NGO societal and political partners, and is less prone to homogenizing the actors. Finally, anthropology is more attuned to maintaining the creative tension between social structure and actor agency, and more resistant to resolving the tension one way or the other than are sociology, economics, or comparative politics and IR within political science.

Our contribution in this context is to identify the two "anchoring practices" that all NGOs perform in common. However, for this effort to contribute to institutional theory, and to participate in the intra- and inter-disciplinary dialogue on international institutions, it must have an entry point into a larger scholarly conversation.

We follow Emanuel Adler and Vincent Pouliot in understanding that "action is behavior imbued with meaning," and that practices are "patterned actions that are embedded in particular organized contexts and, as such, are articulated into specific types of action and are socially developed through learning and training."[11] In short, practices are more or less "competent performances" that are accepted or rejected within particular social contexts and communities.[12] Furthermore, the "anchoring practices" of NGOing can be understood as mid-level institutional practices that are embedded within the broader international practices of world politics.[13] This is the step necessary to link practice theory to broader institutional theory on the one hand, and to the two anchoring practices of NGOs on the other hand.

How do we know that the two practices identified below and their corollaries are the anchoring practices of NGOing? Because these are the only practices that all NGOs perform all the time, wherever they are. To recognize this, an observer's scrutiny must shift from what NGOs say they are doing to what they actually do. To understand NGOs deeply, we need to turn our scholarly gaze away from their emancipatory promises, away from the crying needs of the people or the natural environment, and toward what they consistently do that is distinctive to them.

"NGOing" happens, we have proposed, (1) when private actors claim to pursue public purposes, and (2) when, by the authority so claimed, they partner with societal and political actors in several countries. NGOs make normative claims, establish and maintain partner

302 Conclusions and implications

relations, and thereby grow networks. And they do so, inexorably and indefatigably, every moment of their existence, just by being NGOs.

The first anchoring practice, private actors pursuing public purposes, subsumes all the normative and causal claims discussed above. Such claims are inherently relational, political and contestable, and are contested as often as they are accepted by societal and political partners in the second anchoring practice. Together, the anchoring practices inevitably entail multifaceted bridging dynamics. Each NGO generates and embodies vertical bridging relations between society and state in each country, horizontal (transnational) relations between societies, and transverse relations between each society and other states, and its direct partners connect to additional webs of partners. Hence, the potential scale and complexity of any NGO network is breathtaking.

Crucially, we hold that *actors are part of a network when they share any common partners*. This differs radically from almost all other approaches for studying NGOs and networks, which delimit the scope of network research according to the normative issue areas defined by NGOs themselves. Globalists and pluralists take their bearings in the network from the normative commitments articulated publicly and recognized mutually by other members. Even those few realists who examine NGOs as strategic actors define the scope of NGO competition for scarce resources within the publicly visible normative issue domain. For us, the fact of a direct or indirect organizational link constitutes the network, rather than the shared normative discourse used to legitimize those links. This allows for hidden partners—hidden from the public or even from the NGO itself—and for partners that do not adhere to the NGO norms. An addition, we hold that each societal and political partner of each NGO pursues some latent agenda through linking with the NGO. It may be benign, or may conflict with the NGO's salient agenda or with the latent agendas of other partners. Hence, each NGO may embody both cooperation with its partners on the salient agenda, and conflict over latent agendas.

In sum, NGOs partner and bridge heterogeneously, forming variegated and often conflictive networks. Thus, from *practice*, through *bridging*, we come to *power*. Conflict and asymmetric power may come into play over the transnational movement of people, resources, norms, information, or technologies. Even when a particular partner interface is not actively conflictive, it is still potentially so, especially in war-torn societies, or closed societies with authoritarian politics that lack open institutions for political contestation.

In sum, every NGO is itself a site for power-laced encounters, a nexus of several other cooperating *and* competing actors, with complex interests and agendas. Each NGO bridges and institutionalizes both cooperation and conflict among its own societal and political partners in several countries, as part of routine NGOing. NGO politics is not a pathology to be diagnosed and cured. Without latent agendas, there are no partners; and without partners, there is no NGO. Moreover, savvy and experienced NGO professionals already know this, and consider finessing these tensions to be one measure of their professionalism. Social scientists are only slowly catching up.

This theoretical approach generates profound but simple implications for epistemology, methodology, and ontology. Epistemologically, NGOs can be found by looking for the anchoring practices of NGOing. The common theoretical quest for a taxonomy of NGO operational practices is a losing battle. NGOs adapt and change very quickly, and the most powerful NGO practices tend to be innovative and hidden for some time, precisely by transgressing previous conventions. In many studies, attempts to classify in advance the tactics of NGOs and their partners have made it harder to see the new ones.

Methodologically, to find the politics, *follow the partners*. Follow them especially after you run out of actors that visibly affirm shared norms, and beyond where the conventional theories of IR tell you to stop. Ethnography may be particularly fruitful for following NGO partners, and identifying their heterogeneous norms and rationalities.[14] However, a tenacious investigative reporter, or a savvy national who speaks the language and poses the right questions may be just as successful.[15]

Ontologically, NGOs are permeable and mingled with their partners. NGOing entails partnering, so the NGO *is* the relations with its crucial societal and political partners. Consistent with Morten Andersen's position, we embrace a relational ontology. We have emphasized the recursive social practices by which NGOs recruit partners, and the partners in turn constitute and inhabit the NGOs. However, by our specifying the two anchoring practices of NGOs in such concreteness, we retain more of a foothold in substantialist ontology than Andersen would affirm.

This book, then, has addressed the problem of NGO institutions in a manner that yields a broader conception of international institutions for IR theory. The theoretical groundwork is under construction for a fruitful, inter- and intra-disciplinary conversation about NGO networks and their interactions with other institutionalized anchoring practices in world politics.

Findings: practice as constructive power

How have the contributors to this book followed the partners, and what have they found?

Patrice McMahon finds that many indigenous Bosnian NGOs after the 1995 Dayton Peace Accords did not advance their official mandates of interethnic reconciliation, and yet their donors continued to fund them for years. Clearly, neither the donors nor the Bosnian NGOs were highly committed to the salient normative agenda of ethnic tolerance and peace that ostensibly brought them together. If the NGO operations over these years did not promote interethnic reconciliation, then what other effects might they have had? It seems fair to hypothesize that NGO societal partners in Bosnia were heterogeneous in their rationalities and/or norms, rather than homogeneous as most NGO theories would expect. McMahon hints at possible latent agendas of the donors (containing conflict and preventing refugees) and of the Bosnian NGOs (income generation for their staffs and support for their ethnic communities).

Elizabeth Bloodgood analyzes how national regulations constitute and empower NGOs in the democratic and economically advanced member states of the Organization for Economic Co-operation and Development (OECD). Though states in the OECD are relatively similar, she finds considerable variation in NGO legal identities and relationships with their home governments. All OECD governments regulate NGOs, but only in Poland are they legally identified as "non-governmental organizations." Elsewhere, their legal identities range across the rubrics of nonprofit organization, association, charity, civil society organization, public benefit organization, and corporation. In addition to variation between countries, national regulations may also change over time as in the Japan case, or may vary within countries that have federal systems as in the cases of the United States and Canada.

Several questions merit further investigation:[16] Does the legal heterogeneity of NGO regulations across the OECD and over time indicate variation and change in *norms*, in the strategic *rationality* of NGOs, or in the *incentives* they face with a consistent rationality? How could this survey of national regulations be extended to states outside the OECD in which the rule of law is less well established? To what extent do countries learn from each other's NGO regulations, either to mimic or to counter another country? How can this large-n comparative data be used to suggest structured case studies that would compare selected pairs of countries in more depth, including domestic politics and societal partners?

Morten Andersen sketches two compelling scenes that point to the paradoxical and chameleonic heterogeneity of NGO partners in Liberia. In the first, he was invited to an "NGO wig party" under portable UN shelters at a beachfront condo off a dusty road in

Monrovia. It was not exclusively for NGO workers, but included a variety of expatriates and diplomats, all wearing wigs with no explanation. He interprets the party as somehow emblematic of the paradoxes of UN and NGO aid, perhaps a ritual or parody of "how NGOs are often associated with exactly such informal relations and intermingling, something happening 'below' the level of formal organizations and bureaucracies under a common umbrella (or party tent, as in this case)." The second scene illustrates the Carter Center's extensive partnering throughout Liberia:

> As the CC in Liberia has developed relations with local actors and other NGOs, its borders have become increasingly blurred ... When visiting the headquarters of the National Traditional Council (established with the help of the CC) an NGO worker hinted that it might be time to go back to the CC. The supreme chief responded "this *is* the Carter Center," laughing heartily.

In some real sense, the National Traditional Council of tribal chiefs *is* the Carter Center. NGOs like the Carter Center can be "multiple realities" that are "ontologically intermingled" with their partners. Further study of the heterogeneous societal and political partners of the Carter Center in Liberia over time could be revealing.

Dennis Dijkzeul compares three NGOs that addressed Gender Based Violence (GBV) in a war-torn region of the eastern Democratic Republic of Congo (DRC) during the 2000s: the International Rescue Committee (IRC), with its focus on displacement and health; Malteser International, a German NGO with its support of local systems to address women's health and GBV problems; and Women for Women International (WfWI), with its sponsorship links between local women and women abroad. Cumulatively, the three NGOs engaged with a broad and heterogeneous panoply of societal and political partners in the region. Each organization innovated to address the needs of women in eastern Congo at a micro level, but also transformed global engagement with the region at a macro level, leading to significant increases in humanitarian aid, political attention in support of a large UN peacekeeping mission, and a global anti-GBV campaign with a broad coalition of health, human rights, feminist, and peace networks.

At one level, these NGOs created far reaching institutional bridges with global partners and effected a sweeping transformation of constructivist power. However, while violence against women in the DRC has captured the attention of the world, the world has not prevented violence in the DRC. The paradox and tragedy of this case invites further research on NGO political partners in the DRC. What powers are exercised by traditional leaders, warlords, local government officials, or foreign soldiers and businesses? What powers sustain the violence? Would pursuing such questions about veiled political partners jeopardize the very work of NGO staff and scholars?

Shareen Hertel's chapter offers a conceptual and empirical tour of the vast and expanding world of public–private partnerships (PPPs), in which NGOs form relationships with private sector corporations to promote labor rights. PPPs provide public goods by supplementing inefficient state regulation of worker rights, and private goods by giving progressive companies a competitive advantage among consumers or investors. NGOs involved in PPPs partner with, and mediate between, corporate leaders at headquarters and their workers spread out in a global supply chain of suppliers and subcontractors.

In a three-fold typology, some PPPs are voluntary, cooperative arrangements in which NGOs both negotiate and monitor corporate codes of conduct for labor practices. Local factory managers are essential societal partners in the reporting and monitoring of compliance with these codes of conduct. In the second group, NGOs collect and disseminate data on corporate labor rights performance, provided by the corporations themselves, to consumers, investors and the general public. In the third category, conflictual and radical "fire brigade" NGOs protest and pressure corporations by publicly revealing violations of standards, and catalyzing boycott or divestment.

PPPs have been criticized as a fragmented and uncoordinated global arena providing incomplete accountability. However, Hertel's evidence would support a judgment that no institutional field of global scope other than NGO networks could possibly cope with the breakneck pace of change and variegated local expressions of labor–corporate relations in contemporary capitalism. While Hertel acknowledges that NGOs in PPPs are vulnerable to instrumentalization by the corporations with which they cooperate, she insists "they also resist it." Given this tension, further research comparing societal partner relations at the level of the local factories across the three NGO domains promises to be both empirically interesting and theoretically productive.[17]

Is it possible for scholars of NGOs to go too far in following the partners? William DeMars challenges the theoretical premises and normative commitments that lead many researchers to stop prematurely in looking for network partners. He argues that "color revolutions" against authoritarian rulers were spread through emulation as well as through active transmission and training by a loose network of NGOs, and that the revolutions are strategically isomorphic with each other and with the premises of the strategic nonviolence activist literature.

DeMars follows the partners three steps beyond that circumscribed notion of the conventional NGO network offered by pluralist scholars. First, he shows how all color revolutions address and recruit security actors in the police, military, and intelligence bureaucracies to abandon the dictator and side with the revolution, either actively or passively. This observation seriously undermines the flawed premise of pluralist and globalist theory, as well as some definitions of global governance, that network actors must believe and advocate common norms, and maintain visible and mutual ties. Second, for the Serbian case, DeMars shows that public advocacy by NGOs and diplomats from the United States, Britain and other EU member states was acknowledged by all observers as action within the network, but that parallel support operations by military and intelligence actors from the same governments were ignored. Finally, DeMars follows the partners to delineate comprehensive responses mounted by Russia, China, Iran and their allies to neutralize future color revolutions, especially since 2005. These authoritarian counter-networks are centrally and hierarchically organized, and so do not function as true decentralized networks. However, they counter the color revolutions comprehensively across all modalities of the network, by mobilizing fake NGOs, anti-democratic youth movements, UN Security Council vetoes, new regional IGOs, election monitoring agencies, ideology, and websites.

DeMars argues that the most interesting politics usually happens outside the normative harmony of the publicly visible network. He shows that scholars who stop investigating the network when they run out of homogeneous actors help to conceal the full politics of the network.

In all these empirical cases, NGOs are revealed as partnering profligately with a heterogeneous array of societal and political partners. These encounters are where the politics can be found. Some NGOs are transformed by their encounter with a country or region, and transform it in return. Yet other NGO networks preside over stable situations, contrary to their transformative mandates. The actual effect of a network is not predictable from the intentions articulated through the network's common norms. Instead, the consequences are negotiated and renegotiated in contentious interactions among partners that often carry various overt and latent agendas. The most interesting politics is often revealed by probing *both* the political and societal partners of NGOs.

Among NGO researchers there is often a certain reticence to follow both societal and politics partners; instead, one or the other is privileged in most accounts. When scholars stop following the partners before the politics runs out, there may be good reasons. The research stops before the awkward compromises among partners are exposed that might delegitimize real and hard-won gains.

Findings: power in relationships

We have suggested that our approach can enrich the realist tradition by revealing overlooked power relationships in transnational networks. We have argued that NGO partnering with heterogeneous actors leads to veiled relations of power in the network. However, McMahon and Dijkzeul both highlight the *lack* of NGO power to achieve their mandated normative missions. Reinalda sees NGOs as dependent and ancillary gadflies around the more powerful states and IGOs that states create. Yet, both Balboa and Hertel emphasize that in the last 20–30 years more public goods have been shifted from state provision to provision by market and civil society (meaning NGOs in practice). So, where is the power of NGOs?

A paradox is at play in the color revolutions, DeMars shows, in which NATO is a *weak agent* whose bombs failed to unseat Milosevic in 1999, while at the same time NATO exerts *strong structural power*. The latter is expressed indirectly, as a force to inspire democracy activists with the ideals of democracy and human rights, and attract them with the promises of security and prosperity.

Bob Reinalda analyzes the co-evolutionary expansion of both NGOs and IGOs from a comparative, historical perspective since the American and French revolutions of the late eighteenth century. This long historical view reveals clearly that the affinity for IGO creation by the governments of Britain and the United States is paralleled by an affinity for NGO generation by the societies of the same countries. Reinalda fruitfully combines liberal, realist and constructivist approaches by focusing on international institutions; on the power plays between states, IGOs, NGOs and other actors in the international arena; and on the norms and ideas that led to changes in the functioning of these actors.

Reinalda explains that states, IGOs and NGOs have "co-evolved" by constituting networks in which they instrumentalize each other to realize their different goals. Implicitly, he acknowledges how much social change IGOs and NGOs have wrought, often in opposition to states—and against all odds—as in the antislavery campaign and promotion of human rights and democracy. The cumulative effects of NGO action over more than two centuries are more impressive in retrospect than their frequent setbacks.

Reinalda treats the years 1815, 1919 and 1945 as critical turning points when, after winning a major war, liberal major powers seized the initiative to create a new generation of international organizations to structure world politics. However, he does not treat 1991 as a similar watershed, even though John Ikenberry identifies 1991 as a critical juncture "after victory" in the Cold War.[18] During the 1990s, the United States undertook modest institution building, but the United Nations system and regional security and economic organizations persisted beyond 1991, precluding institution building from scratch.

Was 1991 comparable to 1815, 1919, and 1945 in terms of a surge in international institution building? To what extent are NGOs, not mentioned by Ikenberry, the characteristic organizational form of the new global institutional order after the Cold War? How do some hegemonic states benefit from the expansion of NGOs? Why is the actual power of NGOs so frequently overlooked? More detailed historical study of the tactics of mutual instrumentalization between states, NGOs and IGOs, and the impact this has had on international politics, could illuminate these questions.

Agency, structure, and power

The problem of NGO power is closely intertwined with the elusive relationship between agency and structure. *Agential power* is analytically straightforward. In our framework, as articulated in the Introduction and this Conclusion so far, the practice of NGOing is performed by agents, exercising agential power, even though such agency is only possible within existing structures of meaningful action and social fields. However, here we emphasize the structure of NGO positioning with networks, and the more elusive nature of *structural power*.

We have seen how social theories across many disciplines fail to maintain a balance and creative tension between structure and agency. Instead, they tend to privilege either structure or agency. In terms of IR theory, we seek conceptual alternatives to the false dichotomy of either affirming the agency of international organizations as autonomous from states (a common constructivist claim), or denying their agency as the tools of states (a common realist claim). Our account of NGO practice is intended to convey a balance between agency and structure as mutually constitutive. An increase in one does not necessarily decrease the other. Without a structure of social relationships, there is no agency in social reality. And without actors exercising agency, there are no structured relationships among them. All agency is socially situated and is discernible by the observer only by looking from the point of view of a particular actor in a particular time and

310 *Conclusions and implications*

social location. Structural power is as real as agential power, but is harder to characterize and narrate in a causal explanation.

Further research on agency power and structural power in NGO networks shows great promise. NGOs increasingly emerge as the presumptively legitimate, taken-for-granted organizational form for organizing any political opposition or reform movement. NGO anchoring practices are so deeply embedded in the institutional structure of world politics that everyone assumes the answer to any new problem will include NGOs. NGOs do not impose themselves using agential power. Instead, there is a "structural power" that installs NGOs in the lead of any new political movement, rather than any of the historically alternative actors or organizational forms. In this way structural power is hidden in plain sight.

Because NGOs link societal and political partners, agential and structural dynamics enfold the partners as well. The dynamics of structure and agency play out through a "cycle of NGO social construction" depicted in Figure 11.1. Each corner of the triangle is simultaneously agent and structure. NGOs are structure vis-à-vis the networks they constitute, and agents constituted by their partners. The three arrows indicate the direction of constitutive or structural power; the power to constitute agents within social fields of taken-for-granted organizational forms and conditions:

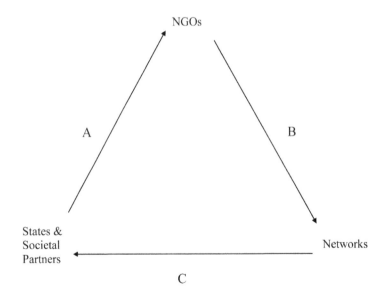

Figure 11.1 Cycle of NGO social construction

Arrow A: Partners (both states and societal actors) shape or constitute NGOs;
Arrow B: NGOs constitute networks;
Arrow C: Networks constitute both states and societal partners; and back to
Arrow A: The cycle begins again with states and societal actors constituting NGOs as partners.

This is not the only cycle of social construction in world politics, nor is it an exhaustive characterization of this cycle, but the diagram points to a significant process that will reward further research.

The triangle is drawn to emphasize the intriguing reality that states of all levels of power occupy a dual position vis-à-vis NGOs and networks. In the structural power relation designated by arrow A, national states are crucial partners for virtually all international NGOs, by authorizing their existence through legal status and regulation in their countries of origin (Bloodgood and Reinalda), and by authorizing and/or resisting their access to countries of operations (Dijkzeul, Hertel, McMahon, Andersen, DeMars). In either role, states may seek either to tighten bonds of accountability by NGO partners to themselves (Balboa, Ohanyan, Mingst and Muldoon), or, conversely, to divest themselves of responsibility by devolving it to NGOs (Hertel, Dijkzeul, DeMars). Here states exercise agency, but they are experienced as structure in the daily life of the NGOs they constitute. In arrow B, as NGOs perform their anchoring practices they generate skeins of relationships with political and societal partners that are thereby constituted as networks. Finally, arrow C indicates the second side of state duality, by which networks constitute and shape states. This is a constructivist form of power, which is often structural.

An important implication of this cycle of NGO social construction is that direct NGO agency to change government policies—which is the focus of most NGO research, may be less important than indirect NGO power, impacting states structurally through networks. Tracing all this requires several rotations around the cycle of NGO social construction, as governments partner with societal actors to constitute NGOs, NGOs constitute networks, and networks sometimes constitute or reconstitute states.

Every chapter of this book addresses both NGO agency and structure in some way. But structural arguments, being more elusive, deserve attention. Reinalda identifies critical historical junctures in the aftermath of major wars at which the victors remake the *structure* of world politics in part by creating new intergovernmental organizations: the

Concert of Europe in 1815, the League of Nations in 1919, and the United Nations in 1945. Mingst and Muldoon document a *structural* shift since the 1990s in both the way governance is conducted in the real world, and in the "global governance" literature to understand those processes. The new structural factors, all of which feature NGOs, include a burgeoning role for nonstate actors, transnational processes of social learning, and a growing global concern for both power and normative accountability. Hertel maps the *structural* terrain of "public-private partnerships"—consisting of NGOs, hybrid organizations, and for-profit corporations which have largely taken over the regulation of labor relations in much of the developing world, thereby displacing both state and IGO regulation.

Other NGO networks extend forms of incomplete and flawed governance, which become part of the political and social *structure* in particular countries or regions, such as NGOs addressing GBV in the DRC (Dijkzeul), or ethnic reconciliation in Bosnia (McMahon). Ohanyan develops an argument emphasizing the *structural* effects on NGO power of their relative positions within different policy networks. She also brings forward the new institutionalist structural argument that NGOs "with unclear technologies and difficult to evaluate outputs" have been particularly sensitive to institutional pressure from their organizational environments, gradually taking on characteristics of their funders since the 1970s.

What is the value added by recasting these arguments in terms of agency and structure? This analytical strategy reveals that every corner of the triangle is an intervening variable. NGOs are not only constituted by their partners, but also go on to constitute networks. States are not only partly constituted by networks, but also contribute to constituting NGOs. This approach provides a more commodious analytical framework that captures more of the politics of each unique network. The influence of NGOs is not only through their agency. NGOs also influence events by creating networks, which become structural realities in the environment that shapes the alternatives available to all actors on the scene. Finally, this approach allows the ironies and paradoxes characteristic of real politics to emerge in the stories of NGOs.

Conclusion: risks of following the partners

To discover the politics of NGOs, and throw off the blinders of IR theory that hide the politics, we have emphasized the need to study NGO practices, in particular the two anchoring practices, using the methodological imperative to "follow the partners" beyond the point when the actors share and articulate common norms. This may reveal latent agendas, expose conflicts and asymmetric power relations among members of the network, or bring to light hidden or normatively deviant partners. These power relations coexist with cooperation in NGO networks. But if you expose the power relations, you may lose the cooperation.

The fundamental research challenge for NGOs is not *epistemological*, as some strands of constructivism argue. The core research challenges are *ontological*—avoiding misleading ontologies that hide the politics or portray NGOs as clearly bounded, hard shelled bureaucracies, as well as *methodological*—mining data and/or getting into the field with enough time and determination and other resources to observe all the faces of NGO practice. Only in this way can we gain an in-depth understanding of NGOs and their networks. A comprehensive research agenda would ideally include:

1   designing detailed and disciplined case studies matched with large-n comparisons;
2   conducting extended, multi-sited, and longitudinal field research;
3   educating and working with local scholars who appreciate and can explain local actors, culture, and history;
4   incorporating multifactor explanations across a broad range of relevant material, ideational, and institutional causes; and
5   directing attention to the details of all actors—whether state or non-state—to their salient and latent agendas, and to the networks in which they operate.

In this way, the partnering and bridging of NGOing, in which NGOs simultaneously resist and embody instrumentalization by their partners, can become the object of research, and their actual politics and power can be understood in more detail. Norms remain important as they proscribe and prescribe NGO action, but the accompanying practices require far more scrutiny. Normative claims and causal chains need to be distinguished.

The serious scholar, who recognizes the subtle, almost mesmerizing, power of NGOs and norms to obscure the real politics from the eyes of even seasoned observers, has a professional duty to consciously set aside the normative lens in order simply to see the broad politics. Then, at a certain point, the normative lens should be brought back in, for a range of reasons including assessing the impact of one's published account on the ongoing politics.

At the same time, there is a countervailing risk of imagining additional "hidden partners" or "latent agendas" in the network that are not really there. Therefore, it remains important both to stay grounded in solid empirical research, and also to acknowledge its practical and ethical limits.

The conventional model of IR research has been dominated by the misleading theoretical trichotomy of liberalism, realism, and constructivism, with the assumption that any particular body of evidence must support only one perspective at the expense of the others. Turning toward the politics of NGOs has demanded that we attempt to transcend this false trichotomy. Instead, we seek to recognize three kinds of things happening simultaneously in the practices of NGOing: institutional cooperation, asymmetric power and conflict, and the transformation of actors' identities and material structures.

For liberals concerned about institutional cooperation, we have proposed a broader conception of institutions by illuminating the transnational networks built by bridging NGOs. For realists concerned about power, we have revealed relationships of power and conflict in those transnational networks that are overlooked in conventional approaches. For constructivists concerned about international political change, our emphasis on NGO practice enhances the power of theory to perceive and explain the origins and reshaping of actors, both normatively and materially. By rejecting the theoretical homogenization of actors and issue areas, we have created a broader conception of politics, particularly in networks, so that the three theoretical traditions can complement each other to better explain the reality of NGOs, and the variety and dynamism of world politics.

Notes

1 Peter A. Gourevitch, David A. Lake, and Janice Gross Stein, eds, *The Credibility of Transnational NGOs: When Virtue is Not Enough* (Cambridge: Cambridge University Press, 2012), 4.
2 Our position may be characterized as methodological pluralism, since we hold that NGOs can change over time and vary over place, and that the politics of NGOs in a particular time and place cannot be assumed and therefore must be observed. We share with post-positivist critical theory the conviction that political reality is socially constructed (see our cycle of NGO social construction below) but find no warrant to abandon the challenge of knowing and describing that process.
3 Brian H, Smith, *More Than Altruism: The Politics of Private Foreign Aid* (Princeton, N.J.: Princeton University Press, 1990), 79.
4 For example, Jonathan G. S. Koppell has published on a range of topics in global governance in the journals *Public Administration Review*; *Journal of Public Administration Research and Theory*; and *Governance: An International Journal of Policy, Administration, and Institutions*.

5 Sara Pantuliano, Kate Mackintosh, Samir Elhawary, and Vicki Metcalfe, "Counter-Terrorism and Humanitarian Action," *HPG Policy Briefs*, no. 43 (October 2011), Humanitarian Policy Group, Overseas Development Institute, London.
6 Andrey Ostroukh, "Russia's Putin signs NGO 'foreign agents' law," Reuters, 21 July 2012 (www.reuters.com/article/2012/07/21/us-russia-putin-ngos-idUSBRE86K05M20120721); and "Amnesty International report criticizes Egypt's NGO restrictions," *Egypt Independent*, 21 February 2013 (www.egyptindependent.com/news/amnesty-international-report-criticizes-egypt-s-ngo-restrictions).
7 See Fiona Terry, *Condemned to Repeat?: The Paradox of Humanitarian Action* (Ithaca, NY: Cornell University Press, 2004); Alex de Waal, *Famine Crimes: Politics and the Disaster Relief Industry in Africa* (Oxford: James Currey, 1997); Peter Uvin, *Aiding Violence: The Development Enterprise in Rwanda* (West Hartford, Conn.: Kumarian Press, 1998); Michael N. Barnett, *Eyewitness to a Genocide: The United Nations and Rwanda* (Ithaca, NY: Cornell University Press, 2003); Roméo Dallaire, *Shake Hands with the Devil: The Failure of Humanity in Rwanda* (London: Arrow Books, 2004); and Alan J. Kuperman, "Provoking Genocide: A Revised History of the Rwandan Patriotic Front," *Journal of Genocide Research* 6, no. 1 (2004): 61–84.
8 Indeed, if donors want to delegate to actors that can be held more accountable than NGOs they have an array of for-profit service agencies (known as "beltway bandits" in Washington, DC) that can be made accountable exclusively to the single donor.
9 While up to seven new institutional theories have been enumerated, we agree with the tripartite division. See B. Guy Peters, *Institutional Theory in Political Science: The "New Institutionalism"* (London: Pinter, 1998).
10 Peter Hall and Rosemary Taylor, "Political Science and the Three New Institutionalisms," *Political Studies* 44 (1996): 954.
11 Emanuel Adler and Vincent Pouliot, "International Practices," *International Theory* 3, no. 1 (2011): 5.
12 Adler and Pouliot, "International Practices," 14–19.
13 On embedded practices, see Anthony Giddens, *The Constitution of Society: Outline of the Theory of Structuration* (Berkeley: University of California Press, 1986), 13. On anchoring practices, see Ann Swidler, "What Anchors Cultural Practices," in *The Practice Turn in Contemporary Theory*, eds Theodore R. Schatzki, Karin Knorr-Cetina and Eike von Savigny (London: Routledge, 2001), 83–101; and Ole Jacob Sending and Iver B. Neumann, "Banking on Power: How Some Practices in IO Anchor Others," in Adler and Pouliot, *International Practices*, 231–254.
14 Dorothea Hilhorst, *The Real World of NGOs: Discourses, Diversity and Development* (London: Zed Books, 2003); David Mosse, *Cultivating Development: An Ethnography of Aid Policy and Practice* (London: Pluto Press, 2004); Harri Englund, *Prisoners of Freedom: Human Rights and the African Poor* (Berkeley: University of California Press, 2006); Mark Schuller, *Killing with Kindness: Haiti, International Aid, and NGOs* (New Brunswick, N.J.: Rutgers University Press, 2012); Anne-Meike Fechter and Heather Hindman, eds, *Inside the Everyday Lives of Development Workers: The Challenges and Futures of Aidland* (Sterling, Va.: Kumarian Press, 2011);

Masooda Bano, *Breakdown in Pakistan: How Aid Is Eroding Institutions for Collective Action* (Stanford, Calif.: Stanford University Press, 2012); and Jon Harald Sande Lie, "Challenging Anthropology: Anthropological Reflections on the Ethnographic Turn in International Relations," *Millennium—Journal of International Studies* 41, no. 2 (2013): 201–20.

15 Bill Birchard, *Nature's Keepers: The Remarkable Story of How the Nature Conservancy Became the Largest Environmental Group in the World* (San Francisco: Jossey-Bass, 2005); Maha M. Abdelrahman, *Civil Society Exposed: The Politics of NGOs in Egypt* (London: Tauris Academic Studies, 2004).

16 For an NGO research agenda focused on acquiring and analyzing data on large numbers of NGOs, see Elizabeth A. Bloodgood and Hans Peter Schmitz, "The INGO Research Agenda: A Community Approach to Challenges in Method and Theory," in *Routledge Handbook of International Organization*, ed. Bob Reinalda (New York: Routledge, 2013), 67–79.

17 Richard M. Locke, *The Promise and Limits of Private Power: Promoting Labor Standards in a Global Economy* (Cambridge: Cambridge University Press, 2013).

18 G. John Ikenberry, *Liberal Leviathan: The Origins, Crisis, and Transformation of the American World Order* (Princeton, N.J.: Princeton University Press, 2011).

Index

6 April Movement in Egypt *see* April 6 Movement

Abbé de Saint-Pierre 110
Abdelrahman, Maha M. 22
accountability of NGOs 3, 77–9, 136, 151; rising calls for 159–161; NGO bridging and 161–3; in traditional literature 163, 166–7; in principal–agent theory 164–6; in new theories 167–71; limits of 171–4; New Life Children's Refuge in Haiti 174–8
Ackerman, Peter 240, 254
Adler, Emanuel 301
Advisory Committee on the Traffic in Women and Children 119
African Union 252
agency: in agenda-setting for multilateral conferences 112, 116–20, 127; of children's NGO in Haiti 174–8; in constructivist theory 18–21; and explanation 253–7; in institutional theories of NGOs 296–300; in liberal theory 9–10, 22; of NATO 247–51; and NGO accountability 164–71; and NGO bridging 161–3; of NGOs in networks 88–97; of NGO partners 282; in pluralist and globalist theory 12–13; in practice theory 46, 53, 58; in principal–agent models 74–7, 133–4, 153, 179, 224–8, 230; in realist theory 15–16; as theoretical and political problem 237–9; in transnational advocacy networks 241–5; *see also* structure and agency

Aix-la-Chapelle/Aachen Conference (1818) 113
Albright, Madeleine 248–9
American Bar Association 50–1
American Declaration of Independence and Constitution 109
Amnesty International 24, 121, 127–8, 136
anchoring practices: in co-evolution of NGOs and IGOs 126–7; and NGO unaccountability 299; and NGO partners in networks 244; of NGOs 4, 22–9; and practice theory of international institutions 301–3; in private–public partnerships for labor rights 192–4, 206; as structural power of NGOs 310–12
Andersen, Morten Skumsrud: encounters in Liberia 41, 49–51, 56; ontologies of substantialism and relationalism 43–5; NGOs and IR theory 45–9, 295, 300–4, 310–11; NGOs in practice 51–7; power expressed to, by, and through NGOs 57–60; research 61–3
Annan, Kofi 124
April 6 Movement in Egypt 125
Arab Spring 237, 240, 257
Ashley, Richard K. 8

Balboa, Cristina M..: limits and myopias of NGO accountability 171–8; NGO bridging as key to accountability 160–3; normative concern for NGO legitimacy 77; research 32, 180, 183; multiple theories of NGO accountability 163–71; IR theory and NGO accountability 178–80, 296–8, 311
Bangladesh 189
Barkin, J. Samuel 18
Barnett, Michael 19–20, 35–6, 48–9, 215, 297
Behn, Robert D. 166–8
Belgrade *see* Serbia
Binnendijk, Anika Locke 246
Bloodgood, Elizabeth A.: national regulations reveal changing NGO–state relations 130–2, new institutionalist views 132–4; comparisons across OECD countries 135–45; cases of U.S., Japan and Poland 145–51; IR theory and NGO regulation 152–3, 181, 304, 311, 316
Bob, Clifford 15–17, 76
Bodin, Jean 108
Bono 3
Börzel, Tanja A. 87
Bosnia and Herzegovina: peacebuilding in 211–216; outcomes of peacebuilding in 216–22; environment and incentives for NGOs in 222–8
Boutros-Ghali, Boutros 124, 211
Bowett, Derek 116
bridging (by NGOs): and accountability 160–3, 178–80; by anchoring practices of NGOing 22–9, 302, 314; of divisions in world politics 5–6; of ethnic divides 211–12, 219, 226, 229; to form networks 244; to generate transnational network institutions 294–300; in global governance perspective 69–71; in network formation and institutionalization 82–4, 87–91; in network institutionalism perspective 93–9; for rule making on labor rights 189–92, 197–200, 203, 206; between states and societies 131;
Bringing Down a Dictator (film) 240, 245, 250, 254
British Antislavery Society 112–13, 127, 292, 308
Britain (British, Great Britain, United Kingdom) 85–6, 88, 112–13, 249–50, 292, 295, 308
Brown, L. David 165, 170–1
Buchanan, Allen 78
Budapest 248, 250
Bulldozer Revolution in Serbia (2000) 239–40, 245–6, 248–51, 254–6
bureaucratization and professionalization of IGOs and NGOs 118–121
Business and Human Rights Resource Centre 200

Campe, Sabine 191–2, 196
CARE 215
Carter, Jimmy 25, 50
Carter Center (CC) 50, 59, 305
Catholic Justice and Peace Commission (Liberia) 50
Catholic Relief Services (CRS) 136, 215, 228
causal claims (implicitly made by NGOs): circumscribed causality 25–7, 194, 201, 290; empowerment 23–26, 173, 274; enforcement causality 23–26, 189, 197, 290–3; magic bullet causality 25–7, 272–4, 290
Cedar Revolution in Lebanon (2005) 239
Center for Applied Nonviolent Action and Strategies (CANVAS) 125
Central Commission for the Navigation of the Rhine 111
Central Intelligence Agency (CIA) 251
Centre Sosame 271
China 252, 257, 307
circumscribed causality *see* causal claims
Citizens United 147
CIVICUS (World Alliance for Citizen Participation) 136

civil society: and counter network against democratization 251–2; "disembedded" civil society 221; in global governance theories 69–70, 78; and League of Nations 117; in liberal theories 22; and NGO accountability 161–5, 176, 178; NGO failure to strengthen civil society in Bosnia 217–19; negative incentives to build civil society 227–30; in network institutionalism theory 94–5; and peacebuilding NGOs in Bosnia 212–15; in pluralist and globalist theories 11–13; provision of public goods shifted from states to civil society 308; in realist theories 7, 14–16; *see also* global civil society

Claude, Jr. Inis 110, 126
Clean Clothes Campaign (CCC) 201
Clinton, Bill 136
Clooney, George 3
Coalition for the International Criminal Court 125
Cobden Clubs 115
Code of Conduct for the International Red Cross and Red Crescent Movement and NGOs in Disaster Relief 136
Cold War, rise of civil society after 11, 124, 214, 263, 309
Color Revolutions: agency of activists in 237–9, 242–3, 254–7; counter network against 251–3; hidden partners in 245–51; and transnational democracy network 239–40; *see also* Bulldozer, Cedar, Dignity, Euromaidan, Green, Lotus, Orange, Rose, Saffron, and Tulip Revolutions
Comité Fronterizo de Obreras (CFO) 202
Commission on Global Governance 69
Commonwealth of Independent States (CIS) 252
communist 139, 151, 219, 239, 247, 253, 256
Community Charter of Fundamental Social Rights of Workers 193

Comparative Nonprofit Sector Project (CNSP) 155
Congress of Vienna (1814–15) 107, 110–13, 120, 122,
constructivism: and challenge of theorizing NGOs 6, 10–14, 16–22, 26–8, 289–91, 293–7, 300–12; and color revolutions 238, 241–5, 253–7; and global governance perspectives 65, 73, 76–7; and labor rights advocacy 190–1, 197–203, 205–7; and network institutionalism 93–100; and NGO accountability 167–74; and peacebuilding 226–30; and practice theory 42, 45–7; and sociological institutionalism 91–3; and state regulation of NGOs 131, 134–6; and violence and women's health in conflict 263–4, 281–3;
consultative status (for NGOs) 113, 121–4
Convention on Cluster Munitions 125
Convention on the Rights of the Child (CRC) 198
Cooley, Alexander 75
corporate codes of conduct 196–9, 306
Council on Economic Priorities (CEP) 202
Council on Foreign Relations (CFR) 252
Cox, Robert 8

Davos consensus 10
Dayton Peace Accords 31, 213–14, 220–1, 249, 304
Declaration of the Rights of Man and the Citizen (France) 109
DeMars, William E. Introduction, 3–38; chapter 9, 237–61; chapter 11, 289–316
democracy promotion 212–15, 238–41
Democratic Republic of Congo (DRC) Chapter 10, 262–86
de Waal, Alex 16
Despines, Michael 268
Diana, Princess of Wales 3
Dignity Revolution in Tunisia (2011) 240

Index

Dijkzeul, Dennis Introduction, 3–38; Chapter 10, 262–86; Chapter 11, 289–316
DiMaggio, Paul G. 93, 98
Dingwerth, Klaus 66
Doctors Without Borders *see* Médecins sans Frontières
Donini, Antonio 22
Drezner, Daniel W. 14–17, 70, 74,
DRC *see* Democratic Republic of the Congo
Duvall, Jack 240, 254–5

Ebrahim, Alnoor 173–4
ECOSOC (Economic and Social Council) 119–123
Edelman Trust Barometer 3
Egypt 22, 125, 240, 299, *see* Lotus Revolution
empowerment causality *see* causal claims
enforcement causality *see* causal claims
environmental NGOs 22, 28, 67–8, 73, 125, 159–60, 191–5, 301
epistemology 8, 16–17, 20–1, 238, 241, 257, 303, 313
Estonia 253
Euromaidan revolution in Ukraine (2014) 237, 253
European Commission 217, 227
European Union (EU) 14–15, 135, 193, 212–16, 221–7, 307
explicit normative claims *see* normative claims
Extractive Industries Transparency Initiative 199

Fair Labor Association (FLA) 192–3
FAO *see* Food and Agriculture Organization
FIFA *see* International Federation of Football Associations
Finnemore, Martha 19–20, 48–9, 297
Fisher, William F. 55
follow the partners 17, 25, 238, 251, 257, 262, 303, 312–14
Food and Agriculture Organization (FAO) 125
French Revolution (1789) 107, 109, 308

gender-based violence (GBV) Chapter 10, 262–86
Geneva 121
Geneva Convention 111
Georgia 124, 239–40, 251, 253, *see also* Rose Revolution
Giddens, Anthony 8
Global Accountability Project (GAP) 169
global civil society 7, 13–15, 22–3, 47, 70, 241, 308, *see also* civil society
Global Compact 124
global moral compass *see* normative claims (explicitly made by NGOs)
Global Reporting Initiative 200
global governance 3, 11–13, 22, 58, 68–70, 211, 297–9, 307, 312; and multi-actor framework 70–1; and network institutionalism 83, 87–8, 91–9; and NGO accountability 160, 164–5; and normative framework 77–9; and transnational networks 71–3; and transnational learning 73; and transnational outcomes 74–7
globalist (theory) 11–14, 24, 27, 241, 290–1, 296, 302, 307
government organized NGO (GONGO) 240, 250, 252
Grant, Ruth W. 166
Great Britain *see* Britain
Green Revolution in Iran (2009–10) 240

Haas, Ernst 8, 118
Hague Peace Conferences (1899, 1907) 113–14
Haiti 159, 174–8
Hall, John A. 18
Hall, Peter 300
Hall, Rodney Bruce 22
Havel, Vaclav 256
Helvey, Robert 250
Hertel, Shareen 31, 36, 207–306, 308, 311–12; labor rights advocacy and governance 189–91, 192–4, 203–7; public-private partnerships (PPPs) 191–2, 194–7, 197–203
Hilhorst, Dorothea 20–1, 76,
Hirsch, Joachim 97

historical institutionalism 89–91, 93, 97, 300
Hopkins, Raymond F. 8
human rights NGOs: in Africa 16, 36, 56, 256, 267, 277–8, 299, 305; idea of 107–9; in the EU 135; in international regimes 9; and labor rights 193, 199–200, 202–4: as representative agents of victims 162; Russian NGO reports on abuses in the west 252; and IR theory 3, 22, 73, 128, 242, 248, 252; *see also* Amnesty International, Human Rights Watch, International Rescue Committee
Human Rights Watch 159, 277,
humanitarian NGOs: and IR theory 3, 16, 22, 28–29, 299, 300; historical development 117, 124; in former Yugoslavia 248–9, in DR Congo 262–70, 276–7, 280–3
Hurrell, Andrew 74

International Fund for Agricultural Development (IFAD) 125
Ikenberry, John 110, 126, 309,
ILO *see* International Labor Organization
implicit causal claims *see* causal claims
INGO Accountability Charter 136
institutionalism *see* rational choice institutionalism, historical institutionalism, sociological institutionalism
Interfaith Center for Corporate Responsibility (ICCR) 202
International Action Network on Small Arms 125
International Association for Labour Legislation 115
International Atomic Energy Agency (IAEA) 164
International Center on Nonviolent Conflict (ICNC) 240, 254–5
International Center for Not-for-Profit Law (ICNL) 135, 152
International Chamber of Commerce 115, 123

International Committee of the Red Cross (ICRC) 111, 123, 136
International Council of Voluntary Agencies (ICVA) 136; ICVA Bosnia 221–2
International Court of Justice (ICJ) 124
International Covenant on Civil and Political Rights (ICCPR) 198
International Covenant on Economic, Social and Cultural Rights (ICESCR) 198
International Criminal Court (ICC) 16, 125
International Federation of Football Associations (FIFA) 193
International Labor Organization (ILO) 115, 117–21, 125, 164, 193–8
International Labor Rights Fund (ILRF) 201
International Monetary Fund (IMF) 48
International Rescue Committee (IRC) 267–70
International Standards Organization (ISO) 193
instrumentalization of NGOs 14–15, 22, 108, 198, 263, 280–3, 313
Iran 240, 251, 307, *see* Green Revolution
ISO 9000 quality standard 193
ISO 14000 environmental standard 193
Ivanov, Sergey 252

Japan 148–52
John Hopkins Center on Civil Society 135
Johnson Sirleaf, Ellen 50
Jolie, Angelina 3
Jordan, Grant 86

Kaan, Christopher 191–2
Kabila, Joseph 265–6
Kabila, Laurent 265
Kantian triangle 10
Kapur, Devesh 73
Keck, Margaret E. 18, 58, 71–2, 242–4

Keohane, Robert O. 67, 78, 166–7
Kimberly Process Certification Scheme (for diamond production) 199
Kirk, Mark 249
Kmara 240–1
Koppell, Jonathan G.S. 160, 167–8, 172
Kosovo Liberation Army (KLA) 249
Kuchma, Leonid 246
Kuperman, Alan J. 16

Latin America 20, 67, 206
League of Nations 117–19, 121–2, 312
Lebanon 239, *see* Cedar Revolution
liberalism: balancing agency and structure in NGO networks 253; and global governance perspectives 65–8; neoliberalism and NGOs 8–10; and NGOs as transnational institutions 6, 22, 153, 205, 294–300; obscuring politics 12–13; and practice theory 45–7
Liberia 41, 49–51, 56, 59, 305
Libya 237
Licht, Sonya 254–5
Lotus Revolution in Egypt (2011) 240

magic bullet causality *see* causal claims
Magone, Claire 22
Malteser International 270–6, 279–82
Marovic, Ivan 246
Marshall, Tim 248–51, 254
McFaul, Michael 255
McMahon, Patrice C.: explaining peacebuilding failure 219–26; future of NGO peacebuilding 227–30; NGOs and peacebuilding 211–19; NGO power and weakness 158, 295–7, 304, 308, 311
Mearsheimer, John J. 68, 70
Médecins sans Frontières (MSF) 22, 123, 127, 267
methodology: imperative to follow the partners 17, 25, 238, 254; methodological individualism or collectivism 8, 43, 82; in network institutionalism 241; in practice theory 61; value of field research 21

Mexico 202
Meyer, John W. 92
Milosevic, Slobodan 124, 239, 245, 248–51, 308
Mingst, Karen A.: emergence of global governance perspective 66–70; multi-actor framework 70–1; normative framework 77–9; research 80–1; transnational learning 73; transnational networks 71–3; transnational outcomes 74–7; understanding NGOs 295, 297–8, 311–12
Mitrany, David 121
modular technique *see* normative claims (explicitly made by NGOs)
Montgomery, William D. 248
MONUC (United Nations Organization Mission in the Democratic Republic of the Congo) 265–7
MONUSCO (United Nations Organization Stabilization Mission in the Democratic Republic of the Congo) 266–7, 278
MSF *see* Médecins sans Frontières
Muldoon, Jr., James P.: emergence of global governance perspective 66–70; multi-actor framework 70–1; normative framework 77–9; research 80–1; transnational learning 73; transnational networks 71–3; transnational outcomes 74–7; understanding NGOs 295, 297–8, 311–12
Multilateral Agreement on Investments 124
Multiple Accountabilities Disorder (MAD) 172, 296
Murphy, Craig 116
Myanmar 239, *see also* Saffron Revolution

Neuman, Michael 22
Neumann, Iver B. 58–9
New Life's Children's Refuge (NLCR) 159, 174–8
New Partnership Initiative 215
new public management (NPM) 161, 164

New York 147
NGO Impact Initiative 136
NGOing: and accountability 161; anchoring practices of 22–9, 290, 297–8, 300–3; concept of 4–5; in global governance perspectives 76; history of 126; in Japan 148–50; and national regulations 130–2, 135–6; in Poland 150–1; in practice theory 55; in the United States 145–8; through agency and structure 309–12
normative claims (explicitly made by NGOs) 23, 26, 290; global moral compass 25, 26, 127, 290; modular technique 25, 26, 28, 127, 277, 290; representative claim 11, 15, 23–4, 26, 126, 228, 290; secular sanction 23–4, 26, 126, 290;
North American Agreement on Labor Cooperation (NAALC) 193
North Atlantic Treaty Organization (NATO): in peacebuilding 215–16, 221; in democracy network 248–51, 253, 308
Nye, Joseph S. 67

Ohanyan, Anna: on networks 72; on network institutionalism 93–100; on new institutional theories 88–93; research 101–2; understanding NGOs 295, 300, 311–12
OHR, Office of the High Representative (Bosnia) 221
ONE Campaign 4
One World Trust 168
Ontology: constructivist 16–17, 19; in global governance perspective 69; NGO permeable ontology 19–21, 303; rationalist 8; relational ontology in practice theory 42–5, 49, 59
Open Society Institute (OSI) 135, 254
Orange Revolution in Ukraine (2004) 239, 246, 252
Organization for Economic Cooperation and Development (OECD) 131–2, 136–45, 304
Organization for Security and Cooperation in Europe (OSCE) 212–15, 218, 223–4, 249

Otpor 124, 240–1, 245–54
Ottawa Convention on Landmines 125

partners: hidden or normatively anomalous partners 18–20, 28, 173–4, 178, 245–51, 291; ironic terminology of NGO partnership 4–5; partnering as NGO anchoring practice 24–9, 302–3; partners of labor rights NGOs 197–203; partners of NGOs responding to rape in war 267–76
Pattberg, Philipp 69
Permanent Court of Arbitration 113, 116
Pettman, Ralph 18
pluralist theory 11–14, 24, 27, 290–2, 296, 307
Poland 150–1
policy network theories 84–8
Pora 240–1
post-communist *see* communist
Pouliot, Vincent 301
Powell, Walter W. 98
practice theory 22–9, 43–5, 52–6, 98–9,136–145, 300–4
principal-agent theory 74–7, 133, 160, 164–6, 224–7, 296
public international union (PIU) 115
public-private partnerships (PPPs) 190–5, 197–203
Puchala, Donald J. 8
Putin, Vladimir 251

rational choice institutionalism 74–7, 89, 164–6, 191–2, 292–3
realism (neorealism) 6–9, 12–16, 28–9, 70, 206, 291–3, 308–9
Reinalda, Bob: multilateral conferences including private actors 110–15; national regulations 130; NGOs subordinate to IGOs 121–5; co-evolution of IGOs and NGOs 125–8
representative claim *see* normative claims (explicitly made by NGOs)
Richardson, Jeremy J. 86
Ron, James 75

324 *Index*

Rose Revolution in Georgia (2003) 124, 239–40, 251
Rosenau, James N. 69
Rowan, Brian 92
Ruggie, John, G. 8, 198
Russia 251–3
Rwanda 274–5

SA8000 human rights standard 193, 203
Saffron Revolution in Myanmar (2007) 239
Schäferhoff, Marco 191–2, 196
Schmidt, Vivien 89
Scott, Richard W. 98
secular sanction *see* normative claims (explicitly made by NGOs)
Selznick, Philip 92
Sending, Ole Jacob 58
Serbia 124, 239–40, 245–51, 254–5, *see also* Bulldozer Revolution
Sese Seko, Mobutu 264
sham standards 15, 70
Shanghai Cooperation Organization 252
Sharp, Gene 125, 250, 256
Shevardnadze, Eduard 124
Shrum, Wesley 54
Sikkink, Kathryn 18, 58, 71–2, 242–4
Smith, Brian H. 20–1, 298
Snyder, Jack 10
Social Accountability International (SAI) 193, 203
sociological institutionalism 73, 85, 91–3, 292–4, 296, 300
Soros Foundations 135
Spector, Regine A. 255
Sperling, Valerie 77
structure and agency 5, 26, 83, 95–8, 162, 179, 243, in Bulldozer Revolution in Serbia 247–53; and color revolutions 237–8; 253–7; and power in NGO cycle of social construction 309–12
Swedish International Development Agency (SIDA) 228

Taylor, Rosemary 300
Third World Network (TWN) 201
Thomas, Albert 117–18
Thompson, Alex 77
Thompson, Kenneth 66
Tierney, Michael J. 77
transnational civil society *see* global civil society
Tulip Revolution in Kyrgyzstan (2005) 239
Tunisia 237, 240, *see also* Dignity Revolution

Uganda 265
Ukraine 237, 239–40, 246, 248, 252–3, *see also* Orange Revolution, and Euromaidan Revolution
UN Charter 121
UN Guiding Principles on Business and Human Rights 198
UN Security Council 124, 252, 269, 278, 307
UN Development Program (UNDP) 120
United Nations (UN) 41, 120, 135, 164, 188, 216, *see also* UN Security Council
United Nations Children's Fund (UNICEF) 269
United States 14–15, 29, 109, 145–8, 249, 295
United Students Against Sweatshops (USAS) 201
US Department of State 148, 243
US Office of Foreign Disaster Assistance 268
US Agency for International Development (USAID) 56, 148, 215

Vanderhill, Rachel 261
Verbeek, Bertjan 130
Versailles Treaty 119

Walt, Stephen M. 7, 10
Waltz, Kenneth N. 7–10
Weaver, Catherine 77
Weissman, Fabrice 22
Wendt, Alexander 47–8
Willetts, Peter 122

Women for Women International (WfWI) 273–5, 279–82, 305
Worker Rights Consortium (WRC) 192–3
World Bank 19, 77, 215, 223
World Food Program (WFP) 125, 269
World Trade Organization (WTO) 193, 195

Young, Dennis R. 94

Zollverein 114

Routledge Global Institutions Series

100 Global Poverty (2nd edition, 2015)
Global governance and poor people in the post-2015 era
by David Hulme *(University of Manchester)*

99 Global Corporations and Global Governance (2015)
by Christopher May *(Lancaster University)*

98 The United Nations Centre on Transnational Corporations (2015)
Corporate conduct and the public interest
by Khalil Hamdani *(Lahore School of Economics) and*
Lorraine Ruffing

97 The Challenges of Constructing Legitimacy in Peacebuilding (2015)
Afghanistan, Iraq, Sierra Leone, and East Timor
by Daisaku Higashi *(University of Tokyo)*

96 The European Union and Environmental Governance (2015)
by Henrik Selin *(Boston University) and*
Stacy D. VanDeveer *(University of New Hampshire)*

95 Rising Powers, Global Governance, and Global Ethics (2015)
edited by Jamie Gaskarth *(Plymouth University)*

94 Wartime Origins and the Future United Nations (2015)
edited by Dan Plesch *(SOAS, University of London) and*
Thomas G. Weiss *(CUNY Graduate Center)*

93 International Judicial Institutions (2nd edition, 2015)
The architecture of international justice at home and abroad
by Richard J. Goldstone *(Retired Justice of the Constitutional Court of South Africa) and* Adam M. Smith *(International Lawyer, Washington, DC)*

92 The NGO Challenge for International Relations Theory (2015)
edited by William E. DeMars (Wofford College) and
Dennis Dijkzeul (Ruhr University Bochum)

91 21st Century Democracy Promotion in the Americas (2014)
Standing up for the Polity
by Jorge Heine (Wilfrid Laurier University) and
Brigitte Weiffen (University of Konstanz)

90 BRICS and Coexistence (2014)
An alternative vision of world order
edited by Cedric de Coning (Norwegian Institute of International Affairs), Thomas Mandrup (Royal Danish Defence College), and Liselotte Odgaard (Royal Danish Defence College)

89 IBSA (2014)
The rise of the Global South?
by Oliver Stuenkel (Getulio Vargas Foundation)

88 Making Global Institutions Work (2014)
edited by Kate Brennan

87 Post-2015 UN Development (2014)
Making change happen
edited by Stephen Browne (FUNDS Project) and
Thomas G. Weiss (CUNY Graduate Center)

86 Who Participates in Global Governance? (2014)
States, bureaucracies, and NGOs in the United Nations
by Molly Ruhlman (Towson University)

85 The Security Council as Global Legislator (2014)
edited by Vesselin Popovski (United Nations University) and
Trudy Fraser (United Nations University)

84 UNICEF (2014)
Global governance that works
by Richard Jolly (University of Sussex)

83 The Society for Worldwide Interbank Financial Telecommunication (SWIFT) (2014)
Cooperative governance for network innovation, standards, and community
by Susan V. Scott (London School of Economics and Political Science) and Markos Zachariadis (University of Cambridge)

82 The International Politics of Human Rights (2014)
Rallying to the R2P cause?
edited by Monica Serrano (Colegio de Mexico) and Thomas G. Weiss (The CUNY Graduate Center)

81 Private Foundations and Development Partnerships (2014)
American philanthropy and global development agendas
by Michael Moran (Swinburne University of Technology)

80 Nongovernmental Development Organizations and the Poverty Reduction Agenda (2014)
The moral crusaders
by Jonathan J. Makuwira (Royal Melbourne Institute of Technology University)

79 Corporate Social Responsibility (2014)
The role of business in sustainable development
by Oliver F. Williams (University of Notre Dame)

78 Reducing Armed Violence with NGO Governance (2014)
edited by Rodney Bruce Hall (Oxford University)

77 Transformations in Trade Politics (2014)
Participatory trade politics in West Africa
Silke Trommer (Murdoch University)

76 Committing to the Court (2013)
Rules, politics, and the International Criminal Court
by Yvonne M. Dutton (Indiana University)

75 Global Institutions of Religion (2013)
Ancient movers, modern shakers
by Katherine Marshall (Georgetown University)

74 Crisis of Global Sustainability (2013)
by Tapio Kanninen

73 The Group of Twenty (G20) (2013)
by Andrew F. Cooper (University of Waterloo) and
Ramesh Thakur (Australian National University)

72 Peacebuilding (2013)
From concept to commission
by Rob Jenkins (Hunter College, CUNY)

71 Human Rights and Humanitarian Norms, Strategic Framing, and Intervention (2013)
Lessons for the Responsibility to Protect
by Melissa Labonte (Fordham University)

70 Feminist Strategies in International Governance (2013)
edited by Gülay Caglar (Humboldt University, Berlin), Elisabeth Prügl (the Graduate Institute of International and Development Studies, Geneva), and Susanne Zwingel (the State University of New York, Potsdam)

69 The Migration Industry and the Commercialization of International Migration (2013)
edited by Thomas Gammeltoft-Hansen (Danish Institute for International Studies) and Ninna Nyberg Sørensen (Danish Institute for International Studies)

68 Integrating Africa (2013)
Decolonization's legacies, sovereignty, and the African Union
by Martin Welz (University of Konstanz)

67 Trade, Poverty, Development (2013)
Getting beyond the WTO's Doha deadlock
edited by Rorden Wilkinson (University of Manchester) and James Scott (University of Manchester)

66 The United Nations Industrial Development Organization (UNIDO) (2012)
Industrial solutions for a sustainable future
by Stephen Browne (FUNDS Project)

65 The Millennium Development Goals and Beyond (2012)
Global development after 2015
edited by Rorden Wilkinson (University of Manchester) and David Hulme (University of Manchester)

64 International Organizations as Self-Directed Actors (2012)
A framework for analysis
edited by Joel E. Oestreich (Drexel University)

63 Maritime Piracy (2012)
by Robert Haywood (One Earth Future Foundation) and Roberta Spivak (One Earth Future Foundation)

62 United Nations High Commissioner for Refugees (UNHCR) (2nd edition, 2012)
by Gil Loescher (University of Oxford), Alexander Betts (University of Oxford), and James Milner (University of Toronto)

61 International Law, International Relations, and Global Governance (2012)
by Charlotte Ku (University of Illinois)

60 Global Health Governance (2012)
by Sophie Harman (City University, London)

59 The Council of Europe (2012)
by Martyn Bond (University of London)

58 The Security Governance of Regional Organizations (2011)
edited by Emil J. Kirchner (University of Essex) and Roberto Domínguez (Suffolk University)

57 The United Nations Development Programme and System (2011)
by Stephen Browne (FUNDS Project)

56 The South Asian Association for Regional Cooperation (2011)
An emerging collaboration architecture
by Lawrence Sáez (University of London)

55 The UN Human Rights Council (2011)
by Bertrand G. Ramcharan (Geneva Graduate Institute of International and Development Studies)

54 Responsibility to Protect (2011)
Cultural perspectives in the Global South
*edited by Rama Mani (University of Oxford) and
Thomas G. Weiss (The CUNY Graduate Center)*

53 The International Trade Centre (2011)
Promoting exports for development
*by Stephen Browne (FUNDS Project) and
Sam Laird (University of Nottingham)*

52 The Idea of World Government (2011)
From ancient times to the twenty-first century
by James A. Yunker (Western Illinois University)

51 Humanitarianism Contested (2011)
Where angels fear to tread
*by Michael Barnett (George Washington University) and
Thomas G. Weiss (The CUNY Graduate Center)*

50 The Organization of American States (2011)
Global governance away from the media
by Monica Herz (Catholic University, Rio de Janeiro)

49 Non-Governmental Organizations in World Politics (2011)
The construction of global governance
by Peter Willetts (City University, London)

48 The Forum on China-Africa Cooperation (FOCAC) (2011)
by Ian Taylor (University of St. Andrews)

47 Global Think Tanks (2011)
Policy networks and governance
*by James G. McGann (University of Pennsylvania) with
Richard Sabatini*

46 United Nations Educational, Scientific and Cultural Organization (UNESCO) (2011)
Creating norms for a complex world
by J.P. Singh (Georgetown University)

45 The International Labour Organization (2011)
Coming in from the cold
*by Steve Hughes (Newcastle University) and
Nigel Haworth (University of Auckland)*

44 Global Poverty (2010)
How global governance is failing the poor
by David Hulme (University of Manchester)

43 Global Governance, Poverty, and Inequality (2010)
*edited by Jennifer Clapp (University of Waterloo) and
Rorden Wilkinson (University of Manchester)*

42 Multilateral Counter-Terrorism (2010)
The global politics of cooperation and contestation
by Peter Romaniuk (John Jay College of Criminal Justice, CUNY)

41 Governing Climate Change (2010)
*by Peter Newell (University of East Anglia) and
Harriet A. Bulkeley (Durham University)*

40 The UN Secretary-General and Secretariat (2nd edition, 2010)
by Leon Gordenker (Princeton University)

39 Preventive Human Rights Strategies (2010)
by Bertrand G. Ramcharan (Geneva Graduate Institute of International and Development Studies)

38 African Economic Institutions (2010)
by Kwame Akonor (Seton Hall University)

37 Global Institutions and the HIV/AIDS Epidemic (2010)
Responding to an international crisis
by Franklyn Lisk (University of Warwick)

36 Regional Security (2010)
The capacity of international organizations
by Rodrigo Tavares (United Nations University)

35 The Organisation for Economic Co-operation and Development (2009)
by Richard Woodward (University of Hull)

34 Transnational Organized Crime (2009)
by Frank Madsen *(University of Cambridge)*

33 The United Nations and Human Rights (2nd edition, 2009)
A guide for a new era
by Julie A. Mertus *(American University)*

32 The International Organization for Standardization (2009)
Global governance through voluntary consensus
by Craig N. Murphy *(Wellesley College) and*
JoAnne Yates (Massachusetts Institute of Technology)

31 Shaping the Humanitarian World (2009)
by Peter Walker *(Tufts University) and*
Daniel G. Maxwell (Tufts University)

30 Global Food and Agricultural Institutions (2009)
by John Shaw

29 Institutions of the Global South (2009)
by Jacqueline Anne Braveboy-Wagner *(City College of New York, CUNY)*

28 International Judicial Institutions (2009)
The architecture of international justice at home and abroad
by Richard J. Goldstone *(Retired Justice of the Constitutional Court of South Africa) and Adam M. Smith (Harvard University)*

27 The International Olympic Committee (2009)
The governance of the Olympic system
by Jean-Loup Chappelet *(IDHEAP Swiss Graduate School of Public Administration) and Brenda Kübler-Mabbott*

26 The World Health Organization (2009)
by Kelley Lee *(London School of Hygiene and Tropical Medicine)*

25 Internet Governance (2009)
The new frontier of global institutions
by John Mathiason *(Syracuse University)*

24 Institutions of the Asia-Pacific (2009)
ASEAN, APEC, and beyond
by Mark Beeson *(University of Birmingham)*

23 United Nations High Commissioner for Refugees (UNHCR) (2008)
The politics and practice of refugee protection into the twenty-first century
by Gil Loescher (University of Oxford), Alexander Betts (University of Oxford), and James Milner (University of Toronto)

22 Contemporary Human Rights Ideas (2008)
by Bertrand G. Ramcharan (Geneva Graduate Institute of International and Development Studies)

21 The World Bank (2008)
From reconstruction to development to equity
by Katherine Marshall (Georgetown University)

20 The European Union (2008)
by Clive Archer (Manchester Metropolitan University)

19 The African Union (2008)
Challenges of globalization, security, and governance
by Samuel M. Makinda (Murdoch University) and F. Wafula Okumu (McMaster University)

18 Commonwealth (2008)
Inter- and non-state contributions to global governance
by Timothy M. Shaw (Royal Roads University)

17 The World Trade Organization (2007)
Law, economics, and politics
by Bernard M. Hoekman (World Bank) and Petros C. Mavroidis (Columbia University)

16 A Crisis of Global Institutions? (2007)
Multilateralism and international security
by Edward Newman (University of Birmingham)

15 UN Conference on Trade and Development (2007)
by Ian Taylor (University of St. Andrews) and Karen Smith (University of Stellenbosch)

14 The Organization for Security and Co-operation in Europe (2007)
by David J. Galbreath (University of Aberdeen)

13 The International Committee of the Red Cross (2007)
A neutral humanitarian actor
*by David P. Forsythe (University of Nebraska) and
Barbara Ann Rieffer-Flanagan (Central Washington University)*

12 The World Economic Forum (2007)
A multi-stakeholder approach to global governance
by Geoffrey Allen Pigman (Bennington College)

11 The Group of 7/8 (2007)
by Hugo Dobson (University of Sheffield)

10 The International Monetary Fund (2007)
Politics of conditional lending
by James Raymond Vreeland (Georgetown University)

9 The North Atlantic Treaty Organization (2007)
The enduring alliance
*by Julian Lindley-French (Center for Applied Policy,
University of Munich)*

8 The World Intellectual Property Organization (2006)
Resurgence and the development agenda
by Chris May (University of the West of England)

7 The UN Security Council (2006)
Practice and promise
by Edward C. Luck (Columbia University)

6 Global Environmental Institutions (2006)
by Elizabeth R. DeSombre (Wellesley College)

5 Internal Displacement (2006)
Conceptualization and its consequences
*by Thomas G. Weiss (The CUNY Graduate Center) and
David A. Korn*

4 The UN General Assembly (2005)
by M. J. Peterson (University of Massachusetts, Amherst)

3 United Nations Global Conferences (2005)
by Michael G. Schechter (Michigan State University)

2 The UN Secretary-General and Secretariat (2005)
by Leon Gordenker *(Princeton University)*

1 The United Nations and Human Rights (2005)
A guide for a new era
by Julie A. Mertus *(American University)*

Books currently under contract include:

The Regional Development Banks
Lending with a regional flavor
by Jonathan R. Strand *(University of Nevada)*

Millennium Development Goals (MDGs)
For a people-centered development agenda?
by Sakiko Fukuda-Parr *(The New School)*

The Bank for International Settlements
The politics of global financial supervision in the age of high finance
by Kevin Ozgercin *(SUNY College at Old Westbury)*

International Migration
by Khalid Koser *(Geneva Centre for Security Policy)*

Human Development
by Richard Ponzio

The International Monetary Fund (2nd edition)
Politics of conditional lending
by James Raymond Vreeland *(Georgetown University)*

The UN Global Compact
by Catia Gregoratti *(Lund University)*

Institutions for Women's Rights
by Charlotte Patton *(York College, CUNY)* and
Carolyn Stephenson *(University of Hawaii)*

International Aid
by Paul Mosley *(University of Sheffield)*

Global Consumer Policy
by Karsten Ronit (University of Copenhagen)

The Changing Political Map of Global Governance
by Anthony Payne (University of Sheffield) and
Stephen Robert Buzdugan (Manchester Metropolitan University)

Coping with Nuclear Weapons
by W. Pal Sidhu

Global Governance and China
The dragon's learning curve
edited by Scott Kennedy (Indiana University)

The Politics of Global Economic Surveillance
by Martin S. Edwards (Seton Hall University)

Mercy and Mercenaries
Humanitarian agencies and private security companies
by Peter Hoffman

Regional Organizations in the Middle East
by James Worrall (University of Leeds)

Reforming the UN Development System
The Politics of Incrementalism
by Silke Weinlich (Duisburg-Essen University)

The United Nations as a Knowledge Organization
by Nanette Svenson (Tulane University)

The International Criminal Court
The politics and practice of prosecuting atrocity crimes
by Martin Mennecke (University of Copenhagen)

The Politics of International Organizations
Views from insiders
edited by Patrick Weller (Griffith University) and
Xu Yi-chong (Griffith University)

The African Union (2nd edition)
Challenges of globalization, security, and governance
by Samuel M. Makinda (Murdoch University),
F. Wafula Okumu (African Union), and
David Mickler (University of Western Australia)

BRICS
by João Pontes Nogueira (Catholic University, Rio de Janeiro) and
Monica Herz (Catholic University, Rio de Janeiro)

Expert Knowledge in Global Trade
edited by Erin Hannah (University of Western Ontario),
James Scott (University of Manchester), and
Silke Trommer (Murdoch University)

The European Union (2nd edition)
Clive Archer (Manchester Metropolitan University)

Governing Climate Change (2nd edition)
Peter Newell (University of East Anglia) and
Harriet A. Bulkeley (Durham University)

Contemporary Human Rights Ideas (2nd edition)
Bertrand Ramcharan (Geneva Graduate Institute of
International and Development Studies)

Protecting the Internally Displaced
Rhetoric and reality
Phil Orchard (University of Queensland)

The Arctic Council
Within the far north
Douglas C. Nord (Umea University)

For further information regarding the series, please contact:

Nicola Parkin, Editor, Politics & International Studies
Taylor & Francis
2 Park Square, Milton Park, Abingdon
Oxford OX14 4RN, UK
Nicola.parkin@tandf.co.uk
www.routledge.com